The New Sabin

Entries 21753-23828

The New Sabin;

Books Described by Joseph Sabin and His

Successors, Now Described Again on the

Basis of Examination of Originals,

and Fully Indexed by Title, Subject,

Joint Authors, and Institutions and Agencies

by

Lawrence S. Thompson

Entries 21753—23828

Volume IX

The Whitston Publishing Company
Troy, New York
1983

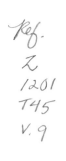

To

William Clement Eaton

1898-1980

PREFACE

This is the third volume of *The New Sabin* to be devoted exclusively to titles in the original Sabin which have been issued on microfiche by the Lost Cause Press. Some others have appeared in other Lost Cause series and are listed by number at the end of this volume. There will be a cumulative index to the first ten volumes, and this should be helpful in locating microfiche editions of around 8,000 Sabin titles by author, title, and subject. The project is growing rapidly, and there will be another volume showing original Sabin titles within the next two or three years.

A large proportion of the works listed by Sabin are extremely scarce, and it would be a major gamble to depend on even the most skillful antiquarian dealer to fill a want list. Indeed, there are thousands of Sabin titles which probably exist only in one or two collections and would turn up solely as lucky finds. Thus the microfiche project is a major contribution both to the "have" and to the "have not" collections.

Most of the titles recorded in the first, fifth, and ninth volumes are represented by printed Library of Congress cards. Entries in the main alphabet and in the index have been based on them. Changes in cataloging policy at the Library of Congress over the years have resulted in some inconsistencies, but every effort has been made to adjust them appropriately.

Lawrence S. Thompson
Lexington, Kentucky
February 1983

21753   An account of a late military massacre at Boston.
        [Boston, Edes & Gill? 1776]
        broadside.   illus.   48 x 39 cm.
        In five columns. Poor printing makes much of the
        text illegible.

21754   An act to block up the harbour of Boston!
        [Boston, 1774]
        broadside.   41½ x 26½ cm.

21755   An address to the true-born Sons of Liberty in the
        government of the Massachusetts-Bay. [Boston? 1772?]
        broadside.   36 x 24½ cm.

21756   Alabama. Laws, statutes, etc.
        A digest of the laws of the state of Alabama: containing
        the statutes and resolutions in force at the end of the
        General Assembly in January, 1823. To which is added,
        an appendix; containing the Declaration of independence;
        the Constitution of the United States; the Act authorizing
        the people of Alabama to form a constitution and state
        government; and the Constitution of the state of Alabama.
        Compiled by appointment, and under the authority of the
        General Assembly, by Harry Toulmin, esq. With a copious
        index.   Cahawba, Published by Ginn & Curtis, J. & J.
        Harper, printers, New York, 1823.
        xxxiv, [2], [9]-1066 p.   23½ cm.

21757   [Alexander, Ann (Tuke)] 1767-1849.
        Remarks on the theatre, and on the late fire at Richmond,
        in Virginia. York, Printed by T. Wilson and son, for
        the author, 1812.
        32 p.   21 cm.

21758   Alexander, William 1726-1783.
        The conduct of Major Gen. Shirley, late general and
        commander in chief of His Majesty's forces in North
        America. Briefly stated. London, Printed for R. & J.

Dodsley [etc.] 1758.
viii, 130 p., 1 l.   20½ cm.
Authorship sometimes attributed to General Shirley
himself. - Sabin 80544.

21759   American Continental Congress, 5 September, 1774.
Extracts from the votes and proceedings of the American
Continental Congress held at Philadelphia on the 5th of
September, 1774. Containing the resolves, the association,
an address to the people of Great-Britain, and a memorial
to the inhabitants of the British American colonies.
Philadelphia, printed; Hartford, re-printed by Eben
Watson [n.d.]
48 p.   19 cm.

21760   The American medical review, and journal of original and
selected papers in medicine and surgery. v. 1-3; June
1824-Aug. 1826. Conducted by John Eberle, M.D. ...
Nathan Smith, M.D. ... George McClellan, M.D. ...
Nathan R. Smith, M.D. ... and assisted by an association
of physicians & surgeons ... Philadelphia, A. Sherman,
1824-26.
3 v.   plates.   22 cm.   quarterly.
Vol. 1 has title: The Medical review, and analectic
journal... Conducted by John Eberle, M.D. ... and George
McClellan, M.D. ...
No more published.

21761   [Angelis, Pedro de] 1784-1859.
Quelques réflexions en reponse à la brochure publiée à
Montevideo, par d. Florencio Varela, sous le titre -
Développement et dénouement de la question française dans
le rio de la Plata. Buenos Aires, Impr. de l'état, 1841.
104 p.   23 cm.

21762   The ardent desire and sincere cry, or a true believer in
Jesus Christ. Newport, Rhode Island, Printed by
J. Franklin, 1728.
broadside.   21 x 15 cm.

21763   Atkins, Thomas Astley, 1839-1916.
Indian wars and the uprising of 1655 -- Yonkers
depopulated. A paper read before the Yonkers historical
and library association by Hon. T. Astley Atkins,
March 18, 1892. Yonkers, The Society, 1892.
14 p.   23½ cm.

21764   Audubon, John James, 1785-1851.
The quadrupeds of North America, by John James Audubon...

and the Rev. John Bachman... New York, V. G. Audubon,
1851-54.
3 v.   clv col. pl.   28 cm.
Vol. 1, 1852; vol. 2, 1851.

21765   Ayres, Philip, 1638-1712, ed.
The voyages and adventures of Capt. Barth. Sharp and
others, in the South Sea: being a journal of the same.
Also Capt. Van Horn with his buccanieres surprizing of
la Vera Cruz. To which is added The true relation of
Sir Henry Morgan his expedition against the Spaniards
in the West-Indies, and his taking Panama. Together
with the president of Panama's account of the same
expedition: translated out of Spanish. And Col.
Beeston's adjustment of the peace between the Spaniards
and English in the West Indies. Published by P. A. esp.;
London, Printed by B. W. for R. H. and S. T., MDCLXXXIV.
12 p.l., 172 p.   17 cm.
This work is in part supplementary to the English
edition of Exquemelin's Bucaniers of America, 1684, and
in part a vindication of the English, especially Capt.
Henry Morgan from the aspersions of that writer. "The
adventures of Capt. Barth, Sharp, and others in the
South Sea" (p. 1-114) differs from both Basil Ringrose's
account, published in "Bucaniers in America, the second
volume, containing the dangerous voyage... of Capt.
Bartholomew Sharp," 1685 and Sharpe's own journal as
printed in William Hack's Collection of original
voyages, 1699.

B

21766   Baqueiro, Serapion, 1838-1900.
Ensayo histórico sobre las revoluciones de Yucatán
desde el año de 1840 hasta 1864, por Serapio Baqueiro...
Mérida, Impr. Lit. dirigida por Gil Canto, 1871-1873.
2 v.   port.   20½ cm.

21767   [Baraga, Friedrich, bp.] 1797-1868.
Jusus obimadisiwin ajonda aking, gwaiakossing anamiewin
ejitwadjig, mi sa Catholique-enamiadjig gewabandangig.
Paris, E. J. Bailly ogimisinakisan manda misinaigan,
1837.
4 p.l., 211 p.   double map.   14 cm.

3

"Approbation" (in French and English) signed
"Frédérick Résé, bishop of Detroit": 3d prelim. leaf.

21768 Barclay, Robert, 1648-1690.
An apology for the true Christian divinity, as the
same is held forth, and preached, by the people, called
in scorn, Quakers: being a full explanation and vindication of their principles and doctrines, by many
arguments, deduced from Scripture and right reason,
and the testimonies of famous authors, both ancient and
modern: with a full answer to the strongest objections
usually made against them. Presented to the King.
Written in Latin and English, by Robert Barclay, and
since translated into High Dutch, Low Dutch, and French,
for the information of strangers. The 6th ed. in English..
Newport, Rhode Island, Printed by James Franklin, 1729.
6 p.l., 524 (i.e. 574), [31] p.   20½ cm.
Page 574 incorrectly numbered 524.
First edition in Latin published under title: Theologiae
verè Christianae apologia. Amstelodami, 1676.

21769 [Barnum, George Henry]
Rube Burrows, the famous outlaw, murderer and train
robber, with a complete history of his eventful life,
from his birth to his startling capture and sensational
death on October 8th, 1890... Chicago, G. H. Barnum,
1890.
64 p.   illus. (incl. ports.)   19 cm.

21770 Barrett, Jonathan Fay, 1817-1885.
Concord: a poem, delivered before the Lyceum, Concord,
Mass., January 22, 1851, and published by request.
Boston, Tickner, Reed, and Fields, 1851.
32 p.   18 cm.

21771 Barry, John Stetson, 1819-1872.
The history of Massachusetts... By John Stetson Barry...
4th ed. Boston, The author [cl856-57]
3 v.   24 cm.
Contents. - [v. 1] Colonial period [1492-1692] -
[v. 2] Provincial period [1692-1775] - v. 3. Commonwealth
period [1775-1820]

21772 Bartlett, William Henry, 1809-1854.
The history of the United States of North America;
from the discovery of the western world to the present
day. By W. H. Bartlett... continued by B. B. Woodward...
New York, Virtue & Yorston [1855-56]
3 v.   fronts., plates, map, facsim.   26 cm.

4

Added t.-p., engr., with vignette, in each volume;
that of v. 2 (apparently taken from another edition) has
title: The history of the United States of America,
continued to the southern secession, by Charles Mackay...
London & New York, J. S. Virtue. In the present edition
the history extends to 1856.
"The first three books in the first volume are from
the pen of Mr. Bartlett; the remainder of the work is by
the continuator of his labors, B. B. Woodward." - Pref.

21773   Barton, William, 1754-1817.
         Memoirs of the life of David Rittenhouse, LLD. F.R.S.,
         late president of the American philosophical society. &c
         interspersed with various notices of many distinguished
         men: with an appendix, containing sundry philosophical
         and other papers, most of which have not hitherto been
         published. Philadelphia, E. Parker, 1813.
         614 p.   fold. facsim., port.   26 cm.

21774   Barton, William Paul Crillon, 1786-1856.
         Compendium florae philadelphicae: containing a des-
         cription of the indigenous and naturalized plants found
         within a circuit of ten miles around Philadelphia.
         By William P. C. Barton... Philadelphia, Published by
         M. Carey and son, 1818.
         2 v.   19 cm.

21775   Bates, Mrs. D   B
         Incidents on land and water, or four years on the
         Pacific Coast. Being a narrative of the burning of the
         ships Nonantum, Humayoon and Franchon, together with
         many startling and interesting adventures on sea and
         land. By Mrs. D. B. Bates. Fifth edition. Boston,
         E. O. Libby and company, 1858.
         336 p.   illus.   19½ cm.

21776   [Bath, William Pulteney, earl of] 1684-1764.
         A review of all that hath pass'd between the courts
         of Great Britain and Spain, relating to our trade and
         navigation from the year 1721, to the present convention;
         with some particular observations upon it. London,
         H. Goreham, 1739.
         2 p.l., 60 p.   20 cm.

21777   [Beauchamp, Alphonse de] 1767-1832.
         Historia do Brazil desde seu descobrimento em 1500 até
         1810, vertida de francez, e accrescentada de muitas notas
         por Pedro José de Figueiredo. Offerecida a Sua Alteza
         Real o serenissimo senhor dom Pedro de Alcantara,

5

principe do Brazil... Com estampas finas... Lisboa,
Na typ. de Marques Leão, 1817-34 [v. 1, '22]
12 v.   plates (part fold.)   14½ cm.
Vols. 2-4 have imprint: Lisboa, Na officina de J. F. M.
de Campos, 1817-18; v. 5-   Na impr. de J. B. Morando,
1818-20.
Vol. 1, "Segunda edicão mais correcta."
Subtitle of v. 2-6 varies: Vertida de francez, e
accrescentada de muitas notas do traductor...
Vols. 7-12 have title: Historia do Brazil desde 1807
até ao presente: originalmente composta em portuguez
para servir de continuaçao a que se publicou vertida do
francez... (These volumes continue the history to 1826,
and are by Pedro Cyriaco da Silva and Antonio Candido
Cordeiro Pinheiro Furtado. cf. Silva, Dicc. bibl. portuguez, v. 6, p. 401-402; v. 17, p. 197)
Translated by Pedro Cyriaco da Silva.
Beauchamp's work is largely a compilation and translation from the first volume of Southey's History of Brazil.
cf. Southey, Robert. History of Brazil, 1817-22, v. 2,
pref.; Netscher, P. M. Les Hollandais au Brésil, 1853,
p. xxi.

21778 Beck, Lewis Caleb, 1798-1853.
A gazetteer of the states of Illinois and Missouri;
containing a general view of each state, a general view
of their counties, and a particular description of their
towns, villages, rivers, &c., &c. With a map, and other
engravings. By Lewis C. Beck... Albany, Printed by
C. R. and G. Webster, 1823.
vii, [1] p., 1 l., [11]-352 p.   front. (fold. map)
v pl. (incl. plans, part fold.)   22 cm.

21779 Beers, Fannie A
Memories. A record of personal experience and
adventure during four years of war [1861-65] Philadelphia, Lippincott Co., 1891.
336 p., port., pl.   19½ cm.
From the Southern viewpoint.

21780 Belknap, Jeremy, 1744-1798.
American biography: or, An historical account of those
persons who have been distinguished in America, as adven-
turers, statesmen, philosophers, divines, warriors,
authors, and other remarkable characters... By Jeremy
Belknap... Printed at Boston, by Isaiah Thomas and E. J.
Andrews, 1794-98.
2 v.   21½ cm.
Imprint of v. 2: Printed at Boston, by Isaiah Thomas

6

and E. T. Andrews, sold by them, and the other book-
sellers in Boston; by I. Thomas, Worcester; by Thomas,
Andrews & Penniman, Albany; and by Thomas, Andrews &
Butler, Baltimore. July, 1798.
The 3d vol., which the author intended to issue, was
never published.

21781 Belsham, William, 1752-1827.
Memoirs of the reign of George III. to the session of
Parliament ending A.D. 1793. By W. Belsham... Dublin,
Printed for J. Milliken, 1796.
4 v. 21½ cm.

21782 Benzoni, Girolamo, b. 1519.
Beschryvinghe van West-Indien, waer in verhaelt wordt,
de eerste vindingh van de eylanden, steeden, plaetsen,
en rivieren, van het selve, als mede hoe de Spangiaerts
het landt verworest, verbrandt ende ingenomen hebben.
Mitsgaders: de natuer, zeden, huysen, en kleedingh
der Indianen, oock van de goudt en silver-mijnen, ende
haer levens-middelen. Beschreven door Jeronimus
Benzonius van Milanen; en uyt het Italiaens overgeset
door Carel Vermander. t' Amsterdam, Gedruckt by G. J.
Saeghman [circa 1660-70]
56 p. illus. 19 cm.
Extract from van Mander's translation of Benzoni's
Historia del Mondo nvovo, pub. Haerlem, 1610.
"Beschryvinge van de regeeringh van Peru, beechreven
door... Pedro de Madriga": p. 49-56.

21783 Benzoni, Girolamo, b. 1519.
Novae Novi orbis historiae, id est, rerum ab Hispanis
in India Occidentali hactenus gestarum, & acerbo illorum
in eas gentes dominatu, libri tres, Vrbani Calvetonis
opera industriaque ex italicis Hieronymi Benzonis Medio-
lanensis, qui eas terras XIIII. annorum peregrinatione
obijt, commentarijs descripti, latini facti, ac perpetuis
notis, argumentis & locupleti memorabilium rerum
accessione, illustrati. His ab eodem adiuncta est,
De Gallorum in Floridam expeditione, & insigni Hispanorum
in eos saeuitiae exemplo, breuis historia. Genevae,
apvd Evstathivm Vignon, 1578.
16 p.l., 480, 13 p. 16½ cm.
Printer's mark on t.-p.
First Latin edition. First Italian edition, 1565.
"Brevis insularvm qvae Canariae appellantur... des-
criptio": p. 417-426.
Appended, with half-title, "De Gallorum in Floridam
expeditione..." translated into Latin by L. Apollonius

from the French account of this expedition by N. Le Challeux, published in Dieppe, 1566.

21784   Bernard, Francis.
A proclamation for a general fast. Boston, Richard Draper, 1769.
broadside.   38 x 30 cm.

21785   Bishop, Albert Webb, 1832-1901.
Loyalty on the frontier, or, Sketches of union men of the south-west; with incidents and adventures in rebellion on the border. By A. W. Bishop, lieut. col. First Arkansas Cavalry Volunteers. St. Louis, R. P. Studley and co., printers, 1863.
228 p.   19 cm.

21786   Bishop, Mrs. Harriet E   1817-1883.
Dakota war whoop; or, Indian massacres and war in Minnesota, of 1862-63. By Harriet E. Bishop McConkey... Rev. ed. St. Paul, The author, 1864.
429 p. incl. illus., 9 port.   19½ cm.
Printed in Auburn, N. Y.

21787   [Blackburne, Francis] 1705-1787.
Memoirs of Thomas Hollis... London, 1780.
2 v.   fronts., illus. (coat of arms) plates, ports.
35 cm.
Privately printed.
Vol. 2 has title: Appendix to the Memoirs of Thomas Hollis.
The plates are engraved by Bartolozzi, Basire and Cipriani.

21788   Bliss, Sylvester, d. 1863.
Memoirs of William Miller, generally known as a lecturer on the prophecies, and the second coming of Christ. By Sylvester Bliss... Boston, J. V. Himes, 1853.
vi, 426 p.   front. (port.) illus.   19½ cm.
"These memoirs were commenced by Elder Apollos Hale, who prepared the first three chapters." - Pref.

21789   [Blome, Richard] d. 1705.
L'Amérique angloise, ou Description des isles et terres du roi d'Angleterre, dans l'Amérique. Avec de nouvelles cartes de chaque isle & terres. Traduit de l'anglois. Amsterdam, A. Wolfgang, 1688.
2 p.l., 331, [1] p.   7 fold. maps.   15 cm.
"Ce livre a été composé en anglois, par monsieur

Richard Blome." - Avertissement, 2d prelim. leaf.
English original, London, 1687, pub. under title:
The present state of His Majesties isles and territories
in America.

21790 A bloody butchery by the British Troops: or, The runaway
fight of the regulars. Salem, Ezekiel Russell [1775]
broadside. 39 x 50 cm.

21791 Blowe, Daniel.
A geographical, commercial, and agricultural view of
the United States of America: forming a complete
emigrant's directory throughout every part of the
republic, particularly the western states and territories... Likewise a concise account of the British
possessions of Upper and Lower Canada. To which is
annexed a correct list of roads and distances, with the
conveyances by water, throughout the Union. Illustrated
with a whole-sheet map of the United States, a quarto
map of Canada, and octavo plans of Boston, New York,
Philadelphia, and Baltimore. Compiled from all the
best authorities, and from original documents. By Daniel
Blowe. Liverpool, Printed for the editor by H. Fisher
[1820?]
vii, [3]-758, xxiv, [12] p.   maps (2 fold.)   fold.
tab.   22 cm.

21792 Blundeville, Thomas, fl. 1561.
Mr. Blundevil his exercises, contayning eight treatises...
which treatises are very necessary to be read and
learned of all young gentlemen, that have not been
excercised in such disciplines, and yet are desirous
to have knowledge as well in cosmographie, astronomie,
and geographie, as also in the art of navigation, in
which art it is impossible to profit without the help
of these or such like instructions. To the furtherance
of which art of navigation, the said Mr. Blundevil
specially wrote the said treatises... 7th ed. cor. and
somewhat enl. by Ro. Hartwell philomathematicus.
London, Printed by R. Bishop, 1636.
Contents. - Of arithmetick. [To which is added] A
briefe description of the tables of three speciall right
lines belonging to a circle, called sines, tangents,
and secants. - A plaine treatise of the first principles
of cosmography, and specially of the spheare, representing the shape of the world. - A plaine description
of Mercator his two globes, that is to say, of the
terrestriall globe, and of the celestiall globe, and of
either of them, together with the most necessary uses

9

thereof. - A plaine and full description of Petrus
Plancius his universall map, serving both for sea and
land, and by him... put forth in... 1592. - A very briefe
and most plaine description of Mr. Blagrave his astrolabe,
which he called the Mathematicall jewell. - A nevv and
necessary treatise of navigation, containing all the
chiefe principles of that art. - A briefe description of
universall maps and cards, and of their use. And also
the use of Ptolomey his tables, together with the true
order of making the sayd tables.

21793 Blunt, Joseph, 1792-1860.
       An anniversary discourse, delivered before the New York
       historical society, Thursday, Dec. 13, 1827. By Joseph
       Blunt. New York, G. and C. Carvill, 1828.
           52 p.   22 cm.

21794 Blunt, Joseph, 1792-1860.
       Speeches, reviews, reports, &c. by Joseph Blunt.
       New York, J. Van Norden & co., 1843.
           2 p.l., 338 p.   22½ cm.
       Contents. - Discourse before the New York historical
       society, 1827. - Review of the principles of the Holy
       alliance. - Report to American institute proposing
       annual fairs. - Argument in case of Erastus Root v. Chas.
       King, &c. - Historical view of the formation of the
       American union. - Review of the Cherokee question. -
       Address before the New York historical society, 1839. -
       Report on common roads. - Review of Ivanhoe. - Address
       of the Home league to the people of the United States,
       1842. - Report to the National convention, 1842. -
       Lecture on coal, before the American institute.

21795 Bohn, Henry George, 1796-1884.
       A pictorial hand-book of modern geography, on a
       popular plan, compiled from the best authorities,
       English and foreign, and completed to the present time;
       with numerous tables and a general index. By Henry G.
       Bohn... Illustrated by 150 engravings on wood, and 51
       accurate maps engraved on steel. London, H. G. Bohn,
       1861.
           x, [2], 529 p.   illus., 51 maps (1 fold.) 18 cm.

21796 Bohun, Edmund, 1645-1699.
       A geographical dictionary, representing the present
       and antient names and states of all the countries,
       kingdoms, provinces, remarkable cities, universities,
       ports, towns, mountains, seas, streights, fountains,
       and rivers of the whole world. Their distances,

longitudes, and latitudes, with a short historical
account of the same... begun by Edmund Bohun, esquire.
Since continued, corrected and enlarged with great
additions... The 4th ed. To which are added the general
praecognita of geography, and the doctrine of the sphere...
by John Augustine Bernard... London, C. Brome, MDCXCV.
4 p.l., 23, 4, 16, 437 (i.e. 445), [20] p.   30½ cm.

21797   Bokee, David A   1805-1860.
        Oration delivered by Hon. David A. Bokee, in the First
        Baptist church, Brooklyn, July 4th, 1851, on the
        occasion of the seventy-sixth anniversary of our national
        independence. Brooklyn, Lees & Foulkes, printers, 1851.
        11 p.   21½ cm.

21798   [Bollan, William] d. 1776.
        A succinct view of the origin of our colonies, with
        their civil state, founded by Queen Elizabeth, corro-
        borated by succeeding princes, and confirmed by act of
        Parliament; whereby the nature of the empire established
        in America, and the errors of various hypotheses formed
        thereupon, may be clearly understood. With observations
        on the commercial, beneficial and perpetual union of the
        colonies with this kingdom. Being an abstract from an
        essay lately published, entitled The freedom of speech
        and writing, &c. ... London, M.DCC.LXVI.
        1 p.l., 46 p.   20 cm.

21799   Bolton, William.
        A narrative of the last cruise of the U.S. steam
        frigate Missouri, from the day she left Norfolk, until
        the arrival of her crew in Boston, including a full and
        circumstantial detail of the general conflagration,
        which took place at Gibraltar, resulting in her total
        loss. Interspersed with explanatory notes and remarks.
        By William Bolton, one of the crew. 4th ed. Boston,
        S. N. Dickinson, printer, 1843.
        iv, [5]-33 p.   21 cm.

21800   [Boltwood, Lucius Manlius] 1825-1905.
        Genealogies of Hadley families, embracing the early
        settlers of the towns of Hatfield, South Hadley,
        Amherst and Cranby. Northampton, Metcalf & company,
        printers, 1862.
        2 p.l., [7]-168 p.   23 cm.
        Pub. also as part of Judd's History of Hadley. 1863.

21801   Bond, Henry, 1790-1859.
        Family memorials. Genealogies of the families and

and descendants of the early settlers of Watertown,
Massachusetts, including Waltham and Weston; to which is
appended the early history of the town... By Henry Bond...
Boston, Little, Brown & Company; New York, J. Wiley;
[etc., etc.] 1855.
2 v. in 1. front., illus., plates, ports., 2 maps
(1 fold.) 23 cm.
Paged continuously.

21802 Bonnet, J [Esprit]
États-Unis de l'Amérique à la fin du XVIIIe siècle.
Par J. E. Bonnet... Paris, Maradan [1802]
2 v. 21 cm.
First edition published at Lausanne in 1788, under
title: Réponse aux principales questions qui peuvent
être faites sur les États-Unis de l'Amérique, par un
habitant de la Pensylvanie. cf. Sabin and Cushing.

21803 Booth, Mary Louise, 1831-1889.
History of the city of New York. By Mary L. Booth...
New York, E. P. Dutton Company, 1880.
2 p.l., [3], 920 p. front., illus., plates, ports.
25 cm.

21804 Bordentown Institute, Bordentown, N. J.
Catalogue of the officers and students. Philadelphia.
v. 24 cm.
Library has 1837.

21805 Bordley, John Beale, 1727-1804.
Essays and notes on husbandry and rural affairs.
By J. B. Bordley... Philadelphia, Printed by Budd and
Bartram, for Thomas Dobson, 1799.
viii, 646, 7, [8] p., 4 pl. (part fold.) 22 cm.

21806 Boston, December 1, 1773. Boston, Edes and Gill, 1773
broadside. 43 x 35 cm.
On meeting in Faneuil Hall to protest importation of
tea.

21807 Bosworth, Newton, d. 1848.
Hochelaga depicta; the early history and present
state of the city and island of Montreal... Ed. by
Newton Bosworth, F.R.A.S. Montreal, W. Greig, 1839.
[Toronto, Congdon & Britnell, 1901]
6 p.l., [9]-284 p. front., plates, fold. map, fold.
plan. 20 cm. (Added t.-p.: Facsimile reprints
of early Canadian books, no. 1)
Added t.-p., illustrated.

21808   Botero, Giovanni, 1540-1617.
        Relations of the most famovs kingdomes and common-
        wealths thorowout the world: discoursing of their
        situations, religions, languages, manners, customes,
        strengths, greatnesse and policies. Translated out of
        the best Italian impression of Boterus. And since the
        last edition by R. I. now once againe inlarged according
        to moderne observation; with addition of new estates and
        countries... London, Printed by Iohn Haviland, and are
        to be sold by Iohn Partridge, 1630.
            4 p.l., 644, [3] p.   front. (fold. map)   19 cm.
            Revised edition of R. Johnson's translation, editor
        not known.
            First English edition published, London, 1601, under
        title: The traveller's breviat, or an historicall des-
        cription of the most famous kingdomes in the world.

21809   Bouton, Nathaniel, 1799-1878.
        An historical discourse in commemoration of the two-
        hundredth anniversary of the settlement of Norwalk, Ct.,
        in 1651; delivered in the First Congregational church in
        Norwalk, July 9, 1851. By Rev. Nathaniel Bouton...
        New York, S. W. Benedict, 1851.
            80 p.   23 cm.

21810   Boutwell, George Sewall, 1818-1905.
        Speeches and papers relating to the rebellion and the
        overthrow of slavery. By George S. Boutwell. Boston,
        Little, Brown, and company, 1867.
            vii, 628 p.   20 cm.

21811   Bowen, Eli, b. 1824.
        ... The pictorial sketch-book of Pennsylvania. Or,
        its scenery, internal improvements, resources, and
        agriculture, popularly described, by Eli Bowen...
        Illustrated with over 200 engravings, and a colored map.
        8th ed., rev. and greatly enl. Philadelphia, W. W.
        Smith, 1854.
            4 p.l., [7], 309, [2], [13], 207, [2] p. incl. front.
        illus., plates, fold. map.   24 cm.
            Contents. - Off-hand sketch: pt. I. The valley of
        the Schuylkill; pt. II. The anthracite coal formation;
        pt. III. Wyoming - Locomotive sketches, with pen and
        pencil. - Pedestrian sketches; pt. IV. Sunbury to
        Lake Erie.

21812   Boykin, Edward M
        The falling flag. Evacuation of Richmond, retreat and
        surrender at Appomattox. By Edward M. Boykin, lt. col.,

7th regt., S. C. cavalry. 3rd ed. New York, R. J. Hale & son, 1974.
67 p.   18 cm.

21813 Bradford, Alden, 1765-1843.
       Biographical notices of distinguished men in New England statesmen, patriots, physicians, lawyers, clergymen, and mechanics. By Alden Bradford... Boston, S. G. Simpkins, 1842.
       464 p.   18½ cm.

21814 A brief outline for a national bank, by a native citizen. [Cincinnati, Pugh & Dodd, printers, 1837]
       8 p.   22½ cm.
       Caption title.

21815 Brooks, Edward, 1784-1859.
       An answer to the pamphlet of Mr. John A. Lowell, entitled "Reply to a pamphlet recently circulated by Mr. Edward Brooks," with new facts and further proofs, by Edward Brooks. Boston, Eastburn's press, 1851.
       xix, 836 p.   25 cm.

21816 Brown, Abiel.
       Genealogical history, with short sketches and family records, of the early settlers of West Simsbury, now Canton, Conn., by Abiel Brown, esq., with an introductory and commendatory notice, by Rev. J. Burt. Hartford, Press of Case, Tiffany and company, 1856; New York, reprinted, 1899.
       151 p.   24 cm.

21817 [Brown, Charles Brockden] 1771-1810.
       The British treaty. With an appendix of state papers; which are now first published. America: Printed, unknown where, or by whom sold; London: Re-printed for John Joseph Stockdale, 1808.
       xvi, [17]-147 p.   21½ cm.
       Treaty of "amity, commerce and navigation," signed at London, December 1806, by Pinckney and Monroe, but refused ratification by President Jefferson, without consultation of the Senate.
       Appendix contains Jay's treaty, 1794, a letter from Thomas Jefferson, September 5, 1793, Ratification of the United States, the Treaty, His Majesty's explanatory notes of the new treaty, and a copy of a letter from Mr. Merry, late minister from the court of Great Britain to the United States.

21818   Brown, Deidamia (Covell)
        Memoir of the late Rev. Lemuel Covell, missionary to
        the Tuscarora Indians and the province of Upper Canada;
        comprising a history of the origin and progress of
        missionary operations in the Shaftsbury Baptist associa-
        tion, up to the time of Mr. Covell's decease in 1806.
        Also a memoir of Rev. Alanson L. Covell, son of the former,
        and late a pastor of the First Baptist church in the city
        of Albany, N. Y. By Mrs. D. C. Brown, daughter and sister
        of the deceased... Brandon [Vt.] Telegraph office, 1839.
        2 v. in 1.   18 cm.

21819   Brown, James Bryce.
        Views of Canada and the colonists embracing the experience
        of an eight years' residence; views of the present state,
        progress, and prospects of the colony; with detailed and
        practical information for intending emigrant. By James
        B. Brown. 2d ed. cor. ... and greatly enl. Edinburgh,
        A. and C. Black [etc.] 1851.
        xxxii, 468 p.   front. (fold. map)   18 cm.

21820   Brown, James D
        The Arcade hotel guide, for the use of strangers
        visiting Philadelphia, containing an account of places
        of interest, public buildings, churches, places of
        amusement, and with directions for visiting the same.
        By J. D. Brown... Philadelphia, King & Baird, printers,
        1859.
        cover-title, 32 p.   15 cm.

21821   Bryant, William Cullen 1794-1878, ed.
        Tales of Glauber-Spa. By several American authors...
        [Ed. by W. C. Bryant] New York, J. & J. Harper, 1832.
        2 v.   18 cm.   (Library of select novels. 27-28)
        Contents. - v. 1. [Sedgwick, Catherine] Le Bossu.
        [Paulding, J. K.] Child Roeliff's pilgrimage. [Bryant,
        W. C.] The skeleton's cave. Medfield. - v. 2. [Leggett,
        W.] The block-house. [Sands, R. C.] Mr. Green.
        [Paulding, J. K.] Selim. [Sands, R. C.] Boyuca.

21822   Burgoyne, Arthur Gordon, 1863-1914.
        Homestead. A complete history of the struggle of
        July, 1892, between the Carnegie Steel Company, Limited,
        and the Amalgamated Association of Iron and Steel
        Workers, by Arthur C. Burgoyne. Pittsburgh, Pa.
        [Press of Rawsthorne Engraving and Printing Co.] 1893.
        viii, 298 p.   illus.   21 cm.

21823 Butler, Charles.
       The American lady. By Charles Butler, esq.
       Philadelphia, Hogan & Thompson, 1836.
       xii, [13]-288 p.   front.   14½ cm.
       Added t.-p., engr.

                            C

21824 [Cabell, Mrs. Margaret Couch (Anthony)] 1814-1882.
       Sketches and recollections of Lynchburg. By the
       oldest inhabitant [pseud.] Richmond, C. H. Wynne, 1858.
       vii, [9]-363 p.   19½ cm.
       Mainly biographical sketches.
       An index, compiled by William Frederic Holcombe, was
       published in 1920 as Bulletin of the Virginia state
       library, v. 13, no. 3.

21825 Cabell, Nathaniel Francis, 1807-1891.
       Early history of agriculture in Virginia, by N. F.
       Cabell... Washington, D. C., Printed by L. Towers
       [18--]
       41 p.   23 cm.

21826 Cabello de Balboa, Miguel, 16th cent.
       Histoire du Pérou, par Miguel Cavello Balboa.
       Inédite. Paris, A. Bertrand, 1840.
       vii, 331 p.   21 cm.   (Added t.-p.: Voyages,
       relations et mémoires originaux pour servir à l'histoire
       de la découverte de l'Amérique, pub. .... par H. Ternaux-
       Compans [t. 15])

21827 The cabinet conference; or Tears of ministry. Present
       the King, Duke of Richmond, Earl of Shelburne, Lord
       North, Lord G. Germaine. London, Printed for G.
       Kearsly, 1779.
       iv, 78 p.   18½ cm.

21828 Call, Richard Keith, 1791-1862.
       Union. - Slavery. - Secession. Letter from Governor
       R. K. Call, of Florida, to John S. Littell, of German-
       town, Pennsylvania. Philadelphia, C. Sherman & son,
       printers, 1861.
       31 p.   24 cm.

21829   [Cameron, Hugh]
        The troublesome trio. [Washington, 1867]
        11 p.   17 cm.
        Entered for copyright by Hugh Cameron. Verses,
        eulogistic of President Johnson. The "troublesome trio"
        are "envy, malice, hate."

21830   [Campbell, John] 1708-1775.
        The Spanish empire in America. Containing, a succinct
        relation of the discovery and settlement of its several
        colonies; a view of their respective situations, extent,
        commodities, trade, &c. ... By an English merchant.
        London, Printed for M. Cooper, 1747.
        viii, 4 , 330 p.   20 cm.
        The "Concise history of Spanish America," published
        1741, with a new t.-p.
        "Memoir concerning the settlements of the Jesuits in
        Paraguay," by a French officer: p. 321-330.

21831   Campbell, John Nicholson, 1798-1864.
        A discourse on the occasion of the death of James
        King, esq. Delivered in the First Presbyterian church
        of Albany, on the evening of the communion Sabbath,
        June 27, 1841. By Rev. J. N. Campbell... Pub. by
        request. Albany, Printed by J. Munsell, 1841.
        21 p.   23 cm.

21832   Campbell, John Richard.
        A history of the county of Yarmouth, Nova Scotia.
        By the Rev. J. R. Campbell. Saint John, N. B.,
        Published by J. & A. McMillan, 1876.
        xvi, 200 p.   illus.   20½ cm.

21833   Campbell, William Henry, 1808-1890.
        A funeral discourse, occasioned by the death of Rev.
        Andrew Yates, D.D., delivered before the Classis of
        Schenectady, in the R. P. Dutch church, Schenectady,
        on Sabbath, Nov. 17, 1844.
        34 p.   23½ cm.

21834   Campe, Joachim Heinrich, 1746-1818.
        Cortez; or, The conquest of Mexico; as related by a
        father to his children, and designed for the instruction
        of youth. Tr. from the German of J. H. Campe, by
        Elizabeth Helme... A new ed., with the translator's
        last corrections and improvements. London, Printed for
        Baldwin, Cradock, and Joy, 1826.
        iv, 259 p.   front. (fold. map)   17½ cm.

From v. 2 of the author's Die entdeckung von Amerika, of which the first edition was published Hamburg, 1780-81.

21835 Canal policy of the state of New York. [n.p., 184-]
8 p.   22 cm.   [With Morris, Thomas. Speech ...
February 9, 1839... Utica, 1844]
Caption title.

21836 [Canby, Margaret T   ]
Flowers from the battle-field, and other poems. By
M. T. C. Philadelphia, H. B. Ashmead, printer, 1864.
36 p.   15½ cm.

21837 A candid appeal to the present ruling party in the United
States, by a citizen. Alexandria, Printed by S.
Snowden, 1816.
52 p.   22 cm.

21838 A candid examination of the Address of the minority of
the Council of censors to the people of Pennsylvania:
together with remarks upon the danger and inconve-
niences of the principal defects of the constitution
of Pennsylvania. By one of the majority. Philadelphia,
1784.
40 p.   16 cm.

21839 [Canning, Josiah Dean] 1816-1892.
The harp and plow. By the "Peasant bard". Greenfield
[Mass.] M. H. Tyler, 1852.
viii, [9]-204 p.   19 cm.
Title vignette.

21840 Cardozo, Jacob Newton.
Reminiscences of Charleston. By J. N. Cardozo.
Charleston, J. Walker, printer, 1866.
144 p.   19 cm.

21841 Carey, Eustace, 1791-1855.
Memoir of William Carey, D. D., late missionary to
Bengal; professor of Oriental languages in the college
of Fort William, Calcutta. By Eustace Carey. With an
introductory essay, by Jeremiah Chaplin... Hartford,
Canfield and Robins, 1837.
468 p.   front. (port.)   16½ cm.

21842 Carey, Mathew, 1760-1839.
Brief view of the system of internal improvement of
the state of Pennsylvania; containing a glance at its

18

rise, progress, retardation, --the difficulties it
underwent, --its present state, --and its future
prospects... By M. Carey... Pub. by order of the
Society for the promotion of internal improvement.
Philadelphia, Printed by L. Bailey, 1831.
vii, [1], [9]-36 p.   22 cm.

21843   [Carey, Mathew] 1760-1839.
Common sense addresses, to the citizens of the
southern states... 3d ed., enl., and improved. By a
citizen of Philadelphia. Philadelphia, Printed by
Clark & Raser, 1829.
xii, 42 p.   21½ cm.
Signed: Hamilton.

21844   [Carey, Mathew] 1760-1839.
The crisis. An appeal to the good sense of the nation,
against the spirit of resistance and dissolution of the
Union... 2d ed. Philadelphia, Printed by W. F. Geddes,
1832.
28 p.   23½ cm.
At bottom of title: July 11, 1832. Gratuitous.
Preface signed: M. Carey.
"A list of the author's pamphlets on political
economy, as far as preserved": p. 28.

21845   [Carey, Mathew] 1760-1839.
The crisis: a solemn appeal to the President, the
Senate and House of representatives, and the citizens
of the United States, on the destructive tendency of the
present policy of this country, on its agriculture,
manufactures, commerce, and finances. With a comparison
between the extraordinary prosperity of Great Britain,
and the general depression in the United States. By a
Pennsylvanian... Philadelphia, H. C. Carey & I. Lea,
1823.
viii, [9]-79 p.   21 cm.

21846   [Carey, Mathew] 1760-1839.
The olive branch: or, Faults on both sides, Federal
and Democratic. A serious appeal on the necessity of
mutual forgiveness and harmony, to save our common
country from ruin. 7th ed. enlarged... Philadelphia,
Published by M. Carey, 1815.
486 p.   21 cm.
Author's presentation copy to the Senate.

21847   Carey, Mathew, 1760-1839.
A plumb pudding for the humane, chaste, valiant,

enlightened Peter Porcupine. Philadelphia [1799]
48 p.   21 cm.

21848   Carey, Mathew, 1760-1839.
A short account of the malignant fever, lately
prevalent in Philadelphia: with a statement of the
proceedings that took place on the subject in different
parts of the United States. By Mathew Carey. Philadelphia, Printed by the author, 1793.
103, [9] p.   21 cm.

21849   Carmen miserabile, a solemn lacrymatory for the grave of
Jonathan Marse, junior-sophister: who deceas'd at
Harvard College in Cambridge: June the 10th, 1708.
Born at Hingham: aged eighteen years and ten months.
[Cambridge? 1708?]
broadside.   21½ x 33 cm.
Unique copy in Boston Athenaeum is defective (torn in
lower right corner)

21850   [Cass, Lewis] 1782-1866.
Remarks on the policy and practice of the United
States and Great Britain in their treatment of the
Indians [anon.] From the North American review, no. LV,
for April, 1827. Boston, F. T. Gray, 1827.
78 p.   23 cm.

21851   Cassegrain, Arthur.
La grand-tronciade; ou, Itinéraire de Québec à la
Rivière-du-Loup; poème badin par Arthur Cassegrain.
Ottawa, G. E. Desbarats, 1866.
vii, 96 p.   17½ cm.

21852   [Castell, William] d. 1645.
A petition of W. C. exhibited to the high covrt of
Parliament new assembled, for the propagating of the
Gospel in America, and the West Indies; and for the
setling of our plantations there; which petition is
approved by 70 able English divines. Also by Master
Alexander Henderson, and some other worthy ministers
of Scotland. [London] Printed in the yeare, 1641.
1 p.l., 5-19 p.   19 cm.

21853   Castelnau, Francis, comte de, 1812-1880.
Expédition dan les parties centrales de l'Amérique
du Sud, de Rio de Janeiro à Lima, et de Lima au Para;
exécutée par ordre du gouvernement français pendant les
annés [!] 1843 à 1847, sous la direction de Francis de

Castelnau... Paris, P. Bertrand, 1850-59.
19 v. in   plates (part col.) maps, charts.
22 -31 cm.
Each part, except pt. 1, Histoire du voyage, has also
special t.-p., with date in some cases differing from
that of general t.-p.

21854 Castleman, Alfred Lewis, 1809-1877.
The Army of the Potomac. Behind the scenes. A diary
of unwritten history; from the organization of the
army... to the close of the campaign in Virginia, about
the first day of January, 1863. By Alfred L. Castleman...
Milwaukee, Strickland & co., 1863.
3 p.l., 288 p.   19½ cm.

21855 A catalogue of books lately imported from Britain and to
be sold by A[ndrew] Barclay... [Boston, 1765]
broadside.   36 x 22 cm.

21856 Chadbourne, Paul Ansel, 1823-1883.
The influence of history on individual and national
action. Annual address before the State historical
society of Wisconsin, Thursday evening, January 30th,
1868. By Paul A. Chadbourne... Published by order
of the Legislature. Madison, Atwood & Rublee, state
printers, 1868.
22 p., 1 l.   22½ cm.

21857 Chaffee, Calvin C   b. 1811.
The Lecompton constitution; a measure to Africanize
the territories of the United States. Speech of
Hon. Calvin C. Chaffee, of Massachusetts. Delivered
in the House of representatives, February 24th, 1858.
[Washington, D. C., Buell & Blanchard, printers, 1858]
8 p.   24 cm.

21858 Chaffin, William Ladd, 1837-
The President's death and its lessons. A discourse
on Sunday morning, April 23d, 1865, before the Second
Unitarian society of Philadelphia, by its pastor,
William L. Chaffin... Philadelphia, King & Baird,
printers, 1865.
18 p.   23 cm.

21859 Challen, Howard.
Publishers & stationers trade list directory. 1867-
1869. Philadelphia, H. Challen.[1867]-69.
3 v.   illus., col. plates.   26½ cm.

21

Title varies: 1867, The Uniform trade list circular.
For the benefit of publishers, booksellers, newsdealers,
and stationers [etc.]
    1868, Publishers' uniform trade list directory, com-
prising all the books, old and new, of upwards of two
hundred publishers...
    1869 ("Advance ed."), Publishers & stationers trade
list directory.
    Monthly lists appeared in Challen's "Uniform trade list
circular" November, 1866-   ("Publishers' and
stationers uniform trade list circular."
    No more published?

21860 [Chalmers, George] 1742-1825.
    An answer from the electors of Bristol, to the letter
of Edmund Burke, esq., on teh [!] affairs of America.
London, Printed for T. Cadell, 1777.
    2 p.l., 85, 5 p.   20½ cm.

21861 Chalmers, George, 1742-1825.
    An estimate of the comparative strength of Great
Britain during the present and four preceding reigns;
and of the losses of her trade from every war since
the revolution. By George Chalmers. A new edition to
which is added a dedication to Dr. James Currie...
London, Printed for John Stockdale, Piccadilly, 1794.
    2 p.l., cxvi, [v]-xi, 254, 15 p.   1 fold. tab.
20½ cm.

21862 Chalmers, George, 1742-1825.
    An introduction to the history of the revolt of the
American colonies; being a comprehensive view of its
origin, derived from the state papers contained in the
public offices of Great Britain. By George Chalmers...
Boston, J. Munroe and co., 1845.
    2 v.   24 cm.
    Vol. 1 appeared in 1782 and was suppressed. The
present ed. reprints that volume and gives the remaining
contents of the original manuscripts. cf. Pref.

21863 Chalmers, George, 1742-1825.
    Political annals of the present united colonies, from
their settlement to the peace of 1763; compiled chiefly
from records, and authorised often by the insertion of
state-papers. By George Chalmers, esq. Book I.
London, Printed for the author; and sold by J. Bowen,
1780.
    5 p.l., 695 p.   30 x 25 cm.

No more published in separate form. Book II appeared
in the collections of the New York historical society,
1868. Publication fund series v. 1.
Ms. note on fly leaf: To Sir John Dalrymple bart.
the author presents these Annals, which had never been
written but for his advice..."

21864 Champneys, John, fl. 1775-1778.
An account of the sufferings and persecution of John
Champneys, a native of Charles-town, South Carolina;
inflicted by order of Congress, for his refusal to take
up arms in defence of the arbitrary proceedings carried
on by the rulers of said place. Together with his
protest, &c. London, Printed in the year 1778.
1 p.l., ii, 20 p.   21½ cm.

21865 Chandler, Samuel, 1713-1775.
A sermon preached at Glocester, Thursday, November 29,
1759. Being the day of the provincial anniversary Thanks-
giving. Published at the desire of some of the hearers.
By Samuel Chandler, A.M. Pastor of a church in Glocester [!]...
Boston, New England, Printed by Green & Russell, at their
Office in Queen Street [1759]
30 p.   20 cm.

21866 Chanler, John Winthrop, 1826-1877.
Down with the black flag of confiscation; up with the
union jack. Speech of Hon. John W. Chanler, of New
York, in the House of representatives, December 10, 1867.
In reply to Mr. Stevens, of Pennsylvania, on his
southern confiscation bill. [Washington, 1867]
8 p.   24 cm.
Caption title.

21867 Channing, Walter, 1786-1876.
Thoughts on the origin, nature, principles and
prospects of the temperance reform. By Walter Channing...
Boston, Perkins, Marvin, & co., 1834.
27 p.   23½ cm.
"From the American quarterly observer."

21868 Chapin, Edwin Hubbell, 1814-1880.
The relation of the individual to the republic. A
sermon delivered before His Excellency Marcus Morton,
governor, His Honor Henry H. Childs, lieutenant governor,
the honorable Council, and the legislature of Massachusetts, at the annual election, on Wednesday, January 3,
1844. By E. H. Chapin... Boston, Dutton and Wentworth,

23

printers to the state, 1844.
36 p.   23 cm.
Printed by order of the Massachusetts House of
representatives.

21869 Chapin, William, 1802-1888, comp.
A complete reference gazetteer of the United States
of North America; containing a general view of the
United States, and of each state and territory, and a
notice of the various canals, railroads and internal
improvements... together with all the post offices
in the United States... By William Chapin. New York,
W. Chapin and J. B. Taylor, 1839.
347, [3] p.   23 cm.

21870 Chapman, Frederick William, 1806-1876.
The Pratt family: or, The descendants of Lieut.
William Pratt, one of the first settlers of Hartford
and Say-Brook, with genealogical notes of John Pratt,
of Hartford; Peter Pratt, of Lyme; John Pratt (Taylor)
of Say-Brook. By Rev. F. W. Chapman... Hartford,
Printed by Case, Lockwood and company, 1864.
420 p., 1 l.   front. (coat of arms) ports.   23½ cm.

21871 Chappell, Edward, 1792-1861.
Narrative of a voyage to Hudson's bay in His Majesty's
ship Rosamond, containing some account of the northeastern
coast of America and of the tribes inhabiting that
remote region. By Lieut. Edward Chappell, R. N. ...
London, Printed for J. Mawman, 1817, 1817.
6 p.l., 279 p.   front. (fold. map) illus., pl.
21 cm.

21872 Chappell, Edward, 1792-1861.
Voyage of His Majesty's ship Rosamond to Newfoundland
and the southern coast of Labrador, of which countries
no account has been published by any British traveller
since the reign of Queen Elizabeth. By Lieut. Edward
Chappell, R. N. ... London, Printed for J. Mawman,
1818.
5 p.l., xix, 270 p.   front., illus., fold. map.
22½ cm.

21873 Charlevoix, Pierre François Xavier de, 1682-1761.
The history of Paraguay. Containing... a full and
authentic account of the establishment formed there
by the Jesuits, from among the savage whites...
establishments allowed to have realized the sublime

ideas of Fenelon. Sir Thomas More, and Plato. Written
originally in French by the celebrated Father Charlevoix...
London, L. Davis, 1769.
2 v.   21½ cm.
An abridged translation.

21874   Charlevoix, Pierre François Xavier de, 1682-1761.
Letters to the Dutchess of Lesdiguières; giving an
account of a voyage to Canada, and travels through that
vast country, and Louisiana, to the Gulf of Mexico.
Undertaken by order of the present king of France, by
Father Charlevoix... London, Printed for R. Goadby
[etc.] 1763.
xiv, 2 , 384 p.   front. (fold. map)   20 cm.
Marginal notes.
Not the same translation as "Journal of a voyage to
North America", 1761; and lacking the Preliminary
discourse and letter I, there given.

21875   Chase, Lucien Bonaparte, 1817-1864.
History of the Polk administration. By Lucien B.
Chase... New York, G. P. Putnam, 1850.
viii, 9-512 p.   23½ cm.

21876   Chase, Mary M   1822-1852.
Mary M. Chase and her writings. Henry Fowler, editor.
Boston, Ticknor and Fields, 1855.
xlvi p., 1 l., 336 p.   19 cm.
Sketch of life, containing "Last days - an account
prepared by C. Thurston Chase": p. [xl]-xlvi.

21877   Chase, Salmon Portland, 1808-1873.
A sketch of the history of Ohio. By Salmon P. Chase.
Cincinnati, Corey and Fairbank, 1833.
1 p.l., 40 p.   26 cm.
Reissue of "Preliminary sketches of the Ohio" from
Chase's edition of "The statutes of Ohio", 1833, v. 1,
p. 9-48.

21878   Chase, Samuel, 1741-1811, defendant.
Report of the trial of the Hon. Samuel Chase, one of
the associate justices of the Supreme court of the
United States, before the High court of impeachment,
composed of the Senate of the United States, for charges
exhibited against him by the House of representatives,
in the name of themselves, and of all the people of the
United States, for high crimes and misdemeanors,
supposed to have been by him committed; with the

necessary documents and official papers, from his
impeachment to final acquittal. Taken in short hand,
by Charles Evans, and the arguments of counsel revised
by them from his manuscript. [Augmented ed.] Baltimore,
Printed for Samuel Butler and George Keatinge, 1805.
3 p.l., 12, [3]-268 (i.e. 316), 63 p.   23½ cm.

21879   Chasles, Philarète, 1798-1873.
        Études sur la littérature et les moeurs des Anglo-
        Américains au XIXe siècle, par m. Philarète Chasles...
        Paris, Amyot pref. 1851
        2 p.l., viii, 515 p.   18 cm.

21880   Chastellux, François Jean, marquis de, 1734-1788.
        Voyage de Mr. le chevalier de Chastellux en Amérique.
        [Cassel] 1785.
        228 p.   17½ cm.
        A surreptitious edition, being a reprint of the
        extracts from his ms. journal first published in a Gotha
        periodical. cf. The Paris edition of 1786, p. 7.

21881   Chateaubriand, François Auguste René, vicomte de, 1768-1848.
        Recollections of Italy, England and America, with
        essays on various subjects, in morals and literature, by
        F. A. de Chateaubriand. Philadelphia, Published by
        M. Carey, no. 121 Chestnut street, 1816.
        iv, [ix]-xiii p., 1 l., [17]-364 p.   23½ cm.

21882   Chatterton, Augustus.
        The buds of beauty; or, Parnassian sprig. Being a
        collection of original poems, upon various subjects.
        By Augustus Chatterton, esq. ... New York, Printed
        for the Author, by Francis Childs, 1787.
        x, 11 -106 p.   16 cm.
        Dedication to Franklin, dated Baltimore, January 22,
        1787. Book-plate: Henry B. Anthony.

21883   Chaudron, Mrs. Adelaide de Vendel.
        ... The first reader, designed for the use of primary
        schools. 2d ed. Adopted for use in the public schools
        of Mobile. By A. de V. Chaudron. Mobile, Ala., W. G.
        Clark & co., 1864.
        57 p.   front.   18 cm.   (Chaudron's series)

21884   Chaudron, Jean Simon.
        Funeral oration on Brother George Washington;
        delivered January 1st, 1800, before the French lodge
        l'Aménité. By Brother Simon Chaudron. Translated from

26

the French by Samuel F. Bradford. Philadelphia,
Printed by John Ormrod, no. 41 Chestnut street, 1800.
26 p.   21 cm.
Title vignette.

21885   Chauncey, Charles, 1777-1849.
An oration, delivered before the society of the
at their anniversary meeting, in the city of New Haven,
on the evening preceding commencement, anno Domini 1797.
By Charles Chauncey, jun. Published at the request of
the society. Printed by T. and S. Green, New Haven [1798]
34 p.   20 cm.

21886   Chauncy, Charles, 1705-1787.
Man's life considered under the similitude of a vapour
... A sermon the death of that honorable & vertuous
gentlewoman Mrs. Sarah Byfield, the amiable consort of
the Honorable Nathaniel Byfield, esq.; who died December
21st, 1730. In the 58th year of her age. By Charles
Chauncy, M.A., one of the pastors of the First church in
Boston... Boston, Printed by B. Green, 1731.
2 p.l., 42 p.   19 cm.

21887   Chauncy, Charles, 1705-1787.
Marvellous things done by the right hand and holy arm
of God in getting him the victory. A sermon preached
the 18th of July 1745. Being a day set apart for solemn
thanksgiving to almighty God, for the reduction of
Cape-Breton by His Majesty's New England forces, under
the command of the Honourable William Pepperrell, esq.
... and cover'd by a squadron of His Majesty's ships
from Great Britain, commanded by Peter Warren, esq.;
by Charles Chauncy... Boston, Printed and sold by
J. Fleet at the Heart and Crown in Cornhill, 1745.
23 p.   20½ cm.

21888   [Chauncy, Charles] 1705-1787.
A second letter to a friend; giving a more particular
narrative of the defeat of the French army at Lake-
George, by the New England troops, than has yet been
published: representing also the vast importance of
this conquest to the American-British colonies. To
which is added, such an account of what the New England
governments have done to carry into effect their design
against Crown-Point, as will shew the necessity of their
being help'd by Great Britain, in point of money.
Boston, Printed and sold by Edes and Gill, at their
printing office, next to the prison in Queen-street, 1755.

27

16 p. 19½ cm.
Signed: T. W. (pseud.) and dated: Boston, September 29th, 1755.
Binder's title: Chauncy's Battle of L. George.
The first letter, published earlier the same year, gives an account of Braddock's defeat.

21889 Chauveau, P[ierre] J[oseph] O[livier]
Discours prononcé le mercredi, 18 juillet 1855, par l'honorable P. J. O. Chauveau... a la cérémonie de la pose de la pierre angulaire du monument dédié... à la mémoire des braves tombés sur la Plaine d'Abraham, le 28 avril 1760... Québec, De la presse de E. R. Fréchette 1855.
8 p. 26 cm.

21890 [Checkley, John] 1680-1754.
A defence of a book lately re-printed at Boston, entituled, A modest proof of the order and government settled by Christ and his apostles in the church in a reply to a book entituled, Sober remarks on the Modest proof, &c. In a letter to a friend... Boston, Printed by T. Fleet, 1724.
2 p.l., 3-73, 14 p., 1 l. 17 cm.
Half-title: ... With some strictures on J. Dickinson's Defence of Presbyterian ordination, by way of postscript. Also, Animadversions upon two pamphlets, the one entituled, An essay upon that paradox, Infallibility may sometimes mistake [by Thomas Walter] The other, The ruling and ordaining power of Congregational bishops or presbyters defended [by Thomas Foxcroft] &c.
A defence of the author's "Modest proof", written in reply to Edward Wigglesworth's "Sober remarks on a book lately re-printed at Boston, entituled, "A modest proof... Boston, 1724.
"Errata": 1 leaf at end.

21891 [Checkley, John] 1680-1754.
A modest proof of the order & government settled by Christ and his apostles in the church. By shewing I. What sacred offices were instituted by them. II. How these offices were distinguished. III. That they were to be perpetual and standing in the church. And, IV. Who succeeded in them, and rightly execute them to this day... Boston, Reprinted by Tho. Fleet, and are to be sold by Benjamin Eliot in Boston, Daniel Aurault in Newport, Gabriel Bernon in Providence, Mr. Gallop in Bristol, Mr. Jean in Stratford, and in most other towns

within the colonies of Connecticut and Rhode-Island,
1723.
First published in London, 1645. cf. Halkett & Laing,
2d ed.
Though called a reprint, there seems no doubt that the
present edition is the first and that Checkley is the
author.
With this are bound: Wigglesworth, Edward. Sober
remarks on... A modest proof of the order and government...
in the church. Boston, 1724; Foxcroft, Thomas. The
ruling & ordaining power of congregational bishops...
defended. Boston, 1724, and Dickinson, Jonathan. A
defence of Presbyterian ordination. Boston, 1724.

21892 Checkley, John, 1680-1754.
The speech of Mr. John Checkley, upon his trial at
Boston in 1724, with an introduction by Rev. E. H.
Gillett, D.D. of Harlem, N. Y. Morrisania, N. Y.,
1868.
[4], vii-xx p.   22 cm.

21893 Checkley, John, 1680-1754.
The speech of Mr. John Checkley upon his tryal, at
Boston in New England, for publishing the Short and easy
method with the deists: To which was added, a discourse
concerning episcopacy; in defense of Christianity, and
the Church of England, against the deists and the
dissenters. To which is added: The jury's verdict;
his plea in arrest of judgment; and the sentence of the
court. The 2d ed. London, printed by J. Applebee,
in Bolt-Court, Fleet street, 1738.
[2], 3-31 p.   22 cm.
Reprinted from: Boston historical discourses, v. 2,
1831.

21894 Checkley, Samuel, 1696-1769.
A day of darkness. A sermon preach'd before His
Excellency William Shirley, esq; the honorable His
Majesty's Council, and House of representatives, of
the province of the Massachusetts-Bay, in New England.
May 28th 1755. Being the anniversary for the election
of His Majesty's Council for said province. By Samuel
Checkley, A. M., pastor of the New South church in
Boston. Boston, Printed by John Draper, printer to
His Excellency the governor and the honorable His
Majesty's Council, MDCCLV.
35 p.   19½ cm.

21895 Checkley, Samuel, 1723-1768.
The duty of God's people when engaged in war. A
sermon preached at the North-church of Christ in Boston,
Sept. 21. To Captain Thomas Stoddard, and his company;
on occasion of their going against the enemy. By Samuel
Checkley, A. M., pastor of said church... Boston,
Printed and sold by D. Fowle, in Ann street, and Z. Fowle,
in Middle-street, below the Mill bridge, 1755.
31 p.   19 x 14½ cm.
Half-title: Mr. Checkley's sermon to a company of
soldiers, going against Crown-Point.

21896 Cheetham, James, 1772-1810.
Letters on our affairs with Spain. By James Cheetham.
New York, Printed for the author, 1804.
59 p.   23 cm.

21897 Cheetham, James, 1772-1810.
The life of Thomas Paine. By James Cheetham...
America printed: London; Reprinted for A. Maxwell,
Bell Yard, Temple Bar. W. Pople, Printer, 67, Chancery
Lane, 1817.
xxvii, [17]-187 p.   22 cm.
Unfriendly to Paine. cf. Conway's Life of Paine, 1892,
v. 1, p. xvi-xvii.

21898 Cheetham, James, 1772-1810.
A reply to Aristides, by James Cheetham... New York,
Printed for James Chetham; H. C. Southwick, printer,
1804.
145 p.   23 cm.
In 1802 Cheetham published "A view of the political
conduct of Aaron Burr." which elicited a reply from
W. P. Van Ness, issued in 1803 under the pseudonym
Aristides, with title: An examination of the various
charges exhibited against Aaron Burr... The present
publication is a reply to that of Van Ness.

21899 [Cheetham, James] 1772-1810.
A view of the political conduct of Aaron Burr, esq.,
vice-president of the United States. By the author of
the "Narrative." New York, Printed by Denniston &
Cheetham, 1802.
120 p.   21 cm.

21900 Cheever, George Barrell, 1807-1890, comp.
The American common-place book of prose, a collection
of eloquent and interesting extracts from the writings

of American authors. By G. B. Cheever. Boston,
Russell, Shattuck and co. [cl828]
468 p.   18 cm.

21901   Cheever, George Barrell, 1807-1890.
        The curse of God against political atheism; with some
        of the lessons of the tragedy at Harper's Ferry. A
        discourse delivered in the Church of the Puritans, New
        York, on Sabbath evening, Nov. 6, 1859. By Rev. George
        B. Cheever, D. D. Boston, Walker, Wise & co., 1859.
        24 p.   23½ cm.
        Cover title: Two sermons on the tragedy at Harper's
        Ferry. Appended: Causes and consequences of the affair
        at Harper's Ferry... By J. F. Clarke.

21902   Cheever, George Barrell, 1807-1890.
        God's hand in America. By the Rev. George B. Cheever.
        With an essay, by the Rev. Dr. Skinner. New York,
        M. W. Dodd; London, Wiley & Putnam, 1841.
        xx, [21]-168 p.   19 cm.

21903   Cheever, Henry Theodore, 1814-1897.
        The whale and his captors; or, The whaleman's adventures,
        and the whale's biography as gathered on the homeward
        cruise of the "Commodore Preble." By Rev. Henry T.
        Cheever... New York, Harper & brothers, 1850 [cl849]
        xiii, [15]-314 p. incl. front., plates.   17½ cm.

21904   Cheever, Samuel, 1639-1724.
        God's sovereign government among the nations asserted
        in a sermon preached before His Excellency the Governour,
        the Honourable Council, and Representatives of the
        province of the Massachusetts Bay in New England, on
        May 28, 1712, being the day for election of Her Majesties
        council for that province. By Samuel Cheever... Boston,
        Printed by B. Green; Sold at the Booksellers Shops, 1712.
        1 p.l., 53 p.   14 cm.

21905   Cheney, Theseus Apoleon, 1830-1878.
        Historical sketch of the Chemung Valley, etc. by
        T. Apoleon Cheney. Watkins, N. Y., 1868.
        1 p.l., 59 p.   22½ cm.
        Appended, "Antiquarian researches. By T. Apoleon
        Cheney [with a criticism of his work]" Reprinted from
        the Art journal, [12] p.

21906   Cheney, Timothy Collingwood, 1808-1871.
        Reminiscences of Syracuse, by Timothy C. Cheney.

31

Comp. by Parish B. Johnson from personal recollections
of the author; first pub. in the Syracuse daily standard.
Syracuse, Summers & brother, printers, 1857.
(In Onondaga historical association, Syracuse, N. Y.
Annual volume, 1914. Syracuse, N. Y. [1915] 23 cm.
p. [88]-187. port.)
"Some notes on the Cheney reminiscences by the Rev.
W. M. Beauchamp... with additions from others": p. 163-
187.

21907 Cherokee nation.
Memorial of the delegates of the Cherokee nation to
the President of the United States, and the Senate and
House of representatives in Congress. [Washington, D.C.]
Washington chronicle print, 1866.
12 p.   23 cm.
Signed: Smith Christie... James McDaniel... Thomas
Pegg... White Catcher... Daniel H. Ross... J. B. Jones...
S. H. Benge... Cherokee delegation.

21908 Chesapeake and Ohio canal company.
Acts of Virginia, Maryland, and Pennsylvania, and of
the Congress of the United States, in relation to the
Chesapeake & Ohio canal company; together with all the
acts and resolutions concerning the Potomac company:
to which are appended the by-laws, list of officers, &c.
of the Chesapeake and Ohio canal company. Printed by
order of the company. Washington, Printed by Gales &
Seaton, 1828.
106, 6 p.   22½ cm.
Lettered on cover: Chesapeake and Ohio canal company,
1784-1828.

21909 Chesapeake and Ohio canal company.
Reports and letters from the engineers employed in the
revised location of the western section of the Chesapeake
and Ohio canal: with the estimates of the cost of the
same... (In its First annual report. Washington, 1829.
22 cm. 104 p. at end)
Reports made by Benjamin Wright and Nathan S. Roberts.

21910 [Chetwood, William Rufus] d. 1766.
Les voyages et avantures du capitaine Robert Boyle;
où l'on trouve l'histoire de mademoiselle Villars,
avec qui il se sauva de Barbarie; celle d'un esclave
italien, & celle de dom Pedro Quilio, qui fournit des
éxemples des coups les plus surprenans de la fortune;
avec la Relation du voyage, du naufrage & de la conser-

vation miraculeuse du Sr. Castelman, où l'on voit une
description de la Pensylvanie & de Philadelphie sa
capitale. Tr. de l'anglois... Amsterdam, Wetsteins &
Smith, 1730.
2 v. fronts., plates. 16½ cm.
"This work has been attributed to Benjamin Victor,
also to Daniel Defoe." - Sabin, Bibl. amer.
"Boyle's narrative is probably fictitious, but that
of Castelman bears mark of authenticity." - Rich,
Bibl. amer. nova.

21911 ... Chicago city directory and business advertiser...
Chicago, 18
v. fold. front., plates, maps. 18-23½ cm.
Library has 1849.

21912 Chipman, Daniel, 1765-1850.
The life of Col. Seth Warner, with an account of the
controversy between New York and Vermont, from 1763 to
1775. By Daniel Chipman, LL. D. Burlington, C. Goodrich
& company, 1858.
iv, [5]-84 p. 15 cm.
First edition, Middlebury, Vt., 1848, published under
title, "Memoir of Colonel Seth Warner, by Daniel Chipman...
to which is added, the life of Colonel Ethan Allen, by
Jared Sparks." The life of Allen is omitted from the
present edition.

21913 Chipman, Daniel, 1765-1850.
The life of Hon. Nathaniel Chipman, LL.D., formerly
member of the United States Senate, and chief justice
of the state of Vermont. With selections from his
miscellaneous papers. By his brother, Daniel Chipman.
Boston, C. C. Little and J. Brown, 1846.
xii, [5]-402 p. 24 cm.

21914 The Christian Baptist... Ed. by Alexander Campbell.
Bethany, Brooke county, Va. [etc.] A. Campbell,
1823-1830.
v. 18½ cm.
Library has v. 1-7, 1823-1830. V. 1 and 2 are 2d ed.
Published from Aug. 3, 1823-July 5, 1830. Superseded
by the Millennial Harbinger. cf. Union list of serials.

21915 The Christian register, and moral and theological review.
v. 1-2, no. 1; July 1816-July 1817. New York, T. and J.
Swords.
2 v. 23 cm. semiannual.
Edited by T. Y. How.

21916　The Christian's duty to render to Caesar the things that
are Caesar's, considered; with regard to the payment
of the present tax of sixty thousand pounds, granted
to the king's use. In which all the arguments for the
non-payment thereof are examined and refuted. Addressed
to the scrupulous among the people called Quakers.
By a lover of his king and country. Philadelphia,
Printed [by Franklin & Hall] 1756.
27 p.　　19 cm.

21917　Christie, James, jr., fl. 1774-1775.
The case of James Christie, jun. late of the province
of Maryland, merchant. [n.p., 1776?]
24 p.　　20 cm.
Caption title; signed: James Christie, jun.
Christie was imprisoned by the Baltimore Committee of
safety and later fined and banished by the Provincial
convention of Maryland for having in a letter expressed
sentiments "altogether inimical to the rights and
liberties of America".

21918　Christie, Robert, 1788-1856.
Memoirs of the administration of the colonial government
of Lower-Canada, by Sir James Henry Craig, and Sir
George Prevost. From the year 1807 until the year 1815.
Comprehending the military and naval operations in the
Canadas during the late war with the United States of
America. By Robert Christie. Quebec, 1818.
150, [9], 5 p., 1 l.　　22½ cm.
Issued also, in 1818, under title: The military and
naval operations in the Canadas, during the late war
with the United States. Including also, the political
history of Lower Canada... from... 1807 until... 1815.

21919　Church, Samuel, 1785-1854.
A historical address, delivered at the commemoration
of the one hundredth anniversary of the first annual
town meeting of the town of Salisbury, October 20, 1841.
By Samuel Church. New Haven, Hitchcock & Stafford,
printers, 1842.
96 p.　　23 cm.

21920　Church, Sanford Elias, 1815-1880.
Speech by Hon. Sanford E. Church, at Batavia,
October 13, 1863. [Batavia? N. Y.] 1863.
8 p.　　23½ cm.
Criticism of the administration's war policy, etc.

21921   Church, William.
        An analysis of the waters of the Bedford mineral
        springs, &c. by Dr. William Church... Bedford, Pa.,
        Printed by C. M'Dowell [1825?]
        1 p.l., 8 p.   22½ cm.
        Read before the Pittsburg medical society.

21922   Cincinnati. Chamber of commerce and merchants' exchange.
        ... Bridging the Ohio and Mississippi rivers.
        Memorial of Cincinnati Chamber of commerce and merchants'
        exchange... Cincinnati, Gazette steam printing esta-
        blishment, 1868.
        cover-title, 36 p., 1 l.   21½ cm.
        At head of title: To the Congress of the United States.

21923   Cincinnati. Chamber of commerce and merchants' exchange.
        Reply of the Chamber of commerce of Cincinnati, to the
        inquiries made by S. B. W. McLean, esq., collector of
        the port of Cincinnati, on the subject of the improve-
        ment of the falls of the Ohio River. Cincinnati,
        G. W. Tagart & co., 1853.
        20 p.   22½ cm.

21924   Cincinnati. Citizens.
        Memorial of the citizens of Cincinnati, to the Congress
        of the United States, relative to the navigation of
        the Ohio and Mississippi rivers. Cincinnati, Printed
        at the Daily Atlas office, 1844.
        53 p.   22 cm.

21925   Cincinnati. Committee on the explosion of the Moselle.
        Report of the committee appointed by the citizens of
        Cincinnati, April 26, 1838, to enquire into the causes
        of the explosion of the Moselle, and to suggest such
        preventive measures as may be best calculated to guard
        hereafter against such occurrences. Cincinnati, A.
        Flash, 1838.
        76 p.   front., illus.   22 cm.

21926   Cincinnati. Fire department.
        Annual report of the chief engineer of the Cincinnati
        fire department. Cincinnati, 1854-19
        v.   front.   22 cm.
        Library has only first annual report.

21927   Cincinnati. House of refuge.
        The charter, rules and regulations for the government
        of the House of refuge and its inmates, and the by-laws

of the Board of directors. Cincinnati, Daily times book
and job rooms, 1850.
ii, 19, 3 p.   front., plates, plan.   23 cm.

21928 Cincinnati. Ordinances, etc.
Charter, amendments, and general ordinances, of the
city of Cincinnati. Revised, A.D. 1850. Pub. by order
of the City council. [Cincinnati] Day & co., printers,
1850.
3 p.l., [3]-486 p.   23 cm.
Collated by George W. Allen, Jonah Martin, Wm. Bromwell,
law committee.

21929 Cincinnati. Ordinances, etc.
An act incorporating the city of Cincinnati, and a
digest of the ordinances of said city, of a general
nature, now in force, with an appendix. Rev. and pub.
by order of the City council. Cincinnati, Lodge,
L'Hommedieu and co., printers, 1835.
3 p.l., [5]-164 p.   21 cm.

21930 Cincinnati colonization society.
Proceedings of the Cincinnati colonization society,
at the annual meeting, January 14, 1833. Pub. by order
of the managers. Cincinnati, Printed by F. S. Benton,
1833.
17 p., 1 l.   23 cm.

21931 [Cincinnatus, L. Quincius] pseud.
A letter to the freeholders and other inhabitants of
the Massachusetts-Bay, relating to their approaching
election of representatives... Boston, Rogers & Fowle
[1749?]
8 p.   19½ cm.

21932 Cist, Charles, 1792-1868.
Cincinnati in 1841; its early annals and future
prospects. By Charles Cist. Cincinnati, Printed and
pub. for the author, 1841.
xi, 13-300 p.   plates.   19 cm.

21933 Civilization; or, The Indian chief and British pastor...
London, Printed for T. Egerton, 1818.
3 v.   18 cm.

20934 Civis anglicus, pseud.
A voice from the motherland, answering Mrs. H. Beecher
Stowe's appeal. By Civis anglicus. London, Trübner

and co., 1863.
2 p.l., 46 p.   22½ cm.

21935 Clapp, Theodore, 1792-1866.
Slavery: a sermon, delivered in the First Congrega-
tional church in New Orleans, April 15, 1838. By
Theodore Clapp. Pub. by request. New Orleans,
J. Gibson, printer, 1838.
67 p.   20 cm.

21936 Clark, Edward L   , of Philadelphia, comp.
A record of the inscriptions on the tables and grave-
stones in the burial grounds of Christ church, Philadelphia. Compiled and arranged at the request of vestry.
By Edward L. Clark... Philadelphia, Collins, printer,
1864.
ix, 637 p.   front., plates, plans.   20½ cm.

21737 Clark, Ferdinand.
The American captives in Havana, being Ferdinand
Clark's reply to Nicholas P. Trist, consul at that
place. Boston, Press of J. Howe, 1841.
36 p.   24 cm.

21938 Clark, George Rogers, 1752-1818.
Col. George Rogers Clark's sketch of his campaign in
the Illinois in 1778-9; with an introduction by Hon.
Henry Pirtle, of Louisville, and an appendix containing
the public and private instructions to Col. Clark, and
Major Bowman's journal of the taking of Post St.
Vincents. Cincinnati, R. Clark & co., 1869.
vi p., 1 l., 119 p.   front. (port.)   25 cm.
(Ohio valley historical series, no. 3)

21939 Clark, Joseph Sylvester, 1800-1861.
An historical sketch of Sturbridge, Mass., from its
settlement to the present time. By Joseph S. Clark...
Brookfield, E. and L. Merriam, printers, 1838.
48 p.   23 cm.

21940 Clark, Rufus Wheelwright, 1813-1886.
A review of the Rev. Moses Stuart's pamphlet on
slavery, entitled Conscience and the Constitution,
by Rufus W. Clark... Boston, C. C. P. Moody, 1850.
103 p.   22½ cm.
Originally published in the Boston daily atlas.

21941 Clark, Samuel Adams, 1822-1875.
The Episcopal church in the American colonies.

37

The history of St. John's church, Elizabethtown, New
Jersey, from the year 1703 to the present time. Compiled
from original documents, the manuscript records and
letters of the missionaries of the Society for propagating the gospel in foreign parts, and from other
sources. By Samuel A. Clark... Philadelphia, J. B.
Lippincott and co.; New York, T. N. Stanford, 1857.
  4 p.l., [vii]-xi, [13]-203 p.   front., plates.
18½ cm.

21942 Clarke, Samuel, 1599-1682.
  The lives of sundry eminent persons in this later age.
In two parts, I. Of divines. II. Of nobility and gentry
of both sexes. By Samuel Clark... Printed and reviewed
by himself just before his death. To which is added his
own life, and the lives of the countess of Suffolk,
Sir Nathan Barnardiston, Mr. Richard Blackerby, and Mr.
Samuel Fairclough, drawn up by other hands... London,
Printed for Thomas Simmons at the Princes Arms in
Ludgate-street, 1683.
  1 p.l., 216 p.   front., illus. (ports.)   32½ cm.
  Irregular foliation and pagination; for explanation
see "Directions to the Book-binder" on errata page.

21943 Clarke, Samuel, 1599-1682.
  A true and faithful account of the four chiefest
plantations of the English in America. To wit, of
Virginia. New England. Bermudus. Barbados.
With the temperature of the air: the nature of the
soil: the rivers, mountains, beasts... fruits, etc.
As also, of the natives of Virginia, and New England,
their religion, customs... &c. Collected by Samuel
Clarke... London, Printed for R. Clavel, T. Passenger,
W. Cadman, W. Whitwood, T. Sawbridge, and W. Birch,
1670.
  85 (i.e. 91) p.   29 cm.   (In his A mirrour or
looking-glass. 4th ed. 1671. v. 1, [pt. 3])
  "The description of the island of Barbados" (beginning
p. 57) appears to be condensed from "A true & exact
history of the island of Barbadoes" by Richard Ligon,
London, 1657.
  This account is appended to the author's "Geographical
description of all the countries," London, 1671, which
forms the 2d part of v. 1 of the "Mirrour."
  "Examples of the wonderful works of God in the
creatures": 35 p. at end.
  Paging irregular.

21944   Clarke, Samuel, 1791-1859.
        The character and reward of the righteous. A sermon,
        occasioned by the death of John Adams: preached in
        Princeton, July 16, 1826. By Samuel Clarke, minister
        of the Congregational church in Princeton. Worcester,
        William Manning, printer [1826?]
        23 p.   21 cm.

21945   Clarke, Samuel Clarke, b. 1806.
        Records of some of the descendants of John Fuller,
        Newton, 1644-98. Compiled from Jackson's history of
        Newton, and other sources. By Samuel C. Clarke.
        Boston, Printed by D. Clapp & son, 1869.
        16 p.   28½ cm.

21946   Clarke, Samuel Clarke, b. 1806.
        Records of some of the descendants of Richard Hull,
        New Haven, 1639-1662. Comp. by Samuel C. Clarke.
        Boston, Printed by D. Clapp & son, 1869.
        20 p.   24 cm.

21947   Clarke, Samuel Clarke, b. 1806.
        Records of some of the descendants of Thomas Clarke,
        Plymouth, 1623-1697. Comp. by Samuel C. Clarke.
        Boston, Printed by D. Clapp & son, 1869.
        43 p.   23½ cm.

21948   Clarke school for the deaf, Northampton, Mass.
        Annual report. Northampton, Mass. [etc.] 1868-
        v.   plates.   23 cm.
        Library has 1867/68.

21949   [Clarke, Sidney] 1831-1909.
        Remonstrance against the treaty with the Great and
        Little Osage Indians... Washington, Gibson brothers,
        printers, 1868.
        11 p.   22 cm.

21950   [Clarke, William] M.D., fl. 1755.
        Observations on the late and present conduct of the
        French, with regard to their encroachments upon the
        British colonies in North America. Together with
        remarks on the importance of these colonies to Great
        Britain. To which is added, wrote by another hand;
        Observations concerning the increase of mankind,
        peopling of countries, &c. Boston, Printed and sold
        by S. Kneeland, in Queen street, 1755.
        4 p.l., iv, 47, 15 p.   18½ cm.

39

Dedication signed: William Clarke.
Title of London reprint of same date reads "By William
Clarke, M.D. of Boston, in New England."
"Observations concerning the increase of mankind" was
written by Benjamin Franklin, in 1751.

21951   Clarkson, Thomas, 1760-1846.
A portraiture of Quakerism. Taken from a view of the
education and discipline, social manners, civil and
political economy, religious principles and character,
of the Society of Friends. By Thomas Clarkson... New
York, Published by Samuel Stansbury, no. 11, Water-
street, 1806.
3 v.   front. (port.)   21½ cm.

21952   Clausson, L   J
Précis historique de la révolution de Saint-Domingue.
Réfutation de certains ouvrages publiés sur les causes
de cette révolution. De l'etat actuel de cette colonie,
et de la nécessité d'en recouvrer la possession. Par
L. J. Clausson... Paris, Pillet aîné, 1819.
2 p.l., xii, 155 p.   8°

21953   Clavijero, Francisco Javier, 1731-1787.
Historia de la Antigua ó Baja California. Obra
postuma del padre Francisco Javier Clavijero... Tr. del
italiano por el presbitero Don Nicolas Garcia de San
Vicente. Méjico, Impr. de J. R. Navarro, 1852.
4 p.l., v, 252, [6] p.   26½ cm.
"Relación histórica de la vida del venerable padre
fray Junipero Serra," [por F. Palou]: p. [125]-252.

21954   Clay, Jehu Curtis, 1792-1863.
Annals of the Swedes on the Delaware. By the Rev.
Jehu Curtis Clay... To which is added the charter of
the United Swedish churches. Philadelphia, J. C. Pechin,
1835.
180 p. incl. pl.   front. (port.)   15 cm.

21955   Cleaveland, John, 1722-1799.
An essay, to defend some of the most important
principles in the Protestant reformed system of
Christianity, on which the churches of Christ in New
England, were originally founded: more especially;
the doctrine of Christ's sacrifice and atonement, as
being absolutely necessary to the pardon of sin,
consistently with God's infinite and unchangeable
rectitude; against the injurious aspersions cast on

the same, by Jonathan Mayhew, D.D., in his late Thanksgiving sermons on Psal. CXLV. 9. In which some of the
doctor's mistakes, inaccuracies and inconsistencies,
are pointed out. By John Cleaveland... Boston, Printed
and sold by D. and J. Kneeland, opposite to the prison
in Queen-street, 1763.
108 p.   19 cm.

21956 Cleaveland, John.
The banking system of the state of New York, with notes
and references to adjudged cases; including also an
account of the New York clearing house. By John Cleaveland... New York, J. S. Voorhies, 1857.
2 p.l., [iii]-lxxvi, 361 p.   23½ cm.

21957 Cleaveland, Nehemiah, 1796-1877.
The first century of Dummer academy. A historical
discourse, delivered at Newbury, Byfield parish,
August 12, 1863. With an appendix. By Nehemiah Cleaveland. Boston, Nichols & Noyes, 1865.
4 p.l., [5]-71, xliii p.   23½ cm.

21958 Cleaveland, Nehemiah, 1796-1877.
Green-wood: a directory for visitors. By N.
Cleaveland... New York, 1850.
vii, [1], [3]-271, [1] p. incl. plates.   front.,
fold. plan.   17 cm.

21959 Clemens, Jeremiah, 1814-1865.
Letter from Hon. Jere. Clemens. [Philadelphia,
1864]
16 p.   18½ cm.
Issued by the Union league of Philadelphia.

21960 Clerkships in Washington. A letter to Hon. ...
member of Congress. By a clerk. Washington, The
author, 1851.
32 p.   22½ cm.

21961 Cleveland, Edward, 1804-1886.
A sketch of the early settlement and history of
Shipton, Canada East; by Rev. Edward Cleveland...
Canada East, S. C. Smith, printer, "Richmond county
advocate", 1858.
x, [11]-78 p.   17½ cm.

21962 Cleveland, Mrs. E[meline] H
Introductory lecture on behalf of the faculty to the

41

class of the Female medical college of Pennsylvania, for the session of 1858-59. By Mrs. E. H. Cleveland... Philadelphia, Merrihew & Thompson, printers, 1858. 16 p. 23 cm.

21963 Cleveland, Richard Jeffry, 1773-1860.
A narrative of voyages and commercial enterprises, by Richard J. Cleveland... Cambridge, J. Owen, 1842. 2 v. 20½ cm.

21964 Cobbett, William, 1763-1835.
An address to the clergy of Massachusetts. Written in England, Nov. 13, 1814. By William Cobbett, with a prefatory epistle, to certain priests, by Jonathan [pseud.] one of the people called Christians... Boston, Printed at the Yankee office, 1815.
24 p. 17 cm.
Caption title of address: To the Cossack priesthood of the state of Massachusetts.
Jonathan, pseud. of William Cobbett.

21965 [Cobbett, William] 1763-1835.
Observations on the debates of the American Congress, on the addresses presented to General Washington, on his resignation; with remarks on the timidity of the language held towards France; the seizures of American vessels by Great Britain and France; and, on the relative situations of those countries with America. By Peter Porcupine... To which is prefixed, General Washington's address to Congress; and the answers of the Senate and House of representatives. Philadelphia, printed; London, reprinted, D. Ogilvy & son, 1797.
1 p.l., 38 p. 20 cm.

21966 Cobbett, William, 1763-1835.
Selections from Cobbett's political works; being a complete abridgement of the 100 volumes which comprise the writings of "Porcupine" and the "Weekly political register." With notes, historical and explanatory. By John M. Cobbett and James P. Cobbett... London, A. Cobbett; [etc., etc., pref. 1835]
6 v. 22½ cm.
Contents. - I. 1794-1805. - II. 1805-1809. - III. 1809-1811. - IV. 1811-1816. - V. 1816-1820. - VI. 1820-1835.

21967 Codman, John, 1814-1900.
Ten months in Brazil: with incidents of voyages and

travels, descriptions of scenery and character, notices
of commerce and productions, etc. By John Codman.
Boston, Lee and Shepard, 1867.
208 p.   front., plates.   19½ cm.

21968   Codman, John, 1814-1900.
Winter sketches from the saddle, by a septuagenarian,
John Codman. New York [etc.] G. P. Putnam's sons [1888]
2 p.l., 205 p.   front.   16 cm.

21969   Coe, Joseph, comp.
The true American; containing the inaugural addresses,
together with the first annual addresses and messages of
all the presidents of the United States, from 1789 to
1839... and a variety of other matter useful and entertaining. By Joseph Coe. Concord, N. H., I. S. Boyd,
1841.
2 v.   front., ports. (v. 2)   19 cm.
First published 1840 in 1 v. Vol. 2 is additional
matter.
Title-page of v. 2: The true American; containing the
portraits of Washington, Adams and Jefferson, with a
sketch of their lives and political characters; together
with all their messages, excepting those already
published in the first volume of this work... Concord,
N. H., Morrill, Silsby, & co., 1841.

21970   Coffin, Charles, 1779-1851, comp.
History of the battle of Breed's Hill, by Major-
Generals William Heath, Henry Lee, James Wilkinson and
Henry Dearborn. Compiled by Charles Coffin.   Saco
[Me.] Printed by W. J. Condon, 1831.
(In Heath, William. Memoirs... New York, 1901.
31½ cm.   p. 357-401)

21971   Coffin, Charles, 1779-1851.
The lives and services of Major General John Thomas,
Colonel Thomas Knowlton, Colonel Alexander Scammell,
Major General Henry Dearborn. Comp. by Charles Coffin.
New York, Egbert, Hovey & King, printers, 1845.
222 p.   18 cm.
Contains "letters from Generals Washington, Lee, and
Schuyler, and from John Adams, never before published."

21972   Cohen, Bernard.
Compendium of finance: containing an account of the
origin, progress, and present state, of the public
debts, revenue, expenditure, national banks and

43

currencies, of France, Russia, Prussia, the Netherlands,
Austria, Naples, Spain, Portugal, Denmark, Norway,
Hanover, and other German states, U. S. of America,
Buenos Ayres, Columbia, and Chili. And shewing the
nature of the different public securities, with the
manner of making investments therein. Also an historical
sketch of the national debt of the British Empire.
Authenticated by official documents. By Bernard Cohen.
London, W. Phillips [etc.] 1822.
    xxxi, [1], 264, 280 p.   fold. tab.   25 cm.
    "Documents": p. 280 p.

21973   Colesworthy, Daniel Clement 1810-1893.
    Chronicles of Casco Bay... Portland, Sanborn and
Carter, 1850.
    cover-title, [9]-56 p., 1 l.   pl.   23 cm.
    Table of contents on p. 2-3 of cover.
    "Marriages in Portland" and "Deaths in Portland"
[1804]: p. 38-42.
    Contents. - First settlement of Casco Bay. - First
attack of the Indians on Falmouth. - Chronicles of
eighteen hundred and four. - George Burroughs. -
Chronicles of eighteen hundred and seven.

21974 The Comet. no. 1-13; Oct. 19, 1811-Jan. 11, 1812.
    Boston, J. T. Buckingham.
    172 p.   24 cm.
    Edited by Walter Wildfire, pseud.

21975 Conant, William C
    Narratives of remarkable conversations and revival
incidents: including a review of revivals, from the
day of Pentecost to the great awakening in the last
century--conversions of eminent persons--instances of
remarkable conversions and answers to prayer--an
account of the rise and progress of the great awakening
of 1857-'8. By William C. Conant... New York,
Derby & Jackson, 1858.
    1 p.l., ix-xi, 444 p.   19 cm.
    Imperfect: 1st prelim. leaf wanting, p. xi mutilated.

21976 Conductor Generalis, Or the Office, Duty and Authority
of Justices of the Peace, High-Sheriffs, Under-Sheriffs,
Goalers, Coroners, Constables, Jury-Men, Over-seers of
the Poor, and also The Office of Clerks of Assize and
of the Peace, &c. Collected out of all the books hitherto
written on those subjects, whether of Common or Statute-
Law. To which is added, A Collection out of Sir Matthew

Hales concerning The Descent of Lands. The whole
alphabetically digested under the several titles, with
a table directing to the ready finding out the proper
matter under those titles. Printed and sold by Andrew
Bradford in Philadelphia, 1722.
4 p.l., xii, 299, [1] p.   19 x 15 cm.

21977   Confederate States of America. Navy dept.
Ordnance instructions for the Confederate States
navy relating to the preparation of vessels of war for
battle, to the duties of officers and others when at
quarters, to ordnance and ordnance stores, and to
gunnery. 3d ed. Pub. by order of the Navy department.
London, Saunders, Otley, & co. [Printed by Spottiswoode
and co.] 1864.
xix, 171, cix p.   21 pl.   24 cm.

21978   Confederate States of America. Treaties, etc.
Treaty with the Cherokees. October 7th, 1861. A
treaty of friendship and alliance, made and concluded at
Tahlequah, in the Cherokee nation, on the seventh day
of October... one thousand eight hundred and sixty-one,
between the Confederate States of America, by Albert
Pike, commissioner with plenary powers, of the Confederate States, of the one part, and the Cherokee
nation of Indians, by John Ross, the principal chief,
Joseph Verner, assistant principal chief, James Brown,
John Drew and William P. Ross, executive councillors,
constituting... the Executive council of the nation
and authorized to enter into this treaty by a general
convention of the Cherokee people, held at Tahlequah...
on the twenty-first day of August... one thousand
eight hundred and sixty-one... of the other part.
[Richmond? 1861?]
26 p.   22½ cm.

21979   Confessions, trials, and biographical sketches of the
most cold-blooded murderers, who have been executed
in this country from its first settlement down to the
present time... containing also, accounts of various
other daring outrages committed in this and other
countries... Boston, G. N. Thomson and E. Littlefield,
1840.
vi, [7]-408 p. incl. front., illus.   18 cm.
Caption title: Murders & daring outrages. Copy-
right by Geo. N. Thomson.

21980   Conklin, Alfred, 1789-1874.
A treatise on the organization, jurisdiction and

practice of the courts of the United States: to which
is added an appendix, containing... rules... and also a
few practical forms. By Alfred Conkling. Albany,
W. & A. Gould & co.; New York, Gould, Banks & co., 1831.
vii, [1], 538 p., 1 l.   22 cm.

21981   Cooper, James Fenimore, 1789-1851.
        Lives of distinguished American naval officers. By
        J. Fenimore Cooper... Philadelphia, Carey and Hart,
        1846.
        2 v.   18½ cm.
        Contents. - v. 1. Bainbridge. Somers. Shaw. Shubrick
        Preble. - v. 2. Jones. Woolsey. Perry. Dale.

21982   [Cooper, James M   ]
        The government the partner of the manufacturer.
        [Pittsburgh, W. S. Haven, printer, 1865]
        cover-title, 8 p.   22½ cm.
        Caption title: The government and the manufactures.

21983   Cooper, Samuel, 1725-1783.
        A sermon preached before His Excellency John Hancock,
        esq; governour, the honourable the Senate, and House
        of representatives of the commonwealth of Massachusetts,
        October 25, 1780. Being the day of the commencement
        of the Constitution, and inauguration of the new govern-
        ment. By Samuel Cooper, D.D. [Boston] Commonwealth of
        Massachusetts, Printed by T. and J. Fleet, and J. Gill
        [1780]
        2 p.l., 55 p.   20 cm.
        Half-title: Dr. Cooper's sermon on the commencement
        of the Constitution, &c.

21984   Cooper, Samuel, 1725-1783.
        A sermon preached before His Excellency Thomas
        Pownall, esq; captain general and governor in chief,
        the Honourable His Majesty's Council and House of
        representatives, of the province of the Massachusetts-
        Bay in New-England, October 16th, 1759. Upon occasion
        of the success of His Majesty's arms in the reduction
        of Quebec. By Samuel Cooper... Boston, Printed by
        Green & Russell, and Edes & Gill, by order of His
        Excellency the governor, and both houses of Assembly
        [1759]
        xi, [13]-53 p.   20 cm.

21985   Cooper, Susan Fenimore, 1813-1894.
        Mount Vernon; a letter to the children of America,

by the author of "Rural hours," etc., etc. New York,
Appleton, 1859.
70 p.   port., plate.   17 cm.
Cover title: Miss Cooper's Mount Vernon letter.

21986 Cooper, Thomas, 1759-1839, defendant.
An account of the trial of Thomas Cooper, of Northumberland; on a charge of libel against the President
of the United States; taken in short hand. With a
preface, notes, and appendix, by Thomas Cooper. Philadelphia, Printed by John Bioren, no. 83, Chestnut
street, for the author, April 1800.
64 p.   21 cm.
Caption-title: Proceedings in the Circuit court of
the United States... under the Act of Congress, passed
July 14th, 1798... commonly called the Sedition law.

21987 Cooper, Thomas, 1759-1839.
The case of Thomas Cooper, M.D., president of the
South Carolina college; submitted to the legislature
and the people of South Carolina, December, 1831...
Columbia, S.C., Printed at the Times and gazette office
[1831]
vii, 44, 17, 5 p.   22 cm.
Dr. Cooper was accused of infidelity.

21988 Cooper, Thomas, 1759-1839.
Political essays, originally inserted in the Northumberland gazette, with additions, by Thomas Cooper,
esq. Northumberland [Pa.] Printed by Andrew Kennedy,
1799.
1 p.l., 64 p.   23½ cm.

21989 Cooper, Thomas, 1759-1839.
Some information respecting America, collected by
Thomas Cooper, late of Manchester. London, Printed
for J. Johnson, 1794.
iv, 240 p., 1 l.   front. (fold. map.)   21½ cm.

21990 Cotton, John, 1584-1652.
The covenant of Gods free grace most sweetly unfolded
and comfortably applied to a disquieted soul, from that
text of 2 Sam. 23, ver. 5. Also a doctrinall conclusion
that there is in all such who are effectually called,
in-dwelling spirituall gifts and graces, wrought and
created in them by the Holy Ghost. Whereunto is added,
A profession of faith, made by John Davenport, in
New England, at his admission into one of the churches

there. London, M. Simmons, 1645.
40 p.   20 cm.

21991 Crèvecoeur, Michel Guillaume St. Jean de, called Saint
John de Crèvecoeur, 1735-1813.
Lettres d'un cultivateur américain addressées à W.^{m}
S... ou esq.^{r} depuis l'année 1770 jusqu'en 1786. Par
M. St. John de Crèvecoeur, traduites de l'anglois...
Paris, Cuchet, 1787.
3 v.   front. (v. 1-2) plates, fold. maps, plan.
20 cm.
A free translation, by the author, of "Letters from
an American farmer."
Greatly enlarged from the edition of 1784.

21992 The crisis. Or, A full defence of the colonies. In which
it is incontestibly proved that the British constitution
has been flagrantly violated in the late Stamp act, and
rendered indisputably evident, that the mother country
cannot lay any arbitrary tax upon the Americans, without
destroying the essence of her own liberties. London,
Printed for W. Griffin, 1766.
1 p.l., 80 p.   20½ cm.
Erroneously attributed to Samuel Cooper.

21993 Cummings, Asa, 1791-1856.
A memoir of the Rev. Edward Payson, D.D., late of
Portland, Maine. By Rev. Asa Cummings. 3d ed. New
York, American Tract Society [n.d.]
1 p.l., 486 p.   15½ cm.

21994 Cunny, Phil M
The letter of Phil. M. Cuny to Judge John C. Watrous,
in reply to the aspersions cast upon the writer, the
Legislature, and the people of Texas, by Judge Watrous,
in answer to the memorial of Jacob Mussina, for his
impeachment, before the Committee on the judiciary of
the House of representatives of the U.S. Austin,
Printed at the Southern intelligencer book office, 1858.
17 p.   24 cm.

21995 [Curtis, Benjamin Robbins] 1809-1874.
An article on the debts of the states. From the North
American review, for January, 1844. Cambridge [Mass.]
Metcalf, Keith, and Nichols, printers, 1844.
48 p.   24 cm.

21996 Curtis, Jonathan, 1786-1861.
A topographical and historical sketch of Epsom, New

Hampshire. By Jonathan Curtis... Published in 1823.
(Republished by request.) Pittsfield, N. H., Analecta
publishing house, 1885.
cover-title, 12 p.   21 cm.

21997   Cushing, Caleb, 1800-1879.
A eulogy on John Adams and Thomas Jefferson, pronounced
in Newburyport July 15, 1826, at the request of the
municipal authorities of the town. By Caleb Cushing.
Cambridge [Mass.] Printed by Hilliard and Metcalf, 1826.
60 p.   23 cm.

21998   Cushing, Caleb, 1800-1879.
Outlines of the life and public services, civil and
military, of William Henry Harrison. By Caleb Cushing.
Boston, Weeks, Jordan and company, 1840.
71 p. incl. front. (port.)   15 cm.

21999   Cushing, Christopher, 1820-1881.
A discourse at the funeral of Dea. Tyler Batcheller,
at North Brookfield, Mass., Oct. 10, 1862. By Rev.
Christopher Cushing. Boston, Wright & Potter, printers,
1864.
32 p.   front. (port.)   23 cm.
Appendix: Genealogy of the Batcheller family, p. 31-32.

22000   Cushing, Jacob, 1730-1809.
Divine judgments upon tyrants: and compassion to the
oppressed. A sermon, preached at Lexington, April 20th,
1778. In commemoration of the murderous war and rapine,
inhumanly perpetrated, by two brigades of British
troops, in that town and neighbourhood, on the nineteenth
of April, 1775. By Jacob Cushing... Massachusetts-
state; Boston, Printed by Powars and Willis, 1778.
28 p.   19½ cm.

22001   Cushing, John, 1744-1823.
A discourse, delivered at Ashburnham, July 4th,
1796, at the request of the militia officers in said
town; who, with the infantry under their command, and
a troop of cavalry, were assembled under arms, to
celebrate the anniversary of the independence of the
United States of America. By John Cushing, A.M.,
minister of the Gospel in Ashburnham... Leominster
(Massachusetts) Printed by Charles Prentiss, 1796.
24 p.   19½ cm.

22002   Cushing, Luther Stearns, 1803-1856.
Manual of parliamentary practice; rules of proceeding

and debate in deliberative assemblies. By Luther S.
Cushing. Boston, W. J. Reynolds & co., 1851.
189 p.   14½ cm.
First edition, 1845.

22003 Cushman, Austin S
Address of Major A. S. Cushman, grand commander,
department of Mass. G. A. R. delivered at the annual
meeting of the department in Boston, January 8, 1868.
Boston, H. J. Hallgreen, printer, 1868.
16 p.   24 cm.

22004 [Cushman, Frederick E   ] 1843?-
History of the 58th regt. Massachusetts vols. From
the 15th day of September, 1863, to the close of the
rebellion. By F. E. C. Washington, D. C., Gibson
brothers, printers, 1865.
38 p.   17½ cm.

22005 Cushman monument association.
Proceedings at the consecration of the Cushman monument at Plymouth, September 16, 1858: including the
discourse and poem delivered on that occasion, together
with a list of contributors to the monument. Boston,
Little, Brown & co., 1859.
viii, [9]-96 p.   front.   24 cm.
Prepared by Nathaniel B. Shurtleff and Henry W.
Cushman for the Cushman monument association.

22006 Cushman, Robert, 1579?-1625.
A sermon preached at Plimmoth in New England, December
9, 1621. Supposed to be the earliest printed sermon
delivered in the English colonies in America. With an
historical and bibliographical pref. Boston [J. K.
Wiggin] 1870.
xvi p., facsim.: [8], 19 p.   33 cm.

22007 Cushman, Robert, 1579?-1625.
The sin and danger of self-love, described in a
sermon preached at Plymouth, in New England, 1621.
By Robert Cushman. London: Printed. Plymouth [Massa-
chusetts] Reprinted by Nathaniel Coverly, 1785.
Boston, Rebecca Wiswell, 1846.
viii, [2], 11-35 p.   19 cm.
First published in 1622 under title: A sermon
preached at Plimmoth in New England.

22008 Cushman, Robert Woodward, 1800-1868.
A calm review of the measures employed in the religious

50

awakening in Boston, in 1842. Being a discourse
delivered in Bowdoin square church, June 28, 1846.
By R. W. Cushman. Boston, W. D. Ticknor & co., 1846.
28 p.   24 cm.

22009   Cussy, Ferdinand de Cornot, baron de, 1795-1866.
Phases et causes célèbres du droit maritime des
nations. Par le baron Ferdinand de Cussy... Leipzig,
F. A. Brockhaus, 1856.
2 v.   22½ cm.

22010   Cussy, Ferdinand de Cornot, baron de, 1795-1866.
Règlements consulaires des principaux états maritimes
de l'Europe et de l'Amérique; fonctions et attributions
des consults: prérogatives, immunités et caractère
public des consults envoyés... Par le Bᵃ Ferdinand de
Cussy... Leipzig, F. A. Brockhaus, 1851.
2 p.l., 492 p.   21½ cm.

22011   Cust, Sir Edward, bart., 1794-1878.
Annals of the wars of the nineteenth century, comp.
from the most authentic histories of the period.   By the
Hon. Sir Edward Cust...   London, J. Murray, 1862-63.
4 v.   16½ cm.
Contents. - v. 1. 1800-1806. - v. 2. 1807-1809. -
v. 3. 1810-1812. - v. 4. 1813-1815.

22012   Cust, Sir Edward, bart., 1794-1878.
Reflection on West Indian affairs, after a recent
visit to the colonists.   Addressed to the consideration
of the Colonial office.   By Lieutenant Colonel the
Hon. Sir Edward Cust.   London, J. Hatchard and son,
1839.
88 p.   23 cm.

22013   Cust, Sir Reginald John, 1828-1913.
A treatise on the West Indian incumbered estates
acts, 17 and 18 Vict., c. 117-21 and 22 Vict., c. 96.
With an appendix, containing the acts, general rules,
forms and directions, local acts, tables of fees,
reports of cases, and index.   By Reginald John Cust...
London, W. Amer, 1859.
viii, 191 p.   18 cm.

22014   Custis, George Washington Parke, 1781-1857.
An address occasioned by the death of General Lingan,
who was murdered by the mob at Baltimore.   Delivered
at Georgetown, September 1, 1812, by George Washington

Park Custis. Boston, Published by Bradford & Read, 1812.
16 p.   23 cm.

22015 Custis, George Washington Parke, 1781-1857.
Recollections and private memoirs of Washington, by G. W. Parke Custis... Washington, D. C., Printed by W. H. Moore, 1859.
104 p., 1 l.   23 cm.
"Compiled from files of the National intelligencer, printed at Washington, D. C."

22016 Cutler, Elbridge Jefferson, 1831-1870.
... Liberty and law. A poem for the hour. By Elbridge Jefferson Cutler. Boston, American Unitarian association, 1861.
11 p.   22 cm.   ([American Unitarian association. Tracts] Army series. no. 4)

22017 Cutler, Elbridge Jefferson, 1831-1870.
War poems. By Elbridge Jefferson Cutler. Boston, Little, Brown, and company, 1867.
59 p.   17½ cm.

22018 Cutter, Benjamin, 1803-1864.
A history of the Cutter family of New England. The compilation of the late Dr. Benjamin Cutter... Rev. and enl. by William Richard Cutter... Boston, Printed by D. Clapp & son, 1871.
xi, 363, [1] p.   front., illus., ports.   23½ cm.

22019 Cutter, Orland Phelps.
Out battery; or, The journal of Company B, 1st O. V. A., by O. P. Cutter. Cleveland, Nevens' book and job printing establishment, 1864.
152 p.   17 cm.

22020 Cutting, H   P
The crisis -- slavery or freedom. A discourse preached in Williston and Hinesburgh, on Sundays, June 25th, and July 2d, 1854. By H. P. Cutting... Burlington, S. B. Nichols, 1854.
21 p.   21½ cm.

22021 Cuvier, Georges, baron, 1769-1832.
Essay on the theory of the earth. By M. Cuvier... With mineralogical notes, and an account of Cuvier's geological discoveries, by Professor Jameson. To which

are now added, Observations on the geology of North
America; illustrated by the description of various
organic remains, found in that part of the world. By
Samuel L. Mitchill... New York, Kirk & Mercein, 1818.
xxiii, [1], [25]-431 p.   viii pl. (incl. front.)
22 cm.

22022 Cyr, Narcisse, 1823?-1894.
Memoir of the Rev. C. H. O. Cote, M.D., with a memoir
of Mrs. M. Y. Cote, and a history of the Grande Ligne
mission, Canada east. By the Rev. N. Cyr. Philadelphia,
American Baptist publication society [1852]
144 p.   front. (port.)   illus.   15 cm.

22023 Daggett, Herman, 1766-1832.
A discourse, delivered at East Hampton, Long Island,
Lord's day, July 22, 1798. Occasioned by the death of
the Rev. Samuel Buell, D.D., and pastor of the church
there. Who departed this life, July 19, 1798. By
Herman Daggett, A.M. and pastor of the church in West
Hampton. New London, Printed by Samuel Green, 1799.
23 p.   22 cm.

22024 Daggett, Naphtali, 1727-1780.
The excellency of a good name. A sermon delivered
in the chapel of Yale-college, in New-Haven, December
4th, 1768. Occasioned by the death of Mr. Job Lane,
one of the tutors of the college; who departed this
life at New Haven, September 16, 1768, in the 27th year
of his age. By the Reverent Naphtali Daggett...
New Haven, Printed by Thomas and Samuel Green [1768]
26 p.   20 cm.

22025 Daggett, Naphtali, 1727-1780.
The faithful serving of God and our generation, the
only way to a peaceful and happy death. A sermon
occasioned by the death of the Reverend Thomas Clap,
(president of Yale-college, in New-Haven) who departed
this life, Jan, 7th, 1767; delivered in the college-
chapel, Jan. 8th, by the Rev'd Naphtali Daggett...
New-Haven, Printed by B. Mecom [1767]
39 p.   20½ x 16½ cm.

22026 Dale cemetery, Ossining, N. Y.
The Dale cemetery, (at Claremont, near Sing-Sing,)
its incorporation, rules and regulations, and the
dedication addresses. New York, C. C. Childs, printer,
1852.
40 p.   22½ cm.

22027 Dalmas, Antoine, 1757-1830.
Histoire de la révolution de Saint-Domingue, depuis le commencement des troubles, jusqu'à la prise de Jérémie et du Môle S. Nicolas par les Anglais; suivie d'un Mémoire sur le rétablissement de cette colonie. Par m. Dalmas... Paris, Mame frères, 1814.
2 v.   20½ cm.

22028 Dallas, Alexander James, 1759-1817.
An exposition of the causes and character of the late war. [Attributed to the pen of Mr. Secretary Dallas] [Boston, Printed and published by Thomas G. Bangs, 1815?]
47, [1] p.   24 cm.

22029 Dallas, George Mifflin, 1792-1864.
Great speech of the Hon. George Mifflin Dallas, upon the leading topics of the day, delivered at Pittsburgh, Pa., with a brief biographical sketch, &c., &c. Philadelphia, Times and Keystone job office, 1847.
28 p.   22 cm.

22030 Dallas, George Mifflin, 1792-1864.
Obsequies in honor of Andrew Jackson. Eulogium by George M. Dallas, vice president of the United States, on the occasion of the Jackson obsequies at Washington square, in the city of Philadelphia, 26th June, 1845: with a notice of the civic and military procession on that day... Philadelphia, Mifflin & Parry, printers, 1845.
16 p.   21½ cm.
Published by request of the Committee of arrangement.

22031 Dallas, Sir Robert 1756-1824.
Considerations upon the American enquiry... London, Printed for J. Wilkie, 1779.
2 p.l., 55 p.   23½ cm.
Relates to the parliamentary inquiry into the conduct of the American war.

22032 [Dalzell, James McCormick] 1838-1924.
John Gray, of Mount Vernon; the last soldier of the revolution. Born near Mount Vernon, Va., January 6, 1764; died at Hiramsburg, Ohio, March 29, 1868. Aged 104 years... Washington, Gibson brothers, printers, 1868.
64 p.   22 cm.
Author's name in cover-title.

22033 Damon, David, 1787-1843.
A sermon delivered before His Excellency Marcus Morton, governor, His Honor George Hull, lieutenant governor, the honorable Council, and the legislature of Massachusetts, at the annual election, January 6, 1841. By David Damon... Boston, Dutton and Wentworth, printers to the state, 1841.
34 p. 23 cm.
Printed by order of the Massachusetts Senate.

22034 Damon, Samuel Chenery, 1815-1885.
The history of Holden, Massachusetts, 1667-1841. By Samuel C. Damon. [Worcester, Mass. Wallace and Ripley, printers, 1841]
viii, 154 p. incl. front. 22 cm.
Added t.-p.: An historical address, delivered at Holden, Mass., May 4th, 1841, the first centennial celebration of the municipal organization of the town; with notes and an appendix...

22035 Dampier, William, 1652-1715.
A collection of voyages. In four volumes. Containing I. Captain William Dampier's Voyages around the world... II. The voyages of Lionel Wafer... III. A voyage round the world... By W. Funnell... IV. Capt. Cowley's voyage round the globe. V. Capt. Sharp's journel [!] over the Isthmus of Darien, and expedition into the South-seas. VI. Capt. Wood's voyage through the Streights of Magellan. VII. Mr. Robert's adventures and sufferings amongst the corsairs of the Levant: his description of the Archipelago islands, &c. Illustrated with maps and draughts: also several birds, fishes and plants... London, Printed for J. and J. Knapton, 1729.
4 v. illus., plates (part fold.) maps (part fold., incl. fronts.: v. 1, 3, 4) tables. 20½ cm.
A collected issue (with additions) of Dampier's voyages, previously published in separate volumes, London, 1698 to 1709.

22036 Dana, Charles Anderson, 1819-1897, ed.
The United States illustrated; in views of city and country. With description and historical articles, edited by Charles A. Dana. New York, H. J. Meyer [1855?]
2 v. in 1. plates. 30 cm.
Engraved t.-p. added to the first volume has subtitle "East, vol. 1"; that added to second volume, "West, vol. 1".

22037 Dana, Daniel, 1771-1859.
       A discourse on the character and virtues of General
       George Washington: delivered on the twenty-second of
       February, 1800: the day of national mourning for his
       death. By Daniel Dana, minister of a church in Newbury-
       port... Newburyport, From the press of Angier March,
       sold at his bookstore [1800]
       31 p.   22½ cm.

22038 Dana, Daniel, 1771-1859.
       A sermon delivered at the annual election on Wednesday,
       January 4, 1837, before His Excellency Edward Everett,
       governor, His Honor George Hull, lieutenant governor,
       the honorable Council, and the legislature of Massa-
       chusetts. By Daniel Dana... Boston, Dutton and Went-
       worth, printers to the state, 1837.
       44 p.   22½ cm.
       Printed by order of the Massachusetts Senate.

22039 [Dana, Mrs. Eliza A   (Fuller)]
       Gathered leaves. Cambridge [Mass., Printed by H. O.
       Houghton] 1864.
       2 p.l., [vii]-viii, 160 p.   21 cm.
       Dedication signed: Eliza A. Dana.

22040 Danforth, John, 1660-1730.
       Greatness & goodness elegized, in a poem upon the
       much lamented decease of the Honourable vertuous Madam
       Hannah Sewall, late consort of the Honourable Judge
       Sewall, in Boston, in New-England. She exchanged this
       life for a better, October 19th, Anno Dom. 1717.
       Aetatis sua 60. [Boston? 1717?]
       broadside.   21½ x 31 cm.

22041 Darwin, Charles Robert, 1809-1882.
       Journal of researches into the natural history and
       geology of the countries visited during the voyage of
       H. M. S. Beagle round the world, under the command of
       Capt. Fitz Roy, R. N. By Charles Darwin... New ed.
       London, J. Murray, 1852.
       viii, 519 p.   illus.   18 cm.

22042 Davenport, Bishop.
       A history and new gazetteer, or geographical
       dictionary, of North America and the West Indies...
       Compiled from the most recent and authentic sources.
       A new and much improved edition. By Bishop Davenport.
       New York, S. W. Benedict & co., 1842.
       592 p.   illus. (incl. maps, coats of arms)   23½ cm.

22043 Davis, Daniel, 1762-1835.
An oration, delivered at Portland, July 4th, 1796.
In commemoration of the anniversary of American inde-
pendence. By Daniel Davis... Printed at Portland, by
Thomas Baker Wait [1796]
20 p.   20½ cm.

22044 Davis, Emerson, 1798-1866.
The half century; or, A history of the changes that
have taken place, and events that have transpired,
chiefly in the United States, between 1800 and 1850.
With an introduction by Mark Hopkins, D.D. By Emerson
Davis, D.D. Boston, Tappan & Whittemore, 1851.
xxiii, 444 p.   20½ cm.

22045 Davis, Emerson, 1798-1866.
A historical sketch of Westfield. By Emerson Davis
... Westfield [Mass.] J. Root, 1826.
36 p.   21½ cm.

22046 Davis, George.
A historical sketch of Sturbridge and Southbridge.
By George Davis. West Brookfield, Mass., Press of O. S.
Cooke and co., 1856.
v, [7]-233 p.   22 cm.

22047 Davis, William Watts Hart, 1820-1910.
History of the battle of the Crooked Billet, fought
May 1st, 1778. By W. W. H. Davis... Doylestown, Pa.,
Printed at the Democrat office, 1860.
19 p.   23 cm.

22048 Davis, William Watts Hart, 1820-1910.
History of the Hart family, of Warminster, Bucks
county, Pennsylvania. To which is added the genealogy
of the family, from its first settlement in America.
By W. W. H. Davis. [Doylestown, Pa.] Print. priv.
[W. W. H. Davis, printer] 1867.
139, 20 p.   col. front. (coat of arms)   24 cm.

22049 Davis, William Watts Hart, 1820-1910.
Sketch of the life and character of John Lacey,
a brigadier general in the revolutionary army. By
W. W. H. Davis, A. M. Printed privately. [Doylestown?
Pa.] 1868.
118, 6 p.   24½ cm.
Lacey was a captain in the 4th Pennsylvania line, 1776,
and from 1777 to the end of the war served in the state

militia as sub-lieutenant for Bucks Co. and colonel
and brigadier general in the field.

22050 Dawson, Henry Barton, 1821-1889.
Battles of the United States, by sea and land:
embracing those of the revolutionary and Indian wars,
the war of 1812, and the Mexican war: with important
official documents. By Henry B. Dawson... Illustrated...
from original paintings by Alonzo Chappel... New York,
Johnson, Fry, and company 1858
2 v.   fronts., plates, ports.   28 cm.
Contents. - I. The war of the revolution. 1775-1783. -
II. The Indian, French, and Algerine wars, the war of
1812, and the Mexican war. 1790-1847.

22051 [Dawson, Henry Barton] 1821-1889.
Reminiscences of the Park and its vicinity. New
York, 1855.
64 p.   front., plates, ports.   21 cm.
, Contents. - The Park and its vicinity. By Henry B.
Dawson. - The old Bridewell. By William J. Davis.

22052 Dawson, John Littleton, 1813-1870.
Speech of Hon. John L. Dawson, of Pa., on the bill
granting one quarter section of the public land to
actual settlers. Delivered in the House of representatives, March 3, 1852. Washington, Printed at the
Congressional globe office, 1852.
15 p.   24 cm.

22053 Dawson, Sir John William, 1820-1899.
Acadian geology. The geological structure, organic
remains, and mineral resources of Nova Scotia, New
Brunswick, and Prince Edward Island. By John William
Dawson... 2nd ed., rev. and enl. London, Macmillan
and Co., Edinburgh, Oliver and Boyd [etc., etc.] 1868.
[4], v-xxvi, [1], 1-694 p.   illus., 4 pl., fold.
map, diagrs.   18½ cm.
"Acadia" - Geological Bibliography of the Acadian
Province: p. [1]-13.
Appendix: Micmac language and supersitions:
p. [673]-687.

22054 Dawson, Sir John William, 1820-1899.
Air-breathers of the coal period: a descriptive
account of the remains of land animals found in the
coal formation of Nova Scotia, with remarks on their
hearing on theories of the formation of coal and of

the origin of species, by J. W. Dawson... Montreal,
Dawson brothers; New York, Bailliere brothers; [etc.,
etc.] 1863.
2 p.l.,[iii]-iv, 81 p.   front., vi pl.   22 cm.

22055 Dealtry, William.
Money, its history, evils and remedy. By William
Dealtry... Albany, Printed by B. Taylor, 1858.
48 p.   22 cm.

22056 Dean, Gilbert, 1819-1870.
The emancipation proclamation and arbitrary arrests!!
Speech of Hon. Gilbert Dean, of New York, on the governor's
annual message, delivered in the House of assembly of
the state of New York, February 12, 1863. Albany,
Atlas & Argus print, 1863.
15 p.   23 cm.

22057 Dean, John Ward, 1815-1902.
A memoir of the Rev. Nathaniel Ward, A.M., author of
The simple cobbler of Agawam in America. With notices
of his family. By John Ward Dean. Albany, J. Munsell,
1868.
viii, [9]-213 p.   illus.   25 cm.

22058 Dean, John Ward, 1815-1902.
Sketch of the life of Rev. Michael Wigglesworth,
A.M., author of the Day of doom. By John Ward Dean...
To which is appended a fragment of his autobiography,
some of his letters, and a catalogue of his library.
Albany, J. Munsell, 1863.
20 p.   25 cm.

22059 Dean, Silas, 1815-1906.
A brief history of the town of Stoneham, Mass.,
from its first settlement to the present time; with an
account of the murder of Jacob Gould, on the evening
of Nov. 25, 1819. By Silas Dean... Boston, Printed
at S. R. Hart's, 1843.
36 p.   19 cm.

22060 Deane, Charles, 1813-1889.
A bibliographical essay on Governor Hutchinson's
historical publications. By Charles Deane. Boston,
Priv. print., 1857.
39 p.   22 cm.

22061 Deane, Charles, 1813-1889.
The forms in issuing letters-patent by the crown of

England, with some remarks on the Massachusetts
charter of the 4th of March, 1628-9; a paper read
before the Massachusetts historical society, 21st
December, 1869, by Charles Deane... Cambridge, Press
of J. Wilson and son, 1870.
24 p.   24½ cm.

22062 [Deane, Charles] 1813-1889.
Some notices of Samuel Gorton, one of the first
settlers of Warwick, R. I., during his residence at
Plymouth, Portsmouth, and Providence; chiefly derived
from early manuscripts; with a brief introductory
memoir... Boston, Printed by Coolidge and Wiley, 1850.
41 p.   24 cm.

22063 Deane, Samuel, 1784-1834.
History of Scituate, Massachusetts, from its first
settlement to 1831. By Samuel Deane. Boston, J.
Loring, 1831.
2 p.l., 406, [2] p.   22 cm.
Family sketches: p. 211-394.

22064 Deane, William Reed, 1809-1871.
A genealogical memoir of the Leonard family;
containing a full account of the first three generations
of the family of James Leonard, who was an early settler
of Taunton, Ms., with incidental notices of later descendants... By Wm. R. Deane... Boston, Office of the
New England historic-genealogical register, 1851.
20 p.   24½ cm.

22065 Dearborn, Henry, 1751-1829.
An account of the battle of Bunker Hill. Written for
the Port folio, at the request of the editor. By
H. Dearborn, maj. gen. U.S.A. Illustrated by a map
drawn by Henry de Berniere, Tenth Royal British infantry;
and corrected by Gen. Dearborn. Philadelphia, Published
by Harrison Hall, No. 133 Chestnut street, J. Maxwell,
printer, 1818.
16 p.   fold. map.   22½ cm.
An attack on the conduct of Gen. Israel Putnam during
the battle of Bunker Hill.

22066 Dearborn, Nathaniel, 1786-1852.
Boston notions; being an authentic and concise account
of "that village," from 1630 to 1847. By Nathaniel
Dearborn... Boston, Printed by N. Dearborn, sold by
W. D. Ticknor & co. [etc.] 1848.

xx p., 1 l., 7 -426 p.   front., illus., plates
(part fold.) ports., maps (part fold.) fold. plans,
facsims. (part fold.)   16 cm.
Sources: p. [v]-vi.

22067 De Boilieu, Lambert.
Recollections of Labrador life. London, Saunders,
Otley & co., 1861.
vii, [9]-251 p.

22068 De Camp, John, 1812-1875.
Reply of Com. John De Camp, to aspersions upon his
character contained in an article published in the
Charleston Mercury, of November 6, 1855, entitled
"Commander Thomas Petigru and the Naval board."
[n.p.] 1856.
cover-title, 12 p.   23 cm.

22069 Decatur, Stephen, 1779-1820.
Correspondence, between the late Commodore Stephen
Decatur and Commodore James Barron, which led to the
unfortunate meeting of the twenty second of March.
Boston, Printed by Russell & Gardner, 1820.
22 p.   26 cm.

22070 De Coin, Robert L
History and cultivation of cotton and tobacco. By
Colonel Robert L. De Coin. London, Chapman and Hall,
1864.
vi, 306 p.   illus., fold. map.   20½ cm.

22071 De Costa, Benjamin Franklin, 1831-1904.
The Northmen in Maine; a critical examination of
views expressed in connection with the subject, by
Dr. J. H. [i.e. G.] Kohl, in volume 1 of the new series
of the Maine historical society. To which are added
criticisms on other portions of the work, and a chapter
on the discovery of Massachusetts bay. By the Rev.
B. F. De Costa... Albany, J. Munsell, 1870.
2 p.l., 146 p.   22½ cm.

22072 De Costa, B[enjamin] F[ranklin] 1831-1904.
Notes on the history of Fort George during the colonial
and revolutionary periods, with contemporaneous documents and an appendix. By B. F. De Costa... New York,
London, J. Sabin & sons, 1871.
3 p.l., 78 p.   front. (plan) illus. (map)   24½ cm.

22073 Deering, Richard.
Louisville: her commercial, manufacturing and social
advantages. Including a sketch of her history, geography, topography, schools, health, railroad and
steamboat facilities, water power, &c.... By Richard
Deering. Louisville, Ky., Hanna & co., printers, 1859.
99 p. incl. front., illus. (incl. map) plates.
23 cm.

22074 A defence of the constitution of England against the libels
that have been lately published on it; particularly in
Paine's pamphlet on the Rights of man... London,
Printed for R. Baldwin, 1791.
2 p.l., 67 p.   21½ cm.

22075 A defence of the legislature of Massachusetts, or The
rights of New England vindicated. Boston, Printed at
the Repertory office, 1804.
28 p.   20½ cm.
Relates to two measures adopted: a proposition to
amend the Constitution of the U.S. by apportioning
representatives among the states according to the number
of free inhabitants, and to provide for the choice of
electors of president and vice president by a general
ticket.

22076 Defoe, Daniel, 1661?-1731.
Daniel Defoe: his life and recently discovered
writings; extending from 1716 to 1729. By William
Lee... London, J. C. Hotten, 1869.
3 v.   front., plates, ports., facsims.   22 cm.

22077 [De Forest, T   R   ]
Olden time in New York. By those who knew. New York,
Anderson and Smith, 1833.
54 p.   18 cm.
Introduction signed: T. R. De Forest.

22078 Defrees, John Doughterty, b. 1810 or 11-1882.
Remarks made by John D. Defrees, before the Indiana
Union club of Washington, D. C., Monday evening,
August 1, 1864. Published and circulated by the
Indiana Union club. [Washington] L. Towers, printer
[1864]
14, [2] p.   illus.   22 cm.

22079 Degrand, Peter Paul Francis, d. 1855, comp.
Revenue laws and custom house regulations, comp. by

P. P. F. Degrand for his weekly report of public sales
and of arrivals, under the direction of General H. A. S.
Dearborn... 2d ed. [Boston] E. Bellamy, printer, 1821.
146 p.   17 cm.

22080   Degrand, Peter Paul Francis, d. 1855, comp.
Tariff of duties, on importations into the United
States; and revenue laws and custom-house regulations.
Comp. by P. P. F. Degrand for his Boston weekly report
of public sales and of arrivals under the direction of
General H. A. S. Dearborn...   Boston E. Bellamy,
printer, 1821.
84 p.   17 cm.

22081   De Kroyft, Mrs. Helen (Aldrich) 1818-1915.
A place in thy memory... By S. H. DeKroyft. New
York, J. F. Trow, printer, 1850.
191 p.   front., port.   18½ cm.
Letters to her friends.

22082   Delacroix, Jacques Vincent, 1743-1832.
A review of the constitutions of the principal states
of Europe, and of the United States of America. Given
originally as lectures by M. De la Croix... Now first
translated from the French, with notes, by the translator of the Abbe Raynal's letter to the National
assembly of France, &c. [Elizabeth Ryves] London,
Printed for G. G. J. and J. Robinson, 1792.
2 v.   22 cm.
A translation of the first 2 vols. of "Constitutions
des principaux états de l'Europe et des États-Unis de
l'Amérique".

22083   Delafaye-Brehier, Mme. Julie.
Les Portugais d'Amérique: souvenirs historiques de
la guerre du Brésil en 1635, contenant un tableau
intéressant des moeurs et usages des tribus sauvages,
des détails instructifs sur la situation des colons dans
cette partie du Nouveau-monde; ouvrage destiné à la
jeunesse, par Mme Julie Delafaye-Bréhier... Illustré
de 12 dessins imprimés en 2 couleurs. Paris, P.-C.
Lehuby, 1847.
2 p.l., 453 p., 1 l.   front., plates.   22 cm.

22084   Delusion; or, The witch of New England... Boston,
Hilliard, Gray and company, 1840.
iv, 160 p.   18 cm.

63

22085 Democratic party. National committee, 1848-1852.
       ... A refutation of Andrew Stewart's fabrication
       against General Lewis Cass. A gross misrepresentation
       of the public documents, by Andrew Stewart and the
       Whig central committee at Washington, exposed.
       Washington, 1848
         16 p.   24 cm.
       At head of title: Published under authority of the
       National and Jackson Democratic association committee.

22086 Derby, Elias Hasket, 1803-1880.
         Boston: a commercial metropolis in 1850. Her
       growth, population, wealth and prospects. As originally
       pub. in Hunt's merchants' magazine for November, 1850.
       By E. H. Derby. Boston, Redding & co., 1850.
         16 p.   22½ cm.

22087 Derby, Elias Hasket, 1803-1880.
         The position and prospects of the United States with
       respect to finance, currency and commerce. With the
       financial policy of Massachusetts... by... E. H. Derby.
       Boston, A. Williams & co., 1868.
         cover-title, 32 p.   23 cm.

22088 Desjardins, Ernest Émile Antoine, 1823-1886.
         Rapport sur les deux ouvrages de bibliographie améri-
       caine de M. Henri Harrisse... par M. Ernest Desjardins,
       lu à la séance de la commission centrale, le 18 janvier
       1867. Extrait du Bulletin de la Société de géographie.
       Paris, Impr. de E. Martinet, 1867.
         20 p.   22½ cm.
       "Les deux ouvrages... sont intitulés Notes on
       Columbus, New York, 1864-66... et, Bibliotheca americana
       vetustissima. New York, 1866."

22089 [Destut de Tracy, Antoine Louis Claude] comte, 1754-1836.
         A commentary and review of Montesquieu's Spirit of
       laws. Prepared for press from the original manuscript,
       in the hands of the publisher. To which are annexed
       Observations on the thirty-first [!] book by the late
       M. Cordorcet: and Two letters of Helvetius on the
       merits of the same work... Philadelphia, Printed by
       William Duane, No. 98, Market street, 1811.
         viii, 292 p.   21½ cm.
       Originally written in French about 1807. Later the
       manuscript was "committed" to Thomas Jefferson, by whom
       the present translation was revised and forwarded to
       Duane. The French edition appeared in 1819 under title:

Commentaire sur l'Esprit des lois. cf. Gilbert Chinard's
Jefferson et les idéologues, 1925, p. 45-55.
The word "thirty-first" in the title is an error for
"twenty-ninth", which is correctly given at the
beginning of Condorcet's Observations on p. 261, and
on the t.-p. of the French edition of this work, Paris,
1819.

22090   The detail and conduct of the American war, under Generals
Gage, Howe, Burgoyne, and vice admiral Lord Howe: with
a very full and correct state of the whole of the
evidence, as given before a committee of the House of
commons: and the celebrated fugitive pieces, which are
said to have given rise to that important enquiry. The
whole exhibiting a circumstantial, connected and complete
history of the real causes, rise, progress and present
state of the American rebellion. 3d ed. London, Sold
by Richardson & Urquhart, 1780.
190 p.   20½ cm.
Interleaved. A new and enlarged edition of "A view
of the evidence relative to the conduct of the American
war."

22091   Devèze, Jean, 1753-1829.
An enquiry into, and observations upon the causes
and effects of the epidemic disease, which raged in
Philadelphia from the month of August till towards the
middle of December, 1793. By Jean Devèze... Printed
by Parent, Philadelphia, 1794.
vii, 1 , 145 p.   22 cm.
Added t.-p.: Recherches et observations, sur les
causes et les effets de la maladie épidémique qui a
régné à Philadelphie, depuis les mots d'août jusques
vers le milieu du mois de décembre de l'année 1793.
English and French on opposite pages.

22092   Devlin, John S   ed.
The Marine corps in Mexico; setting forth its conduct
as established by testimony before a general court
martial, convened at Brooklyn, N. Y., September, 1852,
for the trial of First Lieut. John S. Devlin, of the
U. S. Marine corps. Washington, Printed by L. Towers,
1852.
viii, 62 p.   23 cm.

22093   Devotion, Ebenezer, 1714-1771.
The civil ruler, a dignify'd servant of the Lord,
but a dying man. A sermon preached before the General

assembly of the colony of Connecticut, at Hartford, on the day of the anniversary election, May 10th, 1753. By Ebenezer Devotion, A.M., pastor of a church in Windham... N. London: [Printed and sold by Timothy Green, printer to the gov. & company, 1753]

2 p.l., 59 p.   16 cm.

Imperfect: half-title wanting; title and first and last leaves of text mutilated. Printer and date supplied from Evans's American bibliography.

22094 Dew, Thomas Roderick, 1802-1846.
Lectures on the restrictive system; delivered to the senior political class of William and Mary college. By Thomas R. Dew... Richmond [Va.] Printed by S. Shepherd & co., 1829.

viii, 195 p.   22½ cm.

22095 Dewart, Edward Hartley, 1828-1903, ed.
Selections from Canadian poets; with occasional critical and biographical notes, and an introductory essay on Canadian poetry. By Edward Hartley Dewart. Montreal, Printed by J. Lovell, 1864.

xix, [21]-304 p.   20 cm.

22096 Dewey, Chester, 1784-1867.
An appeal to the friends of temperance, delivered in Pittsfield, Mass., on Sabbath evening, October 7, 1832. By Rev. C. Dewey. Pittsfield, Printed by P. Allen and son [1832]

24 p.   21½ cm.

22097 Dewey, Orville, 1794-1882.
The claims of Puritanism. A sermon preached at the annual election, May 31, 1826. Before His Excellency, Levi Lincoln, governor. The honorable Council, and the Legislature of Massachusetts. By Rev. Orville Dewey. Pastor of the First Congregational church, in New-Bedford. Boston, Printed by True & Greene, 1826.

32 p.   23½ cm.

22098 Dewey, Orville, 1794-1882.
The Old world and the New; or, A journal of reflections and observations made on a tour in Europe. By the Rev. Orville Dewey... New York, Harper & brothers, 1836.

2 v.   18½ cm.

22099 Dewey, Orville, 1794-1882.
On patriotism. The condition, prospects, and duties

of the American people. A sermon delivered on fast
day at Church Green, Boston. Boston, Ticknor and
Fields, 1859.
39 p.   23½ cm.

22100 Dewey, Orville, 1794-1882.
A sermon, on occasion of the late fire, in the city
of New York... By the Rev. Orville Dewey... New York,
D. Felt & co., 1836.
17 p., 1 l.   24 cm.

22101 DeWitt, Thomas, 1791-1874.
Christ the resurrection and the life. A sermon,
preached on the occasion of the death of the Rev. David
S. Bogart, on the evening of Aug. 4, 1839, in the
Middle Dutch church. By Thomas DeWitt... New York,
Printed by G. P. Scott, 1839.
22 p.   23 cm.

22102 DeWitt, Thomas, 1791-1874.
A discourse delivered in the North Reformed Dutch
church (Collegiate) in the city of New York, on the
last Sabbath in August, 1856. By Thomas DeWitt...
New York, Board of publication of the Reformed
Protestant Dutch church, 1857.
3 p.l., [5]-100 p.   front., plates.   23 cm.

22103 DeWitt, William Radcliffe, 1792-1867.
A discussion on the order of the Sons of temperance,
between Rev. W. R. De Witt... and Rev. W. Easton...
together with a letter from Rev. W. Easton, in reply
to Rev. H. Harbaugh, on the same secret order...
Philadelphia, T. R. Simpson, 1847.
viii, [9]-278 p.   19½ cm.

22104 Dewsbury, William, 1621-1688.
A sermon preached at Grace-church-street, the 6th
of the 3d month, 1688. By William Dewsbury, one of
the Christian people called Quakers. Providence,
Printed and sold by John Waterman, at the new printing
office, at the paper-mill, 1768.
23 p.   21 cm.
Half-title: William Dewsbury's sermon.
Printed at Philadelphia in 1740 under title: A
sermon on the important doctrine of regeneration.
"A short account of the life, and convincement of
William Dewsbury": p. [22]-23.

22105 Dexter, Henry Martyn, 1821-1890.
The Congregationalism of the last three hundred
years, as seen in its literature: with special
reference to certain recondite, neglected, or disputed
passages. In twelve lectures, delivered on the South-
worth foundation in the Theological seminary at Andover,
Mass., 1876-1879. With a bibliographical appendix.
By Henry Martyn Dexter... New York, Harper & brothers,
1880.
    xxxviii p., 1 l., 716, 326 p.   26 cm.
Head and tail pieces (include facsimile autographs)

22106 [Dexter, Henry Martyn] 1821-1890.
Memoranda, historical, chronological &c. prepared
with the hope to aid those whose interest in Pilgrim
memorials, and history, is freshened by this jubilee
year, and who may not have a large historical library
at hand. Boston, Printed (but not published) for the
use of Congregational ministers, 1870.
    39 p.   23½ cm.
Published by the Jubilee executive committee of the
convention held in New York, March 2, 1870, to take
action concerning the commemoration of the 250th anniversary of the landing of the Pilgrims.
An edition of 25 copies was issued the same year with
title: Pilgrim memoranda.

22107 Dhormoys, Paul, 1829-
... Sous les tropiques; souvenirs de voyages.
Paris [etc.] Jung-Treuttel, 1864.
    3 p.l., 252 p., 1 l.   18½ cm.

22108 The Dial: a monthly magazine for literature, philosophy
and religion. M. D. Conway, editor... v. 1; Jan.-
Dec. 1860. Cincinnati, 1860.
    1 p.l., [v]-vi, [9]-778 p.   23 cm.
No more published.

22109 A dialogue on peace, an entertainment, given by the senior
class at the anniversary commencement, held at Nassau-
Hall, September 28th, 1763. Philadelphia, Printed by
William Bradford, 1763.
    27 p.   19½ cm.
Contains 7 folded leaves of music not included in
paging.
"The odes, etc., were set to music by a resident
graduate at Princeton. All in verse." - Sabin, Bibl.
amer.

22110　A dialogue on the principles of the constitution and
　　　　legal liberty, compared with despotism; applied to the
　　　　American question; and the probable events of the war,
　　　　with observations on some important law authorities...
　　　　London, Printed for W. Owen, 1776.
　　　　　　2 p.l., 92 p.　　21 cm.
　　　　　　Slip of errata mounted on verso of title.
　　　　　　A conversation between Aristocraticus and Philodemus.

22111　...Diary of the great rebellion.　Containing a complete
　　　　summary of each day's events, from the inauguration of
　　　　the rebellion at Charleston, S. C., December 20th,
　　　　1860, to the 1st of January, 1862.　Prepared with
　　　　great care from "Official reports" and files of the
　　　　New York and Philadelphia daily papers...　Washington,
　　　　Bixler & Winchester, 1862.
　　　　　　64 p.　　14½ cm.

22112　Díaz del Castillo, Bernal, 1492-1581?
　　　　　　The true history of the conquest of Mexico, by
　　　　Captain Bernal Díaz del Castillo, one of the conquerors.
　　　　Written in the year 1568...　Translated from the
　　　　original Spanish, by Maurice Keatinge, esq.　London,
　　　　Printed for J. Wright, by J. Dean, 1800.
　　　　　　viii, 514, [1] p.　　front. (map)　　27½ cm.

22113　Dillaway, Charles Knapp, 1804-1889.
　　　　　　A history of the Grammar school, or, "The free schoole
　　　　of 1645 in Roxburie."　With biographical sketches of
　　　　the ministers of the First church, and other trustees.
　　　　By C. K. Dillaway...　Roxbury, J. Backup, 1860.
　　　　　　viii, [7]-202 p.　　fold. front. (facsim.)　　19½ cm.

22114　Dillingham, William Henry, 1790-1854.
　　　　　　A tribute to the memory of Peter Collinson.　With
　　　　some notice of Dr. Darlington's Memorials of John
　　　　Bertram and Humphry Marshall.　2d ed., with additional
　　　　notes and an appendix.　By Wm. H. Dillingham.　Phila-
　　　　delphia, H. Longstreth, 1852.
　　　　　　48 p.　　23½ cm.

22115　Dillon, Peter, 1785?-1847.
　　　　　　Narrative and successful result of a voyage in the
　　　　South seas performed by order of the government of
　　　　British India, to ascertain the actual fate of La
　　　　Pérouse's expedition...　By the Chevalier Capt. P.
　　　　Dillon...　London, Hurst, Chance and co., 1829.
　　　　　　2 v.　　fronts., pl., fold. map.　　22 cm.

22116   Dimmick, Luther Fraseur, 1790-1860.
          Memoir of Mrs. Catharine M. Dimmick. By L. F.
        Dimmick... Boston, T. R. Marvin, 1846.
          2 p.l., [7]-214 p.   19½ cm.

22117   Dingley, Amasa.
          An oration on the improvement of medicine. Pronounced
        ... in the Federal Hall, in the city of New York;
        according to the appointment of the Medical society of
        the state of New York, at their anniversary meeting,
        on the 16th January, 1794. By Amasa Dingley... New
        York, Printed by J. Buel [1794]
          39 p.   20½ cm.

22118   Dinmore, Richard, 1765-1811, comp.
          Select and fugitive poetry. A compilation... With
        notes biographical and historical. By Richard Dinmore.
        Washington city, Printed at the Franklin press, 1802.
          xi, [13]-288 p.   16 cm.
          "Probably the first volume of verse printed at the
        national capital." cf. Wegelin, Early American poetry.
          "Subscribers' names": p. [iv]-vi.

22119   Dinsmoor, Robert, 1757-1836.
          Incidental poems accompanied with letters, and a few
        select pieces, mostly original, for their illustration,
        together with a preface, and a sketch of the author's
        life. By Robert Dinsmoor, the "Rustic bard". Haverhill
        [Mass.] A. W. Thayer, printer, 1828.
          xxiv, 264 p.   18 cm.
          "Glossary": p. [255]-264.

22120   Dinsmore, John, of Winslow.
          A golden wedding and the Dinsmore genealogy, from
        about 1620 to 1865. Augusta, Printed at the Maine
        farmer office, 1867.
          24 p.   21½ cm.
          The golden wedding was that of Arthur and Patty
        Dinsmore of Anson, Maine, September 10, 1865.

22121   A discourse of the duties on merchandise, more particularly
        of that on sugars, occasionally offer'd, in answer to
        a pamphlet, intituled, The groans of the plantations,
        &c. Exposing the weakness of the said pamphlet, and
        plainly demonstrating, that the taking off the imposition
        on sugars would not be one farthing advantage to the
        plantations,... By a merchant. London, 1695.
          2 p.l., 32 p.   22 x 16½ cm.

22122 A discourse on government and religion, calculated for
the meridian of the thirtieth of January. By an
independent... Boston, Printed and sold by D. Fowle
in Queen street, and by D. Gookin in Marlborough
street, 1750.
1 p.l., ii, [7]-56 p.   20½ cm.

22123 A discourse on the times. The 2d ed. Norwich, Printed
by Judah P. Spooner, for the author, 1776.
16 p.   19½ cm.
"The authorship of the tract is credited by a former
owner to Jabez Huntington." - List of rare Americana
issued by George D. Smith, 29 Wall st., New York.

22124 [Disney, John] 1746-1816.
Memoirs of Thomas Brand-Hollis... London, Printed
by T. Gillet, 1808.
vii, 60 p.   front. (port.) 9 pl. (1 double)   37 cm.

22125 The dispute with America, considered in a series of
letters from a cosmopolite to a clergyman... London,
Printed by A. J. Valpy [1812]
viii, 220 p.   22 cm.

22126 A dissertation on the rise, progress, views, strength,
interests and characters, of the two parties of the
Whigs and Tories. Boston, Printed for Joseph Greenleaf,
and sold at his Printing Office in Hanover Street, 1773.
71 p.   18½ cm.

22127 District of Columbia. Laws, statutes, etc.
Compilation of the laws in force in the District of
Columbia, April 1, 1868. Washington, Govt. print. off.,
1868.
1 p.l., 494 p.   23 cm.

22128 Disturnell, John, 1801-1877.
A trip through the lakes of North America; embracing
a full description of the St. Lawrence river, together
with all the principal places on its banks, from its
source to its mouth: commerce of the lakes, etc.,
forming altogether a complete guide for the pleasure
traveler and emigrant. With maps and embellishments.
New York, J. Disturnell, 1857.
xi, [1], [13]-386 p. incl. front., illus., pl.
plates, 2 maps (1 fold.)   19 cm.

22129 Dix, Morgan, 1827-1908.
Historical recollections of S. Paul's chapel, New York.

By the Rev. Morgan Dix... To which is prefixed an
account of the three days' services held in that chapel
on occasion of the celebration of its centennial anniversary, Oct. 28th, 29th, and 30th, 1866. Printed by
order of the vestry of Trinity church. New York,
F. J. Huntington and company, 1867.
64 p.   front., plan, facsim.   24½ cm.

22130 Dix, William Giles, d. 1898.
The deck of the Crescent City. A poem. By William
Giles Dix. Part first. Boston and Cambridge, J. Monroe
and company, 1852.
46 p.   18 cm.

22131 Dixon, Benjamin Homer, b. 1819.
Brief memoir of the family at Shelton of Connecticut.
Boston, 1857.
5 p.   24 cm.
"Reprinted from the New England historical and geneal-
ogical register," v. 11, 1857, p. 271-272.

22132 Dixon, William Hepworth, 1821-1879.
Robert Blake, admiral and general at sea. Based on
family and state papers. By Hepworth Dixon. London,
Chapman and Hall, 1852.
xv, 366 p.   front. (port.)   19½ cm.

22133 Doane, George Washington, bp., 1799-1859.
America and Great Britain: the address, at Burlington
college, on the seventy-second anniversary of American
independence, July 4, 1848; by the Right Rev. George
Washington Doane... Burlington [N.J.] E. Morris, at
the Missionary press, 1848.
14 p.   21½ cm.

22134 Doane, George Washington, bp. 1799-1859.
The bush that burned with fire: the sermon at the
consecration of St. John's church, Elizabethtown, on
the eve of the feast of circumcision, December 31,
1840; by the Rt. Rev. George Washington Doane...
Burlington [N.J.] J. L. Powell, printer, 1841.
56 p.   23 cm.

22135 Doane, George Washington, bp. 1799-1859.
One world; one Washington: the oration, in the City
hall, Burlington, on Washington's birth-day, 1859;
by request of the lady managers of the Mount Vernon
association, and many citizens of Burlington: by the

Rt. Rev. George Washington Doane... Burlington, N. J.,
Pub. for the Ladies' Mount Vernon association, 1859.
32 p.   23 cm.

22136   Dobson, John, fl. 1760.
Chronological annals of the war; from its beginning
to the present time. In two parts. Part I. Containing
from April 2, 1755, to the end of 1760. Part II. - From
the beginning of 1761, to the signing of the preliminaries
of the peace. With an introductory preface to each part...
By Mr. Dobson. Oxford, Clarendon press, 1763.
1 p.l., xv, 327, [8] p.   21 cm.

22137   ... The doctrines and policy of the Republican party,
as given by its recognized leaders, orators, presses,
and platforms... Washington city, National Democratic
executive committee, 1860.
16 p.   24½ cm.

22138   Documents and official reports, illustrating the causes
which led to the revolution in the government of the
Seneca Indians, in the year 1848, and to the recognition
of their representative republic constitution, by the
authorities of the United States, and the State of
New York. Baltimore, Printed by W. Wooddy & son, 1857.
92 p.   20 cm.
Apparently a publication of the Society of Friends
(Hicksite)

22139   Dodd, Stephen, 1777-1856.
A family record of Daniel Dodd, who settled with the
colony of Branford, 1644, where he died in 1665, and
also of his descendants in New Jersey. Comp. by
Stephen Dodd. Printed for the author. [New Haven]
1839.
24 p.   18 cm.

22140   Doddridge, Jose, 1769-1826.
Logan. The last of the race of Shikellemus chief
of the Cayuga nation. A dramatic piece. To which is
added, the dialogue of the backwoodsman and the dandy,
first recited at the Buffaloe seminary, July the 1st
1821. By Dr. Joseph Doddridge... Buffalo Creek,
Brooke county, Va., Printed for the author, by S. Sala,
1823.
47 p.   19 x 11 cm.
"A dialogue between a dandy and a back woods-man"
(p. 37-47) wanting. Preface (p. 3-4) mutilated.

22141 Doddridge, Joseph, 1769-1826.
       Notes, on the settlement and Indian wars, of the
       western parts of Virginia & Pennsylvania, from the
       year 1763 until the year 1783 inclusive. Together
       with a view, of the state of society and manners of
       the first settlers of the western country. By the
       Rev. Dr. Jos. Doddridge. Wellsburgh, Va., Printed at
       the office of the Gazette, for the author, 1824.
       5 p.l., [v]-xiii, [1], [15]-316 p.   17½ cm.

22142 Dodge, Allen Washington, 1804-1878.
       A prize essay on fairs. By Allen W. Dodge...
       Boston, J. H. Eastburn's press, 1858.
       16 p.   24 cm.

22143 Dodge, Joshua.
       A sermon, delivered in Haverhill, December 22, 1820,
       being the second centesimal anniversary of the landing
       of New England fathers, at Plymouth. By Joshua Dodge...
       Haverhill [Mass.] Printed by Burrill & Hersey, 1821.
       28 p.   22 x 14 cm.

22144 [Dodge, Mary Abigail] 1833-1896.
       A battle of the books, recorded by an unknown writer
       for the use of authors and publishers... Ed. and pub.
       by Gail Hamilton [pseud.]... Cambridge [Mass.] Printed
       at the Riverside press, for sale by Hurd and Houghton,
       New York, 1870.
       2 p.l., 288 p.   19 cm.
       "Account of her business relations with her former
       publishers, Ticknor and Fields [under assumed names]"
       cf. Sabin.

22145 Dodge, Paul, 1777-1808.
       A poem: delivered at the commencement of Rhode Island
       college, September 6, A.D. 1797. By Paul Dodge...
       Providence, Printed by Carter and Wilkinson, and sold
       at their bookstore, opposite the market, 1797.
       8 p.   19 cm.

22146 Dodge, Robert, 1820-1899.
       Memorials of Columbus, read to the Maryland historical
       society, by Robert Dodge, 3 April 1851. Baltimore,
       Printed for the Society, 1851.
       28 p.   23 cm.
       Contents. - [Introductory paper]: Autograph letters
       at Genoa. - Appendix: [Letters to Nicolo Oderigo (no. 1
       dated Seville, Mar. 21, 1502; no. 2 dated Seville,

Dec. 27, 1504)] no. 3, Copy of a letter written by the
magistrate of St. George's to Columbus [dated Genoa,
Dec. 8, 1502] no. 4, [Letter from Columbus to the Bank
of St. George, Genoa, dated Seville, Apr. 2, 1502
(Italian and English)] Martin Behaim and his globe, at
Nurembergh.

22147 Dodge, William Earl, 1805-1883.
Speech of Hon. William E. Dodge, of New York, on
reconstruction; delivered in the House of representatives,
January 21, 1867. Washington, Printed at the Congressional globe office, 1867.
8 p.   23½ cm.

22148 Doggett, David Seth, 1810-1880.
A nation's Ebenezer. A discourse delivered in the
Broad St. Methodist church, Richmond, Virginia,
Thursday, September 18, 1862: the day of public
thanksgiving, appointed by the President of the Confe-
derate States. By Rev. D. S. Doggett... Richmond, Va.,
Enquirer book and job press, 1862.
18 p.   21½ cm.

22149 Doheny, Michael, 1805-1862.
The history of the American revolution. By Michael
Doheny. 2d ed. Dublin, J. Duffy; [etc., etc.] 1847.
xv, [13]-248 p.   14 cm.

22150 Dole, Benjamin.
An examination of Mr. Rantoul's report for abolishing
capital punishment in Massachusetts. By Benjamin Dole
... Boston, Printed for the author, 1835.
36 p.   19 cm.

22151 [Donaldson, William]
North America, a descriptive poem. Representing the
voyage to America; a sketch of that beautiful country;
with remarks upon the political humour and singular
conduct of its inhabitants. To which are subjoined,
notes, critical and explanatory. London, Printed for
J. Shepheard, 1757.
2 p.l., [3]-19 p.   25½ x 19½ cm.

22152 [Donck, Adriaen van der] d. 1655.
Remonstrance of New Netherland, and the occurrences
there. Addressed to the High and Mighty States
general of the United Netherlands, on the 28th July,
1640. With Secretary Van Tienhoven's answer. Tr. from

a copy of the original Dutch ms., by E. B. O'Callaghan,
M.D. Albany, Weed, Parsons and company, 1856.
   2 p.l., iii p., 1 l., [7]-65 p., 1 l.   29½ x 23½ cm.
Van Tienhoven's answer (p. [53]-56) has special t.-p.:
Brief statement or answer to some of the points contained
in the written remonstrance laid by Adrinen van der
Donck... before the... States general...

22153   Donkin, Robert, 1727-1821.
      Military collections and remarks... Pub. by Major
   Donkin. New York, Printed by H. Gaine, 1777.
      2 p.l., vi, [22], 264 p.   front.   21 cm.
      Published to assist in providing funds "to relieve
   and support the innocent children and widows of the
   valiant soldiers inhumanly and wantonly butchered"
   when "peaceably marching to and from Concord the 19th
   April, 1775". cf. Pref.
      A treatise on military science. Occurrences of the
   American revolution are used in several cases as
   illustrative material.

22154   Donnant, Denis Francois.
      Statistical account of the United States of America.
   By D. F. Donnant... Tr. from the French, by William
   Playfair... London, Greenland and Norris, 1805.
      xiii, [15]-72 p.   fold. col. diagr.   22 cm.

22155   Doolittle, Mark, d. 1855.
      Historical sketch of the Congregational church in
   Belchertown, Mass., from its organization, 114 years,
   with notices of the pastors and officers, and list of
   communicants chronologically arranged, tracing
   genealogies, intermarriages and family relatives.
   Also, embracing numerous facts and incidents relating
   to the first settlers and early history of the place.
   By Hon. Mark Doolittle... Northampton, Mass., Hopkins,
   Bridgman & co., 1852.
      xii, [13]-282 p., 1 l.   19 cm.

22156   Doran, John, 1807-1878.
      New pictures and old panels. By Dr. Doran...
   London, R. Bentley, 1859.
      viii, 376 p.   front. (port.)   19½ cm.
      Imaginary and historical character sketches.

22157   Drake, Joseph Rodman, 1795-1820.
      The American flag. By Joseph Rodman Drake. Illus-
   trated from original drawings by F. O. C. Darley.

Illuminated cover by John A. Hows. Music from Bellini,
by Geo. Danskin. New York, J. G. Gregory, 1861.
  cover-title, 4 l., [4] p. (music)   illus.   16 cm.
Poem.

22158 Drury, Luke.
    A report of the examination of Rev. Ephraim K. Avery,
for the murder of Sarah Maria Cornell. By Luke Drury.
[Providence, R.I.?] 1833.
    64 p.   20½ cm.

22159 Dwight, Timothy, 1752-1817.
    The duty of Americans at the present crisis, illus-
trated in a discourse, preached on the Fourth of July,
1798; by the Reverend Timothy Dwight, D.D., president
of Yale-college; at the request of the citizens of
New Haven. New Haven, printed by Thomas and Samuel
Green, 1798.
    32 p.   21½ cm.
    Half-title: President Dwight's discourse on the 4th
of July, 1798.

22160 Dye, John Smith.
    Life and public services of Gen. U. S. Grant, the
nation's choice for president in 1868. By Deacon Dye.
Philadelphia, S. Loag, printer, 1868.
    48 p.   21½ cm.
    On cover: 2d edition.

E

22161 [Eardley-Wilmot, John] 1750-1815.
    A short defence of the opposition; in answer to a
pamphlet intitled, "A short history of the opposition"...
London, Printed for J. Almon [etc.] 1778.
    2 p.l., 80 p.   21½ cm.

22162 Eastwick, Edward Backhouse, 1814-1883.
    Venezuela: or, Sketches of life in a South American
republic; with the history of the loan of 1864. By
Edward B. Eastwick... 2d ed. London, Chapman & Hall,
1868.
    viii p., 1 l., [ix]-xi, 418 p.   fold. map.   23 cm.

22163 Eaton, Amos, 1776-1842.
    North American botany; comprising the native and

common cultivated plants, north of Mexico. Genera
arranged according to the artificial and natural
methods. By Amos Eaton... In the present edition the
author is associated with John Wright... 8th ed.;
with the... additions of the Properties of plants,
from Lindley's New medical flora... Troy, N. Y.,
E. Gates, 1840.
    vii, [1], 625 p.   22½ cm.
"Eaton's Botanical dictionary, 5th ed.": p. 567-625.

22164 Eaton, Cyrus, 1784-1875.
    Annals of the town of Warren; with the early history
of St. George's, Broad Bay, and the neighboring settle-
ments on the Waldo patent. By Cyrus Eaton, A.M.
Hallowell, Masters, Smith & co., 1851.
    xi, [1], 437 p. incl. port.   fold. maps.   20 cm.
Genealogical table: p. 375-437.
Edited by Emily Eaton.

22165 Eaton, John Henry, 1790-1856.
    The life of Major General Andrew Jackson, comprising
a history of the war in the South; from the commencement of the Creek campaign to the termination of hostilities before New Orleans. Addenda: containing a
brief history of the Seminore war, and cession and
government of Florida. By John Henry Eaton... 3d ed.
Rev. and corr. by the author. Philadelphia, McCarty &
Davis, 1828.
    iv, [5]-355 p.   front. (port.)   18 cm.
    Chapters I to IV were written by Major John Reid, an
eye-witness of the late events related; chapters V to XI,
from the papers and notes left at his death, were
edited by Eaton. (cf. Preface to 1st edition. Philadelphia, 1817, p. v.
    Addenda: Seminole war (p. 277-317), by Eaton (publishe
for the first time in this edition.)

22166 Edwards, Richard, ed.
    Statistical gazetteer of the states of Virginia and
North Carolina; embracing important topographical and
historical information, from recent and original
sources... with the results of the last census... in
many cases to 1855... Ed. by Richard Edwards...
Richmond, Pub. for the proprietor, 1856.
    6 p.l., 601 p.   illus.   23½ cm.

22167 An elegy composed on the death of Elder Josiah Shepard,
       who died in Gilmanton, of a scald and burn, which he
       received by the overflowing of the copper, in the
       distillery, on the night of 21st of April, 1814, and
       expired after twenty six hours... aged 32 years.
       [Gilmanton, N.Y.?] 1814?
         broadside.   31½ x 25½ cm.
       In verse.

22168 An elegy occasioned by the melancholy [!] catastrophe
       which happen'd in the night of the 19th of August,
       1774. [Boston] Sold in the printing-office in Milk-
       street. [John Kneeland? 1774?]
         broadside.   24 x 37 cm.
       Death of five persons in a fire.

22169 An elegy occasioned by the sudden and awful death of
       Mr. Nathanael Baker [of] Dedham: a young man just
       upon the point of marriage. And son to Lieutenant
       John Baker. He fell from his horse on Monday night
       the 7th of May, 1733: and died the Wednesday following.
       Aetat 27. [Boston? 1733?]
         broadside.   illus.   22 x 30 cm.

22170 An elegy on the much lamented death of Nathan Starr,
       B.A. who departed this life, June 9th, Anno Domini,
       1752. Aged nineteen years. [New London, Conn.?
       Timothy Green? 1752?]
         broadside.   27 x 41 cm.

22171 An elegy upon His Excellency William Burnet, Esq.;
       who departed this life Sept. 7th, 1729. Aetat 42.
       Boston, Thompson Fleet [1729?]
         broadside.   illus.   21 x 35 cm.

22172 Elliot, Jonathan, 1784-1846, ed.
         The debates, resolutions, and other proceedings,
       in convention, on the adoption of the federal Consti-
       tution, as recommended by the general convention at
       Philadelphia, on the 17th of September, 1787: with
       the yeas and nays on the decision of the main question.
       Collected and revised, from contemporary publications,
       by Jonathan Elliot... Washington, Printed by and for
       the editor, 1827-30.
         4 v.   21 cm.

22173 Ellis, Samuel.
The history of the order of the Sons of temperance,
from its organization on the 29th September, 1842, to the
commencement of the year 1848; also, an account of its
formation and introduction into the several states of
the Union. By Samuel Ellis... Boston, Stacy, Richardson
& co., 1848.
iv, [5]-238 p.   18½ cm.

22174 Ellis, William, 1794-1872.
The American mission in the Sandwich islands: a
vindication and an appeal, in relation to the proceedings
of the Reformed Catholic mission at Honolulu. By Rev.
W. Ellis... London, Jackson, Walford, and Hodder,
1866.
2 p.l., 108 p.   21½ cm.

22175 Ellison, Thomas, 1833-1904.
Slavery and secession in America, historical and
economical. By Thomas Ellison... With map and appendices
London, S. Low, son & co.   pref. 1861
1 p.l., xvi, 371, 1 p.   front. (fold. map)   19 cm.

22176 Elmer, Jonathan, 1745-1807.
An eulogium on the character of Gen. George Washington,
late president of the United States: delivered at
Bridge-Town, Cumberland County, New Jersey, January 30th,
1800. By Jonathan Elmer... Trenton, Printed by G.
Craft, 1800.
25 p.   front. (port.)   23 cm.
The first journal, for the year 1811, was pub. in
New York in 1812, and repub. in London, 1813 under title
"Visits of mercy," after which there were several
editions. The second journal was also issued under
title "Visits of mercy."

22177 [Ely, Ezra Stiles] 1786-1861.
The second journal of the stated preacher to the
hospital and almshouse in the city of New York, for a
part of the year of Our Lord 1813. With an appendix...
Philadelphia, Pub. by M. Carey, G. Palmer, printer,
1815.
xi, [13]-255 p.   20 cm.

22178 Ely, Zebulon, 1759-1824.
The death of Moses the servant of the Lord. A
sermon preached at the funeral solemnity of His Excellency Jonathan Trumbull, esq., L.L.D., late
governor of the state of Connecticut, August 19, 1785.

By Zebulon Ely, A.M., pastor of the First church of
Christ in Lebanon... Hartford, Printed by Elisha
Babcock, 1786.
   28 p.   18 cm.

22179 Emerson, Charles Noble, 1821-1869, ed.
   Emerson's internal revenue guide, 1867, containing the
law of June 30, 1864, as amended March 3, 1865, July 13,
1866, and March 2, 1867, with sections codified and
arranged in their appropriate places... with decisions,
rulings, circulars, schedules of rates of tax, exemptions,
stamp duties, with analysis and full directions for the
pending assessment of the income tax, with complete
digest and alphabetical index. By Charles N. Emerson...
Springfield, Mass., S. Bowles & Company, 1867.
   vi, [iii]-vi, [2], [9]-401, [1] p. incl. tables.
22½ cm.
   Also published as The internal revenue guide.

22180 Emerson, Gouverneur, 1796-1874.
   Medical statistics; consisting of estimates relating
to the population of Philadelphia, with its changes as
influenced by the deaths and births, during ten years,
viz. from 1821 to 1830, inclusive. By Gouverneur
Emerson... Philadelphia, Printed by J. R. A. Skerrett,
1831.
   32 p.   tables.   21½ cm.
   "Extracted from the American journal of medical
sciences, for November, 1831.

22181 Emerson, Joseph 1700-1767.
   Advice of a father to a son engaging in the work of
the Evangelical ministry: a sermon preach'd at the
ordination of the Reverend Mr. Joseph Emerson, to the
work of the ministry, and pastoral office over the
Second church of Christ in Groton, in the province of
the Massachusett's Bay, N. E. on Wednesday, Feb. 25th,
1746, 7. By his father, pastor of the First church of
Christ in Malden... Boston, Printed and sold by S.
Kneeland and T. Green, 1747.
   2 p.l., 19 p.   19½ cm.
   Half-title: Mr. Emerson's sermon at the ordination
of his son.

22182 Emerson, Ralph, 1787-1863.
   Life of Rev. Joseph Emerson, pastor of the Third
Congregational church in Beverly, Ms., and subsequently
principal of a female seminary. By Rev. Ralph Emerson...

Boston, Crocker and Brewster; New York, Leavitt, Lord
& Co., 1834.
454 p.   20 cm.

22183   Emery, Samuel Hopkins, 1815-1901.
The ministry of Taunton, with incidental notices of
other professions. By Samuel Hopkins Emery... With
an introductory notice by Hon. Francis Baylies...
Boston, J. P. Jewett & co.; Cleveland, O., Jewett,
Proctor & Worthington; etc., etc. 1853.
2 v.   front., ports.   19 cm.
Includes reprints of published sermons of William
Hooke, Samuel Danforth, and Ephraim Judson.

22184   Emott, James, 1771-1850.
Speech of the Hon. James Emott, in the House of representatives of the U. States, February 6, 1811, in
relation to the non-intercourse. [Washington? 1811]
37 p.   22 cm.

22185   The end of the irrepressible conflict. By a merchant
of Philadelphia. Printed for the author. Philadelphia,
King & Baird, printers, 1860.
47 p.   23 cm.
A criticism of Mr. Seward's speeches in the campaign.

22186   Endicott, Charles Moses, 1793-1863.
Account of Leslie's retreat at the North bridge in
Salem, on Sunday, February 26, 1775. By Charles M.
Endicott... From the proceedings of the Essex institute. Salem, Mass., W. Ives & G. W. Pease, printers,
1856.
1 p.l., 47 p.   23 cm.

22187   Endicott, Charles Moses, 1793-1863.
A genealogy of the Peabody family, as compiled by the
late C. M. Endicott, of Salem. Rev. and cor. by
William S. Peabody, of Boston. With a partial record
of the Rhode Island branch by B. Frank Pabodie, of
Providence... Boston, D. Clapp & son, 1867.
2 p.l., 60, [1] p.   illus., col. pl. (coat of arms)
24 cm.

22188   Engel, Samuel   1702-1784.
Essai sur cette question: quand et comment l'Amérique
a-t-elle été peuplée d'hommes et d'animaux? Par E. B.
d'E. Amsterdam, M. M. Rey, 1767.
xi, [5], 610 p.   26½ x 21½ cm.
E. B. d'E. [i.e. Engel, bailli d'Echalens]

22189   Everett, Edward, 1794-1865.
          The great issues now before the country. An oration
       by Edward Everett. Delivered at the New York Academy
       of music, July 4, 1861. New York, G. Q. Cotton, 1861.
          52 p.   20 cm.
          Issued also under title: The questions of the day.

22190   Exquemelin, Alexandre Olivier.
          Histoires des avanturiers qui se sont signalez dans
       les Indes, contenant ce qu'ils ont fait de plus
       remarquable depuis vingt années. Avec la vie, les
       moeurs, les coûtumes des habitans de Saint Domingue &
       de la Tortuë, & une description exacte de ces lieux;
       ou l'on voit l'établissement d'une chambre des
       comptes dans les Indes, & un etat, tiré de cette
       chambre, des offices tant ecclesiastiques que seculiers,
       où le roy d'Espagne pourvoit, les revenus qu'il tire
       de l'Amerique, & ce que les plus grands princes de
       l'Europe y possedent... Par Alexandre Olivier Oexmelin.
       Paris, J. de Febvre, 1686.
          2 v.   4 pl., 3 fold maps.   17½ cm.
          "First French edition, of extreme rarity, translated
       from the Spanish. The author's name is rather singularly
       changed. The translation was made by M. de Frontignières.
       In 1689 the Journal of Raveneau de Lussan first appeared,
       and was republished in 1692, and is afterwards generally
       added to the work. Editions of Oexmelin, with this
       addition, appeared in 3 vols., 12 mo. in 1699." -
       Sabin, Bibl. amer., v. 6, p. 312.
          The dedicatory letter is signed by the translator, who
       while utilizing the Spanish version by Bonne-Maison
       practically rewrote the work, rearranging it as to
       details and giving it a more literary form. cf. Barros
       Arana, Notas, p. 72.
          Dutch original, Amsterdam, 1678, published under
       title: De Americaeusche zee-roovers...

                              F

22191   Fargo, Frank F
          A full and authentic account of the murder of
       James King, of Wm., editor of the San Francisco Evening
       bulletin, by James P. Casey, and the execution of
       James P. Casey and Charles Cora, by the Vigilance
       committee, compiled from the columns of the Alta
       California and originally written for that paper, by

Frank F. Fargo. [San Francisco, J. W. Sullivan, 1856?]
24 p.   22 cm.
Caption title. Cover-title: A true and minute history
of the assassination of James King... and the execution
of Casey and Cora. Portrait of James King on cover.

22192 Farine, Charles, b. 1818.
Benjamin Franklin, docteur en droit, membre de la
Société royale de Londres, et de l'Académie des sciences
de Paris, ministre plénipotentiare des États-Unis
d'Amérique à la cour de France, etc. D'après les
documents authentiques recueillis dans ses oeuvres
posthumes et dans ses papiers de famille. Par Charles
Farine... Tours, R. Pornin et cie, 1846.
2 p.l., 284 p.   plates, port.   18 cm.

22193 Farley, Harriet.
Operatives' reply to... Jere. Clemens, being a
sketch of factory life and factory enterprise, and a
brief history of manufacturing by machinery. By
Harriet Farley... Lowell, S. J. Varney, 1850.
cover-title, 24 p.   23 cm.

22194 Farmer, John, 1789-1838.
Memorials of the graduates of Harvard university,
in Cambridge, Massachusetts, commending with the first
class, MDCXLII. By John Farmer... Concord, N. H.,
Marsh, Capen and Lyon, 1833.
48 p.   22 cm.

22195 Federmann, Nikolaus, 16th cent.
Belle et agréable narration du premier voyage de
Nicolas Federmann le jeune, d'Ulm aux Indes de la
mer océane, et de tout ce qui lui est arrivé dans ce
pays jusqu'à son retour en Espagne... Haguenau. -
1557. [Paris, A. Bertrand, 1837]
3 p.l., [3]-227 p.   21 cm.   (Added t.-p.:
Voyages, relations et mémoires originaux pour servir
à l'histoire de la découverte de l'Amérique, pub. pour
la première fois en francais, by Henri Ternaux. [t. 1])
The original account of Federmann's expedition,
written in Spanish by a "notario scribano publico"
was translated into German by Federmann and pub. for
the first time with his additions by his brother-in-law,
Hans Kiffhaber, under title, "Indianische historia.
Ein schöne kurtzweilige historia Niclaus Federmanns
des jüngern von Ulm erster raise... [Hagenaw, Gedruckt

84

von Sigmund Bund] 1557." (Reprinted in "Bibliothek des Literarischen vereins in Stuttgart XLVII")

22196 A few thoughts compos'd on the sudden and awful death of Mrs. Fessenden, wife of Mr. Nathanael Fessenden, of Cambridge, who was shot May 30, 1770. [Boston? Seth Adams and John Kneeland? 1770?]
   broadside.   22 x 36 cm.

22197 Fisher, George, b. 1795.
   Memorials of George Fisher, late secretary to the expedition of Gen. Jose Antonio Mexia, against Tampico, in November, 1835. Presented to the Fourth and Fifth congresses of the Republic of Texas, praying for relief in favor of the members of the said expedition. Houston, Printed at the Telegraph office, 1840.
   87 p.   2 port. (incl. mounted phot.)   22 cm.
   Prefixed to the Memorials is a biographical sketch of the author, extracted from John Livingston's Portraits of eminent Americans now living. New York, 1853-54, v. 3, p. 441-446.

22198 Follett, Frederick, 1804-1891.
   History of the press in western New York from the beginning to the middle of the nineteenth century, by Frederick Follett. With a preface by Wilberforce James. With facsimile. New York, Charles F. Heartman, 1928.
   xv, 65 p.   front. (fold. facsim.)   23 cm.

22199 The following lines were occasioned by the death of Miss Mary Hedges, who departed this life February 17th, 1768, in the 19th year of her age. [New York? 1768?]
   broadside.   26 x 36 cm.

22200 Foster, J[ohn] W[ells] 1815-1873.
   Report upon the mineral resources of the Illinois central railroad; made at the request of the president, by J. W. Foster, March 4th, 1856. New York, G. S. Roe, printer, 1856.
   29 p.   fold. pl.   22 cm.

22201 Foster, John Young.
   New Jersey and the rebellion: a history of the services of the troops and people of New Jersey in aid of the Union cause. By John Y. Foster. Published by authority of the state. Newark, M. R. Dennis & co., 1868.

viii, 872 p. incl. maps.   front. (port.)
fold. map.   23½ cm.

22202 Foster, Lillian, comp.
       Andrew Johnson, president of the United States;
       his life and speeches. By Lillian Foster... New York,
       Richardson & co., 1866.
       316 p.   19 cm.

22203 Fowle, Daniel, 1715-1787.
       A total eclipse of liberty, being a true and faithful
       account of the arraignment and examination of Daniel
       Fowle before the honorable House of representatives
       of the province of the Massachusetts-Bay in New-England,
       October 24th, 1754, barely on suspicion of his being
       concern'd in printing and publishing a pamphlet
       intitled, The monster of monsters. Also his inprison-
       ment and sufferings... Written by himself... Boston,
       Printed in the year 1755. [Tarrytown, N. Y., Reprinted,
       W. Abbatt, 1930]
       (In The Magazine of history with notes and queries.
       Tarrytown, N. Y., 1930.   26½ cm.   Extra number.
       no. 158 (v. 40, no. 2) p. [5]-34)

22204 Franklin, Benjamin, 1706-1790.
       Memoirs of Benjamin Franklin. Written by himself,
       and continued by his grandson and others. With his
       social epistolary correspondence, philosophical,
       political, and moral letters and essays, and his
       diplomatic transactions as agent at London and minister
       plenipotentiary at Versailles. Augmented by much
       matter not contained in any former ed. With a post-
       liminious preface... Philadelphia, M'Carty & Davis,
       1837.
       2 v.   front., v. 1, port., illus., 11 pl. (7 fold.)
       fold. map. facsim.   23½ cm.

22205 Fraser, Donald, 1755?-1820.
       A collection of select biography; or, The bulwark
       of truth; being a sketch of the lives and testimonies
       of many eminent laymen, in different countries, who
       have professed their belief in, and attachment to the
       Christian religion... To which are prefixed two
       letters to Thomas Paine, containing some important
       queries and remarks relative to the probable tendency
       of his Age of reason... By D. Fraser... New York,
       Printed for the author, at the Literary printing-
       office, 1798.
       vi p., 1 l., 255, [9] p.   16½ cm.

22206 Freeman, Edward Augustus, 1823-1892.
Some impressions of the United States, by Edward A.
Freeman... London, Longmans, Green, and co., 1883.
xi p., 1 l., 289 p.   19½ cm.

22207 Freeman, Peyton Randolph, 1775-1868.
A refutation of sundry aspersions in the "Vindication"
of the present trustees of Dartmouth college, on the
memory of their predecessors. By Peyton R. Freeman.
Portsmouth, Printed by Beck & Foster, 1816.
32 p.   24 cm.

22208 Frémont, John Charles, 1813-1890, defendant.
... Message of the President of the United States,
communicating the proceedings of the court martial in
the trial of Lieutenant Colonel Frémont. [Washington?
1848]
447 p.   22   cm.   (30th Cong., 1st sess. [Senate]
Ex. [doc.] 33)

22209 French, George.
An answer to a scurrilous libel, intitled A letter to
Mr. G. French, occasion'd by his History of Col. Parke's
administration, &c. To which is added the character
and conduct, as well of Walter Hamilton, esq; the
present captain-general of the Leeward islands, as of
the principal fomentors and actors in the rebellion
and murder mention'd in that history. By Mr. George
French... London, Printed for J. Bettenham, 1719.
xxiv, 3-239 p.   20 cm.

22210 Frisbie, Levi, 1748-1806.
A discourse, before the Society for propagating the
gospel among the Indians, and others, in North America.
Delivered on the 1st of November, 1804. By Rev. Levi
Frisbie, A.M. pastor of the First church in Ipswich.
Charlestown, Printed by Samuel Etheridge, 1804.
38 p.   21½ cm.

22211 Frost, Griffin.
Camp and prison journal, embracing scenes in camp,
on the march, and in prisons... Also, scenes and
incidents during a trip for exchange, from St. Louis,
Mo., via Philadelphia, Pa., to City Point, Va. By
Griffin Frost. Quincy, Ill.   Printed at the Quincy
herald book and job office 1867.
vi p., 1 l., 303 p. incl. front.   20½ cm.
The author's experiences in northern prisons.

22212 Frost, Mrs. Jennett Blakeslee.
       The rebellion in the United States; or, The war of
       1861; being a complete history of its rise and progress,
       commencing with the presidential election... comp.
       from government documents and other reliable sources.
       By Mrs. J. Blakeslee Frost. Boston, Degen, Estes, and
       Priest [c1862]
          xiv, 11-388 p.   front., ports.   23 cm.
       Another edition published in 2 vols., Hartford,
       1862-63.

22213 [Frost, John] 1800-1859.
       An illustrated history of Washington and his times:
       embracing a history of the seven years' war, the
       revolutionary war, the formation of the federal Consti-
       tution, and the administrations of Washington... With
       an appendix, containing maxims of Washington, the
       Declaration of independence, the Articles of confede-
       ration, the Constitution of the United States, and
       Washington's farewell address. Ed. by Rev. William
       Hutchison... Norwich, Conn., H. Bill, 1868.
          8, 13-626 p. incl. illus., plates.   front. (port.)
       9 pl.   24 cm.
       1st edition, Philadelphia, 1847, pub. under title:
       Pictorial life of George Washington.

22214 Frost, John, 1800-1859.
       Pictorial life of George Washington: embracing a
       complete history of the seven years' war, the revolu-
       tionary war, the formation of the federal Constitution,
       and the administration of Washington. By J. Frost...
       With upwards of one hundred engravings, by Croome &
       Devereux. Philadelphia, C. J. Gillis, 1847.
          2 p.l., [3]-588 p. incl. illus., plates.   front.
       23 cm.

22215 Fry, Joseph Reese, 1811-1865.
       A life of Gen. Zachary Taylor; comprising a narrative
       of events connected with his professional career,
       derived from public documents and private correspondence;
       by J. Reese Fry; and authentic incidents of his early
       years, from materials collected by Robert T. Conrad.
       With... portrait and eleven... illustrations... by
       F. O. C. Darley. Philadelphia, Grigg, Elliot & co.,
       1847.
          x, [11]-322 p. incl. map.   front. (port.) 7 pl.,
       2 plans.   18½ cm.

22216 A full and free inquiry into the merits of the peace;
       with some strictures on the spirit of party...
       London, Printed for T. Payne, 1765.
          2 p.l., 160 p.   21 cm.

22217 Fuller, Richard, 1804-1876.
          A city or house divided against itself. A discourse
       delivered by Rev. Richard Fuller, D.D., on the first
       day of June, 1865, being the day of national fasting
       and humiliation. Baltimore, J. F. Weishampel, jr.,
       1865.
          20 p.   23 cm.

22218 Fuller, Samuel, 1802-1895.
          Early days of the church in the Helderberg. Two
       sermons preached in Trinity church, Rensselaerville,
       N. Y., Sunday, April 24, 1842, on the death of its
       founder and first rector, the Rev. Samuel Fuller, who
       died on the ninth, in the 75th year of his age, and
       50th of his ministry. By his son, the Rev. Samuel
       Fuller... Andover, Printed by Allen, Morrill and
       Wardwell, 1843.
          52 p.   23 cm.

22219 Fulton, Ambrose Cowperthwaite.
          A portion of life's voyage. Ambrose C. Fulton's
       talk to the Scott County pioneer settlers' association
       respecting some of his acts and his experiences during
       near a century. Davenport, Ia., The Osborn-Skelley
       co., printers, 1902.
          cover-title, 144 p.   23 cm.

22220 A funeral elegy, occasioned by the tragedy, at Salem,
       near Boston, on Thursday afternoon the seventeen of
       June, 1773. [n.p., 1773?]
          broadside.   26½ x 45 cm.
       Death of ten persons in a shipwreck.

22221 A funeral elegy upon the death of that excellent and
       most worthy gentleman John Winthrop Esq. late governour
       of his Majestyes Colonel of Connecticut, who deceased
       April, 1676. [Boston? John Foster? 1676?]
          broadside.   21½ x 31 cm.

22222 Furman, Gabriel, 1800-1854.
          Notes geographical and historical, relating to the
       town of Brooklyn, in Kings County on Long Island. By
       Gabriel Furman... Brooklyn, Printed by A. Spooner,

1824.
  3 p.l., [5]-116 p., 1 l.   20 cm.
  7 views and a portrait of Washington are inserted
in this copy.

G

22223 Gabriac, Alexis, comte de.
       ... Promenade à travers l'Amérique du Sud, Nouvelle-
       Grenade, Équateur, Pérou, Brésil, ouvrage orné de
       vingt-et-une gravures sur bois et de deux cartes
       géographiques. Paris, Michel Lévy frères, 1868.
       4 p.l., [3]-304 p.   illus. (music) 21 pl., 2 maps.
       24½ cm.

22224 Gallaudet, Thomas Hopkins, 1787-1851.
       An address on female education, delivered, Nov. 21st,
       1827, at the opening of the edifice erected for the
       accommodation of the Hartford female seminary. By
       T. H. Gallaudet... Published at the request of the
       trustees. Hartford, H. & F. J. Huntington, 1828.
       34 p.   22½ cm.

22225 Ganilh, Anthony.
       Odes, and fugitive poetry. By the Rev. Anthony
       Ganilh. Boston, Printed by W. Smith, 1830.
       36 p.   20½ cm.
       Includes: The Mississippi - an ode; A night in the
       woods of Louisiana; A crevasse in the levee of the
       Mississpi [!]

22226 Gannett, Ezra Stiles, 1801-1871.
       The religion of politics. A sermon delivered before
       His Excellency John Davis, governor, His Honor George
       Hull, lieutenant governor, the honorable Council, and
       the legislature of Massachusetts, at the annual
       election, January 5, 1842. By Ezra S. Gannett...
       Boston, Dutton and Wentworth, printers to the state,
       1842.
       46 p.   21½ cm.

22227 Gannett, Ezra Stiles, 1801-1871.
       A sermon preached in the Arlington-street church,
       Boston, on Sunday, July 3, 1864, at the close of the
       fortieth year of his ministry. By Ezra S. Gannett.
       Boston, Printed by J. Wilson and son, 1864.
       22 p.   23 cm.

22228 García Calderón, Francisco, 1834-1905.
Diccionario de la legislacion peruana, por Francisco
Garcia Calderon... Lima, Imprenta del estado, por
E. Aranda, 1860-62.
2 v.   32½ cm.

22229 Garrison, Joseph Fithian, 1823-1892.
The teachings of the crisis. Address delivered in
St. Paul's church, Camden, N. J., on the occasion of
the funeral of Abraham Lincoln, April 19, 1865. By
Rev. J. F. Garrison, M.D. 2d ed. Camden, N. J.,
Printed by S. Chew, 1865.
20 p.   22½ cm.

22230 Gasca, Mariano de la, 1776-1839.
Genera et species plantarum, quae aut novae sunt,
aut nondum recte cognoscuntur. Auctore Mariano Lagasca...
Matriti, ex Typographia regia, 1816.
4 p.l., 35 p.   2 pl. (1 fold.)   20½ cm.

22231 Gaspar da Madre de Deos (originally Teixeira de Azevedo)
1715-1800.
Memorias para a historia da capitania de S. Vicente,
hoje chamada de S. Paulo, do estado do Brazil,
publicadas de ordem da Academia R. das sciencias, por
fr. Gaspar da Madre de Deos, monge benedictino, e
correspondente da mesma academia. Lisboa, Na typografia
da Academia, 1797.
4 p.l., 242 p.   22 cm.

22232 Gasparin, Agénor Étienne, comte de, 1810-1871.
Une parole de paix sur le différend entre l'Angleterre et les États-Unis, par le Cte A. de Gasparin.
Paris, Michel Lévy frères, 1862.
31, [1] p.   21½ cm.

22233 Gass, Patrick, 1771-1870.
Voyage des capitaines Lewis et Clarke, depuis
l'emboulure du Missouri, jusqu'à l'entrée de la
Colombia dans l'océan Pacifique; fait dans les
années 1804, 1805 et 1806, par ordre du gouvernement
des États-Unis: contenant le journal authentique
des événements les plus remarquables du voyage,
ainsi que la description des habitants, du sol, du
climat, et des productions animales et végétales des
pays situés à l'ouest de l'Amérique Septentrionale.
Rédigé en anglais par Patrice Gass, employé dans
l'expédition; et traduit en française par A. J. N.

Lallemant... Avec des notes, deux lettres du
capitaine Clarke, et une carte gravée par J. B.
Tardieu. Paris, Arthus-Bertrand, 1810.
xviii, 443 p.   fold. map.   22 cm.

22234   Gautier du Tronchoy.
Journal de la campagne des isles de l'Amérique, qu'à
fait Monsieur D***. La prise & possession de l'isle
Saint Christophe, avec une description exacte des
animaux, des arbres, & des plantes les plus curieuses
de l'Amérique. La manière de vivre des sauvages,
leurs moeurs, leur police & religion. Avec la
relation de la surprise que voulut faire la garnison
de Fribourg sur les deux Brissack. Par G. D. T.,
enseigné dans le vaisseau du roy, le Zeripsée. Troyes,
J. le Febvre, 1709.
174 (i.e. 274) p.   16½ cm.

22235   Gay, Ebenezer, 1696-1787.
A beloved disciple of Jesus Christ characterized.
In a sermon preached at the West church in Boston,
July 27... 1766. The third Lord's day from the
decease of the reverend pastor, Jonathan Mayhew, D.D.
By Ebenezer Gay... Boston, Printed by R. and S. Draper
[etc.] 1766.
30 p.   20 cm.

22236   Geoffroy, William.
Facts connected with the cruise of the United States
steam frigate Merrimac, commanded by R. B. Hitchcock,
commander, late the flag ship of the Pacific squadron,
during the years 1857, 1858, 1859 & 1860. By William
Geoffroy... Baltimore, Printed by Kelly, Hedian &
Piet, 1860.
40 p. incl. tables.   front.   23 cm.

22237   Georgia. General assembly, 1806.
Memorial of the legislature of the state of Georgia
[to the Congress of the United States]... City of
Washington, A. & G. Way, printers, 1806.
45 p.   21 cm.   [U.S. 9th Cong., 1st sess. House.
Doc. Jan. 13, 1806]

22238   Georgia. General assembly.
Resolutions passed by the General assembly of Georgia,
on the 19th day of March, 1864, declaring the late
Act of Congress for the suspension of the writ of
habeas corpus unconstitutional; also, resolutions,

passed on the same day, setting forth the principles involved in the contest with the Lincoln government, and the terms upon which peace should be sought. Milledgeville, Ga., Boughton, Nisbet, Barnes & Moore, state printers, 1864.
   8 p.   21 cm.

22239 Gibbes, Robert Wilson, 1809-1866.
   ... A memoir on Mosasaurus and the three allied new genera, Holcodus, Conosaurus, and Amphorosteus. By Robert W. Gibbes...   Washington, Smithsonian institution, 1850
   13 p.   III pl.   31 cm.   (Smithsonian contributions to knowledge, vol. II, art. 5)

22240 Giddings, Joshua Reed, 1795-1864.
   History of the rebellion: its authors and causes. By Joshua R. Giddings. New York, Follet, Foster & co., 1864.
   viii, 9-498 p.   23 cm.

22241 Gilbert, Amos.
   Memoir of Frances Wright, the pioneer woman in the cause of human rights. By Amos Gilbert. Cincinnati, Pub. for the author, by Longley brothers, 1855.
   vi, 7-86, [2] p.   front. (port.)   15½ cm.

22242 Gillette, Abram Dunn, 1807-1882.
   God seen above all national calamities. A sermon on the death of President Lincoln, April 23, 1865. By A. D. Gillette... Washington, D. C., McGill & Witherow, printers, 1865.
   15 p.   23 cm.

22243 Gillette, Walter Bloomfield.
   Memoir of Rev. Daniel Holbrook Gillette, of Mobile, Alabama. By his brothers Rev. W. B. Gillette... and Rev. A. D. Gillette... Philadelphia, J. B. Lippincott & co., 1846.
   vi, 234 p.   front. (port.)   18½ cm.

22244 Gillies, John, 1712-1796.
   Memoirs of the life of the Reverend George Whitefield, M.A., late chaplain to the Right Honourable the Countess of Huntingdon... Faithfully selected from his original papers, journals, and letters... To which are added, a particular account of his death and funeral; and extracts from the sermons, which were preached on

that occasion. Compiled by the Rev. John Gillies...
London, E. and C. Dilly; [etc., etc.] 1772.

22245 Gilman, Samuel, 1791-1858.
Contributions to literature; descriptive, critical,
humorous, biographical, philosophical, and poetical.
By Samuel Gilman, D.D. Boston, Crosby, Nichols and
company, 1856.
viii, 564 p.   19½ cm.

22246 [Gilpin, Mrs. Eliza] comp.
A memorial of Henry D. Gilpin. Philadelphia, 1860.
1 p.l., iii p., 2 l., 211 p.   front. (port.)
24½ cm.

22247 Glasscock, Lemuel, b. 1801.
The life and travels of Lemuel Glasscock. [Maysville,
Ky., 1841?]
27 p.   24 cm.

22248 Glazier, Willard, 1841-1905.
Headwaters of the Mississippi; comprising biographical
sketches of early and recent explorers of the great
river, and a full account of the discovery and location
of the true source in a lake beyond Itasca. By Captain
Willard Glazier... Chicago and New York, Rand, McNally
& company, 1893.
527 p. incl. front., illus., maps.   19½ cm.

22249 Gleason, Benjamin, 1777-1847.
An oration, pronounced at the Baptist meeting-house
in Wrentham, February 22, 1800. At the request of the
Society, in memory of Gen. George Washington, first
president and late commander in chief of the armies
of the United States of America... By Benjamin Gleason.
Printed at Wrentham, Massachusetts, by Nathaniel and
Benjamin Heaton, 1800.
31, [1] p.   22½ cm.
"An occasional ode, sung at the Baptist meeting-house,
in Wrentham, February 22, 1800": p. [32]

22250 Glorious news. Boston, Friday 11 o'clock, 16th May
1766. This instant arrived the brig Harrison. Boston,
1766.
broadside.   33½ x 21 cm.

22251 Gobineau, [Joseph] A[rthur] de.
Voyage à Terre-Neuve par le comte A. de Gobineau...

Paris, L. Hachette et c^{ie}, 1861.
2 p.l., 309 p., 1 l.

22252   González de Mendoza, Juan, bp., 1545-1618.
        The history of the great and mighty kingdom of China
and the situation thereof. (Comp. by the padre Juan
González de Mendoza, and now reprinted from the early
translation of R. Parke. Ed. by Sir George T. Staunton,
bart. with an introduction by R. H. Major... London,
Printed for the Hakluyt society, 1853-54.
        2 v.   22 cm.   (Half-title: Works issued by the
Hakluyt society. [no. xiv-vi])
        "Second part... is diuided into three parts. The
first containeth such thinges as the fathers, Frier
Martin de Herrada, prounciall of the order of Sainte
Augustine, in the ilands Philipinas, and his companion
Fryer Geronimo Martin, and other souldiers that went
with them, did see and had intelligence of in that
kingdom. The second containeth the miraculous voiage
that was made by Frier Pedro de Alfaro, of the order of
S. Francis, and his companions, vnto the said kingdome.
The third containeth a briefe declaration by the said
frier, and of Frier Martin Ignacio, that went out of
Spaine into China and returned into Spain againe by
the Orientall India, after that he had compassed the
world."

22253   Gordon, Thomas Francis, 1787-1860.
        A gazetteer of the state of Pennsylvania. Part first...
general description of the state... geological construction, canals and rail-roads, bridges, revenue,
expenditures, public debt, &c. Part second...
counties, towns, cities, villages, mountains, lakes,
rivers, creeks, &c., alphabetically arranged. By
Thomas F. Gordon. To which is added a table of all the
post offices in the state, their distances from
Washington and Harrisburg, and the names of the post
masters... Philadelphia, T. Belknap, 1832.
        2 p.l., 9-63, 508 p.   front. (fold. map)   22½ cm.

22254   Gordon, Thomas Francis, 1787-1860.
        The history of Pennsylvania, from its discovery by
Europeans, to the Declaration of independence in 1776.
By Thomas F. Gordon. Philadelphia, Carey, Lea & Carey,
1829.
        vii, viii, 628 p., 1 l.   22½ cm.

22255   Gorham, John, 1783-1829.
        Inaugural address, delivered in the chapel of the

University at Cambridge, December 11, 1816. By John
Gorham... Boston, Printed by Wells and Lilly, 1817.
23 p.   22 cm.
"I propose... to confine myself to a cursory detail
of the state of science [chemistry], as it has existed
at different periods, and to conclude with a view of
the philosophy of the present age." - p. 7.

22256   Gorman, John C
Lee's last campaign, with an accurate history of
Stonewall Jackson's last wound. By Capt. J. C. Gorman.
2d ed. 10th thousand. Raleigh, W. B. Smith & company,
1866.
iv, [5]-71 p.   14 cm.

22257   Gough, John Bartholomew, 1817-1886.
An autobiography, by John B. Gough... 8th thousand.
Boston, The author, 1845.
2 p.l., 172 p.   15½ cm.

22258   Gould, Marcus Tullius Cicero, 1793-1860, comp.
Debate, in the Senate of New York, on Mr. Granger's
motion, of the 3d of March, to amend the 6th section
of the Convention bill, by increasing the number of
delegates to 165, and equalizing that number among the
several districts and counties in the state, conformable
to actual population and the principles of justice and
equity. Together with Mr. Granger's address, to the
conventions of the two Republican parties in the
Western district. By M. T. C. Gould. Albany, Printed
by E. & E. Hosford, 1821.
37, [1] p., 1 l.   23½ cm.

22259   Graah, Wilhelm August, 1793-1863.
Narrative of an expedition to the east coast of
Greenland, sent by order of the king of Denmark, in
search of the lost colonies, under the command of
Captain W. A. Graah... Tr. from the Danish by the
late G. Gordon Macdougall, F.R.S.N.A., for the Royal
geographical society of London, with the original
Danish chart completed by the expedition. London,
J. W. Parker, 1837.
xvi, 199, [1] p.   fold. map.   22 cm.

22260   Gracey, Samuel Levis, 1835-1911.
Annals of the Sixth Pennsylvania cavalry. By Rev.
S. L. Gracey, chaplain... Published for the officers
of the regiment. [Philadelphia] E. H. Butler & Co.,

1868.
4 p.l., 13-372 p.   fold. map.   23 cm.

22261 Graham, David.
The pioneer, consisting of essays, literary, moral
and theological. v. 1, no. 1-7; Feb. 28-Oct. 8, 1812.
Pittsburgh, Printed by S. Engels.
301 p.   20 cm.   monthly (irregular)

22262 Graham, Mrs. Isabella (Marshall) 1742-1814.
The unpublished letters and correspondence of
Mrs. Isabella Graham, from the year 1767 to 1814;
exhibiting her religious character in the different
relations of life. Selected and arranged by her
daughter, Mrs. Bethune... New York, J. S. Taylor,
1838.
xii, [13]-314 p.   19 cm.

22263 Graham, James.
The life of General Daniel Morgan, of the Virginia
line of the army of the United States, with portions
of his correspondence; comp. from authentic sources.
By James Graham... New York, Derby & Jackson, 1859.
xv, 17-475 p.   18 cm.

22264 Graham, John, b. 1794.
Autobiography and reminiscences of Rev. John Graham,
late pastor of the Associate, not the United Presbyterian
congregation of Bovina, Delaware co., N. Y. With an
appendix containing some interesting and important
letters to the author from Rev. Dr. McCrie... and
other eminent ministers of Scotland of a former day.
To which are added a few of his sermons. Philadelphia,
W. S. Rentoul, 1870.
vi, 206 p.   19½ cm.
"A brief sketch of Rev. Andrew Arnot": p. 124-129.

22265 Graham, Samuel, 1756-1831.
Memoir of General Graham, with notices of the campaigns
in which he was engaged from 1779 to 1801. Ed. by
his son, Colonel James J. Graham. Edinburgh, Priv.
print. by R. & R. Clark, 1862.
xvii p., 1 l., 318 p.   front. (port.) 4 pl., 2 maps.
20 cm.

22266 Graham, William Alexander, 1804-1875.
Discourse in memory of the life and character of the
Hon. Geo. E. Badger, delivered by William A. Graham...

(by request of the bar of Wake County,) at Raleigh,
July 19th, 1866. Raleigh, Nichols, Gorman & Neathery,
printers, 1866.
34 p.   22½ cm.

22267 Graham, William Sloan, 1818-1847.
Remains of William S. Graham... With a memoir...
Ed. by George Allen. Philadelphia, J. W. Moore, 1849.
viii, [13]-278 p.   front. (port.)   20 cm.
"Memoir [by his wife]": p. [13]-156. "Translations
[from Horace, Lessing, Goethe, Schiller, Körner, and
Uhland]": p. 226-250.
Verse and prose.

22268 Gray, Asa, 1810-1888.
Field, forest, and garden botany, a simple introduction
to the common plants of the United States, east of the
Mississippi, both wild and cultivated. By Asa Gray...
New York, Ivison, Phinney, Blakeman, & co.; Chicago,
S. C. Griggs & co., 1868.
2 p.l., [9]-386 p.   21½ cm.
"This book is designed to be the companion of the
First lessons in botany, which serves as grammar and
dictionary." - Pref.

22269 Gray, Thomas, d. 1849.
Change: a poem pronounced at Roxbury, October VIII,
MDCCCXXX, in commemoration of the first settlement of
that town. By Thomas Gray, jr., M.D. Roxbury [Mass.]
C. P. Emmons, 1830.
25 p.   21 cm.

22270 Gt. Brit. Treaties, etc., 1760-1820 (George III)
Treaty of amity, commerce, and navigation, between
His Britannic Majesty, and the United States of
America, conditionally ratified by the Senate of the
United States, at Philadelphia, June 24, 1795. To
which is annexed a copious appendix. 2d ed. Phila-
delphia, Printed by Lang & Ustick, for Mathew Carey,
No. 118, Market-street, Nov. 2, 1795.
190 p.   21½ cm.

22271 Greeley, Horace, 1811-1872.
Recollections of a busy life: including reminiscences
of American politics and politicians, from the opening
of the Missouri contest to the downfall of slavery;
to which are added miscellanies... also, a discussion
with Robert Dale Owen of the law of divorce. By Horace

Greeley. New York, J. B. Ford & co.; Boston, H. A. Brown
& co.; [etc., etc.] 1868.
2 p.l., [vii]-xv, [17]-624 p.   front. (port.) illus.,
2 pl., facsim.   22½ cm.

22272 Green, Ashbel, 1762-1848.
The life of Ashbel Green, V.D.M., begun to be written
by himself in his eighty-second year and continued to
his eighty-fourth. Prepared for the press... by
Joseph H. Jones... New York, R. Carter & bros., 1849.
1 p.l., 628 p.   front. (port.)   22½ cm.

22273 Greenleaf, Jonathan, 1785-1865.
Sketches of the ecclesiastical history of the state
of Maine, from the earliest settlement to the present
time. By Jonathan Greenleaf... Portsmouth N.H.
H. Gray, 1821.
vi, [7]-293, 77, [1] p.   17½ cm.

22274 Grimshaw, William, 1782-1852.
History of the United States, from their first
settlement as colonies, to the peace of Ghent:
comprising, every important political event... By
William Grimshaw... Philadelphia, Published by
Benjamin Warner, no. 171, Market street, Lydia R.
Bailey, printer, 1820.
1 p.l., 306, [6] p.   18½ cm.

22275 Griswold, Rufus Wilmot, 1815-1887.
The republican court: or, American society in the
days of Washington. By Rufus Wilmot Griswold. A new
ed., with the author's last additions and corrections.
With twenty-five portraits of distinguished women,
engraved from original pictures by Wollaston, Copley,
Gainsborough, Stuart, Peale, Trumbull, Pine, Malborne,
and other contemporary painters. New York, London,
D. Appleton and company, 1867.
iv p., 2 l., 481 p.   25 port. (incl. front.)   24 cm.

22276 Guizot, François Pierre Guillaume, 1787-1874.
Washington, por M. Guizot. Madrid, Impr. de D. A.
Espinosa y compañía, 1846.
2 p.l., xxi p., 1 l., [5]-148 p.   16½ cm.

22277 Guthrie, William, 1708-1770.
A new system of modern geography: or, A geographical,
historical, and commercial grammar; and present state
of the several kingdoms of the world... By William

Guthrie, esq. The astronomical part by James Ferguson, F.R.S. To which have been added, the late discoveries of Dr. Herschell [!] and other eminent astronomers. The 6th ed., cor., and greatly enl. London, Printed for C. Dilly etc. MDCCXCV.

6 p.l., 1098, [28] p.   27½ x 21½ cm.   and atlas.

The original edition (1770) and many others have title "A new geographical, historical, and commercial grammar"; other later editions, "A universal geography."

"Of this popular grammar, Knox, the bookseller, is said to be the real compiler." - Watt, Bibl. brit., 1824, v. 1, 452 s.

A table of the coins of all nations, and their value in English money: p. 1062-1076.

A chronological table of remarkable events from the creation to the present time: p. [1077]-1098.

22278 [Gutiérrez de Lafuente, Antonio]
Manifiesto que di en Trujillo en 1824 sobre los motivos que me obligaron á deponer a D. José de la Riva-Aguero, y conducta que observé en ese acontecimiento. Lima, Impreso por J. M. Masias, 1829.

1 p.l., 29, xxviii p., 1 l.   29½ cm.

H

22279 Haas, J   C   of Philadelphia.
Geographie von Amerika und ins besondere von den Vereinigten Staaten. Bearb. von J. C. Haas. Philadelphia und Leipzig, Schäfer und Koradi, 1867.

69 p.   12 cm.

22280 Hacke, William, ed.
A collection of original voyages: containing I. Capt. Cowley's voyage round the globe. II. Captain Sharp's journey over the Isthmus of Darien, and expedition into the South seas, written by himself. III. Capt. Wood's voyage thro' the Streights of Magellan. IV. Mr. Roberts's adventures among the corsairs of the Levant; his account of their way of living; description of the Archipelago islands, taking of Scio, &c. Illustrated with several maps and draughts. Published by Capt. William Hacke. London, Printed for J. Knapton, 1699.

8 p.l., 45, 100 [i.e. 84], 53 p.   illus., 2 pl. (1 fold.) 2 fold. maps, fold. plan.   19½ cm.

22281 Häcker, Ludwig.
Amerikanische reise-skizzen aus dem gebiete der
technik, landwirthschaft und des socialen lebens. Von
Ludwig Häcker... Braunschweig, F. Vieweg und sohn,
1867.
x, 199, [1] p.   22½ cm.

22282 Haco, Dion, pseud.?
J. Wilkes Booth, the assassinator of President
Lincoln, by Dion Haco, esq.... New York, T. R. Dawley,
1865.
1 p.l., [15]-102 p.   19 cm.   (On cover: Dawley's
new war novels, no. 9)

22283 Hagthorpe, John, fl. 1627.
Englands-exchequer. Or A discovrse of the sea and
navigation, with some things thereto coincident concerning plantations. Likewise some particular remonstrances
how a sea-force might be profitably imployed. Wherein
by the way, is likewise set downe the great commodities
and victories the Portingalls, Spaniards, Dutch, and
others, haue gotten by nauigation and plantations, in
the West-Indies, and elsewhere. Written as an incourage-
ment to our English nation to affect the like, who are
better prouided than any of those. By Iohn Hagthorpe
gent.... London, Printed for N. Butter and N. Bourne,
1625.
2 p.l., 49 [i.e. 47] p.   17 cm.

22284 Hair, James T   comp.
Iowa state gazetteer... Comp. and ed. by James T.
Hair. Chicago, Bailey & Hair, 1865.
722 p.   23½ cm.

22285 Hakluyt, Richard, 1552?-1616, comp.
Divers voyages touching the discovery of America and
the islands adjacent. Collected and published by
Richard Hakluyt... in the year 1582. Edited, with
notes and an introduction, by John Winter Jones...
London, Printed for the Hakluyt society, 1850.
3 p.l., cxi, 171, 6 p.   3 fold. facsim. (incl.
2 maps)   22 cm.   (Half-title: Works issued by the
Hakluyt society. [No. 7])

22286 Hall, Edward Brookes, 1800-1866.
Memoir of Mary L. Ware, wife of Henry Ware, jr.
By Edward B. Hall. 11th thousand. Boston, American

By Edward B. Hall. 11th thousand. Boston, American
Unitarian association, 1867.
    vii, 434 p.   front. (port.)   19½ cm.

22287 Hall, Edward Hepple, comp.
    The northern counties gazetteer and director, for
1855-6: a complete and perfect guide to northern
Illinois. Containing a concise description of the
cities, towns & principal villages, with the names
of the public officers, professional and business
men, in the counties of Boone, Cook, De Kalb, Du
Page, Jo Daviess, Kane, Lake, McHenry, Stephenson,
Winnebago; and a variety of other useful and interesting
information. Brought down to November, 1855... E. H.
Hall, compiler. Chicago, R. Fergus, book & job printer,
1855.
    vii, [1], [17]-152 p.   23½ cm.

22288 [Hall, Fayr]
    A short account of the first settlement of the
provinces of Virginia, Maryland, New York, New Jersey,
and Pennsylvania, by the English. To which is annexed
a map of Maryland, according to the bounds mentioned
in the Charter, and also of the adjacent country,
anno. 1630. London, 1735.
    22 p.   fold. map.   24 cm.
    The map has title: A map of Virginia according to
Captain John Smiths map published anno 1606, also
of the adjacent country called the Dutch Niew
Nederlant anno 1630. By Iohn Senex, 1735.

22289 Hall, Henry, 1845-
    The history of Auburn, by Henry Hall...   Auburn
N. Y. Dennis bros. & co., 1869.
    xvi, 579, [1] p.   18½ cm.

22290 Hall, Hiland, 1795-1885.
    The history of Vermont, from its discovery to its
admission into the Union in 1791. By Hiland Hall.
Albany, N. Y., J. Munsell, 1868.
    xii, 521, [1] p. incl map.   fold. front.   24 cm.
    Running title: Early history of Vermont.
    "Biographical sketches of the principal persons
mentioned in this work": p. [451]-476.

22291 Hall, Joseph, bp. of Norwich, 1574-1656.
A common apologie of the Chvrch of England: against
the vniust challenges of the ouer iust sect, commonly
called Brownists. Wherein the grounds and defences,
of the separation are large discussed: occasioned by a
late pamphlet published vnder the name, of An answer to
a censorious epistle, which the reader shall finde in
the margent. By J. H. London, Printed for E. Edgar,
1610.
3 p.l., 145, [4] p.   19 cm.

22292 Halleck, Henry Wager, 1815-1872.
Elements of international law and laws of war. By
H. W. Halleck... Prepared for the use of colleges and
private students. Philadelphia, J. B. Lippincott & co.,
1878.
xxxviii, 17-380 p.   21 cm.
Abridgment of the author's International law.

22293 Halliday, Samuel Byram, 1812-1897.
The lost and found; or, Life among the poor. By
Samuel B. Halliday... New York, Blakeman & Mason, 1859.
356 p.   front.   19½ cm.
Also published under title: The little street sweeper;
or, Life among the poor.

22294 Hamilton, Alexander, 1757-1804.
The official and other papers of the late Major-General
Alexander Hamilton: comp. chiefly from the originals
in the possession of Mrs. Hamilton... Vol. I. New York,
and London, Wiley & Putnam, 1842.
iv, 496 p.   22½ cm.
Composed by Francis L. Hawks.
No more published.

22295 Hammond, James Henry, 1807-1864.
An address delivered before the South-Carolina
institute, at its first annual fair, on the 20th
November, 1849. By James H. Hammond... Charleston,
S. C., Press of Walker and James, 1849.
54, [2] p.   23 cm.
"Report of the Committee on premiums of the South-
Carolina institute": p. [39]-50.
Members of the South-Carolina institute": p. [51]-54.

22296 Hancock, John, 1702-1744.
A memorial of God's goodness. Being the substance of
two sermons, preach'd in the First church of Christ in

Braintre, Sept. 16th, 1739. On compleating the first
century since the gathering of it. By John Hancock...
Printed at the earnest desire of the hearers; in remembrance of God's mercy. Together with some marginal
illustrations... Boston, Printed and sold by S. Kneeland
& T. Green, over against the prison in Queenstreet, 1739.
2 p.l., ii, 37 p.   19 cm.

22297 Harden, Edward Jenkins, 1813-1873.
        The life of George M. Troup. By Edward J. Harden.
        Savannah, E. J. Purse, 1859.
            viii, 536, xxii p.   front. (port.)   24 cm.

22298 [Harding, W   M   ]
        Trans-Atlantic sketches, by "Porte Plume." New York,
        G. F. Nesbitt & co., printers, 1870.
            87 p.   23 cm.
        "A small portion of the... 'Sketches' appeared as
        'Letters to the Brooklyn Union,' with the signature of
        'Porte Plume' in that journal in the fall of 1868."-
        Pref.

22299 Hare, Francis, bp. of Chichester, 1671-1740.
        The allies and the late ministry defended against
        France, and the present friends of France. In answer to
        a pamphlet, entitled, The conduct of the allies. London,
        Printed for E. Sanger, 1711-12.
            4 v. in 1.   20 cm.
        In answer to Swift's "The conduct of the allies".

22300 Hare, Robert, 1781-1858.
        A brief exposition of the injury done to the community,
        and especially to the poor, by the prohibition of bills
        under five dollars, while such bills are permitted to
        circulate in adjoining states. In a letter to William
        B. Reed, esq., also, a subsequent letter, on the
        failure of the late effort to resume specie payments.
        By Robert Hare, M.D. Philadelphia, 1841.
            8 p.   23 cm.

22301 Harford, John Scandrett, 1785-1866.
        Some account of the life, death, and principles of
        Thomas Paine, together with remarks on his writings,
        and on their intimate connection with the avowed
        objects of the revolutionists of 1793, and of the
        radicals in 1819. By John S. Harford... Bristol,
        J. M. Gutch, 1819.
            viii, 93 p.   21 cm.

22302 Harlow, Samuel R
    Life sketches of the state officers, senators and
members of the Assembly of the state of New York, in
1867. By S. R. Harlow and H. H. Boone. Albany, Weed,
Parsons & co., 1867.
    418 p.   front. (port.)   21½ cm.

22303 Harlow, Samuel R
    Life sketches of the state officers, senators, and
members of the Assembly, of the state of New York, in
1868. By S. R. Harlow and S. C. Hutchins. Albany, Weed,
Parsons & company, printers, 1868.
    402 p.   front. (port.)   21½ cm.

22304 Harris, Mary, defendant.
    Official report of the trial of Mary Harris, indicted
for the murder of Adoniram J. Burroughs, before the
Supreme court of the District of Columbia (sitting as
a criminal court) Monday, July 3, 1865. Prepared by
James O. Clephane, official reporter. Washington, D. C.,
W. H. & O. H. Morrison, 1865.
    181 p.   23 cm.

22305 [Harris, Miriam (Coles)] 1834-1925.
    Louie's last term at St. Mary's. By the author of
"Rutledge"... New York, C. Scribner & company, 1871.
    3 p.l., [v]-vi, 7-239 p.   19 cm.

22306 Harris, William Wallace.
    The battle of Groton Heights: a collection of
narratives, official reports, records, &c., of the
storming of Fort Griswold, and the burning of New
London by British troops, under the command of Brig.
Gen. Benedict Arnold, on the sixth of September, 1781.
With an introduction and notes. By William W. Harris...
New London, 1870.
    x, 123 p.   23½ cm.

22307 Harrison, Helen Dortch, comp.
    Life and correspondence of James Iredell, by
Griffith J. McRee. Index compiled by Helen Dortch
Harrison. Chapel Hill, N.C., University of North
Carolina Library, 1955.
    151 p.   28 cm.

22308 Harrison, Jesse Burton, 1805-1841.
    A discourse on the prospects of letters and taste in
Virginia, pronounced before the Literary and philoso-

phical society of Hampden-Sydney college, at their
fourth anniversary, in September, 1827. By J. B.
Harrison... Cambridge [Mass.] Hilliard and Brown,
1828.
    42 p.   22 x 13½ cm.

22309   Harrison, Richard Almgill, 1824-1904.
        The suppression of the rebellion. Speech of Hon.
    Richard A. Harrison, of Ohio. Delivered in the House
    of representatives, January 23, 1862. [Washington,
    L. Towers & co., printers, 1862]
        8 p.   24½ cm.

22310   Harrison, Walter.
        Pickett's men: a fragment of war history. By Walter
    Harrison... New York, D. Van Nostrand, 1870.
        202 p.   front. (port.) pl.   19 cm.

22311   [Harrisse, Henry] 1829-1910.
        Bibliotheca americana vetustissima. A description
    of works relating to America, published between the
    years 1492 and 1551... New York, G. P. Philes, 1866.
        4 p.l., liv p., 1 l., 519, [1] p.   25 cm.

22312   [Harrisse, Henry] 1830-1910.
        Notes on Columbus. New York, Priv. print. Cambridge,
    Riverside press 1866.
        vli, 1 , 227 p.   front. (port.) pl., facsims.
    32 cm.
        Bibliographical and historical notes and extracts
    from documents and printed books: a contribution to
    American bibliography and to the documentary history
    of Columbus.

22313   Harrisson, David, jr.
        A voice from the Washingtonian home; being a history
    of the foundation, rise, and progress of the Washington-
    ian home, an institution established at No. 36 Charles
    street, Boston, for the reformation of the inebriate.
    Also, a review of some of the evils of intemperance in
    England. Together with a sketch of the temperance
    reform in America. By David Harrison, jr... Boston,
    Redding & co., 1860.
        xii, 324 p.   front. (port.)   20 cm.

22314   Hart, Burdette, 1821-1906.
        The Mexican war. A discourse delivered at the
    Congregational church in Fair Haven, on the annual fast

of 1847. By Rev. Burdett Hart. New Haven, Peck & Stafford, printers, 1847.
    16 p.   23 cm.

22315   Hart, Frederick Weber
        Exposition of the Houmans land claim, and of the second section of the Missouri land bill, approved June 2, 1858... Washington, 1859.
        30 p.   22½ cm.

22316   Hartley, Cecil B
        Life and adventures of Lewis Wetzel, the Virginia ranger; to which are added biographical sketches of General Simon Kenton, General Benjamin Logan, Captain Samuel Brady, Governor Isaac Shelby, and other heroes of the West. By Cecil B. Hartley. Illustrated with engravings from original designs, by G. G. White. Philadelphia, G. G. Evans, 1860.
        1 p.l., 820 p.   front., 3 pl.   19 cm.

22317   Hartley, Oliver Cromwell, 1823-1859.
        A digest of the laws of Texas: to which is subjoined an appendix containing the acts of the Congress of the United States on the subjects of the naturalization of aliens, and the authentication of records, etc., in each state or territory, so as to take effect in every other state of territory; and to which are prefixed the constitutions of the United States, of the provisional government of Texas, of the republic of Texas, and of the state of Texas. By Oliver C. Hartley... Philadelphia, Thomas, Cowperthwait & co., 1850.
        1 p.l., [v]-viii, 1041, [1] p.   26 cm.

22318   [Hartley, Thomas] 1748-1800.
        Observations on the propriety of fixing upon a central and inland situation for the permanent residence of Congress. Humbly offered to the consideration of the honorable the members of the Senate and House of representatives of the United States. By the author. [New York] Printed in the year MDCCLXXXIX.
        11 p.   21 x 12 cm.
        Signed: Phocion.
        In favor of York, Pa.

22319   Hartpence, Alanson.
        Our national crisis: a sermon preached in the Presbyterian church, Holmesburg, Pa., September 14, 1862, by Rev. A. Hartpence... Philadelphia, 1862.
        cover-title, 8 p.   21 cm.

22320   Hartt, Charles Frederick, 1840-1878.
            Thayer expedition. Scientific results of a journey
        in Brazil. By Louis Agassiz and his travelling compa-
        nions. Geology and physical geography of Brazil. By
        Ch. Fred. Hartt... Boston, Fields, Osgood & co., 1870.
            xxiii, 620 p.   front., illus., plates, maps (part
        fold.) diagrs.   22½ cm.

22321   Hartwell, Abraham.
            Memoir of the late Rev. John Pierce. By Abraham Hart-
        well. To which is added original sermons, miscellaneous
        pieces, &c., selected from the writings of Mr. Pierce.
        Lunenburg [Mass.] The editor, W. J. Merriam-printer,
        Fitchburg, Mass., 1842.
            x p., 1 l., [13]-180 p.   front. (port.)   20 cm.

22322   Hartwig, Georg Ludwig, 1813-1880.
            The polar world: a popular description of man and
        nature in the Arctic and Antarctic regions of the globe.
        By Dr. G. Hartwig... With additional chapters... New
        York, Harper & brothers, 1869.
            xvi, [17]-486 p. incl. front., illus.   25½ cm.

22323   Hartwig, Georg Ludwig, 1813-1880.
            The tropical world: a popular scientific account of
        the natural history of the animal and vegetable kingdoms
        in the equatorial regions. By Dr. G. Hartwig...
        London, Longman, Green, Longman, Roberts, and Green,
        1863.
            xx, 566 p.   illus., 8 col. pl. (incl. front.)
        22½ cm.

22324   Harvard college and its benefactors. Boston, C. C. Little
        and J. Brown, 1846.
            37 p.   25 cm.

22325   The Harvard register. no. I-XII; March, 1827-Feb. 1828.
        Cambridge, Hilliard and Brown, 1828.
            2 p.l., 334 p.   21½ cm.   monthly.
        No more published.

22326   Harvard university.
            Addresses at the inauguration of the Hon. Edward
        Everett, LL.D., as president of the University at
        Cambridge, Thursday, April 30, 1846. Boston, C. C.
        Little and J. Brown, 1846.
            66 p.   24 cm.

22327 Harvard university.
A memorial concerning the recent history and the
constitutional rights and privileges of Harvard college;
presented by the president and fellows to the legislature, January 17, 1851. Cambridge, J. Bartlett, 1851.
56 p.   23 cm.

22328 Harvey, George, A.N.A.
Harvey's illustrations of our country, with an outline
of its social progress, political development, and
material resources, being an epitome of a part of eight
lectures... before... the Royal institution of Great
Britain, in 1849... entitled the Discovery, resources,
and progress of North America, north of Virginia...
Boston, Printed by Dutton & Wentworth, 1851.
36 p.   23½ cm.

22329 Harvest, George, d. 1776.
Sermon preached before the honourable Trustees for
establishing the colony of Georgia in America, and the
Associates of the late Reverend Dr. Bray; at their
anniversary meeting, March 16, 1748-9. In the parish
church of St. Margaret, Westminster. By George Harvest...
London, Printed for W. Meadows [etc.] 1749.
2 p.l., [3]-22 p.   21½ x 16½ cm.

22330 Harvey, William Woodis, 1798-1864.
Sketches of Hayti; from the expulsion of the French,
to the death of Christophe. By W. W. Harvey... London,
L. B. Seeley and son, 1827.
xvi, 416 p.   fold. front.   22 cm.

22331 Harward, Thomas, 1700-1736.
Electuarium novum alexipharmacum. Or, A new cordial,
alexiterial and restorative electuary; which may serve
for a succedaneum to the grand theriaca andromachi.
The theriaca examined, with reasons humbly offered why
the troches should be ejected, as well as a great number
of the rest of the ingredients. A new correction of
theriaca most humbly proposed, and, with due deference,
submitted to the superior and impartial judgment of the
Royal college of physicians; and dedicated to the most
honoured the president, the justly honoured the censors,
with their most worthy brethren the elect, and the rest
of the fellows of that most honourable society. By the
Reverend Mr. Harward... Boston, Printed by B. Green,
and sold by the booksellers, 1732.
2 p.l., 26 p.   18 cm.

22332　Harwood, John Edmund, 1771-1806.
　　　　Poems, by John Edmund Harwood. New York, Published
　　　　by M. & W. Ward, no. 4 City-hotel, for Joseph Osborn,
　　　　1809.
　　　　1 p.l., 107 p.　　17½ cm.

22333　Haskins, Roswell Wilson, 1796-1870.
　　　　New England and the West. By R. W. Haskins...
　　　　Buffalo, A. W. Wilgus, 1843.
　　　　36 p.　　21 cm.
　　　　"Reprinted from the Boston (Mass.) atlas."

22334　Hassard, John Rose Greene, 1836-1888.
　　　　Life of the Most Reverend John Hughes, D.D., first
　　　　archbishop of New York. With extracts from his private
　　　　correspondence. By John R. G. Hassard. New York,
　　　　D. Appleton and company, 1866.
　　　　519 p.　　front. (port.) fold. facsim.　　23 cm.

22335　Hassaurek, Friedrich, 1832-1885.
　　　　Four years among Spanish-Americans. By F. Hassaurek...
　　　　New York, Hurd and Houghton, 1867.
　　　　x, 401 p.　　18½ cm.
　　　　Life in Ecuador.

22336　Hastings, Hiram P
　　　　An essay on constitutional reform; treating of state
　　　　credit,-special legislation,-election of all officers
　　　　by the people,.. &c. By Hiram P. Hastings... New
　　　　York, Printed at the Globe job office, 1846.
　　　　35 p.　　22 x 13 cm.

22337　Hatfield, Edwin Francis, 1807-1883.
　　　　History of Elizabeth, New Jersey; including the early
　　　　history of Union county. By Rev. Edwin F. Hatfield...
　　　　New York, Charlton & Lanahan, 1868.
　　　　701 p.　　front., pl., port., fold. map.　　23 cm.
　　　　With manuscript appendix (16 p.)

22338　Hathaway, Levi, b. 1790.
　　　　The narrative of Levi Hathaway, giving an account of
　　　　his life, experience, call to the ministry of the
　　　　gospel of the Son of God, and travels as such to the
　　　　present time... Providence, Printed for the author, by
　　　　Miller & Hutchens, 1820.
　　　　140 p.　　17½ cm.
　　　　The author's travels and experiences as a minister of
　　　　the Christian church, chiefly in New York and New England

22339   Hathaway, Warren, 1828-1909.
        A discourse occasioned by the death of Abraham Lincoln:
        preached at Coxsackie, on Wednesday, April 19, 1865, by
        Warren Hathaway. Albany, J. Munsell, 1865.
        24 p.   23½ cm.

22340   Hattersley, John.
        The conquest of America, and minor poems, by John
        Hattersley. London, Baldwin and Cradock, and I. Contes,
        Darlington, 1831.
        viii, 207, [1] p.   17 cm.

22341   Hauch, Johannes Carsten, 1790-1872.
        Robert Fulton, an historical novel, by John Carsten
        Hauch... Tr. [from the Danish] by Paul C. Sinding...
        New York, Printed by Macdonald & Palmer, 1868.
        vii, [2], 450 p.   19 cm.

22342   Hautefeuille, Laurent Basile, 1805-1875.
        ... Propriétés privées des sujets belligérants sur
        mer. Par M. L.-B. Hautefeuille. Paris, A. Franck,
        1860.
        39 p.   23½ cm.

22343   Haven, Charles Chauncy.
        Annals of the city of Trenton, with random remarks
        and historic reminiscences by C. C. Haven. Trenton,
        N. J., Printed at the "State gazette" office, 1866.
        31 p.   21½ cm.

22344   Haven, Charles Chauncy.
        Thirty days in New Jersey ninety years ago: an essay
        revealing new facts in connection with Washington and
        his army in 1776 and 1777, by C. C. Haven... Trenton,
        Printed at the "State gazette" office, 1867.
        72 p.   col. front., maps.   21½ cm.

22345   Haven, Gilbert, bp., 1821-1880.
        Te Deum laudamus. The cause and the consequence of
        the election of Abraham Lincoln; a Thanksgiving sermon
        delivered in the Harvard st. M. E. church, Cambridge,
        Sunday evening, Nov. 11, 1860, by Rev. Gilbert Haven...
        Boston, J. M. Hewes, printer, 1860.
        44 p.   23 cm.

22346   Haven, John, 1733-1803.
        A sermon, preached at Stoughton, on Wednesday, the
        18th of June, 1783. At the funeral of the Rev. Mr.

Samuel Dunbar, late pastor of the First church and
and society, in that town; who died the preceeding Lord's
day; in the 79th year of his age, and the 56th of his
ministry. By Jason Haven... Boston, Printed by N.
Willis, 1783.
23 p.   20 cm.

22347   Haven, Jason, 1733-1803.
A sermon preached before His Excellency Sir Francis
Bernard, baronet, governor: His Honor Thomas Hutchinson,
esq; lieutenant-governor, the honorable His Majesty's
Council, and the honorable House of representatives, of
the province of the Massachusetts-Bay in New England,
May 31st, 1769. Being the anniversary of the election
of His Majesty's Council for said province. By Jason
Haven, A.M., pastor of the First church in Dedham.
Boston, Printed by Richard Draper, printer to His
Excellency the governor, and the honorable His Majesty's
Council, 1769.
55 p.   21½ cm.

22348   Haven, Nathaniel Appleton, 1790-1826.
The remains of Nathaniel Appleton Haven. With a
memoir of his life, by George Ticknor. [Cambridge,
Mass., Hilliard, Metcalf, & company, printers] 1827.
xl, 351 p.   24 cm.

22349   Haven, Samuel, 1727-1806.
Joy and salvation by Christ; his arm displayed in
the Protestant cause. A sermon preached in the South
parish in Portsmouth; occasioned by the remarkable
success of His Majesty's arms in the late war, and by
the happy peace of 1763. By Samuel Haven, A.M., pastor
of the South-church in Portsmouth, Portsmouth, in
New Hampshire, Printed and Sold by Daniel Fowle, 1763.
1 p.l., [5]-39 p.   20½ cm.

22350   Haven, Samuel Foster, 1806-1881.
An historical address delivered before the citizens
of the town of Dedham, on the twenty-first of September,
1836, being the second centennial anniversary of the
incorporation of the town. By Samuel F. Haven.
Dedham, Printed by H. Mann, 1837.
79 p.   23 cm.

22351   Hawes, Mrs. Angelica H
The grafted bud; a memoir of Angelica Irene Hawes.
By Mrs. A. H. Hawes... New York, Redfield, 1853.
vi, [7]-102 p.   front. (port.)   17 cm.

22352 Hawes, Mrs. Elizabeth.
       The harp of Accushnet: poems by Mrs. Elizabeth
       Hawes. Boston, Otis, Broaders and company, 1838.
       viii, 172 p.   18½ cm.

22353 Hawes, J   H
       Manual of United States surveying. System of rectangular
       surveying employed in subdividing the public lands of the
       United States; also instructions for subdividing sections
       and restoring lost corners of the public lands. Illus-
       trated with forms, diagrams, and maps; constituting a
       complete text-book of government surveying... To which
       is added an appendix containing information in regard
       to entering, locating, purchasing, and settling lands
       under the various land laws, etc., etc. By J. H.
       Hawes... Philadelphia, J. B. Lippincott & co., 1868.
       xxiv, 25-234 p.   illus.   21½ cm.

22354 Hawes, Joel, 1789-1867.
       An address delivered at the request of the citizens
       of Hartford, on the 9th of November, 1835. The close
       of the second century, from the first settlement of
       the city. By Joel Hawes... Hartford, Belknap &
       Hamersley, 1835.
       80 p.   19½ cm.

22355 Hawes, Joel, 1789-1867.
       A tribute to the memory of the Pilgrims, and a
       vindication of the Congregational churches of New
       England. By Joel Hawes... Hartford, Cooke & co. [etc.]
       1830.
       vi p., 1 l., 226 p.   18 cm.

22356 Hawker, Peter, 1786-1853.
       Instructions to your sportsmen, in all that relates
       to guns and shooting. By Lieut. Col. P. Hawker. First
       American, from the 9th London ed. To which is added the
       hunting and shooting of North America, with descriptions
       of the animals and birds... collated from authentic
       sources. By Wm. T. Porter... Philadelphia, Lea and
       Blanchard, 1846.
       xvi, [17]-459 p.   front., illus., plates.   24 cm.

22357 Hawkins, Alfred, d, 1854.
       Hawkins's picture of Quebec; with historical
       recollections. Quebec, Printed for the proprietor by
       Neilson & Cowan, 1834.
       2 p.l., [iii]-viii p., 2 l., 477 p.   front., 12 pl.
       18½ cm.

Added t.-p. engraved.
Compiled, and in part written, by J. C. Fisher.
cf. Pref.

22358 Hawkins, Sir Richard, 1562?-1622.
The observations of Sir Richard Havvkins knight, in
his voiage into the South Sea. Anno Domini 1593...
London, Printed by I. D. for I. Iaggard, 1622.
3 p.l., 169, [6] p.   30 cm.

22359 Hawkins, William George, 1823-1909, comp.
Life of John H. W. Hawkins. Comp. by his son, Rev.
William George Hawkins... Boston, J. P. Jewett and
company; New York, Sheldon, Blakeman & co.; [etc., etc.]
1859.
vii, 433 p.   front. (port.) illus.   19 cm.

22360 Hawles, Sir John, 1645-1716.
The Englishman's right: a dialogue between a barris-
ter at law and a juryman; plainly setting forth, I. The
antiquity, II. The excellent designed use, III. The
office, and just privileges, of juries, by the law of
England. By Sir John Hawles, knight, solicitor-general
to the late King William. London, 1771.
vi p., 1 l., 51 p.   16 cm.
"Appeared first in the year 1680."

22361 Hawley, William Fitz, 1804-1855.
Quebec, The harp, and other poems. By W. F. Hawley.
Montreal, Printed at the Herald and New gazette office,
1829.
4 p.l., [v]-viii p., 1 l., [11]-172 p.   15 cm.

22362 Hawley, Zerah Kent.
Congregationalism and Methodism. By Z. K. Hawley...
New York, Leavitt, Trow and company, 1846.
2 p.l., [7]-311 p.   20 cm.

22363 [Hay, George] 1765-1830.
A treatise on expatriation. Washington, A. & G. Way,
printers, 1814.
1 p.l., 90 p.   22 cm.

22364 Hayden, Mrs. Caroline A
Our country's martyr. A tribute to Abraham Lincoln
our beloved and lamented president. By Mrs. Caroline
A. Hayden. Boston, Press of Dakin and Metcalf, 1865.
23 p.   19½ cm.
Poems.

22365   Hayden, William Benjamin, 1816-1893.
        A brief abstract of remarks by Rev. Wm. B. Hayden, at
        the New Jerusalem church, on the funeral of the President,
        April 19, 1865. Cincinnati, Mallory, Power & co.,
        printers, 1865.
        cover-title, 10 p.   21½ cm.

22366   Hayes, Isaac Israel, 1832-1881.
        An Arctic boat journey, in the autumn of 1854. By
        Isaac I. Hayes... Boston, Brown, Taggard and Chase;
        New York, Sheldon & co.; [etc., etc.] 1860.
        3 p.l., [vii]-xvii, 375 p.   2 fold. maps (incl.
        front.)   20 cm.
        A partial account of the second Grinnell expedition.

22367   Hayne, Robert Young, 1791-1839.
        Defence of the South. General Hayne, in reply to
        Mr. Webster... Charleston, S. C., A. E. Miller, 1830.
        20 p.   22 cm.
        Caption title: General Hayne's complete answer to all
        Mr. Webster's arguments. Mr. Foot's resolution, pro-
        posing an inquiry into the expediency of abolishing the
        office of surveyor general of public lands, and to
        suspend further surveys, &c. being under consideration...

22368   Hayne, Robert Young, 1791-1839.
        An oration, delivered in the Independent or Congrega-
        tional church, Charleston, before the State rights &
        free trade party, the state Society of Cincinnati, the
        Revolution society, the '76 association, and several
        volunteer companies of militia; on the 4th of July,
        1831, being the 55th anniversary of American independence.
        By the Hon. Robert Y. Hayne... Charleston, A. E. Miller,
        1831.
        2 p.l., 47 p.   21 cm.

22369   Hayne, Robert Young, 1791-1839.
        The several speeches made during the debate in the
        Senate of the United States, on Mr. Foot's resolution,
        proposing an inquiry into the expediency of abolishing
        the office of surveyor general of public lands, and to
        suspend further surveys, &c. By General Hayne, of
        South Carolina, and Mr. Webster, of Massachusetts.
        Charleston, S. C., A. E. Miller, 1830.
        22, 112 p.   21½ cm.

22370   Hayward, John, 1781-1862.
        The book of religions; comprising the views, creeds,

sentiments, or opinions, of all the principal religious
sects in the world, particularly of all Christian deno-
minations in Europe and America, to which are added
church and missionary statistics, together with biographical sketches. By John Hayward... 3d ed. Boston,
J. Hayward, 1843.
432 p. 19 cm.

22371 Hayward, John Henry, comp.
Poetical pen-pictures of the war: selected from our
Union poets. By J. Henry Hayward... New York, The
editor, 1863.
xiii, [3], [17]-400 p. 19 cm.
"Published for the purpose of founding a building fund
for the 'Union home and school,' established for the
education and maintenance of our volunteers' children
who may be left unprovided for. Organized May, 1861.
Chartered by act of Legislature, April, 1862."

22372 Hazard, Benjamin, 1770-1841.
Letters addressed to the Hon. John Quincy Adams, in
refutation of charges made by that gentleman against a
committee of the legislature of Rhode-Island, and
against the legislature itself. By B. Hazard...
Providence, Marshall, Brown & co., 1834.
46 p. 19 cm.
The committee was appointed to inquire into the
charges against masonry and masons in Rhode Island.

22373 Hazard, Rowland Gibson, 1801-1888.
A discourse delivered before the Rhode-Island historical
society, on... January 18th, 1848: on the character
and writings of Chief Justice Durfee. By Rowland G.
Hazard... Providence, C. Burnett, jr., 1848.
45 p. 24 cm.

22374 Hazard, Rowland Gibson, 1801-1888.
Finance and hours of labor. By R. G. Hazard. New
York, C. Scribner & company, 1868.
50 p. 23 cm.
Various articles reprinted from magazines and
newspapers.

22375 [Hazard, Rowland Gibson] 1801-1888.
Our resources. A series of articles on the financial
and political condition of the United States. By a
citizen of this state. 2d ed. Providence [R.I.]
S. S. Rider & brother, 1864.
32 p. 22½ cm.

22376   Hazard, Samuel, 1784-1870.
        Annals of Pennsylvania, from the discovery of the
        Delaware. By Samuel Hazard... 1609-1682. Philadelphia,
        Hazard & Mitchell, 1850.
            viii, 664 p.   22½ cm.

22377   Hazard, Thomas Robinson, 1797-1886.
        An appeal to the people of Rhode Island, in behalf of
        the constitution and the laws; b [!] Thomas R. Hazard...
        [n.p.] 1857.
            163, [1] p.   plan.   24½ cm.
        Papers concerning the case of Robert H. Ives versus
        Charles T. Hazard.

22378   [Hazard, Thomas Robinson] 1797-1886.
        Facts for the laboring man: by a laboring man...
        [no. 1-12] Newport, R.I., J. Atkinson, printer, 1840.
            102 p.   22 cm.
        Originally published in the Newport (R.I.) Herald
        of the times, over the signature Narragansett.

22379   Hazlitt, William, 1811-1893.
        Manual of the law of maritime warfare, embodying the
        decisions of Lord Stowell and other English judges,
        and of the American courts, and the opinions of the
        most eminent jurists: with an appendix of the official
        documents and correspondence in relation to the present
        war. By William Hazlitt & Henry Philip Roche...
        London, V. & P. Stevens and G. S. Norton; [etc., etc.]
        1854.
            xvi, 457, [1] p.   18½ cm.

22380   Headley, Joel Tyler, 1813-1897.
        The Adirondack; or, Life in the woods. By J. T.
        Headley... New and enl. ed. New York, C. Scribner,
        1869.
            9 p.l., xi, [13]-451 p.   front., 7 pl.   18½ cm.
        First edition, New York, 1849.

22381   Headley, Joel Tyler, 1813-1897
        Letters from the backwoods and the Adirondac. By
        The Rev. J. T. Headley. New York, J. S. Taylor, 1850.
            iv, [5]-105 p.   front. (port.)   19½ cm.
        "The Fire Islands": p. 86-105.

22382   Headley, Joel Tyler, 1813-1897.
        The lives of Winfield Scott and Andrew Jackson. By
        J. T. Headley... New York, C. Scribner, 1852.
            xi, [13]-341 p.   2 port. (incl. front.)   18 cm.

22383 Headley, Jhineas Camp, 1819-1903.
　　　　The life of General Lafayette, marquis of France,
　　　general in the U.S. Army, etc., etc., by P. C. Headley...
　　　New York, Miller, Orton & co., 1857.
　　　　vi, 3 -377 p.　　front. (port.)　　19½ cm.

22384 Headley, Phineas Camp, 1819-1903.
　　　　The patriot boy; or, The life and career of Major-
　　　General Ormsby M. Mitchel.　By Rev. P. C. Headley...
　　　New York, W. H. Appleton, 1865.
　　　　278 p.　　front., illus., plates, ports., map.　　18 cm.

22385 [Heady, Morrison] 1829-1915.
　　　　The farmer boy, and how he became commander-in-chief.
　　　By Uncle Juvinell [pseud.] Ed. by William M. Thayer...
　　　Boston, Walker, Wise, and company, 1864.
　　　　2 p.l., 3 -321 p.　　4 pl. (incl. front.)　　18½ cm.
　　　A narrative, for children, of the life of George
　　　Washington before 1775.

22386 Heard, John T
　　　　A historical account of Columbian lodge of Free and
　　　accepted masons of Boston, Mass.　By John T. Heard...
　　　Boston, Printed by A. Mudge and son, 1856.
　　　　xi, [2], 10-592 p.　　19 cm.

22387 Heath, Herman H　　　d. 1874.
　　　　Address of General H. H. Heath, at Santa Fé, New
　　　Mexico, of the night of the 12th of November, '68, on
　　　the occasion of the Republican jubilee and torchlight
　　　procession in honor of Grant's election to the presi-
　　　dency.　Santa Fe, Manderfield & Tucker, printers, 1869.
　　　　cover-title, [3]-10 p.　　20½ cm.

22388 Heath, William, 1737-1814.
　　　　Memoirs of Major General Heath.　Containing anecdotes,
　　　details of skirmishes, battles, and other military
　　　events, during the American war.　Written by himself...
　　　Boston, Printed by I. Thomas and E. T. Andrews, 1798.
　　　　vi, 7 -388 p.　　21½ cm.

22389 Heathcote, George
　　　　A letter to the Right Honourable the lord mayor, the
　　　worshipful aldermen, and common-council; the merchants,
　　　citizens and inhabitants, of the city of London.　From
　　　an old servant.　The 2d ed....　London, Printed for W.
　　　Nicoll, 1762.
　　　　1 p.l., 90 p.　　20½ cm.
　　　Concerning the proposed peace with France.

22390   Heaviside, John T   C
        American antiquities; or, The New world the old, and
        the Old world the new. By John T. C. Heaviside...
        London, Trubner and company, 1868.
            45, 2 p.   illus.   23 cm.

22391   Heckewelder, John Gottlieb Ernestus, 1743-1823.
        A narrative of the mission of the United Brethren among
        the Delaware and Mohegan Indians, from its commencement,
        in the year 1740, to the close of the year 1808.
        Comprising all the remarkable incidents which took place
        at their missionary stations during that period. Inter-
        spersed with anecdotes, historical facts, speeches of
        Indians, and other interesting matter. By John Heckewelder,
        who was many years in the service of that mission.
        Philadelphia, Published by M'Carty & Davis, 1820.
            xii, 17 -429 p., 1 l.   front. (port.) $21\frac{1}{2}$ cm.

22392   Hedge, Frederic Henry, 1805-1890.
        Discourse on Edward Everett, delivered in the church
        of the First parish, Brookline, on the twenty-second
        January. By Frederic Henry Hedge. Boston, Press of
        G. C. Rand & Avery, 1865.
            23 p.   26 cm.

22393   Hedge, Frederic Henry, 1805-1890.
        The national weakness: a discourse delivered in the
        First church, Brookline, on Fast day, Sept. 26, 1861.
        By Rev. F. H. Hedge, D.D. Boston, Walker, Wise and
        company, 1861.
            19 p. $19\frac{1}{2}$ cm.

22394   Hedges, Henry Parsons, 1817-1911.
        An address, delivered on the 26th of December, 1849,
        on the occasion of the celebration of the two hundredth
        anniversary of the settlement of the town of East-
        Hampton, together with an appendix, containing a general
        history of the town from its first settlement to the
        year 1800: by Henry P. Hedges. Sag-Harbor, L. I.,
        Corrector office, 1850.
            2 p.l., iii -iv p., 1 l., 100, 1 p. $22\frac{1}{2}$ cm.

22395   Hedges, Isaac A
        Sorgo, or The northern sugar plant, by Isaac A.
        Hedges... with an introduction by William Clough...
        Sorgo culture. Cincinnati, Applegate & co., 1863.
            xviii, 19-204 p.   illus., plates (1 col., 1 fold.)
        28 cm.

22396 Heeren, Arnold Hermann Ludwig, 1760-1842.
       A manual of the history of the political system of
       Europe and its colonies, from its formation at the close
       of the fifteenth century, to its re-establishment upon
       the fall of Napoleon. By A. H. L. Heeren... Translated
       from the 5th German ed. London, H. G. Bohn, 1846.
       xxxii, 540 p.   22 cm.
       Translated by D. A. Talboys.

22397 [Heermans, J   ]
       ... War power of the President -- summary imprisonment --
       habeas corpus. [New York, 1863]
       10 p.   22 cm.

22398 Helmer, Charles Downes, 1827-1879.
       Two sermons. I. Signs of our national atheism. II.
       The war begun. By C. D. Helmer... Preached in Plymouth
       church on the evenings of April 21st and 28th, 1861...
       Milwaukee, Terry & Cleaver, 1861.
       35 p.   21½ cm.

22399 Helms, Anton Zacharias, 1751-1803.
       Travels from Buenos Ayres, by Potosi, to Lima. With
       notes by the translator, containing topographical de-
       scriptions of the Spanish possessions in South America,
       drawn from the last and best authorities. By Anthony
       Zachariah Helms... London, Printed for R. Phillips,
       1807.
       viii, [9]-92 p.   21 cm.
       German original, Dresden, 1798, has title: Tagebuch
       einer reise durch Peru...

22400 Helps, Sir Arthur, 1813-1875.
       The life of Columbus, the discoverer of America.
       Chiefly by Arthur Helps... London, Bell and Daldy,
       1869.
       xvi, 262 p., 1 l.   19 cm.

22401 Helps, Sir Arthur, 1813-1875.
       The life of Las Casas, "the apostle of the Indies".
       By Arthur Helps... 2d ed. London, Bell and Daldy, 1868.
       xix, 292 p.   front. (fold. map)   19 cm.

22402 Hemmenway, Moses, 1735-1811.
       A discourse delivered at Wells, on the 22d February,
       1800; occasioned by the lamented death of General George
       Washington. By Moses Hemmenway... Portsmouth, Printed
       at the United States' oracle-office, by Charles Peirce,

1800.
16 p.   21 cm.

22403   Hemphill, John, 1803-1862.
Eulogy on the life and character of the Hon. Thomas
J. Rusk, late U.S. senator from Texas. Delivered in the
hall of the House of representatives of the state of
Texas, on the seventh of November, 1857. By John Hemphill... Austin, Printed by J. Marshall & co., 1857.
24 p.   21 cm.
Printed by order of the House of representatives of the
7th Legislature of Texas.

22404   Henderson, Alexander, of Belize, Honduras.
A grammar of the Moskito language, by Alexander
Henderson, Belize, Honduras. New York, Printed by J.
Gray, 1846.
iv, [5]-47 p.   22 cm.

22405   Henderson, George.
A short view of the administrations in the government
of America, under the former presidents, the late General
Washington and John Adams; and of the present administration under Thomas Jefferson: with cursory observations
on the present state of the revenue, agriculture,
commerce, manufacture, and population of the United
States. By George Henderson, esq. ... London, Printed
for J. Hatchard [etc.] 1802.
viii, 71 p.   21½ cm.

22406   Henderson, George Donald, 1832-1875.
Address on the death of Gen. Nathaniel Lyon. Delivered at Manhattan, Kansas, September 26th, 1861, by
Rev. George D. Henderson... [n.p., 1861]
cover-title, 8 p.   20 cm.

22407   Henderson, James.
A history of the Brazil; comprising its geography,
commerce, colonization, aboriginal inhabitants, &c. &c.
&c. By James Henderson... Illustrated with twenty-
eight plates and two maps. London, Longman, Hurst,
Rees, Orme, and Brown, 1821.
xxiii, 522, [2] p.   front., plates, fold. maps.
28 x 22 cm.

22408   Henderson, John J
Annual statement of the trade and commerce of
Buffalo for the year 1854, together with a review of the

general business of the city, its progress in improvements and manufactures, the state of trade during the
season, the tonnage of the western lakes, &c. By John J.
Henderson, commercial editor of the 'Democracy', as
compiled by him for that journal. Buffalo, Democracy
print, 1855.
    56 p. incl. tables.   22½ cm.

22409   Henfrey, Benjamin.
        A plan with proposals for forming a company to work
mines in the United States; and to smelt and refine the
ores, whether of copper, lead, tin, silver, or gold.
By Benjamin Henfrey... Philadelphia, Printed by Snowden
& M'Corkle, 1797.
    v, [7]-34 p.   fold. tab.   20½ cm.

22410   Henley, David, 1749-1823.
        Proceedings of a court martial, held at Cambridge,
by order of Major General Heath, commanding the American
troops for the northern district, for the trial of
Colonel David Henley, accused by General Burgoyne, of
ill treatment of the British soldiers, &c. Taken in
short hand by an officer, who was present. London,
Printed for J. Almon, 1778.
    2 p.l., 147 p.   21 cm.

22411   [Hennepin, Louis] 17th cent.
        A discovery of a large, rich, and plentiful country,
in the North America; extending above 4000 leagues.
Wherein, by a very short passage, lately found out,
thro' the Mer-Barmejo into the South-Sea; by which a
considerable trade might be carry'd on, as well in the
northern as the southern parts of America. London,
Printed for W. Boreham [1720]
    2 p.l., 22 p.   19 cm.
    An abridgment of Hennepin's A new discovery...
published to raise the credit of the South Sea stock.
cf. Preface.

22412   Henry, Robert R
        Letter to the New-York Chamber of commerce on "discre-
tionary power"... With an appendix... By Robert R.
Henry... New York, Printed for the author, 1830.
    124 p.   23 cm.

22413   Henry, William Seaton, 1816-1851.
        Campaign sketches of the war with Mexico. By Capt.
W. S. Henry... New York, Harper & brothers, 1847.

vi, [7]-331 p. incl. illus., plates.   front., double
plans.   19½ cm.
    A diary of General Taylor's operations, July, 1845 -
June, 1847.

22414 [Henshaw, David] 1791-1852.
    Remarks upon the rights and powers of corporations,
and of the rights, powers, and duties of the legislature
toward them. Embracing a review of the opinion of the
Supreme court of the United States, in the case of
Dartmouth college, in New Hampshire, given in 1819.
By a citizen of Boston. Boston, Beals and Greene, 1837.
    31 p.   22½ cm.

22415 Henshaw, David 1791-1852.
    An address, delivered before an assembly of citizens
from all parts of the commonwealth, at Faneuil hall,
Boston, July 4, 1836. By David Henshaw. Boston,
Beals and Greene, 1836.
    39 p.   22½ cm.

22416 Henshaw, Joshua Sidney.
    A manual for United States consults: embracing their
rights, duties, liabilities, and emoluments... By
J. Sidney Henshaw... New York, J. C. Riker, 1849.
    x p., 1 l., [13]-252 p., 1 l.   15 cm.

22417 Henshaw, Mrs. Sarah Edwards (Tyler) b. 1822.
    Our branch and its tributaries; being a history of the
work of the Northwestern sanitary commission and its
auxiliaries, during the war of the rebellion. By Mrs.
Sarah Edwards Henshaw. Including a full report of
receipts and disbursements, by E. W. Blatchford, treas-
urer; and an introductory chapter, by Hon. Mark Skinner.
Chicago, A. L. Sewell, 1868.
    xvi, 17-432 p.   pl., double maps.   22½ cm.

22418 Hepworth, George Hughes, 1833-1902.
    The criminal; the crime; the penalty. By George H.
Hepworth. Boston, Walker, Fuller, and company, 1865.
    31 p.   19½ cm.
    An invective against Jefferson Davis.

22419 Herbert, Charles, 1757-1808.
    A relic of the revolution, containing a full and
particular account of the sufferings and privations of
all the American prisoners captured on the high seas,
and carried into Plymouth, England, during the revolution

of 1776; with the names of the vessels taken-the names
and residence of the several crews, and time of their
commitment-the names of such as died in prison, and such
as made their escape, or entered on board English men-
of-war; until the exchange of prisoners, March 15, 1779.
Also, an account of the several cruises of the squadron
under the command of Commodore John Paul Jones, prizes
taken, etc., etc. By Charles Herbert, of Newburyport,
Mass., who was taken prisoner in the brigantine Dolton,
Dec., 1776, and served in the U.S. frigate Alliance,
1779-80. Boston, Pub. for the proprietors, by C. H.
Pierce, 1847.
    2 p.l., 258 p.   front.   17 cm.

22420 Herbert, Henry William, 1807-1858.
    Frank Forester's fish and fishing of the United States
and British provinces of North America. By Henry
William Herbert. London, R. Bentley, 1849.
    3 p.l., [ix]-xvi, 455 p.   col. front., illus.,
plates.   23 cm.
    Illustrated from nature by the author.

22421 Herbert, Sir Thomas, 1606-1682.
    A relation of some yeares travaile, begvnne anno 1626.
Into Afrique and the greater Asia, especially the
territories of the Persian monarchie, and some parts of
the Oriental Indies and iles adiacent. Of their religion,
language, habit, discent, ceremonies and other matters
concerning them. Together with the proceedings and
death of the three late ambassadours Sir D. C., Sir
R. S. and the Persian Nogdibeg; as also the two great
monarchs, the king of Persia, and the great mogol. By
T. H. ... London, Printed by W. Stansby, and J. Bloome,
1634.
    5 p.l., 225, [12] p., 1 l.   illus. (incl. maps)
27½ cm.

22422 Héricault, Charles Joseph de Ricault, called d', 1823-1899.
    ... Maximilien et le Mexique; histoire des derniers
mois de l'Empire Mexicain. Paris, Garnier frères,
1869.
    2 p.l., 419 p. incl. plates.   front. (ports.)   18 cm

22423 Herrick, Anson, 1812-1868.
    The disunion policy of the administration. Speech of
Hon. Anson Herrick, made in the House of representatives,
March 26, 1864. Washington, D. C., Printed at Constitu-
tional union office, 1864.
    14 p.   24 cm.

22424 Herrick, Jedediah, 1780-1847.
        A genealogical register of the name and family of
     Herrick, from the settlement of Henerie Hericke, in
     Salem, Massachusetts 1629, to 1846. With a concise
     notice of their English ancestry. By Jedediah Herrick...
     Bangor, S. S. Smith, printer, 1846.
        69 p.   front. (coat of arms)   24½ cm.

22425 Herring, Thomas, abp. of Canterbury, 1693-1757.
        A sermon preached before the incorporated Society for
     the propagation of the gospel in foreign parts; at their
     anniversary meeting in the parish-church of St. Mary-le-
     Bow, on Friday, February 17, 1737-8. By Thomas, lord
     bishop of Bangor. London, J. and J. Pemberton, 1738.
        70 p., 1 l.   19 cm.

22426 Hersey, Charles.
        Reminiscences of the military life and sufferings of
     Col. Timothy Bigelow, commander of the Fifteenth
     regiment of the Massachusetts line in the continental
     army, during the war of the revolution. By Charles
     Hersey. Worcester, Printed by H. J. Howland, 1860.
        vi, [7]-24 p.   24½ cm.

22427 Herttell, Thomas.
        The demurrer; or, Proofs of error in the decision of
     the Supreme court of the state of New York, requiring
     faith in particular religious doctrines as a legal quali-
     fication of witnesses; thence establishing by law a
     religious test, and a religious creed. By Thomas
     Herttell... New York, E. Conrad, 1828.
        iv, 5 -158 p.   21½ cm.
     "The case alluded to, is that of Jackson ex dem.
     Tuttle vs. Gridley, 18th vol. Johnson's Reports,
     page 98. This cause was tried at the Oneida circuit...
     in June, 1819". - p. 6-7.

22428 Herty, Thomas.
        A digest of the laws of Maryland. Being a complete
     system (alphabetically arranged) of all the public acts
     of Assembly, now in force and of general use. From the
     first settlement of the state, to the end of November
     session 1803, inclusive. To which is added, the acts
     of Congress for the District of Columbia, from the
     assumption of jurisdiction to the end of the session,
     which terminated in April 1804, inclusive. Also, a
     variety of precedents, (adapted to the several acts)
     for the use of justices of the peace, &c. And also

a table explanatory of sundry technical law terms. By
Thomas Herty... vol. II. Washington, Printed for the
editor by J. C. O'Reilly, 1804.
2 p.l., 204 (i.e. 206), [2] p.   24 cm.

22429   Hertz, Bram.
Catalogue of the collection of Assyrian, Babylonian,
Egyptian, Greek, Etruscan, Roman, Indian, Peruvian and
Mexican antiquities, formed by B. Hertz... London
[G. Norman, printer] 1851.
iv, [8], 156 p.   front., 5 pl.   27½ cm.

22430   [Hervey, Nathaniel]
The memory of Washington; with biographical sketches
of his mother and wife. Relations of Lafayette to
Washington; with incidents and anecdotes in the lives
of the two patriots... Boston and Cambridge, J. Munroe
and company, 1852.
viii, [9]-320 p.   front.   18½ cm.

22431   Heustis, Jabez Wiggins, 1784-1841.
Physical observations, and medical tracts and
researches, on the topography and diseases of Louisiana.
By Jabez W. Heustis... New York, Printed by T. and
J. Swords, no. 160 Pearl street, 1817.
165 p.   22½ cm.

22432   Hewes, George Whitfield.
Ballads of the war, by George Whitfield Hewes. New
York, Carleton, 1862.
1 p.l., [v]-x, [11]-147 p.   19 cm.

22433   Hewes, Joseph.
A collection of occurrences and facts, known by
living evidences, and also recorded in a public manner,
in printed and written papers, now in being, and
indisputably true. With reflections thereon... This
historical collection is finished by repeating a
prophecy... concerning the present commotions in the
kingdom of Great Britain. By Joseph Hewes, a student
of nature. [n.p.] Printed in the year 1775.
2 p.l., 46 p.   22 cm.

22434   Hewett, J   F   Napier.
European settlements on the west coast of Africa;
with remarks on the slave trade and the supply of cotton.
By Captain J. F. Napier Hewett, F.R.G.S. London,
Chapman and Hall, 1862.
viii, 374, [1] p.   19½ cm.

22435 Hewitt, Abram Stevens, 1822-1903.
On the statistics and geography of the production of
iron: a paper read before the American geographical
and statistical society, on the 21st February, A.D.,
1856... by Abram S. Hewitt, and printed at the request
of the society. New York, W. C. Bryant & co., printers,
1856.
39 p.   fold. diagr.   24 cm.

22436 Hewitt, Abram Stevens, 1822-1903.
... The production of iron and steel in its economic
and social relations. By Abram S. Hewitt... Washington,
Govt. print. off., 1868.
iv, 104 p.   23 cm.

22437 Hewitt, John Hill, 1801-1890.
Miscellaneous poems. By John H. Hewitt. Baltimore,
N. Hickman, 1838.
235 p.   18½ cm.
Includes "Flora's festival: a pastoral oratorio,"
and "The rival harps. A poem. In five parts."

22438 Hewson, William.
Principles and practice of embanking lands from
river-floods, as applied to "levees" of the Mississippi.
By William Hewson, civil engineer; assisted in the
engineering remarks by consultation with M. Butt Hewson...
New York, D. Van Nostrand, 1860.
171 p.   illus., tables.   23½ cm.

22439 Hey, Richard, 1745-1835.
Observations on the nature of civil liberty, and the
principles of government... By Richard Hey... London,
Printed for T. Cadell [etc.] 1776.
2 p.l., 70 p.   20 cm.

22440 Heyden, Thomas, 1798-1870.
A memoir on the life and character of the Rev. Prince
Demetrius A. de Gallitzin, founder of Loretto and
catholicity, in Cambria county, Pa., apostle of the
Alleghanies. By Very Rev. Thomas Heyden... Baltimore,
J. Murphy & co.; New York, Catholic publication society;
[etc., etc.] 1869.
viii p., 1 l., 9 -200 p.   front. (port.) pl.
15½ cm.

22441 Heylen, Louis, 1828-1863?
The progress of the age, and The danger of the age:

127

two lectures, delivered before the St. Xavier conference
of the St. Vincent de Paul brotherhood in the hall of
St. Louis university. By the Rev. Louis Heylen, S.J.
Cincinnati, J. P. Walsh, 1865.
107 p.   18½ cm.

22442   Hibbard, Augustine George, 1833-
In memory of Abraham Lincoln. A discourse delivered in
the First Congregational Unitarian church in Detroit,
Mich., Sunday, April 17th [i.e. 16th] 1865, by A. G.
Hibbard... Detroit, O. S. Gulley's steam book and job
printing office, 1865.
12 p.   22 cm.

22443   Hichborn, Benjamin, 1746-1817.
An oration, delivered March 5th, 1777, at the request
of the inhabitants of the town of Boston; to commemorate
the bloody tragedy of the fifth of March, 1770. By
Benjamin Hichborn... Boston, Printed by Edes and Gill,
1777.
18 p.   25 x 19 cm.

22444   Hickcox, John Howard, 1832-1897.
A history of the bills of credit or paper money issued
by New York, from 1709 to 1789: with a description of
the bills, and catalogue of the various issues. By
John H. Hickcox... Albany, N. Y., J. H. Hickcox & co.,
1866.
3 p.l., 103 p.   diagr.   25½ cm.

22445   Hickcox, John Howard, 1832-1897.
An historical account of American coinage. By John H.
Hickcox... Albany, N. Y., J. Munsell [etc., etc.] 1858.
viii, 151 (i.e. 153) p.   5 pl.   26 cm.

22446   Hickman, Edwin C
Scraps of poetry and prose. By Edwin C. Hickman.
Lexington, Ky., A. W. Elder, printer, 1854.
168, 16, 16, 2 p.   15½ cm.

22447   [Hickman, George H   ]
The life of General Lewis Cass, with his letters and
speeches on various subjects. Baltimore, N. Hickman,
1848.
72 p.   front. (port.)   22 cm.

22448   [Hickman, Nathaniel] ed.
The citizen soldiers at North Point and Fort McHenry,

September 12 & 13, 1814. Resolves of the citizens in
town meeting, particulars relating to the battle, official
correspondence and honorable discharge of the troops.
Baltimore [N. Hickman, J. Young, printer, 1858]
96 p.   19 cm.

22449   Hicks, Elias, 1748-1830.
Journal of the life and religious labours of Elias
Hicks. Written by himself. 5th ed. New York, I. T.
Hopper, 1832.
451 p.   22½ cm.

22450   Hicks, Elias, 1748-1830.
Sermons delivered by Elias Hicks & Edward Hicks;
in Friends' meetings, New York, in 5th month, 1825.
Taken in short-hand, by L. H. Clarke, & M. T. C. Gould...
New York, Sold by J. V. Seaman, 1825.
138 p.   22 cm.

22451   Hicks, Thomas, 1823-1890.
Eulogy on Thomas Crawford, by Thomas Hicks, N. A.
New York, Priv. print. for subscribers, 1865.
103 p.   mounted front. (port.)   mounted plates.
29½ cm.

22452   The Hierophant: or, Monthly journal of sacred symbols and
prophecy. Conducted by George Bush... no. 1-12;
June 1842-May 1843. New York, M. H. Newman, 1844.
2 p.l., 288 p.   23 cm.

22453   [Higgins, Jesse] b. 1763.
Sampson against the Philistines, or The reformation
of lawsuits; and justice made cheap, speedy and brought
home to every man's door: agreeable to the principles
of the ancient trial by jury, before the same was
innovated by judges and lawyers. Compiled for use of
the honest citizens of the United States. To whom it
is dedicated. [Washington, D. C., Printed by W. Duane,
1805]
v, 98, xxiii p.   21 cm.

22454   [Higginson, Stephen] 1743-1828.
Ten chapters in the life of John Hancock. Now first
published since 1789. New York, 1857.
68 p.   24 cm.
Reprint, with reproduction of t.-p., of Stephen
Higginson's The writings of Laco, as published in the
Massachusetts centinel, in the months of February and

March, 1789, with the addition of no. VII, which was
omitted... Printed at Boston, 1789.

22455 [Higginson, Stephen] 1743-1828.
The writings of Laco, as published in the Massachusetts
Centinel, in the months of February and March, 1789 -
with the addition of no. VII, which was omitted...
Printed at Boston, 1789.
39 p.   20 cm.

22456 Higginson, Thomas Wentworth, 1823-1911.
Out-door papers, by Thomas Wentworth Higginson.
Boston, Ticknor and Fields, 1863.
2 p.l., 370 p.   17½ cm.

22457 The "high private," with a full and exciting history of
the New York volunteers, illustrated with facts,
incidents, anecdotes, engravings, &c., &c., including
the mysteries and miseries of the Mexican war. In
three parts - Part first. To which will be appended
the constitution and by-laws of the guerrillas,
banditti, &c., found on Priest Jaurata. By "Corporal
of the guard." New York, Printed for the publishers,
1848.
60 p.   illus.   20 cm.
Copyrighted by Albert Lombard.

22458 Hildebrand, Samuel S   1836-1872.
Autobiography of Samuel S. Hildebrand, the renowned
Missouri "bushwacker"... being his complete confession,
recently made to the writers, and carefully compiled
by James W. Evans and A. Wendell Keith... Together
with all the facts connected with his early history.
Jefferson City, Mo., State times printing house, 1870.
312 p. incl. front., plates.   19 cm.

22459 [Hildreth, Hosea] 1782-1835.
An abridged history of the United States of America.
For the use of schools. Intended as a sequel to
Hildreth's View of the United States [anon.] Boston,
Carter, Hendee & Babcock, 1831.
xii, 248 p.   19 cm.

22460 [Hildreth, Hosea] 1782-1835.
A book for Massachusetts children, in familiar letters
from a father, for the use of families and schools.
Boston, Hilliard, Gray, Little and Wilkins, 1829.
iv, 132 p.   front. (fold. map) illus.   18½ cm.

22461 Hildreth, Hosea, 1782-1835.
A discourse, delivered before the Washington benevolent
society in Exeter, on the day of their anniversary,
May 4th, 1813. By Hosea Hildreth. Exeter [N. H.]
Printed by Charles Norris & co., 1813.
24 p.   21½ cm.

22462 [Hildreth, Richard] 1807-1865.
The contrast: or William Henry Harrison versus Martin
Van Buren... Boston, Weeks, Jordan & company, 1840.
72 p.   16 cm.

22463 [Hildreth, Richard] 1807-1865.
The history of banks: to which is added, a demonstra-
tion of the advantages and necessity of free competition
in the business of banking. Boston, Hilliard, Gray &
company, 1837.
iv, [5]-142, iv p.   19 cm.

22464 Hildreth, Richard, 1807-1865.
A letter to His Excellency Marcus Morton, on banking
and the currency. By R. Hildreth... Boston, Printed
by Kidder & Wright, 1840.
16 p.   24 cm.

22465 [Hildreth, Richard] 1807-1865.
The people's presidential candidate; or The life of
William Henry Harrison, of Ohio. Boston, Weeks, Jordan
and company, 1839.
1 p.l., [5]-211 p.   15 cm.

22466 Hill, Clement Hugh, 1836-1898.
Argument made before a joint committee of the legislature of Massachusetts, May 17, 1869, against the
establishment of a state police in the city of Boston,
by Clement Hugh Hill. Phonographically reported by
Henry Oviatt. Boston, A. Mudge & son, city printers,
1869.
46 p.   23 cm.

22467 Hill, Ebenezer.
The substance of two lectures, on the history of Mason,
delivered before the Lyceum in Mason village... Fitch-
burg [Mass.] W. J. Merriam, 1846.
16 p.   18 cm.

22468 Hill, Mrs. Elizabeth (Freeman)
The widow's offering: an authentic narrative of the

131

parentage, life, trials and travels of Mrs. Elizabeth
Hill. Written by herself. New London, Conn., D. S.
Ruddock, printer, 1852.
179 p.   19½ cm.

22469   Hill, George Canning, 1825-1898.
Capt. John Smith; a biography. By George Canning Hill.
Boston, Hill & Libby, 1858.
viii, [9]-286 p.   plates.   17½ cm.

22470   Hill, George William, 1824-
Memoir of Sir Brenton Halliburton, late chief justice
of the province of Nova Scotia. By Rev. G. W. Hill,
M.A. Halifax, Printed by J. Bowes & sons, 1864.
2 p.l., 207 p.   20½ cm.

22471   Hill, George William, 1824-
Nova-Scotia and Nova-Scotians: a lecture, delivered
before the Literary and debating society of Windsor,
N.S. and afterward at the Temperance hall, Halifax,
in behalf of the Athenaeum... Halifax, J. Bowes & sons,
1858.

22472   Hill, Hamilton Andres, 1827-1895.
The relations of the business men of the United States
to the national legislation. By Hamilton Andrews Hill...
Boston, Barker, Cotter & co., printers, 1870.
32 p.   24½ cm.

22473   Hill, Ira.
Antiquities of America explained. By Ira Hill, A.M....
Hagers-town [Md.] Printed by W. D. Bell, 1831.
ix, [11]-131 p.   illus.   17½ cm.

22474   Hill, Isaac, 1788-1851.
An address, delivered at Concord, N. H., January 8,
1828, being the thirteenth anniversary of Jackson's
victory at New Orleans. By Isaac Hill. Concord, N. H.,
Printed at Manahan, Hoag & co., 1828.
44 p.   21 cm.
Addresses by J. B. Thornton, Nathan B. Felton and
J. M. Harper: p. [33]-44.

22475   [Hill, Isaac] 1788-1851.
Brief sketch of the life, character and services of
Major General Andrew Jackson. By a citizen of New
England. Concord, N. H., Printed by Manahan, Hoag &
co. for I. Hill, 1828.
51 p.   front. (port.)   14½ cm.

22476   Hill, John Boynton, 1796-1886.
        History of the town of Mason, N. H. from the first
grant in 1749, to the year 1858. By John B. Hill.
Boston, L. A. Elliott & co.; Bangor, D. Bugbee & co.,
1858.
        iv, 5 -324 p.   illus., fold. pl., ports.   24½ cm.

22477   Hill, John Boynton, 1796-1886.
        Memoir of the Rev. Ebenezer Hill, pastor of the
Congregational church, in Mason, N. H., from November,
1790, to May, 1854. With some of his sermons, and his
discourse on the history of the town. By John B. Hill.
Boston, L. A. Elliot & co.; Bangor, D. Bugbee & co., 1858.
        113, 1 p.   front. (port.) illus., facsim.   24½ cm.

22478   Hill, John Boynton, 1796-1886.
        Proceedings of the centennial celebration of the one
hundredth anniversary of the incorporation of the town
of Mason, N. H., August 26, 1868. Prepared for publication, under the direction of the committee of arrange-
ments, by J. B. Hill. Boston, Elliott, Thomes & Talbot,
1870.
        115 p.   front., port.

22479   Hill, Joshua, 1812-1891.
        The union record of Hon. Joshua Hill, of Georgia.
A letter in reply to his enemies. Washington, Gibson
brothers, printers, 1870.
        18 p.   22½ cm.

22480   Hill, Richard, 1795-1872.
        Haiti and Spain: a memorial, by Richard Hill.
Dedicated to the Honorable W. H. Seward... Kingston,
Jamaica, M. De Cordova & co., printers, 1862.
        14 p.   20 cm.

22481   [Hill, Richard] 1795-1872.
        A week at Port-Royal... Montego-Bay [Jamaica]
Cornwall chronicle office, 1855.
        2 p.l., 109 p.   18 cm.

22482   [Hill, S   S   ]
        A short account of Prince Edward island, designed
chiefly for the information of agriculturists and
other emigrants of small capital, by the author of
The emigrant's introduction to an acquaintance with
the British American colonies, &c. ... London,
Madden & co., 1839.

133

2 p.l., vi, 90, iii, [1] p.   front. (fold. map)
19½ cm.

22483 Hill, Thomas, 1818-1891.
       Integral education. An inaugural address, delivered
       at Antioch college, of Yellow Springs, Greene County,
       Ohio, September 8, 1859. By Rev. Thomas Hill...
       Boston, Little, Brown and company, 1859.
       31 p.   23 cm.

22484 Hill, William, 1769-1852.
       History of the rise, progress, genius, and character
       of American Presbyterianism: together with a review
       of "The constitutional history of the Presbyterian
       church in the United States of America, by Chas. Hodge..."
       By William Hill... Washington city, J. Gideon, jr.,
       1839.
       xv, 224 p.   24 cm.

22485 Hill, William Henry, b. 1816, comp.
       Genealogical table of the Lee family from the first
       emigration to America in 1641. Brought down to the
       year 1851. Comp. from information furnished by Hon.
       Martin Lee... By the Rev. William H. Hill... Albany,
       Weed, Parsons & co.'s print., 1851.
       31 p.   23 cm.

22486 Hill, William Henry, 1877-
       A brief history of the printing press in Washington,
       Saratoga and Warren Counties, State of New York.
       Together with a check list of their publications prior
       to 1825, and a selection of books relating particularly
       to the vicinity. By William H. Hill. Fort Edward,
       N. Y., Privately printed, 1930.
       117 p.   facsim.   23 cm.

22487 Hillard, George Stillman, 1808-1879.
       Life and campaigns of George B. McClellan, major-
       general U. S. Army. By G. S. Hillard. Philadelphia,
       J. B. Lippincott & co., 1864.
       396 p.   front. (port.)   18½ cm.

22488 Hillard, George Stillman, 1808-1879.
       A memoir of James Brown; with obituary notices and
       tributes of respect from public bodies. By George
       Stillman Hillard. Boston, Priv. print., 1856.
       4 p.l., 138 p.   front. (port.)   23 cm.

22489 Hiller, Oliver Prescott, 1814-1870.
        Pocahontas; or The founding of Virginia. A poem.
     In three cantos. By the Rev. O. Prescott Hiller...
     London, Hatchard and co.; New York, Mason brothers;
     [etc., etc.] 1865.
        vi, [7]-107 p.   17 cm.

22490 Hillhouse, William, 1757-1833.
        A dissertation, in answer to a late lecture on the
     political state of America, read in New-Haven, January
     12th, 1789, during the adjourned sessions of the
     honorable legislature. To which is added, a short poem
     spoken at the same time. By William Hillhouse, jun. ...
     New Haven, Printed by T. & S. Green [1789]
        23 p.   20 cm.

22491 Hillhouse, James Abraham, 1789-1841.
        An oration, pronounced at New Haven, by request of
     the Common council, August 19, 1834, in commemoration
     of the life and services of General Lafayette. By
     James A. Hillhouse. New Haven, H. Howe & co., 1834.
        40 p.   23 cm.

22492 Hines, David Theodore.
        The life, adventures and opinions of David Theo.
     Hines, of South Carolina; master of arts, and, some-
     times, doctor of medicine... in a series of letters
     to his friends. Written by himself... New York,
     Bradley & Clark, 1840.
        iv, [5]-195 p.   19 cm.

22493 Hinman, Royal Ralph, 1785-1868, comp.
        Letters from the English kings and queens Charles II,
     James II, William and Mary, Anne, George II, &c. to the
     governors of the colony of Connecticut, together with
     the answers thereto, from 1635 to 1749; and other original,
     ancient, literary and curious documents, comp. from
     files and records in the office of the secretary of the
     state of Connecticut. By R. R. Hinman... Hartford,
     J. B. Eldredge, printer, 1836.
        vi, [2], 10-372 p.   port., 2 facsim. (incl. front.)
     19 cm.

22494 His jewels; or, A story of New England in war time.
        Founded on facts... Written for the Congregational
     Sabbath-school and publishing society, and approved by
     the Committee of publication. Boston, Cong. Sabbath-
     school and publishing society, 1868.
        iv, 5-281 p.   front.   17½ cm.

22495   Historical & descriptive lessons, embracing sketches of the
        history, character & customs of all nations: designed
        as a companion to Goodrich's, Woodbridge's, Morse's,
        Smiley's, and other school geographies. With numerous
        engravings. Brattleboro [Vt.] Holbrook and Fessenden,
        1828.
           vi, [7]-336 p. incl. front., illus.   15½ cm.

22496   History of American missions to the heathen, from their
        commencement to the present time. Worcester, Spooner &
        Howland, 1840.
           2 p.l., [9]-346, [4], 355-528, 529-620, [529]-615, [709]
        726 p.   illus. (incl. ports.) maps.   24 cm.
           Errors in paging.
           "Missionaries": p. 322-344.

22497   History of the American war, of eighteen hundred and
        twelve, from the commencement until the final termination
        thereof, on the memorable eighth of January 1815, at
        New Orleans: embellished with a striking likeness of
        General Pike, and six other engravings. Philadelphia,
        Wm. M'Carty; printed by M'Carty & Davis, 1816.
           vii, [1], 9-252 p.   front. (port.) 6 pl.   18½ cm.

22498   The history of the second ten years of the reign of George
        the Third, king of Great-Britain, &c. from the conclusion
        of the third session of the thirteenth Parliament, in
        1770, to the end of the last session of the fourteenth
        Parliament of Great Britain, in 1780... London, Printed
        for the author, and sold by T. Evans, 1782.
           2 p.l., xiv, [15]-463 p.   23 cm.

22499   Hitchcock, Benjamin W
           Hitchcock's chronological record of the American
        civil war, giving every event in the order of its
        occurrence from November 8th, 1860, to June 3d, 1865;
        also a complete list of vessels captured by the
        Confederate navy. New York, B. W. Hitchcock, 1866.
           1 p.l., 106, [561]-566 p.   front. (port.)   23 cm.

22500   Hitchcock, David, 1773-1849.
           The poetical works of David Hitchcock. Containing,
        The shade of Plato, Knight and quack, and the subtlety
        of foxes. Boston, Published by Etheridge and Bliss,
        no. 12, Cornhill, 1806, Oliver & Munroe, printers.
           xvi, [17]-164 p.   18 cm.
           "Sketch of author's life": p. [iii]-ix.

22501 Hitchcock, David, 1773-1849.
        The social monitor; or, A series of poems, on some of
        the most important and interesting subjects. By David
        Hitchcock... 2d ed. New York, Printed for Gould, Banks
        & Gould, Prior & Dunnings, Isaac Riley, and Collins &
        co., 1814.
        v, [7]-204 p.   14½ cm.

22502 [Hitchcock, Edward] 1793-1864.
        Catalogues of the animals and plants of Massachusetts.
        With a copious index. Amherst, J. S. and C. Adams,
        1835.
        142 p.   23 cm.

22503 Hitchcock, Edward, 1793-1864.
        Ichnology of New England. A report on the sandstone of
        the Connecticut valley, especially its fossil footmarks,
        made to the government of the commonwealth of Massachu-
        setts. By Edward Hitchcock... Boston, W. White,
        printer to the state, 1858.
        xii, 220 p. incl. illus., fold. tables.   60 pl.
        (part fold.; incl. col. map)   32 x 25 cm.

22504 Hitchcock, Edward, 1793-1864.
        The inseparable trio. A sermon delivered before His
        Excellency George N. Briggs, governor... and the legis-
        lature of Massachusetts, at the annual election,
        Wednesday, January 2d, 1850. By Edward Hitchcock...
        Boston, Dutton and Wentworth, state printers, 1850.
        45 p.   21½ cm.

22505 Hitchcock, Edward, 1793-1864, comp.
        The power of Christian benevolence, illustrated in
        the life and labors of Mary Lyon. Comp. by Edward
        Hitchcock... with the assistance of others. 7th ed.
        Northampton, Hopkins, Bridgman, and company; Phila-
        delphia, Thomas, Cowperthwait, & co., 1852.
        viii, 486 p.   front. (port.) plates.   19½ cm.

22506 Hitchcock, Edward, 1793-1864.
        Reminiscences of Amherst college, historical,
        scientific, biographical and autobiographical: also,
        of other and wider life experiences. (With four plates
        and a geological map) By Edward Hitchcock. Northampton,
        Mass., Bridgman & Childs, 1863.
        vii, [1], 412 p.   front. (port.) 3 pl., fold. map.
        18½ cm.

22507 Hitchcock, Henry Lawrence, 1813-1873.
God acknowledged, in the nation's bereavement. A
sermon delivered in Hudson, Ohio, on the day of the
obsequies of Abraham Lincoln, April 19th, 1865, by Henry
L. Hitchcock. Cleveland, Fairbanks, Benedict & co.,
printers, 1865.
23 p.   22½ cm.

22508 Hitchcock, Roswell Dwight, 1817-1887.
Our national sin: a sermon, preached on the day of the
national fast, September 26, 1861, in the South Reformed
Dutch church, New York city. By Rev. Roswell D.
Hitchcock... New York, Baker & Godwin, printers, 1861.
24 p.   23 cm.

22509 Hobart, Benjamin, 1781-1877.
History of the town of Abington, Plymouth County,
Massachusetts, from its first settlement. By Benjamin
Hobart, A.M. Boston, T. H. Carter and son, 1866.
xix, [1], 453 p.   front. (port.) plates.   20½ cm.

22510 [Hobart, John Henry, bp.] 1775-1830.
A reply to A letter to the Right Rev. Bishop Hobart,
occasioned by the strictures on Bible societies,
contained in his late address to the convention of
New York, by a churchman of the diocese of New York, in
a letter to that gentleman. By Corrector [pseud.]
New York, Printed by T. and J. Swords, 1823.
98 p.   24 cm.

22511 Hobart, Noah, 1706-1773.
An attempt to illustrate and confirm the ecclesiastical
constitution of the consociated churches, in the colony
of Connecticut. Occasioned by a late "Explanation of
the Saybrook platform." By Noah Hobart, A.M., pastor
of a church in Fairfield... New-Haven, Printed by
B. Mecom, 1765.
44 p.   19½ cm.

22512 Hodges, Almon Danforth, 1801-1878.
Genealogical record of the Hodges family in New England,
containing the names of over 1500 persons, from 1633 to
1853, numbering eight generations. By Almon D. Hodges...
Boston, Printed by Dutton and Wentworth, 1853.
71 p.   facsims.   23 cm.

22513 Hodgman, Edwin Ruthven, 1819-1900.
A brief memoir of Rev. Joseph Bancroft Hill, who died

in the service of U.S. Christian commission, at
Chattanooga, Tenn., June 16, 1864. By Rev. Edwin R.
Hodgman. Boston, Printed by A. Mudge & son, 1868.
126 p. 17 cm.

22514 Hodgson, William Brown, b. 1800.
Memoir on the Megatherium, and other extinct gigantic
quadrupeds of the coast of Georgia, with observations
on its geologic features. By William B. Hodgson.
New York, Bartlett & Welford, 1846.
vi, [7]-47 p. pl., map, fold. profile. 25½ cm.

22515 Hoffman, Eugene Augustus, 1829-1902.
The martyr President. A sermon preached in Grace
church, Brooklyn Heights, N. Y., by the Rev. Eugene
Augs. Hoffman... 20 April, A.D. 1865, being the day
of mourning appointed by the governor of the state after
the death of President Lincoln... New York, C. A.
Alvord, printer, 1865.
14, [2] p. 23½ cm.

22516 Hoffman, William.
The monitor; or, Jottings of a New York merchant
during a trip round the globe... By William Hoffman...
New York, Carleton, 1863.
xiv, 448 p. front. (port.) plates. 19½ cm.

22517 [Hogan, Edmund] ed.
The Pennsylvania state trials: containing the
impeachment, trial, and acquittal of Francis Hopkinson,
and John Nicholson, esquires. The former being judge
of the Court of admiralty, and the latter, the
comptroller-general of the commonwealth of Pennsylvania,
vol. I... Philadelphia, Printed by Francis Bailey,
at Yorick's head, no. 116, High-street, for Edmund
Hogan, 1794.
xii, 776 p. 21½ cm.

22518 Hoge, Jane C   (Blaikie) "Mrs. A. H. Hoge."
... Address delivered by Mrs. Hoge, of the North western sanitary commission (branch of the U. S. sanitary
commission), at a meeting of ladies, held at Packer
institute, Brooklyn, L. I., March, 1865, in aid of the
great North western fair, to be held at Chicago, Illinois, May 30th, 1865. New York, Sanford, Harroun &
co., steam printing house, 1865.
21 p. 23 cm. (U[nited] S[tates] sanitary
commission. [Documents] no. 88)

22519 Holbrook, James, 1812-1864.
        Ten years among the mail bags: or, Notes from the
        diary of a special agent of the Post-office department.
        By J. Holbrook... Philadelphia, H. Cowperthwait & co.,
        1855.
            xxiv, 25-432 p.   plates, ports.   19½ cm.

22520 Holbrook, Timothy Washington.
        Address to the people of the United States. The great
        rebellion. Causes, progress, and remedy. By Timothy
        Washington Holbrook... Rochester, N. Y., Printed for
        the author, 1864.
            52 p.   23 cm.

22521 Holcombe, Henry, 1762-1824.
        A sermon occasioned by the death of Lieutenant-General
        George Washington, late president of the United States
        of America; who was born February 11th, 1732, in
        Virginia, and died, December 14th on Mount Vernon, his
        favorite seat in his native country: first delivered
        in the Baptist church, Savannah, Georgia, January 19th,
        1800, and now published at the request of the honorable
        City council. By Henry Holcombe... [Savannah]
        Printed by Seymour & Woolhopter [1800]
            16, [2] p.   20 x 17 cm.

22522 Holden, Frederic Augustus.
        Genealogy of the descendants of Banfield Capron, from
        a.d. 1660 to A.D. 1859. By Frederic A. Holden...
        Boston, Printed by G. C. Rand & Avery, 1859.
            263 p.   front., ports.   19½ cm.

22523 Holden, Horace, b. 1810.
        A narrative of the shipwreck, captivity, and sufferings,
        of Horace Holden and Benj. H. Nute; who were cast away
        in the American ship Mentor, on the Pelew Islands, in
        the year 1832; and for two years afterwards were sub-
        jected to unheard of sufferings among the barbarous
        inhabitants of Lord North's Island. By Horace Holden.
        Boston, Russell, Shattuck, and co., 1836.
            xii, [13]-133 p. incl. front.   pl.   16 cm.

22524 Holdich, Joseph, 1804-1893.
        The life of Wilbur [!] Fisk, D.D., first president of
        the Wesleyan university. By Joseph Holdich... New
        York, Harper & brothers, 1842.
            xvi, [17]-455 p.   23 cm.

22525   Holland, Elihu Goodwin, 1817-1878.
         Memoir of Rev. Joseph Badger. By E. G. Holland.
       3d ed. New York, C. S. Francis and co.; Boston,
       B. H. Greene, 1854.
         vi, [7]-473 p.   front. (port.)   19½ cm.

22526   Holland, Elihu Goodwin, b. 1817.
         Niagara. And other poems. By E. G. Holland. New
       York, Rudd and Carleton, 1861.
         1 p.l., ii, [4], 170 p.   15½ cm.

22527   Holland, Josiah Gilbert, 1819-1881.
         The Bay-path; a tale of New England colonial life.
       By J. G. Holland... New York, Charles Scribners, 1864.
         4 p.l., [7]-418 p.

22528   Holland, Josiah Gilbert, 1819-1881.
         Life of Abraham Lincoln, by J. G. Holland...
       Springfield, Mass., G. Bill, 1866.
         544 p.   front., plates, port.   22 cm.

22529   [Holland, Mrs. Robert]
         Channing, sa vie et ses oeuvres, avec une nouvelle
       préface de m. Charles de Rémusat. 2. éd., rev. et augm.
       Paris, Didier et cie, 1861.
         2 p.l., xxxvi, 439 p.   19 cm.

22530   Holloway, John N
         History of Kansas: from the first exploration of the
       Mississippi valley, to its admission into the Union:
       embracing a concise sketch of Louisiana; American slavery,
       and its onward march; the conflict of free and slave
       labor in the settlement of Kansas, and the overthrow of
       the latter, with all other items of general interest...
       By J. N. Holloway, A.M. Lafayette, Ind., James Emmons
       & co., 1868.
         534 p.   front., illus., plates.   22½ cm.

22531   Holloway, William, fl. 1790-1812.
         The peasant's fate: a rural poem. With miscellaneous
       poems. By William Holloway... London, Printed for
       Vernor and Hood, Poultry, by James Swan and co., 1802.
         x p., 1 l., 128 p.   16 cm.

22532   Holmes, Abiel, 1763-1837.
         The life of Ezra Stiles... a fellow of the American
       philosophical society; of the American academy of arts
       and sciences; of the Connecticut society of arts and

141

sciences; a corresponding member of the Massachusetts historical society; professor of ecclesiastical history; and president of Yale college. By Abiel Holmes... Boston, Printed by Thomas & Andrews, 1798.
　　vi, [7]-403, [1] p.　　front. (port.)　　21½ cm.

22533　Holmes, Abiel, 1763-1837.
　　A sermon, preached at Cambridge, on the Lord's day, December 29, 1799, occasioned by the death of George Washington, commander in chief of the American armies, and late president of the United States of America. By Abiel Holmes... Boston, Printed by Samuel Hall, 1800.
　　22 p., 1 l.　　21 cm.

22534　Holmes, Abraham, 1754-1839.
　　An address delivered before the members of the bar of the county of Bristol, Mass., at New-Bedford, June term, 1834. By Abraham Holmes. New-Bedford, Press of B. T. Congdon, 1834.
　　24 p.　　21½ cm.

22535　[Holmes, Mrs. Elizabeth (Emra] 1804-1843.
　　Scenes in our parish. By a "country parson's" daughter. To which is prefixed, a memoir of the author, by her sister... New York, Stanford and Swords, 1851.
　　xliv, 374 p.　　18½ cm.

22536　Holmes, John, 1773-1843.
　　The statesman; or, Principles of legislation and law. By John Holmes... Augusta [Me.] Severance & Dorr, printers, 1840.
　　viii, [9]-510 p., 1 l.　　23½ cm.

22537　Holmes, Oliver Wendell, 1809-1894.
　　Oration delivered before the city authorities of Boston, on the Fourth of July, 1863, by Oliver Wendell Holmes. Boston, J. E. Farwell & company, printers to the city, 1863.
　　60 p.　　23½ cm.

22538　Holt, Edwin, 1805-1854.
　　Historical sketch of the North church. A discourse delivered at the re-opening and dedication of the North church in Portsmouth, Jan. 31, 1838. By Edwin Holt. Portsmouth, C. W. Brewster, printer, 1838.
　　30 p.　　23 cm.

22539　Holt, Joseph, 1807-1894.
　　Vindication of Judge Advocate General Holt from the

foul slanders of traitors, confessed perjurers and
suborners, acting in the interest of Jefferson Davis.
[Washington] Chronicle print [1866]
9 p.   23 cm.
Concerning the charge of withholding recommendation
for mercy in the case of Mrs. Surratt.

22540   Holton, Isaac Farwell.
New Granada: twenty months in the Andes. By Isaac F
Holton... New York, Harper & brothers, 1857.
1 p.l., [v]-xiv, [2], [17]-605 p. incl. illus., plates,
plans, tab. 2 double maps (incl. front.)   23 cm.

22541   Holyoke, Edward, 1689-1769.
Integrity and religion to be principally regarded,
by such as design others to stations of publick trust.
A sermon preach'd before His Excellency, Jonathan
Belcher, esq; His Majesty's Council, and the Assembly
of the province of the Massachusetts-Bay in New England,
on the anniversary for the election of counsellors for
said province, May 26, 1736. By Edward Holyoke, M.A.,
pastor of a church in Marblehead... Boston, in New
England: Printed by J. Draper, printer to His Excellency
the governour and Council, for J. Eliot, 1736.
2 p.l., 51 p.   22 cm.

22542   Holyoke, Edward Augustus, 1728-1829.
An ethical essay. Or, an attempt to enumerate the
several duties which we owe to God, our Saviour, our
neighbour and ourselves, and the virtues and graces of
the Christian life; contrasted on the opposite pages
with their opposite vices and ill dispositions. To each
of which are subjoined some loose notes, imperfect hints,
and common observations, serving to illustrate, limit,
or enforce them. Intended to assist in the important
duty of self-examination. By the late Edward Augustus
Holyoke... To which is added an appendix, containing
some miscellaneous papers and prayers. With a biographical memoir, by John Brazer. [Salem, Foote & Brown,
printers] 1830.
xxviii, 183 p.   23 cm.
"Memoir": p. xiii-xxviii.

22543   Homans, Isaac Smith   1807-1874.
History of Boston, from 1630 to 1856... Illustrated
with one hundred and twenty engravings. Boston, F. C.
Moore & company, 1856.
xi, [v]-vi, [xiii]-xv, 246 p.   illus., plates.
15 cm.

22544 The home book of the picturesque: or, American scenery,
art, and literature. Comprising a series of essays by
Washington Irving, W. C. Bryant, Fenimore Cooper...
etc., with thirteen engravings on steel, from pictures
by eminent artists... New York, G. P. Putnam, 1852.
4 p.l., [7]-8 p., 2 l., 188 p.   13 pl. (incl. front.)
29½ cm.
Published in 1868, with some changes and additions,
under title: A landscape book.

22545 Home league.
Address of the Home league to the people of the
United States. New York, J. Van Norden & co., printers,
1841.
16 p.   23½ cm.

22546 [Homer, James Lloyd]
Nahant, and other places on the north-shore; being a
continuation of Notes on the sea-shore, by the Shade of
Alden... Boston, Printed by W. Chadwick, 1848.
vii, [9]-48 p.   23 cm.

22547 [Homer, James Lloyd]
Notes on the sea-shore; or, Random sketches. In
relation to the ancient town of Hull, its settlement,
its inhabitants, and its social and political institutions; to the fisheries, fishing parties, and boat sailing
to Boston harbor and its islands... by the "Shade of
Alden." Boston, Redding & co., 1848.
vii, [9]-54, [1] p.   front.   23 cm.

22548 Homer, William Bradford, 1817-1841.
Writings of Rev. William Bradford Homer, late pastor
of the Congregational church in South Berwick, Me.
With an introductory essay and a memoir by Edwards A.
Park... 2d ed. Boston, T. R. Marvin, 1849.
lix, [13]-395 p.   pl.   19½ cm.

22549 Homes of American authors; comprising anecdotical,
personal, and descriptive sketches, by various writers...
New York, G. P. Putnam and co.; [etc., etc.] 1853.
2 p.l., [iii]-viii, 366 p.   front., illus., plates,
ports., facsims. (part double)   21½ cm.
By G. W. Curtis, H. T. Tuckerman, G. W. Greene, C. F.
Briggs, G. S. Hillard, W. C. Bryant, G. W. Peck, R. W.
Griswold, P. Godwin, E. E. Hale, Mrs. C. M. Kirkland.
Many of these papers were printed by G. P. Putnam's
sons in 1896 under title "Little journeys to the homes
of American authors."

Contents. - John James Audubon. - James K. Paulding. -
Washington Irving. - William Cullen Bryant. - George
Bancroft. - Richard Henry Dana. - William H. Prescott. -
Miss C. M. Sedgwick. - J. Fenimore Cooper. - Edward
Everett. - Ralph Waldo Emerson. - William Gilmore Simms. -
Henry W. Longfellow. - Nathaniel Hawthorne. - Daniel
Webster. - John Pendleton Kennedy. - James Russell
Lowell.

22550   Homes of American statesmen: with anecdotical, personal,
and descriptive sketches, by various writers. Illustrated with engravings on wood, from drawings by Döpler
and daguerreotypes; and fac-similes of autograph letters.
New York, G. P. Putnam and co.; London, S. Low, son and
co., 1854.
        2 p.l., [iii]-viii, 469 p.   front. (mounted photo)
illus., plates, facsims. (part fold.)   22½ cm.
        Contents. - Washington, by Mrs. C. M. Kirkland. -
Franklin, by C. F. Briggs. - Jefferson, by P. Godwin. -
Hancock, by R. Hildreth. - John Adams, by C. Cook. -
Patrick Henry, by E. W. Johnston. - Madison, by E. W.
Johnston. - Jay, by W. S. Thayer. - Hamilton, by J. C.
Carter. - Marshall, by R. W. Griswold. - Ames, by J. B.
Thayer. - John Quincy Adams, by D. L. Child. - Jackson,
by P. Godwin. - Rufus King, by C. King. - Clay, by H.
Greeley. - Calhoun, by P. Godwin. - Clinton, by T. R.
Beck. - Story, by F. Howland. - Wheaton.

22551   Hooker, Edward William, 1794-1875.
        Memoir of Mrs. Sarah Lanman Smith, late of the mission
in Syria... By Edward W. Hooker... Boston, Perkins &
Marvin; Philadelphia, H. Perkins, 1839.
        407 p.   front. (Port.)   20 cm.

22552   [Hooker, Edward William] 1794-1875.
        Memorials of the families of Mr. James Thompson and
of Dea. Augustus Thompson, of Goshen, Connecticut.
Hartford, Press of Case, Tiffany and company, 1854.
        iv, [5]-106 p.   23½ cm.

22553   Hooker, Edward William, 1794-1875.
        The life of Thomas Hooker. By Edward W. Hooker...
Boston, Massachusetts Sabbath school society, 1849.
        vi, 7 -324 p.   19 cm.   (Half-title: Lives of
the chief fathers of New England... vol. VI)

22554   [Hooker, Thomas] 1586-1647.
        The sovles exaltation. A treatise containing The
soules vnion with Christ, on I Cor. 6.17. The soules

145

benefit from vnion with Christ, on I Cor. 1.30. The
soules justification, on 2 Cor. 5.21. By T. H. ...
London, Printed by Iohn Haviland, for Andrew Crooke,
and are to be sold at the Black beare in S. Pauls
church-yard, 1638.
8 p.l., 311 p.   18½ cm.

22555   Hooker, Sir W[illiam] J[ackson] 1785-1865.
Notes on the botany of the Antarctic voyage conducted
by Captain James Clark Ross... in Her Majesty's
discovery ships Erebus and Terror; with observations
on the tussac grass of the Falkland Islands. By Sir
W. J. Hooker... London, H. Baillière; [etc., etc.] 1843.
2 p.l., 83 p.   fold. col. front., illus.   21½ cm.

22556   Hooper, William Hulme, 1827-1854.
Ten months among the tents of the Tuski, with
incidents of an Arctic boat expedition in search of Sir
John Franklin, as far as the Mackenzie river, and Cape
Bathurst. By Lieut. W. H. Hooper... London, J. Murray,
1853.
xv, [1], 417, [1] p.   col. front., illus., plates
(part col.) fold. map.   21 cm.
An account of the expedition of H. M. S. Plover, under
Capt. T. E. L. Moore, 1848-51.

22557   Hopkins, Albert, 1807-1872.
A sermon delivered at Williamstown, Mass., on the day
of the annual state fast, March 28, 1839, by Albert
Hopkins... Published by request of the students.
Troy, N. Y., Stevenson and M'Call, printers, 1839.
21 p.   20 cm.

22558   Hopkins, Daniel, 1734-1814.
A sermon, preached December 29, 1799, in the South
meeting house, Salem, the Lord's day after the melancholy
tidings were received of the death of General George
Washington... By Daniel Hopkins... Salem, Printed
by Thomas C. Cushing [1800]
28 p.   19½ cm.

22559   Hopkins, Jesse.
The patriot's manual; comprising various standard
and miscellaneous subjects, interesting to every
American citizen... Comp. by Jesse Hopkins. Utica,
W. Williams, 1828.
xi, [13]-220 p.   18½ cm.
Contents. - Patrick Henry's speech in 1775. - Declara-
tion of independence. - Constitution of the United States

146

Amendments - Washington's farewell address. - Constitution of the state of New York. - Everett's oration in 1824, on the celebration of the landing of the Pilgrims. - Webster's oration on laying the corner stone of the Bunker Hill monument. - Wirt's discourse on Jefferson and Adams. - Webster's speech in Congress, on the Greek revolution.

22560 Hopkins, Mark, 1802-1887.
A sermon delivered before His Excellency Edward Everett, governor, His Honor George Hull, lieutenant governor, the honorable council, and the legislature of Massachusetts, on the anniversary election, January 2, 1839. By Mark Hopkins... Boston, Dutton and Wentworth, printers to the state, 1839.
40 p.   20 cm.

22561 Hopkins, Samuel, 1721-1803.
Sketches of the life of the late, Rev. Samuel Hopkins, d.d., pastor of the First Congregational church in Newport, written by himself; interspersed with marginal notes extracted from his private diary: to which is added; A dialogue, by the same hand, on the nature and extent of true Christian submission; also, A serious address to professing Christians: closed by Dr. Hart's sermon at his funeral: with an introduction to the whole, by the editor. Published by Stephen West, D.D., pastor of the church in Stockbridge. Published according to act of Congress. Hartford, Printed by Hudson and Goodwin, 1805.
xxii, [23]-240 p.   front. (port.)   17 cm.

22562 Hopkins, Samuel Miles, 1772-1837.
An oration, delivered before the Washington benevolent society, in the city of New York, at Zion church, on the twenty-second of February, 1809. By Samuel M. Hopkins, esq. Pub. by the society... New York, Printed by J. Seymour, and sold by Hopkins and Bayard, 1809.
20 p.   21½ cm.

22563 Hopper, Edward.
Republican homes. An address delivered before the Association of the alumni of the University of the city of New York, on the evening preceding the commencement, June 19th, 1861. By the Rev. Edward Hopper... With officers of Association, meeting of alumni, and constitution of Association. [New York] University press, 1861.
27 p.   22½ cm.

22564   [Hornot, Antoine]
        Anecdotes américaines, ou Histoire abrégée des
        principaux événements arrivés dans le Nouveau monde,
        depuis sa découverte jusqu'à l'époque présente. A
        Paris, Chez Vincent, 1776.
        xv, 782 p.   17½ cm.

22565   Horsford, Jedidiah, 1791-1874.
        Speech of Hon. J. Horsford, of New York, in favor of
        the establishment of an agricultural bureau. Delivered
        in the House of representatives, June 24, 1852.
        Washington, Printed at the Globe office, 1852.
        7 p.   23½ cm.

22566   Horton, Rushmore G   b. 1826.
        ... The life and public services of James Buchanan.
        Late minister to England and formerly minister to
        Russia, senator and representative in Congress, and
        secretary of state: including the most important of
        his state papers, by R. G. Horton... New York, Derby &
        Jackson; Cincinnati, H. W. Derby & co., 1856.
        xi, 13-428 p.   front. (port.)   19½ cm.

22567   Hosack, David, 1769-1835.
        Memoir of De Witt Clinton: with an appendix, containing
        numerous documents, illustrative of the principal events
        of his life. By David Hosack... New York, Printed
        by J. Seymour, 1829.
        xxiv, [21]-530 p.   2 pl. (incl. front.)   fold. map.
        28 cm.

22568   Hotchkin, James Harvey, 1781-1851.
        A history of the purchase and settlement of western
        New York, and of the rise, progress, and present state
        of the Presbyterian church in that section. New York,
        M. W. Dodd, 1848.
        xvi, 600 p.   front.   24 cm.

22569   Hotchkiss, Frederick William, 1763?-1844.
        An oration delivered at Saybrook on Saturday
        February 22d, 1800; the day set apart by the recommenda-
        tion of Congress for the people of the United States
        to testify their grief for the death of General George
        Washington... By Fred. W. Hotchkiss. New London,
        Printed by S. Green, 1800.
        32 p.   20½ cm.

22570   Hough, Franklin Benjamin, 1822-1885.
        American biographical notes, being short notices of

deceased persons, chiefly those not included in Allen's or Drake's biographical Dictionaries, gathered from many sources, and arranged by Franklin B. Hough. Albany, Joel Munsell, 1875.
iv, 442 p.   21½ cm.

22571   Hough, Franklin Benjamin, 1822-1885, ed.
Diary of the siege of Detroit in the war with Pontiac. Also a narrative of the principal events of the siege, by Major Robert Rogers; a plan for conducting Indian affairs, by Colonel Bradstreet; and other authentick documents, never before printed. Ed. with notes by Franklin B. Hough. Albany, J. Munsell, 1860.
xxiii p., 1 l., 304 p.   facsim.   21½ x 18 cm.

22572   Hough, Franklin Benjamin, 1822-1885.
A history of Jefferson county in the state of New York, from the earliest period to the present time. By Franklin B. Hough... Albany, J. Munsell; Watertown, N. Y., Sterling & Riddell, 1854.
601 p. incl. illus., pl., ports.   front.   23 cm.

22573   Hough, Franklin Benjamin, 1822-1885.
A history of St. Lawrence and Franklin counties, New York, from the earliest period to the present time. By Franklin B. Hough... Albany, Little & co., 1853.
xv, [17]-719 p., 1 l. incl. illus., plates, ports. front., plates (1 fold.)   ports., fold. maps.   22 cm.

22574   Hough, Franklin B[enjamin] 1822-1885, ed.
Plan for seizing and carrying to New York Coll. [!] Wm. Goffe, the regicide, as set forth in the affidavit of John London, Apr. 20, 1678. Pub. from the original... by Franklin B. Hough, M.D. with other documents... Albany, Weed, Parsons & co., 1855.
17 p.   20½ cm.

22575   Hovey, Alvah, 1820-1903.
A memoir of the life and times of the Rev. Isaac Backus, A.M., by Alvah Hovey... Boston, Gould and Lincoln; New York, Sheldon, Blakeman & co.; [etc., etc.] 1858.
xvi, [17]-369 p.   20 cm.

22576   Hovey, Horace Carter, 1833-1914.
The national fast. A sermon, preached at Coldwater, Mich., January 4, 1861, by Rev. Horace C. Hovey. Coldwater, Mich., Republican print, 1861.
2 p.l., 3-12 p.   23 cm.

22577   How, Thomas Yardley.
        A vindication of the Protestant Episcopal church, in
        a series of letters addressed to the Rev. Samuel
        Miller, D.D., in reply to his late writings on the
        Christian ministry, and to the charges contained in his
        life of the Rev. Dr. Rodgers; with preliminary remarks.
        By Thomas Y. How... New York, Published by Eastburn,
        Kirk, & co., T. & J. Swords, and P. A. Mesier. T. & J.
        Swords, printers, no. 160, Pearl-street, 1816.
        xxxvi, [5]-492 p.   21 cm.

22578   Howard, Bezaleel, 1753-1837.
        A sermon, preached at the ordination of the Rev. Benj.
        R. Woodbridge, to the pastoral office, over the church
        and society in Norwich, October 17th, 1799: by Bezaleel
        Howard, A.M., pastor of the First church in Springfield.
        Springfield [Mass.] Printed by Timothy Ashley, 1800.
        15 p.   20½ cm.

22579   Howard, Simeon, 1733-1804.
        A sermon preached before the honorable Council, and the
        honorable House of representatives of the state of
        Massachusetts-Bay, in New-England, May 31, 1780. Being
        the anniversary for the election of the honorable Council.
        By Simeon Howard, A.M., pastor of the West church in
        Boston. N. B. Several passages omitted in preaching
        are now inserted in the publication of this discourse.
        Boston, Printed by John Gill, in Court-street, 1780.
        48 p.   19½ cm.

22580   Howe, Henry, 1816-1893.
        Historical collections of Virginia; containing a
        collection of the most interesting facts, traditions,
        biographical sketches, anecdotes, &c. relating to its
        history and antiquities. Together with geographical
        and statistical descriptions. To which is appended,
        an historical and descriptive sketch of the District
        of Columbia... By Henry Howe... Charleston, S. C.,
        W. R. Babcock, 1852.
        1 p.l., x, [11]-544 p.   col. front., illus., pl.,
        port., map, plan, facsim.   22½ cm.

22581   Howe, James Blake, d. 1844.
        A sermon, preached at Concord, before His Excellency
        Samuel Bell, governor, the honourable Council, and the
        two houses, composing the legislature of the state of
        New Hampshire, June 8, 1820. Being the anniversary
        election. By Rev. James B. Howe, A.M., rector of Union
        church, Claremont. Concord, Printed by Hill and Moore,

1820.
21 p.   21½ cm.

22582 Howe, Mathanael, 1764-1837.
A century sermon delivered in Hopkinton on Lord's
day, December 24, 1815. By Rev. Nathanael Howe...
Andover, Printed by Flagg and Gould, 1816.
31 p.   21½ cm.

22583 Howitt, Mary (Botham) 1799-1888.
Vignettes of American history... London, S. W.
Partridge & co. [1868]
1 p.l., ii, 138 p.   front., illus., pl.

22584 Howland, Edward.
Grant as a soldier and statesman: being a succinct
history of his military and civil career. By Edward
Howland... Hartford, J. B. Burr & company, 1868.
1 p.l., xi, [1], 11, 631 p.   front. (port.) plates.
23 cm.

22585 Howlett, Thomas Rosling.
The dealings of God with our nation. A discourse
delivered in Washington, D. C. on the day of humiliation
and prayer, June 1, 1865, by Rev. T. R. Howlett,
pastor of the Calvary Baptist church. Washington, D. C.,
Gibson brothers, printers, 1865.
cover-title, 7 p.   22 cm.
On the death of President Lincoln.

22586 Hubard, Edmund W
Speech of Edmund W. Hubard, of Virginia, on the
United States fiscal bank bill: delivered in the House
of representatives, August 4, 1841. Washington,
Printed by Blair and Rives, 1841.
37 p.   23 cm.

22587 Hubbard, George H
Eulogium on Thomas C. Brinsmade, M.D. Read before
the Rensselaer County medical society, by Geo. H.
Hubbard... Albany, Weed, Parsons & co., printers,
1869.
1 p.l., 238-246 p.   24 cm.

22588 Hubbard, William, 1621-1704.
A general history of New England, from the discovery
to MDCLXXX. By the Rev. William Hubbard... Second ed.,
collated with the original ms. ... Boston, Charles C.
Little and James Brown, 1848.

vi, [14], [7]-768 p.   23½ cm.
"Notes": p. [677]-768.

22589 Hudson, Charles, 1795-1881.
       History of the town of Lexington, Middlesex County,
       Massachusetts, from its first settlement to 1868, with
       a Genealogical register of Lexington families. By
       Charles Hudson... Boston, Wiggin & Lunt, 1868.
       xv, [16]-449, 296 p.   front., plates, ports., plan.
       24 cm.

22590 Hudson, Charles, 1795-1881.
       History of the town of Marlborough, Middlesex county,
       Massachusetts, from its first settlement in 1657 to
       1861; with a brief sketch of the town of Northborough,
       a genealogy of the families in Marlborough to 1800,
       and an account of the celebration of the two hundredth
       anniversary of the incorporation of the town. By
       Charles Hudson... Boston, Press of T. R. Marvin & son,
       1862.
       xvi, [13]-544 p., 1 l.   front., plates, ports.,
       plan.   23½ cm.

22591 Hudson, Charles Frederic.
       The imperative nature of duty. A discourse delivered
       in the Congregational church of Sycamore... May 30,
       1852, and repeated at Elk Grove, Sept. 11, 1853. By
       C. F. Hudson. Chicago, Fulton & co., printers, 1853.
       iv, [5]-19 p.   21½ cm.

22592 Hughes, Griffith, fl. 1750.
       The natural history of Barbados. In ten books. By
       the Reverend Mr. Griffith Hughes... London, Printed for
       the author, 1750.
       3 p.l., vii, [1], 314 (i.e. 313), 20 p.   front.
       (fold. map) 29 (i.e. 30) pl.   37 cm.

22593 Huish, Robert, 1777-1850.
       The public and private life of His late... Majesty,
       George the Third, embracing its most memorable incidents.
       and tending to illustrate the causes, progress, and
       effects, of the principal political events of his
       glorious reign. Comprising, also, a... historical
       memoir of the house of Brunswick... translated ex-
       pressly for this history, from the celebrated Latin
       work, entitled Origines Guelphicae... By Robert Huish...
       London, Printed for T. Kelly, 1821.
       2 p.l., ii, viii, 724 p.   6 pl., 11 port. (incl.
       front.)   27½ x 22 cm.

22594 Hull, William, 1753-1825, defendant.
Trial of Brig. Gen. William Hull, for neglect of duty
and un-officerlike conduct. Boston, Printed for Russell,
Cutler & co., 1814.
28 p.   21 cm.

22595 Hume, Hamilton.
The life of Edward John Eyre, late governor of Jamaica.
By Hamilton Hume. London, R. Bentley, 1867.
xvi, 320 p.   front. (port.)   19 cm.

22596 Humphrey, Heman, 1799-1861.
An address, delivered at the Collegiate institution
in Amherst, Ms. By Heman Humphrey, D.D., on occasion
of his inauguration to the presidency of that institution, Oct. 15, 1823. Boston, Printed by Crocker and
Brewster, 1823.
40 p.   21½ cm.
On education.

22597 Humphrey, Heman, 1799-1861.
Death of President Harrison. A discourse delivered
in the village church in Amherst, Mass., on the morning
of the annual state fast, April 8, 1841. By Heman
Humphrey... Amherst, J. S. and C. Adams, 1841.
24 p.   22 cm.

22598 Humphrey, Heman, 1799-1861.
The life and labors of the Rev. T. H. Gallaudet,
LL.D., by Rev. Heman Humphrey, D.D. New York, R. Carter
& brothers, 1857.
viii, [9]-440 p.   front. (port.)   illus., 2 pl.
19 cm.

22599 Humphrey, Heman, 1779-1861.
Memoir of Rev. Nathan W. Fiske, professor of
intellectual and moral philosophy in Amherst college;
together with selections from his sermons and other
writings. By H. Humphrey, D.D. Amherst, J. S. and
C. Adams; Boston, Phillips, Sampson and co.; [etc.,
etc.] 1850.
viii, [9]-392 p.   front. (port.)   19 cm.

22600 Humphreys, Andrew Atkinson, 1810-1883.
Report upon the physics and hydraulics of the
Mississippi river; upon the protection of the alluvial
region against overflow; and upon the deepening of the
mouths... Submitted to the Bureau of topographical
engineers, War department, 1861. Prepared by Captain

A. H. Humphreys and Lieut. H. L. Abbot... Philadelphia,
J. B. Lippincott & co., 1861.
xxiv, 17-456, clxvi p.   xx fold. pl. (incl. maps,
diagrs.) tables.   34 cm.

22601 Humphreys, David, 1689-1740.
       An historical account of the incorporated Society for
       the propagation of the gospel in foreign parts.
       Containing their foundation, proceedings, and the
       success of their missionaries in the British colonies,
       to the year 1728. By David Humphreys, D.D., secretary
       to the honourable society. London, Printed by
       J. Downing, 1730.
       xxxi, 356 p.   2 fold. maps.   20½ cm.

22602 Humphreys, David, 1752-1818.
       The miscellaneous works of Colonel Humphreys. New
       York, Printed by Hodge, Allen, and Campbell; and sold
       at their respective book-stores, 1790.
       348 p.   20½ cm.
       "An essay on the life of... Major-General Israel
       Putnam": p. [185]-330.

22603 Humphreys, David, 1752-1818.
       Poems by Col. David Humphreys, late aid-de-camp to
       His Excellency General Washington. 2d ed., with several
       additions. Philadelphia, Printed by Mathew Carey, 1789.
       1 p.l., 90 p., 1 l.   16½ cm.

22604 Humphreys, David, 1752-1818.
       A valedictory discourse, delivered before the Cincinnati
       of Connecticut, in Hartford, July 4th, 1804, at the
       dissolution of the society. By D. Humphreys...
       Published at the request of the society. Boston,
       Printed by Gilbert and Dean, 1804.
       60 p.   21½ cm.

22605 Humphreys, Edward Rupert, 1820-1893.
       America, past, present and prospective, a lecture,
       by E. R. Humphreys... To which are subjoined essays
       on the higher education of America and England, with an
       historical sketch of the Queen's colleges in Ireland.
       Newport, R. I., C. E. Hammett, jun., 1869.
       77 p.   21 cm.

22606 Hundley, Daniel Robinson, 1832-1899.
       Social relations in our southern states. By D. R.
       Hundley... New York, H. B. Price, 1860.
       vi, [7]-367 p.   19½ cm.

22607   Hunt, Charles Havens.
            Life of Edward Livingston. By Charles Havens Hunt.
        With an introduction by George Bancroft. New York, D.
        Appleton and company, 1864.
            xxiv, 448 p. incl. front.   port.   23 cm.

22608   Hunt, Cornelius E
            The Shenandoah; or, The last Confederate cruiser. By
        Cornelius E. Hunt... New York, G. W. Carleton & co.;
        [etc., etc.] 1867.
            273 p.   front.   19 cm.

22609   Hunt, Ezra M[undy] 1830-1894.
            Words about the war; or, Plain facts for plain people.
        By Ezra M. Hunt... New York, Printed by F. Somers,
        1861.
            39 p.   23 cm.

22610   [Hunt, Freeman] 1804-1858.
            Letters about the Hudson River. And its vicinity.
        Written in 1835 & 1836... By a citizen of New York.
        New York, F. Hunt & co.; Boston, Otis, Broaders & co.,
        1836.
            x, [11]-209 p.   16 cm.

22611   Hunt, Gilbert J
            The historical reader; containing "The late war between
        the United States and Great Britain from June, 1812,
        to February, 1815. In the scriptural style." Altered
        and adapted for the use of schools throughout the United
        States. By G. J. Hunt... 3d ed. With improvements
        by the author. New York, J. Tiebout & son, 1819.
            viii, [9]-233, [2] p.   17 cm.

22612   Hunt, Harriot Kesia, 1805-1875.
            Glances and glimpses; or, Fifty years social, including
        twenty years professional life. By Harriot K. Hunt...
        Boston, J. P. Jewett and company; New York, Sheldon,
        Lamport and Blakeman; [etc., etc.] 1856.
            xii, 418 p.   20 cm.

22613   Hunt, Richard Morris, 1828-1895.
            Designs for the gateways of the southern entrances to
        the Central park. By Richard M. Hunt... with a
        description of the designs, and a letter in relation to
        them, addressed to the commissioners of the park. New
        York, D. Van Nostrand, 1866.
            36 p.   col. front., col. plates, plans.
        30½ x 23½ cm.

22614 Hunter, William, 1774-1849.
         Oration pronounced before the citizens of Provindence,
         on the Fourth of July, 1826, being the fiftieth anniver-
         sary of American independence: by William Hunter. 2d
         ed. Providence, Smith & Parmenter, printers, 1826.
         46, [3] p.   23 cm.

22615 The hunter's guide, and trapper's companion. A complete
         guide in all the various methods by which to capture
         all kinds of game, fur animals &c. Also, full directions
         how to cure and tan all kinds of skins, &c. ... By an
         experienced woodsman. Hinsdale, N. H., Hunter & co.,
         1871.
         74 p.   15 cm.

22616 Huntington, Asahel, 1761-1813.
         A sermon, delivered at Topsfield January 5, 1800.
         Occasioned by the death of George Washington, commander
         in chief of the American armies, and late president of
         the United States. By Ashahel Huntington... Salem,
         Printed by Joshua Cushing, 1800.
         32 p.   20 cm.

22617 [Huntington, Dan] 1774-1864.
         Memories, counsels, and reflections. By an octogenary.
         Addressed to his children and descendants, and printed
         for their use... Cambridge [Mass.] Metcalf and company,
         1857.
         2 p.l., 119 p.   24 cm.

22618 Huntington, Elijah Baldwin, 1816-1877.
         A genealogical memoir of the Huntington family in this
         country: embracing all the known descendants of Simon
         and Margaret Huntington, who have retained the family
         name, and the first generation of the descendants of
         other names. By Rev. E. B. Huntington, A.M. Stamford,
         Conn., The author, 1863.
         xii, [9]-428 p.   front., ports.   23½ cm.

22619 Huntington, Elijah Baldwin, 1816-1877.
         History of Stamford, Connecticut, from its settlement
         in 1641, to the present time, including Darien, which
         was one of its parishes until 1820; by E. B. Huntington,
         A.M. Stamford, The author, 1868.
         4 p.l., 492 p.   front., plates, ports., map.   22 cm.

22620 Huntington, Elijah Baldwin, 1816-1877.
         Stamford soldiers' memorial, by Rev. E. B. Huntington...

156

Stamford, Conn., The author, 1869.
165, [1] p.   22 cm.

22621   Huntington, Enoch, 1739-1809.
A discourse, occasioned by the death of the Honorable
Jabez Hamlin, esq. who departed this life April 25th,
1791, ae. 82. Delivered on the ensuing Lord's day, to
the First church and society in Middletown. By Enoch
Huntington, A.M. pastor of said church and society...
Middletown, Printed by M. H. Woodward, 1791.
24 p.   19 cm.

22622   Hurd, Rollin Carlos, b. 1815.
A treatise on the right of personal liberty, and on the
writ of habeas corpus and the practice connected with it:
with a view of the law of extradition of fugitives. By
Rollin C. Hurd. Albany, W. C. Little & co., 1858.
xxvii, 677 p.   24½ cm.

22623   Hurlbut, Henry Higgins, 1813-1890.
A paper read at a family meeting of some of the
descendants... of Samuel Hurlbut... and his wife Jerusha
(Higgins) Hurlbut... held at Racine, Wis., September 20,
1860. By Henry Higgins Hurlbut. Racine, Wis., Printed
for the author, 1861.
22 p.   fold. geneal. tab.   22 cm.

22624   Huskisson, William, 1770-1830.
Substance of two speeches, delivered in the House of
commons... March, 1825. By the Right Hon. William
Huskisson, respective, the colonial policy, and foreign
commerce of the country. Baltimore, F. Lucas, jr.,
1826.
88 p.   22 cm.

22625   Hutchings, James Mason, 1820-1902.
Scenes of wonder and curiosity in California. Illustrated with over one hundred engravings. A tourist's
guide to the Yo-Semite valley... By J. M. Hutchings...
New York and San Francisco, A. Roman and company, 1870.
292 p.   front., illus.   22 cm.

22626   Hutchins, Levi, 1761-1855.
The autobiography of Levi Hutchins: with a preface,
notes, and addenda, by his youngest son... [Private ed.]
Cambridge [Mass.] Riverside press, 1865.
iv, 188 p.   front. (port.)   19 cm.
Contains genealogical notes of the descendants of William
Hutchins of Rowley, Mass., 1657.

157

22627 [Hutchinson, Thomas] 1711-1780, comp.
A collection of original papers relative to the
History of the colony of Massachusets-bay. Boston,
New England, Printed by Thomas and John Fleet, 1769.
1 p.l., ii, 576 p.   20½ cm.

22628 Hutchinson, Thomas, 1711-1780.
The representations of Governor Hutchinson and others,
contained in certain letters transmitted to England,
and afterwards returned from thence, and laid before the
General-assembly of the Massachusetts-Bay. Together with
the resolves of the two houses thereon. Boston, Printed
and sold by Edes and Gill, 1773.
1 p.l., ii, 3 -94 p.   18½ cm.

22629 Hutchinson, Thomas Joseph, b. 1820.
The Paraná; with incidents of the Paraguayan war,
and South American recollections, from 1861-1868. By
Thomas J. Hutchinson... London, E. Stanford, 1868.
xxvii, 424 p.   front., plates, ports., fold. map.
22 cm.

22630 Hutton, Matthew, successively abp. of York and Canterbury,
1693-1758.
A sermon preached before the incorporated Society for
the propagation of the gospel in foreign parts; at
their anniversary meeting in the parish church of
St. Mary-le-Bow, on Friday, February 21, 1745 [i.e.
1746] By the Right Reverend Father in God, Mathew,
lord bishop of Bangor. London, Printed by E. Owen, and
sold by J. Roberts [etc.] 1746.
74 p.   18½ cm.

22631 Hyde, Alvan, 1768-1833.
Memoir of Rev. Alvan Hyde, D.D., of Lee, Mass.
Boston, Perkins, Marvin, & co.; Philadelphia, H. Perkins,
1835.
xii, [13]-408 p.   front. (port.)   19 cm.

22632 Hyde, John, 1833-1875.
Mormonism: its leaders and designs. By John Hyde,
jun.... New York, W. P. Fetridge & company, 1857.
xii, [13]-335 p.   front., illus., plates, ports.
18½ cm.

22633 Hyde, William, 1806-1888.
An address, delivered at the opening of the new Town-
hall, Ware, Mass., March 31, 1847. Containing sketches
of the early history of that town, and its first settlers.

By William Hyde... Brookfield, Mass., Merriam and
Cooke, printers, 1847.
56 p.   24½ cm.

22634   Hyndman, William, b. 1842 or 43.
History of a cavalry company. A complete record of
Company "A", 4th Penn'a cavalry, as identified with
that regiment... in all the compaigns of the Army of
the Potomac, during the late civil war. By Capt.
William Hyndman. Philadelphia, J. B. Rodgers co.,
printers, 1870.
2 p.l., ix-xxiv, 25-343 p.   19 cm.

I

22635   Illinois. Supreme court.
Reports of cases argued and determined in the Supreme
court of the state of Illinois. [December term, 1832-
December term, 1843] By J. Young Scammon... Philadelphia, J. Kay, jun. & brother; Boston, C. C. Little &
J. Brown; etc., etc. 1841-44.
4 v.   22½-24 cm.

22636   Indian Creek and Jack's Knob coal, salt, lead, lumber, oil
and manufacturing company.
Prospectus... with a geological report on the lands
of the company, by Dr. J. S. Newberry, and the charter
and by-laws of the company. Cincinnati, Wrightson &
co., printers, 1866.
20 p.   22 cm.

22637   Indiana. State geologist.
Report of a geological reconnoisance [!] of the state
of Indiana; made in the year 1837, in conformity to an
order of the Legislature. By David Dale Owen, M.D.,
geologist of the state. Indianapolis, John C. Walker,
State printer, 1859.
69 p.   23 cm.

22638   The Intercourse of nations: being a collection of short,
correct and easy rules for reducing thirteen different
coins and currencies into each other, with a concise
method of calculating federal money. To which is
prefixed, a complete system of vulgar and decimal
fractions, &c. ... New York, Printed for the author,
by G. Forman, no. 46, Wall-street, opposite the Post

159

office, in the 20th year of American independence [1795]
    125, [1] p.   fold. tab.   21½ cm.

22639 Ireland, John B
    Wall-street to Cashmere. A journal of five years in Asia, Africa, and Europe: comprising visits, during 1851, 2, 3, 4, 5, 6, to the Danemora iron mines, the "Seven churches", plains of Troy, Palmyra, Jerusalem, Petra, Scringapatam, Surat; with the scenes of the recent mutinies (Benares, Agra, Cawnpore, Lucknow, Delhi, etc., etc.), Cashmere, Peshawur, the Khyber pass to Afghanistan, Java, China, and Mauritius. By John B. Ireland. With nearly one hundred illustrations, from sketches made on the spot by the author. New York, S. A. Rollo & co.; [etc., etc.] 1859.
    xviii, 13 -531 p.   col. fronts., plates, double map. 23½ cm.

22640 Ixtilxochitl, Fernando de Alva, ca. 1568-1648.
    ... Histoire des Chichimèques ou des anciens rois de Tezcuco, par don Fernando d'Alva Ixtlilxochitl, tr. sur le manuscrit espagnol... inédite. Paris, A. Bertrand, 1840.
    2 v.   21 cm.

J

22641 Jaboatão, Antonio de Santa Maria, 1695-1764?
    Novo orbe serafico brasilico ou Chronica dos frades menores da provincia do Brasil, por Fr. Antonio de Santa Maria Jaboatam. Impressa em Lisboa em 1761 e reimpressa por ordem do Instituto historico e geografico brasileiro... Rio de Janeiro, Typ. brasiliense de M. Gomes Ribeiro, 1858-62.
    5 v.   23 cm.

22642 Jack, Charles James, 1790?-1873.
    A political lecture upon the "influence of slavery on the Constitution and Union," delivered at the request of the citizens of Brooklyn, by C. J. Jack, esq., on... the 22d day of June, 1860, at the Musical hall, Brooklyn. Brooklyn, E. B. Spooner, steam book and job printer, 1860.
    17 p.   22 cm.

22643   Jackson, Albert, d. 1878, defendant.
        Official report of the trial of the Hon. Albert
        Jackson, judge of the Fifteenth judicial circuit,
        before the Senate, composing the High court of impeach-
        ment of the state of Missouri. Reported by Thomas J.
        Henderson. Jefferson City [Mo.] W. G. Cheeney, public
        printer, 1859.
          iv, [5]-480 p.   23 cm.

22644   Jackson, Andrew, pres. U.S., 1767-1845.
          Opinions of Gen. Andrew Jackson, on the annexation
        of Texas. [n.p., 1844]
          8 p.   24½ cm.
          "Letter of Hon. James K. Polk": p. 2-3; "Letter of
        Hon. Levi Woodbury": p. 3-8.

22645   Jackson, Francis, 1789-1861.
          A history of the early settlement of Newton, county
        of Middlesex, Massachusetts, from 1639 to 1800. With a
        genealogical register of its inhabitants, prior to
        1800. By Francis Jackson...   Boston, Printed by Stacy
        and Richardson, 1854.
          iv, 5-555, [1] p.   front. (port.) fold. map.   19 cm.

22646   Jackson, Henry, 1798-1863.
          An historical discourse, delivered in the Central
        Baptist meeting house, Newport, R. I., January 8th, 1854,
        by the pastor Henry Jackson...   Newport, R. I., Cranston
        & Norman, 1854.
          20 p.   23 cm.

22647   Jackson, James, 1777-1867.
          A memoir of James Jackson, jr., M.D., with extracts
        from his letters to his father; and medical cases,
        collected by him. By James Jackson...   Boston, Printed
        by I. R. Butts, 1835.
          3 p.l., [3]-444 p.   24½ cm.

22648   Jackson, James, 1777-1867.
          Memoir on the last sickness of General Washington and
        its treatment by the attendant physicians. By James
        Jackson, M.D. Boston, Priv. print., 1860.
          31 p.   19 cm.

22649   Jackson, James Caleb, 1811-1895.
          American womanhood: its peculiarities and necessities.
        By James C. Jackson...   3d ed. Dansville, N. Y.,
        Austin, Jackson & co.; New York, Baker, Pratt & co.
        [c1870]
          159 p.   front.   19 cm.

22650 Jackson, John Walker.
The Union - The Constitution - peace. A thanksgiving sermon, delivered in the Locust St. M. E. church, Harrisburg, Pa., by John Walker Jackson, pastor, August 6, 1863... Harrisburg, "Telegraph" steam book and job office, 1863.
33 p.   21½ cm.

22651 Jackson, Robert Edmund Scoresby, 1835-1867.
The life of William Scoresby... By his nephew, R. E. Scoresby-Jackson... London, Edinburgh, and New York, T. Nelson & sons, 1861.
3 p.l., [v]-ix, [9]-406 p.   front. (port.) col. plates, fold. map, diagrs.   19½ cm.

22652 Jackson, Samuel Cram, 1802-1878.
Religious principle - a source of public prosperity. A sermon delivered before Hie Excellency John Davis, governor, His Honor George Hull, lieutenant governor, the honorable Council, and the legislature of Massachusetts, at the annual election, on Saturday, January 7, 1843. By Samuel C. Jackson... 2d ed. Andover, W. Peirce, 1843.
32 p.   21½ cm.

22653 Jackson, Thomas, 1783-1873.
The centenary of Wesleyan Methodism: a brief sketch of the rise, progress, and present state of the Wesleyan Methodist societies throughout the world. By Thomas Jackson... New York, T. Mason & G. Lane, for the Methodist Episcopal church, 1839.
240 p.   front. (port.)   18½ cm.

22654 Jackson, Thomas, 1783-1873.
The life of the Rev. Charles Wesley... Comprising a review of his poetry; sketches of the rise and progress of Methodism; with notices of contemporary events and characters. By Thomas Jackson... London, J. Mason, 1841.
2 v.   front. (port.) facsim.   22½ cm.

22655 Jackson, William Ayrault, 1832-1861.
... Address, delivered at Albany, February 22, 1858, by the late Col. William A. Jackson, of the Eighteenth regiment of New York volunteers... presented as a memento of him to the officers and privates of the regiment, by their friend Professor Jackson. [Albany, 1863]

22656 Jacob, Stephen, 1756-1817.
A poetical essay, delivered at Bennington, on the anniversary of the 16th of August, 1777. By Stephen Jacob, A.B. 1778. Hartford, Printed by Watson and Goodwin, 1779.
8 p.   20½ cm..

22657   Jacob, William, 1762?-1851.
        An historical inquiry into the production and con-
        sumption of the precious metals. By William Jacob...
        London, J. Murray, 1831.
        2 v.   21½ cm.

22658   Jacobi, Eduard Adolf, 1796-1865.
        Dictionnaire mythologique universel, ou, Biographie
        mythique des dieux et des personnages fabuleux de la
        Grèce, de l'Italie, de l'Égypte... etc. Ouvrage
        composé sur un plan entièrement neuf, par le dᵣ E.
        Jacobi; traduit de l'allemand, refondu et complété par
        Th. Bernard. Paris, Firmin Didot frères, 1846.
        2 p.l., ii, 515 p.   19 cm.

22659   Jacobs, Bela, 1786-1836.
        Memoir of Rev. Bela Jacobs, A.M., compiled chiefly
        from his letters and journals, by his daughter. With a
        sketch of his character, by Barnas Sears... Boston,
        Gould, Kendall & Lincoln, 1837.
        vii, [9]-305 p.   front. (port.)   16½ cm.

22660   Jaeger, B[enedict]
        Class book of zoology: designed to afford to pupils
        in common schools and academies a knowledge of the
        animal kingdom: with a list of the different species
        found in the state of New York... By Prof. B. Jaeger.
        New York, D. Appleton & company; Philadelphia, G. S.
        Appleton, 1849.
        1 p.l., [5]-179 p.   illus.   16 cm.

22661   Jaeger, Benedict.
        The life of North American insects. By B. Jaeger...
        Assisted by H. C. Preston, M.D. With numerous
        illustrations, from specimens in the cabinet of the
        author. New York, Harper & brothers, 1859.
        xiv, [15]-319 p.   illus.   19 cm.

22662   Jagger, William.
        To the people of Suffolk, of all parties. By William
        Jagger. New York, Printed for the author, by Craighead
        & Allen, 1838.
        16 p.   23 cm.

22663   Jamaica. Assembly.
        To the king's most excellent majesty in council, the
        humble petition and memorial, of the Assembly of Jamaica
        (voted in Assembly on the 28th of December, 1774)
        [n.p., 1775]
        8 p.   20 cm.

22664   Jamaica. Laws, statutes, etc.
        An abridgment of The laws of Jamaica, being an alpha-
        betical digest of all the public acts of Assembly now
        in force, from the thirty-second year of King Charles II.
        to the thirty-second year of His present Majesty King
        George III [1681-1792] inclusive, as published in two
        volumes, under the direction of commissioners appointed
        by 30 Geo. III. cap. XX. and 32 Geo. III. cap. XXIV.
        The 2d ed. St. Jago de la Vega, Jamaica, Printed by
        A. Aikman, printer to the King's Most Excellent Majesty,
        1802.
        6 p.l., 240 p.   28½ x 22½ cm.

22665   James, Edwin.
        Oration delivered before the Young men's association
        of Brooklyn, N. Y., on the fourth of July, 1863. By
        Edwin James. New York, Baker & Godwin, printers, 1863.
        23 p.   22 cm.

22666   James, Edwin John, 1812-1882, ed.
        The Bankrupt law of the United States. 1867. With
        notes, and a collection of American and English decisions
        upon the principles and practice of the law of bank-
        ruptcy. Adapted to the use of the lawyer and merchant.
        By Edwin James... New York, Harper & brothers, 1867.
        v, [7]-325 p.   24 cm.

22667   James, George Payne Rainsford, 1801?-1860.
        The Old Dominion. By G. P. R. James. London, George
        Routledge and sons, limited, 1903.
        1 p.l., iv, 373 p.   19½ cm.

22668   James, George Payne Rainsford, 1801?-1860.
        Ticonderoga, or The Black Eagle. A romance of days
        not far distant. By G. P. R. James... New York, Harper
        & brothers, 1854.
        1 p.l., [5]-133 p.   24½ cm.

22669   James, Henry, 1811-1882.
        The social significance of our institutions: an
        oration delivered by request of the citizens at Newport,
        R. I., July 4th, 1861. By Henry James. Boston, Ticknor
        and Fields, 1861.
        47 p.   24 cm.

22670   James River and Kanawha company, Richmond.
        Annual report. Richmond, 1836-
        v.   map.   22½-24½ cm.
        Library has no. 4, 1838 (1839)

22671 James River company.
[Statement of the situation of the company from its commencement to the present day. Richmond? 1803?]
11 p.   20½ cm.
No t.-p. Title taken from text.

22672 James, Uriah Pierson, 1811-1889.
James' river guide: containing descriptions of all the cities, towns, and principal objects of interest on the navigable waters of the Mississippi valley... Illustrated with forty-four maps. Cincinnati, U. P. James, 1856.
128 p.   illus. (incl. maps)   22½ cm.

22673 James, William, d. 1827.
A full and correct account of the chief naval occurrences of the late war between Great Britain and the United States of America; preceded by a cursory examination of the American accounts of their naval actions fought previous to that period: to which is added an appendix; with plates. By William James... London, Printed for T. Egerton, 1817.
xv, [1], 528, ccxvi, [16] p.   pl.   22 cm.

22674 James, William, d. 1827.
The naval history of Great Britain, from the declaration of war by France in 1793, to the accession of George IV. By William James. A new ed., with additions and notes, and an account of the Burmese war and the battle of Navarino, by Captain Chamier... London, R. Bentley, 1847.
6 v.   fronts., illus., ports., fold. tables.
22½ cm.

22675 Jameson, Mrs. Anna Brownell (Murphy) 1794-1860.
Visits and sketches at home and abroad. With tales and miscellanies now first collected, and a new edition of the "Diary of an ennuyee." By Mrs. Jameson... New York, Harper & brothers, 1834.
2 v.   20½ cm.

22676 Jameson, John Alexander, 1824-1890.
The constitutional convention; its history, powers, and modes of proceeding. By John Alexander Jameson... 3d ed. Rev. and cor. Chicago, Callaghan and company, 1873.
xix, 561 p.   23½ cm.

22677 Jamestown, Va.
Report of the proceedings of the late jubilee at

Jamestown, in commemoration of the 13th May, the second
centesimal anniversary of the settlement of Virginia;
containing the order of procession, the prayer of Bishop
Madison, the orations; the odes and toasts; together
with the proceedings at Williamsburg on the 15th, the
day when the convention of Virginia assembled in the
old capitol, declared her independence and recommended
a similar procedure to Congress and to the other states.
Reported by the Select committee. Petersburg, Published
by William F. McLaughlin, and J. O'Connor, Norfolk,
1807.
    48 p.   21½ cm.

22678   Janeway, Thomas Leiper, 1805-1895.
    Memoir of the Rev. Jacob J. Janeway, D.D. By Thomas
L. Janeway, D.D. Philadelphia, Presbyterian board of
publication, 1861.
    iv, [5]-304 p.   front. (port.)   19 cm.
    "Funeral sermon, by the Rev. Charles Hodge, D.D.":
p. [277]-296.

22679   Janes, Frederic, b. 1808.
    The Janes family. A genealogy and brief history of
the descendants of William Janes the emigrant ancestor
of 1637, with an extended notice of Bishop Edmund S.
Janes, D.D., and other biographical sketches: by the
Rev. Frederic Janes... New York, J. H. Dingman, 1868.
    xiv, [15]-419 p.   front., photos, coat of arms.
24 cm.

22680   Jardine, David, 1794-1860.
    Criminal trials, supplying copious illustrations of
the important periods of English history during the
reigns of Queen Elizabeth and James I.; to which is
added a narrative of the gunpowder plot, with historical
prefaces and notes. By David Jardine... London, M. A.
Nattali, 1847-[5-?]
    2 v.   front. (v. 2) illus.   16½ cm.
    Contents. - I. Introduction. Memoir of Sir Nicholas
Throckmorton. Trial of Sir N. Throckmorton. Remarks.
Memoir of the Duke of Norfolk. Trial of the Duke of
Norfolk. Remarks. Introduction to the trial of Parry.
Trial of William Parry. Remarks. Memoir of the Earl
of Essex. Trial of Robert earl of Essex, and Henry
earl of Southampton. Confession and execution of the
Earl of Essex. Remarks. Introduction to the trial of
Sir Walter Raleigh. Trial of Sir Walter Raleigh. Sir
Walter Raleigh's inprisonment, voyage to Guiana, and
execution. Remarks. - II. Narrative of the gunpowder plot

22681   Jarnagin, Spencer, 1792-1853.
            Speech of Mr. Jarnagin, of Tennessee, on the treaty for
        the annexation of Texas. Delivered in the Senate of the
        United States, in executive session, June 6, 1844.
        [Washington, 1844]
            32 p.   25½ cm.

22682   Jarratt, Devereux, 1733-1801.
            The life of the Reverend Devereux Jarratt, rector of
        Bath parish, Dinwiddie county, Virginia. Written by
        himself, in a series of letters addressed to the Rev.
        John Coleman, one of the ministers of the Protestant
        Episcopal church, in Maryland. Baltimore, Printed by
        Warner & Hanna, 1806.
            1 p.l., iv p., 1 l., [5]-223 p.   16 cm.
        With this is bound the author's Thoughts on some
        important subjects in divinity. Baltimore, 1806.
        "To the reader" signed: John Coleman.

22683   Jarves, James Jackson, 1820-1888.
            The art-idea: sculpture, painting, and architecture
        in America. By James Jackson Jarves. 4th ed. New York,
        Hurd and Houghton, 1877.
            x, 381 p.   16 cm.

22684   Jarves, James Jackson, 1820-1888.
            History of the Hawaiian islands: embracing their
        antiquities, mythology, legends, discovery by Europeans
        in the sixteenth century, re-discovery by Cook, with
        their civil, religious and political history... by
        James Jackson Jarves. 4th ed. Honolulu, Henry M.
        Whitney, publisher, 1872.
            iv, [5]-242 p.   24 cm.

22685   Jarves, James Jackson, 1820-1888.
            Italian sights and papal principles, seen through
        American spectacles. By James Jackson Jarves... New
        York, Harper & brothers, 1856.
            2 p.l., [9]-382 p.   illus.   18½ cm.

22686   Jarvis, Edward, 1803-1884.
            Insanity among the coloured population of the free
        states. By Edward Jarvis... Philadelphia, T. K. &
        P. G. Collins, printers, 1844.
            15 p.   24 cm.
            Extracted from the American journal of the medical
        sciences for January, 1844.

22687   [Jarvis, Russell] 1791-1853.
            A biographical notice of Com. Jesse D. Elliott;

167

containing a review of the controversy between him and
the late Commodore Perry; and a history of the figure-
head of the U. S. frigate Constitution... By a citizen
of New York. Philadelphia, Printed for the author, 1835.
480 p. incl. diagrs.   18 cm.

22688   Jay, Sir James, 1732-1815.
A letter to the universities of Oxford and Cambridge,
&c., in respect to the collection that was made for the
colleges of New York and Philadelphia. By Sir James
Jay... being a vindication of the author, occasioned
by the groundless insinuations, and very illiberal
behaviour of Mr. Alderman Trecothick, with authentic
evidence... London, G. Kearsly [etc.] M.DC.LXXIV.
1 p.l., 20 p.   22 cm.

22689   [Jay, John] 1745-1829.
An address to the people of the state of New York, on
the subject of the Constitution, agreed upon at Philadelphia, the 17th of September, 1787. New York,
Printed by S. and J. London [1788]
19 p.   21½ cm.

22690   Jay, John, 1817-1894.
The American church and the African slave trade.
Mr. Jay's speech in the New York diocesan convention of
the Protestant Episcopal church. On the 27th September,
1860. With a note of the proceedings had in that council
on the subject. New York, R. Lockwood & sons, 1860.
30 p.   21½ cm.

22691   Jay, John, 1817-1894.
The great conspiracy. An address delivered at Mt.
Kisco... New York, on the 4th of July, 1861, the 86th
anniversary of American independence. By John Jay, esq.
New York, R. Lockwood & son; London, Trübner & co.,
1861.
50 p.   23 cm.

22692   Jay, John, 1817-1894.
New plottings in aid of the rebel doctrine of state
sovereignty. Mr. Jay's second letter on Dawson's
introduction to the Federalist... New York, American
news company; [etc., etc.] 1864.
54, viii p.   22 cm.

22693   [Jay, William] 1789-1858.
The Creole case, and Mr. Webster's despatch; with the
comments of the N. Y. America. New York, Pub. at the

office of the "New York American", 1842.
iv, [5]-39 p.   22½ cm.

22694   Jay, William, 1789-1858.
The life of John Jay: with selections from his
correspondence and miscellaneous papers. By his son,
William Jay... New York, J. & J. Harper, 1833.
2 v.   front. (port.)   23 cm.
Portrait wanting.

22695   [Jefferson, Thomas] pres. U.S., 1743-1826.
A summary view of the rights of British America.
Set forth in some resolutions intended for the inspection
of the present delegates of the people of Virginia. Now
in convention. By a native, and member of the House of
Burgesses. Williamsburg, Printed by Clementina Rind
[1774]
23 p.   19 cm.

22696   Jefferys, Thomas, d. 1771.
The American atlas; or, A geographical description
of the whole continent of America; wherein are delineated
at large, its several regions, countries, states, and
islands; and chiefly the British colonies, composed from
numerous surveys, several of which were made by order
of government. By Major Holland, Lewis Evans, William
Scull, Henry Mouzon, Lieut. Ross, J. Cook, Michael Lane,
Joseph Gilbert, Gardner, Hillock, &c. &c. Engraved on
forty-nine copper-plates, by the late Mr. Thomas
Jefferys... London, Printed by R. Sayer and Bennett,
1778.
2 p.l., 30 maps (29 double)   55½ cm.

22697   Jefferys, Thomas, d. 1771.
The natural and civil history of the French dominions
in North and South America. Giving a particular account
of the climate, soil, minerals, animals, vegetables,
manufactures, trade, commerce and languages, together
with the religion, government, genius, character,
manners and customs of the Indians and other inhabitants.
Illustrated by maps and plans of the principal places,
collected from the best authorities, and engraved by
T. Jefferys, geographer to His Royal Highness the
Prince of Wales... London, Printed for T. Jefferys,
1760.
2 pt. in 1 v.   fold. maps, fold. plans.   36 cm.

22698   [Jeffries, Thomas Fayette] b. 1829.
"Crippled Fayette," of Rockingham, detailing his times,

and giving his rhymes... Made helpless by the rheuma-
tism since the 20th of October, 1847... Mountain
Valley, Va., Printed at the office of J. Funk & sons,
1857.
187, [1] p.   14½ cm.
Verse and prose.

22699   Jéhan, Louis François, b. 1803.
Dictionnaire de linguistique et de philologie comparée.
Histoire de toutes les langues mortes et vivantes, ou
Traité complet d'idiomographie... Précédé d'un essai
sur le rôle du langage dans l'évolution de l'intelligence
humaine. Par L. F. Jéhan (de Saint-Clavien)... Paris,
S'imprime et se vend chez J.-P. Migne, éditeur, 1858.
1448 col.   27½ cm.

22700   Jekyll, Nathaniel.
The vindication of N. Jekyll, esq., late captain of
the 43d (or Monmouthshire) regiment; with a copy of the
proceedings of the general court martial held on
Colonel Stewart, of the same regiment; together with
the several memorials and letters addressed to His Royal
Highness the commander in chief, the Right Hon. the
secretary at war, and the judge advocate general, with
their answers... London, E. Lloyd, 1805.
1 p.l., [v]-xliv, 217, [1] p.   21½ cm.

22701   Jenkins, Charles Jones, 1805-1883.
Eulogy on the life and services of Henry Clay,
delivered at the request of the City council, in Augusta
Ga., Nov. 4, 1852. By Charles J. Jenkins. Augusta,
Ga., Steam power press of Chronicle & sentinel, 1853.
19 p.   23½ cm.

22702   [Jenkins, Edward] 1838-1910.
The coolie, his rights and wrongs. Notes on a journey
to British Guiana, with a review of the system and of
the recent commission of inquiry. By the author of
Ginx's baby." London, Strahan & co., 1871.
xii, 446 p.   illus. (incl. map)   20 cm.

22703   Jenkins, Geoffrey, pseud.
Legislative sketches from a reporter's note book.
B Geoffrey Jenkins, state capitals reporters. Albany,
Weed, Parsons & company, printers, 1866.
92 p., 1 l.   18 cm.

22704   Jenkins, John Stilwell, 1818-1852.
The generals of the last war with Great Britain. By

John S. Jenkins... Auburn, Derby, Miller & co.;
Buffalo, G. H. Derby & co., 1849.
xi, [13]-407 p.   5 port. (incl. front.)   20 cm.

22705   Jenkins, John Stilwell 1818-1852.
The life of John Caldwell Calhoun. By John S. Jenkins...
Auburn [N. Y.] J. M. Alden, 1850.
xiv, [15]-454 p.   front. (port.)   20½ cm.

22706   Jenkins, John Stilwell, 1818-1852.
Lives of the governors of the state of New York. By
John S. Jenkins... Auburn [N. Y.] Derby and Miller,
1851.
xxiv, [25]-826 p.   front., ports.   23½ cm.

22707   Jenkins, Warren.
The Ohio gazetteer, and traveler's guide; containing
a description of the several towns, townships and
counties, with their water courses, roads, improvements,
mineral productions... with an appendix, or general
register... rev. ed. By Warren Jenkins. Columbus,
I. N. Whiting, 1841.
xxiv, [51]-578 p.   fold. map at end.   19½ cm.

22708   Jenks, William, 1778-1866.
An eulogy, illustrative of the life, and commemorative
of the beneficence of the late Hon. James Bowdoin,
esquire, with notices of his family; pronounced in
Brunswick, (Maine) at the request of the trustees and
overseers of Bowdoin college, on the annual commencement, Sept. 2d, 1812. By William Jenks... Boston,
Printed by John Eliot, jun. 1812.
40 p.   26 x 21 cm.

22709   [Jerningham, Edward] 1737-1812.
Yarico to Inkle, an epistle. By the author of the
Elegy written among the ruins of an abbey. London,
Printed for J. Dodsley, 1766.
19 p.   24 cm.

22710   Jersey City. Charters.
Charters of and acts relating to Jersey City, and the
ordinances thereof; together with some statistical
information, &c. Jersey City, Southard & Post,
printers, 1844.
92, 80 p.   21½ cm.

22711   Jessup, William, 1797-1868.
Address delivered before the New York state agricultural

171

society at its sixteenth annual fair, held at Watertown,
October 3d, 1856. By Hon. William Jessup... Albany,
Fisk & Little, 1856.
23 p.   22½ cm.
Published by order of the society.

22712   Jevons, William Stanley, 1835-1882.
A serious fall in the value of gold ascertained, and
its social effects set forth... By W. Stanley Jevons...
London, E. Stanford, 1863.
2 p.l., 73 p.   tables (part fold.) 2 diagr. (incl.
front.)   22 cm.

22713   Jewitt, John Rodgers, 1783-1821.
A narrative of the adventures and sufferings, of John
R. Jewitt; only survivor of the crew of the ship Boston,
during a captivity of nearly three years among the
savages of Nootka sound: with an account of the manners,
mode of living, and religious opinions of the natives.
Embellished with a plate, representing the ship in
possession of the savages... Middletown [Conn.] Printed
by S. Richards, 1815.
204 p.   front.   18 cm.

22714   Jewitt, John Rodgers, 1783-1821.
A narrative of the adventures and sufferings, of John
R. Jewitt; only survivor of the crew of the ship Boston,
during a captivity of nearly three years among the
savages of Nootka sound: with an account of the manners,
mode of living, and religious opinions of the natives.
Embellished with a plate, representing the ship in
possession of the savages... Ithaca, N. Y., Andrus
Gaunfleet & co., 1851.
[1] pl., 2 p.l., [1]-166 p.   17 cm.

22715   Johns, John, bp., 1796-1876.
A memoir of the life of the Right Rev. William Meade,
D.D., bishop of the Protestant Episcopal church in the
diocese of Virginia. By the Right Rev. J. Johns, D.D.,
with a memorial sermon by the Rev. William Sparrow,
D.D. Baltimore, Innes & company, 1867.
vi p., 1 l., [v]-vi, [7]-537 p.   2 port. (incl.
front.)   19½ cm.

22716   Johnson, Alexander Bryan, 1786-1867.
A guide to the right understanding of our American
union; or, Political, economical and literary miscellanies... by A. B. Johnson. New York, Derby & Jackson;
Cincinnati, H. W. Derby & co., 1857.

vii, [9]-407 p.   19½ cm.
A collection of articles previously published by the
author in various periodicals.

22717   Johnson, Herrick, 1832-1913.
The banners of a free people set up in the name of
their God. A Thanksgiving sermon preached before the
First and Third Presb. congregations, in the First
Presbyterian church, Pittsburgh, Thursday, November 24,
1864. By Rev. Herrick Johnson... Pittsburgh, Printed
by W. S. Haven, 1864.
34 p.   23 cm.

22718   [Johnson, Samuel] 1696-1772.
Elementa philosophica: containing chiefly, Noetica, or
things relating to the mind or understanding: and Ethica,
or things relating to the moral behaviour. Philadelphia,
Printed by B. Franklin, and D. Hall, at the new-printing-
office, near the market, 1752.
4 p.l., vii-xxiv, 103 p., 1 l., vii, [1], 103 p.
19½ cm.

22719   Johnston, George Harvey, 1860-1921.
The heraldry of the Douglases; with notes on all the
males of the family, descriptions of the arms, plates
and pedigrees, by G. Harvey Johnston... Edinburgh and
London, W. & A. K. Johnston, limited, 1907.
x p., 1 l., [13]-96 p.   front. (col. coat of arms)
VIII col. pl.   26½ cm.

22720   Jones, Amanda Theodocia, 1835-
Poems. By Amanda T. Jones. New York, Hurd and
Houghton, 1867.
vi, [7]-203 p.   17½ cm.

22721   Jones, Anson.
Memoranda and official correspondence relating to the
republic of Texas, its history and annexation. Including
a brief autobiography of the author. New York, D.
Appleton and co., 1859.
1 p.l., 648 p.   front. (port.)

22722   Jones, Charles Colcock, 1831-1893.
Indian remains in southern Georgia. Address delivered
before the Georgia historical society, on its twentieth
anniversary, February 12, 1859, by Charles C. Jones, Jr.
Savannah, Press of J. M. Cooper & co., 1859.
25 p.   23½ cm.

22723 Jones, Edward Conway, 1820-1865.
       The harp of Sylva. By Edward C. Jones... Philadelphia,
       R. S. H. George, 1841.
       viii, [13]-218 p.   19 cm.

22724 Jones, William Alfred, 1817-1900.
       The Library of Columbia College. New York, 1861.
       41-61 p.   22 cm.
       Reprinted from The University Quarterly, April, 1961.

22725 Jordan, Ebenezer Stevens, 1819-1890.
       Death of Abraham Lincoln. A discourse delivered on
       the day of the national fast, June 1, 1865, at the
       Congregational church, Cumberland Center, Me. By Rev.
       E. S. Jordan... Portland [Me.] Printed by D. Tucker,
       1865.
       18 p.   24 cm.

22726 Josselyn, John, fl. 1630-1675.
       An account of two voyages to New-England, wherein you
       have the setting out of a ship, with the charges; the
       prices of all necessaries for furnishing a planter and
       his family at his first coming; a description of the
       countrey, natives and creatures, with their merchantil
       and physical use; the government of the countrey as it
       is now possessed by the English, &c. A large chronologica
       table of the most remarkable passages, from the first
       discovering of the continent of America, to the year
       1673. By John Josselyn, gent.... London, Printed for
       G. Widdows, 1674.
       4 p.l., 279 (i.e. 277), [3] p.   15 cm.

22727 Josselyn, John, fl. 1630-1675.
       New Englands rarities discovered in birds, beasts,
       fishes, serpents, and plants of that country. Together
       with the physical and chyrurgical remedies wherewith
       the natives constantly use to cure their distempers,
       wounds, and sores. Also a perfect description of an
       Indian squa, in all her bravery; with a poem not
       improperly conferrd'd upon her. Lastly a chronological
       table of the most remarkable passage in that country
       amongst the English... By John Josselyn, gent.
       London, Printed for G. Widdowes, 1672.
       2 p.l., 114 p.   illus.   15½ cm.

22728 Journal de la guerre du Micissippi contre les Chicachas,
       en 1739 et finie en 1740, le 1er d'Avril. Par un
       officier de l'armee de M. de Nouaille. Nouvelle York,
       isle de Manate, De la Presse Cramoisy de Jean-Marie

Shea, M.DCCC.LIX.
iv, [5]-92 p.   20½ x 15 cm.

22729   ... A journal of the expedition up the River St. Lawrence:
        containing a true and most particular account of the
        transactions of the fleet and army under the command of
        Admiral Saunders and General Wolfe, from the time of
        their embarkation at Louisbourg 'til after the surrender
        of Quebeck. By the sergeant-major of Gen. Hopson's
        grenadiers. Boston, Printed and sold by Fowle and
        Draper... 1759.
        (In The magazine of history with notes and queries.
        New York, 1913. 27 cm. Extra no. 24, p. [97]-113)

22730   Journal of the voyage of the sloop Mary, from Quebeck,
        together with an account of her wreck off Montauk Point,
        L. I., anno 1701. With introduction and notes by E. B.
        O'Callaghan. Albany, N. Y., J. Munsell, 1866.
        xvii p., 1 l., 50 p.   21 cm.

22731   Joutel, Henry, 1640?-1735.
        A journal of the last voyage perform'd by Monsr. de
        La Sale, to the Gulph of Mexico, to find out the mouth
        of the Mississippi River; containing an account of the
        settlements he endeavour'd to make on the coast of the
        aforesaid bay, his unfortunate death, and the travels
        of his companions for the space of eight hundred leagues
        across that inland country of America, now call'd
        Louisiana... till they came into Canada. Written in
        French by Monsieur Joutel... and translated from the
        ed. just pub. at Paris. With an exact map of that vast
        country, and a copy of the letters patents granted by
        the K. of France to M. Crozat. London, Printed for
        A. Bell etc. 1714.
        1 p.l., xii, [9], 205, [5] p.   fold. map.   19½ cm.
        French original published, Paris, 1713, under title:
        Journal historique du dernier voyage que feu M. de
        La Sale fit...

22732   Judd, Sylvester, 1789-1860.
        Thomas Judd and his descendants. By Sylvester Judd...
        Northampton, Printed by J. & L. Metcalf, 1856.
        112 p.   23 cm.

22733   Judge, Jonathan J   comp.
        The southern orator: being a collection of pieces in
        prose, poetry, and dialogue; designed for exercises in
        declamation, or for occasional reading in schools and
        families. By J. J. Judge... Montgomery, Printed by

Brittan and De Wolf, 1853.
vii, [9]-400 p.   20 cm.

22734 Juge, M   A
The American planter; or, The bound labor interest in
the United States. By M. A. Juge. New York, Long and
brother, 1854.
iv, [5]-42, [1] p.   20½ cm.
In defence of slavery.

K

22735 Kercheval, Samuel, 1786-1845?
A history of the valley of Virginia. By Samuel Kercheva.
Winchester [Va.] S. H. Davis, 1833.
iii -xlvi, [47]-486 p.   19 cm.
"The beginning, progress and conclusion of Bacon's
rebellion by T. M.   p. xxii-xlv.
"Notes on the settlement and Indian wars of the
western parts of Virginia and Pennsylvania" ... by
Joseph Doddridge: p. 148-157, [251]-410.
"Rev. Mr. Jacob's account of Dunmore's war," from his
Biographical sketch of the life of... Cresap: p. 157-187
"Report of C. J. Faulkner relative to the boundary
line between Virginia and Maryland": p. 215-233.
"The affecting history of the dreadful distresses of
Frederick Manheim's family": p. [411]-445.

22736 Kidder, Frederic, 1804-1885.
History of the Boston massacre, March 5, 1770;
consisting of the narrative of the town, the trial of
the soldiers: and a historical introduction, containing
unpublished documents of John Adams, and explanatory
notes, by Frederic Kidder. Albany, N. Y., J. Munsell,
1870.
2 p.l., 291 p.   front., double map.   23½ cm.

22737 Kimball, Emma Adeline, 1847-
The Peaslees and others of Haverhill and vicinity.
By E. A. Kimball. Haverhill, Mass., Press of Chase
bros., 1899.
72 p.   front., plates.   25 cm.

22738 [Knox, William] 1732-1810.
The controversy between Great Britain and her colonies
reviewed; the several pleas of the colonies, in support
of their right to all the liberties and privileges of

British subjects, and to exemption from the legislative
authority of Parliament, stated and considered; and
the nature of their connection with, and dependence on,
Great Britain, shewn, upon the evidence of historical
facts and authentic records. Boston, by Mein and
Fleeming at the London Book-Store, Kent Street, MDCCLXIX.
100 p.   20½ cm.

22739   Kortbondige beschryvinge van de colonie de Berbice...
Vervolgens een beschryving van de negers of slaven;
mitsgaders de staat der Europeanen, die zich aldaar
voorheen bevonden; en verder een beschryving van de
voornaamste producten, welke deeze colonie voortbrengt.
Verrykt met merkwaardige berichten wegens de onlangs
ontstaane en noch aanhondende opstand door de negers,
en de gesteldheid aldaar... Uit de aanteekeningen van
een voornaam heer opgemaakt, die eenige jaaren op de
colonie zyn verblyf gehouden beeft... 2. druk.
Amsteldam, S. J. Baalde, 1763.
3 p.l., 31 p.   pl., map.   21 cm.

22740   Kotzebue, Otto von, 1787-1846.
A new voyage round the world, in the years 1823, 24,
25, and 26. By Otto von Kotzebue... London, H. Colburn
& R. Bentley, 1830.
2 v.   front., 2 fold. maps, fold. plan.   19½ cmm.
"Review of the zoological collection of Fr. Eschscholtz":
v. 2, p. [325]-362.

22741   Kruzenshtern, Ivan Federovich, 1770-1846.
Voyage round the world, in the years 1803, 1804, 1805,
& 1806, by order of His Imperial Majesty Alexander the
First, on board the ships Nadeshda and Neva, under the
command of Capt. A. J. von Krusenstern... Translated
from the original German, by Richard Belgrave Hoppner...
London, Printed by C. Roworth for J. Murray, 1813.
2 v. in 1.   col. fronts., fold. map.   28 x 22 cm.
Original in Russian.

L

22742   Lacroix, Henry.
Opuscule sur le présent et l'avenir du Canada, par
Henry Lacroix. Montréal, En vente chez les principaux
libraires, 1867.
32 p.   21 cm.

22743   La Crosse and Milwaukee Railroad Company.
        Statement of the affairs of the La Crosse and
        Milwaukee Railroad Company, showing the cost of the
        road up to July 1, 1857, with a report of the Chief
        Engineer, showing the progress of the work, etc.,
        July 23, 1857. New York, Baker & Godwin, printers, 1857.
        28 p.   fold. front. (map).   24 cm.

22744   Lacy, B
        Miscellaneous poems compos'd at Newfoundland, on
        board His Majesty's ship the Kinsale. By B. Lacy,
        A.M., then chaplain to the said ship. London, The
        author, 1729.
        1 p.l., vi, 128 (i.e. 120) p.   20 cm.

22745   Ladd, Joseph Brown, 1764-1786.
        The literary remains of Joseph Brown Ladd, M.D.
        Collected by his sister, Mrs. Elizabeth Haskins, of
        Rhode Island. To which is prefixed, A sketch of the
        author's life, by W. B. Chittenden... New York, H. C.
        Slight, 1832.
        xxiv, [13]-228 p.   21 cm.
        Verse and prose.

22746   Ladies' industrial aid association, of Union hall, Boston.
        Report of the Ladies' industrial aid association,
        of Union hall, from July, 1861, to Jan. 1862. Boston,
        J. H. Eastburn's press, 1862.
        16 p., 1 l.   24 cm.

22747   Lafosse, J   F
        Avis aux habitans des colonies, particulièrement à
        ceux de l'isle S. Domingue sur les principales causes
        des maladies qu'on y éprouve le plus communément, & sur
        les moyen de les prevenir. Par J. F. Lafosse... Paris,
        Chez Royez, 1787.
        1 p.l., 8, 236 p.   21 cm.

22748   [Lafragua, José María] 1813-1875.
        Memorandum de los negocios pendientes entre Mexico y
        España, presentado al Exmo. Sr. ministro de estado por
        el representante de la república el dia 28 de julio de
        1857. Poissy, Tip. de Arbieu, 1857.
        2 p.l., 347 p.   23 cm.

22749   La gloire de s. Vrsvle, divisee en devx parties. La
        premiere contient l'histoire & martyre des onze mille
        vierges, auec quelques considerations là dessus. La
        deuxieme est vn abregé de la vie d'aucunes filles de

s. Vrsvle, signalées en sainteté. Recueillie par vn
pere de la Compagnie de Jesus. A Valentiennes, De
l'impr. de I. Bovcher, M.DC.LVI.
   8 p.l., 367 (i.e. 377), [3] p.   18½ cm.

22750 [La Grange de Chessieux, Gilbert Arnaud François Simon de]
      La conduite des François justifiée, ou Observations
      sur un écrit anglois, intitulé: Conduite des François
      à l'égard de la Nouvelle-Écosse... par le sieur D.L.G.D.C.
      ... A Utrecht, et se trouve a Paris, chez Le Breton,
      1756.
      viii, 256 p.   nar. 16½ x 10 cm.

22751 Lahontan, Louis Armand de Lom d'Arce, baron de, 1666-1715?
      Dialogues de Monsieur le baron de Lahontan et d'un
      sauvage, dans l'Amerique. Contenant une description
      exacte des moeurs & des coutumes de ces peuples sauvages.
      Avec les voyages du même en Portugal & en Danemarc,
      dans lesquels on trouve des particularitez trés curieuses,
      & qu'on n'avoit point encore remarquées. Le tout enrichi
      de cartes & de figures. Amsterdam, Veuve de Boeteman;
      et se vend a Londres, chez D. Mortier, 1704.
      222 p.   maps, 4 plates.   16 cm.

22752 Lamentations upon the never enough bewailed death of the
      Reverend Mr. John Reiner, pastor of the Church of Christ
      at Dover who was gathered to his fathers December 21,
      1676. [Boston? John Foster? 1676?]
      broadside.   25 x 30 cm.

22753 Lamon, Ward Hill, 1828-1893.
      The life of Abraham Lincoln; from his birth to his
      inauguration as president. By Ward H. Lamon...
      Boston, J. R. Osgood and company, 1872.
      xiv p., 1 l., 547 p.   front., plates, ports., plan,
      facsim.   23 cm.

22754 Lawson, Dodate, fl. 1693-1698.
      Threnodia, on a mournfull remembrance, of the much
      to be lamented death of the worthy & pious Capt.
      Anthony Collamore... on the 16 day of December 1693.
      Boston, Bartholomew Green, 1694.
      broadside.   28½ x 34½ cm.

22755 Lea, Albert Miller, 1807-1890.
      Notes on Wisconsin territory, with a map. By
      Lieutenant Albert M. Lea... Philadelphia, H. S. Tanner,
      1836.
      vi, [7]-53 p.   fold. map.   15 cm.

22756 Leake, Isaac Q
Memoir of the life and times of General John Lamb, an
officer of the revolution, who commanded the post at West
Point at the time of Arnold's defection, and his correspondence with Washington, Clinton, Patrick Henry, and
other distinguished men of his time. By Isaac Q. Leake.
Albany, J. Munsell, 1850.
x, 431 p.   front. (port.)   plans.   22½ cm.

22757 Le Clercq, Chrétien, fl. 1641-1695.
Nouvelle relation de la Gaspesie, qui contient les
moeurs & la religion des sauvages gaspesiens, Porte-Croix,
adorateurs du soleil, & d'autres peuples de l'Amerique
Septentrionale, dite le Canada. Dedie'e a Madame la
princesse d'Epinoy, par le pere Chrestien le Clercq,
missionnaire recollet... Paris, A. Auroy, 1691.
14 p.l., 572 p.   16½ x 9 cm.

22758 [Lee, Arthur] 1740-1792.
A true state of the proceedings in the Parliament of
Great Britain, and in the province of Massachusetts bay,
relative to the giving and granting the money of the
people of that province, and of all America, in the
House of commons, in which they are not represented.
London, printed: Philadelphia, Re-printed by Joseph
Crukshank, in Market-street, between Second and Third
streets, 1774.
39 p.   21 cm.

22759 Le Maire, Jacob, 1585-1616.
Iovrnal, & miroir de la navigation avstrale du vaillant
& bien renomme Seigneur Iaqves Le Maire, chef & con-
ducteur de deux navires Concorde & Horne. (In Herrera
[y Tordesillas], Antonio de. Description des Indes
Occidentales. Amsterdam, 1622. 29 cm. 2 p.l., p. [105]-
174)

22760 Leonard, Charles C
The history of Pithole: by "Crocus" (Chas. C. Leonard)
Pithole City, Pa., Morton, Longwell & co., 1867.
106 p.   illus.   18½ cm.

22761 Les Jesuites, marchants, usuriers, usurpateurs, et leurs
cruautes dans l'Ancient et le Nouveau continent. La
Haye, Chez les freres Vaillant, 1759.
viii, 388 p., 1 l.   16½ cm.

22762 Liberty, property, and no excise. A poem, composed on
occasion of the sight seen on the great trees, (so-called

180

in Boston, New England, on the 14th of August, 1765.
[Boston, 1765]
    broadside.   35½ x 47 cm.
    Refers to "Liberty Tree" in Boston, celebrated in
Thomas Paine's ballad, "Liberty Tree" and to the Stamp
Act crisis of 14 August 1765.

22763   The life, campaigns, and public services of General Mc-
Clellan. (George B. McClellan) The hero of western
Virginia [!], South Mountain [!] and Antietam [!]...
Philadelphia, T. B. Peterson & brothers [1864]
    1 p.l., [17]-184 p.   19½ cm.

22764   The life and public services of Hon. Abraham Lincoln, of
Illinois, and Hon. Hannibal Hamlin, of Maine. Boston,
Thayer & Eldridge, 1860.
    320 p.   front., ports.   19½ cm.

22765   Life of Luther C. Ladd, the first martyr that fell a
sacrifice to his country, in the city of Baltimore, on
the 19th of April, 1861, while bravely defending the
flag of the nation... Also, an account of the brilliant
naval engagement at Port Royal. By a citizen of
Alexandria... Concord [N. H.] P. B. Cogswell, printer,
1862.
    viii, [9]-40 p.   front. (port.)   22 cm.

22766   Lincoln, Abraham, pres. U.S., 1809-1865.
    Political debates between Hon. Abraham Lincoln and
Hon. Stephen A. Douglas, in the celebrated campaign of
1858, in Illinois; including the preceding speeches of
each, at Chicago, Springfield, etc.; also, the two great
speeches of Mr. Lincoln in Ohio, in 1859, as carefully
prepared by the reporters of each party, and published
at the times of their delivery. Columbus, Follett,
Foster and company; New York, W. A. Townsend & co.;
[etc., etc.] 1860.
    2 p.l., 268 p.   24 cm.

22767   [Lind, John] 1737-1781.
    Remarks on the principal acts of the Thirteenth
Parliament of Great Britain. By the author of Letters
concerning the present state of Poland... Vol. I.
Containing remarks on the acts relating to the colonies.
With a plan of reconciliation. London, Printed for
T. Payne, 1775.
    xvi, [4], 500 p.   22 cm.

22768 Liverpool, Robert Banks Jenkinson, 2d earl of, 1770-1828.
        The speech of the... Earl of Liverpool, in the House
        of lords... 1820, on a motion of the Marquis of Lansdown,
        "That a select committee be appointed to inquire into
        the means of extending and securing the foreign trade
        of that country." With an appendix, containing the
        official accounts referred to in the speech. London,
        J. Hatchard and son, 1820.
        1 p.l., 56, [4] p.   21½ cm.

22769 Liverpool, Robert Banks Jenkinson, 2d earl of, 1770-1828.
        Substance of the speech delivered in the House of lords,
        on the 15th of March, 1824, by the Earl of Liverpool, on
        the Marquess of Lansdowne's motion for the recognition
        of the independence of the late Spanish colonies in
        South America, by the British government. London, J.
        Murray, 1824.
        44 p.   22 cm.

22770 Lowell, Percival, 1571-1776.
        A funeral elegie (written many years since) on the
        death of the memorable and truly honourable John
        Winthrope Esq: Governour of the Massachusetts Colony in
        N-England... who died... March 26, 1649. [Cambridge,
        Mass., before 1665]
        broadside.   23 x 30 cm.

22771 Lyons, W   F
        Brigadier-General Thomas Francis Meagher: his political
        and military career; with selections from his speeches
        and writings. By Capt. W. F. Lyons. New York, D. & J.
        Sadlier & co.; Boston, P. H. Brady;   etc., etc. 1870.
        vi, [7]-357 p.   front. (port.)   18½ cm.

                                M

22772 Mably, Gabriel Bonnot de, 1709-1785.
        Observations sur le gouvernement et les loix des
        États-Unis d'Amérique. Par M. l'abbé de Mably. Paris,
        Volland, 1791.
        2 p.l., 199 p.   17 cm.

22773 Mably, Gabriel Bonnot de, 1709-1785.
        Remarks concerning the government and the laws of the
        United States of America: in four letters, addressed
        to Mr. Adams... From the French of the Abbé de Mably:

with notes, by the translator. London, Printed for J. Debrett, 1784.
  2 p.l., 280 p.   21 cm.

22774 McAlpine, William Jarvis, 1812-1890.
  Report made to the Water committee, of the Common council of the city of Brooklyn, April 15th, on supplying the city with water: by William J. McAlpine, civil engineer. Brooklyn, Printed by T. Van Anden, 1852.
  130 p., 1 l. incl. tables.   23 cm.

22775 McAnally, David Rice, 1810-1895.
  Life and times of Rev. William Patton, and annals of the Missouri conference. By Rev. D. R. M'Anally. St. Louis, Printed at the Methodist book depository, 1858.
  vi, 347 p.   19½ cm.

22776 McArthur, John, 1755-1840.
  Financial and political facts of the eighteenth century; with comparative estimates of the revenue, expenditure, debts, manufactures, and commerce of Great Britain, by John M'Arthur, esq. ... 3d ed., with an appendix of useful and interesting documents. The whole rev., cor., and considerably enlarged. London, J. Wright, 1801.
  xxiii, [1], 337, [19] p. incl. tables.   21½ cm.

22777 McCabe, James Dabney, 1808-1875.
  Substance of a discourse in St. Stephen's church, September 12th, 1858, before the Old defenders of Baltimore, by the Rev. J. D. McCabe... Printed by request, for private circulation only. Baltimore, Printed by J. Robinson, 1858.
  24 p.   22 cm.

22778 McCabe, James Dabney, 1842-1883.
  Life and campaigns of General Robert E. Lee. By James D. McCabe, jr. ... New York etc. Blelock & co.; Richmond, Va. [etc.] National publishing company, 1867.
  717 p.   front. (port.) fold. maps.   21 cm.

22779 McCabe, James Dabney, 1842-1883.
  The life and public services of Horatio Seymour; together with a complete and authentic life of Francis P. Blair, jr. By James D. McCabe, jr. New York, United States publishing company; Cincinnati, O., Jones brothers & co.; [etc., etc.] 1868.
  xiv p., 1 l., [17]-511 p.   2 front. (ports.)   23 cm.

22780 MacCabe, Julius P   Bolivar, comp.
        Directory of the city of Detroit, with its environs,
        and register of Michigan, for the year 1837. Containing
        an epitomised history of Detroit... &c. By Julius P.
        Bolivar MacCabe. Detroit, Printed by W. Harsha, 1837.
        2 p.l., [3]-114 p.   20 cm.

22781 McCaffery, Michael J   A
        The siege of Spoleto; a camp-tale of Arlington Heights,
        by Michael J. A. McCaffery, M.A. New York, P. O'Shea,
        1864.
        90, [4] p.   19 cm.
        Poem, in prose setting.

22782 McCaffrey, John, 1806-1881.
        Oration delivered at the commemoration of the landing
        of the Pilgrims of Maryland, celebrated May 16, 1842, at
        Mt. St. Mary's, Md., by Rev. John M'Caffrey... Gettys-
        burg, Printed by H. C. Neinstedt, 1842.
        32 p.   23½ cm.

22783 M'Caine, Alexander, 1768(ca.)-1856.
        The history and mystery of Methodist episcopacy, or, A
        glance at "the institutions of the church, as we received
        them from our fathers." By Alexander M'Caine...
        Baltimore, Printed by R. J. Matchett, 1827.
        v, [7]-76 p.   21 cm.

22784 McCall, Hext.
        An oration, delivered in St. Michael's church, before
        the inhabitants of Charleston, South-Carolina, on the
        Fourth of July, 1810. In commemoration of American
        independence. By appointment of the American revolution
        society, and pub. at the request of that society, and
        also of the South-Carolina state society of Cincinnati...
        By Hext M'Call... Charleston, Printed by W. P. Young,
        Franklin's head, no. 41, Broad-street, 1810.
        28 p.   19 cm.

22785 McCall, Hugh.
        The history of Georgia, containing brief sketches of
        the most remarkable events, up to the present day. By
        Capt. Hugh M'Call... Savannah, Seymour & Williams
        etc. 1811-16.
        2 v.   port., plans.   21½ cm.

22786 McCall, Peter, 1809-1880.
        Discourse delivered before the Law academy of Phila-

delphia, at the opening of the session, September 5,
1838. By P. M'Call... Philadelphia, Printed for the
Academy by W. F. Geddes, 1838.
51 p.   22 cm.

22787 M'Callum, Pierre Franc.
Travels in Trinidad during the months of February,
March, and April, 1803, in a series of letters, addressed
to a member of the imperial Parliament of Great Britain.
Illustrated with a map of the island. By Pierre F.
M'Callum... Liverpool, Printed for the author by W. Jones,
1805.
xvi, [9], 354 p.   front. (fold. map)   21½ cm.
Giving the author's personal experiences and impressions
of Gov. Picton's rule.
"A cursory view of the historical events in St. Domingo,
from the year 1790 till 1802": p. 313-331.

22788 MacCann, William.
Two thousand miles' ride through the Argentine provinces:
being an account of the natural products of the country,
and habits of the people; with a historical retrospect
of the Rio de la Plata, Monte Video, and Corrientes, by
William McCann... London, Smith, Elder & co.; [etc.,
etc.] 1853.
2 v.   col. fronts., plates, fold. map.   19½ cm.

22789 MacCarthy, Jacques, 1785-1835.
Choix de voyages dans les quatre parties du monde,
ou, Précis des voyages les plus intéressans, par terre
et par mer, entrepris depuis l'année 1806 jusqu'à ce
jour; par J. MacCarthy... Paris, Librairie nationale
et étrangère [etc.] 1821-22.
10 v.   front., plates, port.   20½ cm.

22790 M'Cartney, Washington, 1812-1856.
The origin and progress of the United States. By
Washington M'Cartney, esq. Philadelphia, E. H. Butler
& co., 1847.
xii, [13]-404 p.   19½ cm.

22791 M'Carty, John Mason.
A view of the whole ground: being the whole corre-
spondence between Mr. John M. M'Carty and General A. T.
Mason. District of Columbia, 1818.
2 p.l., [3]-38 p.   23 cm.
A personal controversy between the two men.

22792 McCarty, William, comp.
Songs, odes, and other poems, on national subjects; compiled from various sources. By Wm. McCarty... Philadelphia, W. McCarty, 1842.
3 v.   15 cm.

22793 [Macaulay, Zachary] 1768-1838.
Haïti, ou, Renseignemens authentiques sur l'abolition de l'esclavage et ses résultats à Saint-Domingue et à la Guadeloupe, avec des détails sur l'état actual d'Haïti et des noirs émancipés qui forment sa population. Traduit de l'anglais. Paris, L. Hachette, 1835.
2 p.l., iv, 207 p.   21 cm.

22794 Macauley, James.
The natural, statistical and civil history of the state of New York... By James Macauley. New York, Gould & Banks; Albany, W. Gould & co., 1829.
3 v.   tab.   22 cm.
The historical narrative extends only to 1800.
Indians of New York: v. 2, p. [161]-275.

22795 McCauley, James Andrew, 1822-1896.
Character and services of Abraham Lincoln: a sermon preached in the Eutaw Methodist Episcopal church, on the day of national humiliation and mourning, appointed by the President of the United States, Thursday, June 1, 1865, by Rev. Jas. A. McCauley. Baltimore, J. D. Toy, printer, 1865.
16 p.   22½ cm.

22796 M'Chesney, James.
An antidote to Mormonism; a warning to the church and nation; the purity of Christian principles defended; and truth disentangled from error and delusion. By James M'Chesney. Rev. by G. J. Bennet... New York, Pub. by the author, at the book store of Burnett & Pollard, 1838.
iv, [5]-60 p.   21 cm.

22797 M'Chord, James, 1785-1820.
National safety: a sermon, delivered in the legislative hall, before the hon. the Legislature of Kentucky... on Thursday, the 12th January, 1815: observed by them as a day of national fasting. By James M'Chord... Lexington, Ky., T. T. Skillman, 1815.
32 p.   21½ cm.

22798 McClellan, George, 1796-1847.
       A statement of facts. By George McClellan...
       Philadelphia, 1822.
       24 p.   21½ cm.
       Regarding the controversy caused by the author's
       review of Dr. Gibson's Reflections on the treatment of
       fractures of the thigh.

22799 McClellan, George Brinton, 1826-1885.
       The Army of the Potomac: Gen. McClellan's report of
       its operations while under his command. With maps and
       plans. New York, G. P. Putnam, 1864.
       1 p.l., p. 505-655.   maps, plans.   25 cm.

22800 McClellan, George Brinton, 1826-1885.
       ... Letter of the secretary of war, transmitting report
       on the organization of the Army of the Potomac, and of
       its campaigns in Virginia and Maryland, under the command
       of Maj. Gen. Beorge B. McClellan, from July 26, 1861, to
       November 7, 1862. Washington, Govt. print. off., 1864.
       1 p.l., 242 p.   23 cm.   (38th Cong., 1st sess.
       House. Ex. doc. 15)

22801 McClellan, George Brinton, 1826-1885.
       Oration by Gen. George B. McClellan. New York, C. S.
       Westcott & co., printers, 1864.
       31 p.   22½ cm.
       Oration delivered at the dedication of the Battle
       monument at West Point, and an address at Lake George,
       June 25, 1864.

22802 McClellan, George Brinton, 1826-1885.
       Report on the organization and campaigns of the Army
       of the Potomac: to which is added an account of the
       campaign in western Virginia, with plans of battle-fields.
       By George B. McClellan... New York, Sheldon & company,
       1864.
       480 p.   4 maps (incl. fold. front.)   23½ cm.

22803 McClellan, George Brinton, 1826-1885.
       ... West Point oration, by Gen. George B. McClellan.
       [New York, 1864]
       8 p.   22 cm.
       General McClellan's letter of acceptance: p. 7-8.

22804 M'Clellan, Rolander Guy.
       Republicanism in America: a history of the colonial
       and republican governments of the United States of America,

from the year 1607 to the year 1869. To which is added
constitutions, proclamations, platforms, resolutions,
platforms, resolutions, decisions of courts, laws...
Also, a brief history of all the existing republics of
the world... By R. Guy M'Clellan. San Francisco, R. J.
Trumball & co.; [etc., etc.] 1869.
xii, [13]-665 p. incl. front. ports. 23½ cm.

22805 McClellan's campaign. Reprinted from the World of August 7,
1862... New York, A. D. F. Randolph, 1862.
12 p. 19 cm.
A defence of General McClellan.

22806 [McClenthen, Charles S   ] b. 1827.
Narrative of the fall & winter campaign, by a private
soldier of the 2nd div. 1st army corps, containing a
detailed description of the "battle of Fredericksburg,"
at the portion of the line where the 2nd div. were
engaged. With accurate statements of the loss in killed,
wounded and missing, in each regiment. Syracuse,
Masters & Lee, printers, 1863.
53 p. 17½ cm.

22807 M'Clintock, Sir Francis Leopold, 1819-1907.
... Meteorological observations in the Arctic seas.
By Sir Francis Leopold McClintock, R. N., made on board
the Arctic searching yacht "Fox", in Baffin bay and Prince
Regent's inlet, in 1857, 1858, and 1859. Reduced and
discussed, at the expense of the Smithsonian institution.
By Charles A. Schott... [Washington, Smithsonian institution, 1862]
xii, 5, 146 p. chart, diagrs. 32½ cm. (Smithsonian contributions to knowledge. [vol. XIII, art. 3])

22808 McClintock, John, 1814-1870.
Discourse delivered on the day of the funeral of
President Lincoln, Wednesday, April 19, 1865, in St.
Paul's church, New York, by John McClintock... Reported
by J. T. Butts. New York, Press of J. M. Bradstreet &
son, 1865.
35 p. 23½ cm.

22809 Macclintock, Samuel, 1732-1804.
An oration, commemorative of the late illustrious
General Washington; pronounced at Greenland, February
22d, 1800; according to a recommendation of the Congress
of the United States. By Samuel Macclintock, D.D.
Portsmouth, N. H., Printed at the United States' oracle-

office, by Charles Peirce, 1800.
16 p.   20½ cm.

22810 Macclintock, Samuel, 1732-1804.
A sermon preached before the honorable the Council, and
the honorable the Senate, and House of representatives,
of the state of New Hampshire, June 3, 1784. On occasion
of the commencement of the new constitution and form of
government. By Samuel McClintock, A. M. Portsmouth,
New Hampshire, Printed by Robert Gerrish, 1784.
47 p.   23½ cm.

22811 McClung, John W
Minnesota as it is in 1870. Its general resources
and attractions... with special descriptions of all its
counties and towns... By J. W. McClung...   St. Paul
The author, 1870.
299, [1] p.   front. (map)   illus.   18 cm.

22812 M'Clure, Alexander Wilson.
The life of John Cotton. By A. W. M'Clure...   Boston,
Massachusetts Sabbath school society, 1846.
xii, [13]-300 p.   19 cm.

22813 M'Clure, Alexander Wilson, 1808-1865.
The lives of John Wilson, John Norton, and John Davenport. By A. W. M'Clure...   Boston, Massachusetts Sabbath
school society, 1846.
vi, [7]-305 p.   19 cm.

22814 McClure, David, 1748-1820.
A discourse; commemorative of the death of General
George Washington, first president of the United States
of America... Delivered at East-Windsor, Connecticut,
February 22, 1800. By David M'Clure... East-Windsor,
Printed by Luther Pratt, March 24th, 1800.
23 p.   22½ cm.

22815 McClure, David, 1748-1820.
Memoirs of the Rev. Eleazar Wheelock, D.D., founder
and president of Darthmouth college and Moor's charity
school; with a summary history of the college and school.
To which are added, copious extracts from Dr. Wheelock's
correspondence. By David McClure... and Elijah Parish...
Newburyport, Published by Edward Little & co., and sold
at their book store, Market square, C. Norris & co.,
printers, 1811.
vii, [9]-336 p.   front. (port.)   23½ cm.

22816   McClure, Sir [Robert John Le Mesurier] 1807-1873.
            The north-west passage. Capt. M'Clure's despatches
        from Her Majesty's discovery ship, "Investigator," off
        Point Warren and Cape Bathurst. London, J. Betts, 1853.
            48 p.   fold. map.   23 cm.

22817   Maclure, William, 1763-1840.
            Observations on the geology of the United States of
        America; with some remarks on the effect produced on the
        nature and fertility of soils, by the decomposition of
        the different classes of rocks; and an application to
        the fertility of every state in the Union, in reference to
        the accompanying geological map... By William Maclure.
        Philadelphia, Printed for the author by A. Small, 1817.
            ix, [10]-127, [2] p.   front. (fold. map) fold. pl.
        21 cm.

22818   McClure, William James, 1842-
            Poems. By William James McClure. New York, P. O'Shea,
        1869.
            1 p.l., vii, [9]-148, [1] p.   19½ cm.

22819   Maclure, William, 1763-1840.
            Observations on the geology of the West India Islands,
        from Barbadoes to Santa Cruz, inclusive. By William
        Maclure. New Harmony, Ind., Printed for the author,
        1832.
            17 p.   21 cm.

22820   [Maclure, William] 1763-1840.
            To the people of the United States. Philadelphia,
        1807.
            1 p.l., 2 p., 1 l., 3, [1], [9]-145 p. incl. fold.
        tables.   21 cm.

22821   Maclurian lyceum, Philadelphia.
            Contributions of the Maclurian lyceum to the arts and
        sciences. v. 1, no. 1-3; Jan. 1827-Jan. 1829. Phila-
        delphia, Sold for the Maclurian lyceum by J. Dobson;
        [etc., etc.] 1827-29.
            84 p.   plates (partly col.)   22 cm.

22822   M'Collum, William S
            California as I saw it... Pencillings by way of its
        gold and gold diggers! And incidents of travel by land
        and water. By William S. M'Collum... Buffalo, G. H.
        Derby & co., 1850.
            iv, [5]-72 p.   22½ cm.

22823 [Macomb, Alexander] 1782-1841.
    Pontiac; or, The siege of Detroit. A drama, in three
acts. Boston, S. Colman, 1835.
    60 p.   19½ cm.

22824 Macomb, Alexander, 1782-1841.
    The practice of courts martial. By Alexander Macomb...
New York, S. Colman, 1840.
    1 p.l., [vii]-x p., 1 l., 13-154 p.   24 cm.

22825 Macomb, Alexander, 1782-1841.
    A treatise on martial law, and courts-martial; as
practised in the United States of America. Pub. by order
of the United States military philosophical society. By
Alexander Macomb... Charleston, S. C., J. Hoff, 1809.
    2 p.l., [3]-6, [5]-340 p.   21 cm.

22826 [Macomb, Robert]
    A reply to the resolutions and address of a meeting
convened at Martlings, in the city of New York, February
4, 1811. Containing, the proceedings of the Committee
of safety, of '76, against Mangle Minthorne, chairman of
that meeting. By a Whig of '76. New York, Printed by
Henry C. Southwick, 1811.
    11 p.   25 cm.

22827 M'Connell, Matthew.
    An essay on the domestic debts of the United States of
America. Giving an account of the various kinds of
public securities, and generally in what manner the
debts arose: with the provision made and proposed for
payment of the interest and principal thereof by federal
measures, and of those adopted by individual states. To
which is subjoined, A statement of the foreign debt, as
set forth by the United States in Congress assembled, in
their address and recommendations of the 18th of April,
1783. By Matthew M'Connell. Philadelphia, Printed and
sold by Robert Aitken, at Pope's Head in Market street,
1787.
    iv p., 1 l., 90 p.   22½ cm.

22828 McCord, Thomas.
    Synopsis of the changes in the law effected by the
Civil code of Lower Canada. By T. McCord... Ottawa,
G. E. Desbarats, printer, 1866.
    39 p.   24½ cm.

22829 McCorkle, John, 1838-
    Three years with Quantrell; a true story, told by his

scout John McCorkle, written by O. S. Barton. Armstrong,
Mo., Armstrong herald print [c1914]
    157 p.   front., ports.   24½ cm.

22830 M'Cormick, Charles, 1755?-1807.
    Memoirs of the Right Honourable Edmund Burke; or,
An impartial review of his private life, his public
conduct... interspersed with a variety of curious
anecdotes, and extracts from his secret correspondence...
By Charles M'Cormick. LL.B. London, For the author,
1797.
    383 p.   front. (port.)   28 cm.

22831 McCoskry, Samuel Allen, bp., 1804-1886.
    Trust in God the strength of a nation. A sermon
preached in St. Paul's church, Detroit, on the day of the
national fast, January 4, 1861, by the Rt. Rev. Sam'l
A. McCoskry... Pub. by request of the Vestry of the
church. Detroit, Free press book and job printing house,
1861.
    16 p.   22½ cm.

22832 McCoun, William T
    Address, delivered before the Queen's County agricul-
tural society, at its first anniversary, at Hempstead,
October 13th, 1842, by William T. McCoun. New-York,
Vinten, printer, 1843.
    16 p.   23 cm.

22833 McCoy, A   D   b. 1813.
    Thoughts on labor in the South, past, present and
future, by A. D. McCoy... New Orleans, Blelock & co.,
1865.
    viii p., 2 l., [13]-35 p.   19½ cm.

22834 McCoy, Amasa.
    Funeral oration on the death of Hon. Daniel Webster,
delivered at a commemoration in the Presbyterian church,
Ballston Spa, N. Y.... November 8, 1852, by Prof.
Amasa McCoy. [2d ed.] Boston, C. C. P. Moody, printer,
1853.
    29 p.   22½ cm.

22835 McCrea, Robert Barlow.
    Lost amid the fogs: sketches of life in Newfoundland,
England's ancient colony. By Lieut.-Col. R. B. McCrea...
London, S. Low, son & Marston, 1869.
    xv, 299 p.   col. front.   21 cm.

22836 McCready, Benjamin William, 1813-1892.
        Memoir of John A. Swett, M.D.... By W. W. M'Cready,
        M.D. Read before the N. Y. medical and surgical society,
        and published by its order. New York, D. Appleton and
        company, 1855.
        36 p.   23½ cm.

22837 McCulloch, Hugh, 1808-1895.
        Our national and financial future. Address of Hon.
        Hugh McCulloch, secretary of the Treasury, at Fort Wayne,
        Indiana, October 11, 1865. Fort Wayne, 1865.
        16 p.   23½ cm.

22838 McCulloch, John Ramsay, 1789-1864.
        A dictionary, geographical, statistical, and historical,
        of the various countries, places, and principal natural
        objects in the world. Illustrated with maps. By J. R.
        McCulloch... A new ed. rev., with a supplement...
        London, Longman, Brown, Green, and Longmans, 1854.
        2 v.   fold. fronts., fold. maps.   22 cm.

22839 [McCulloch, John Ramsay] 1789-1864.
        Outlines of political economy: being a republication
        of the article upon that subject contained in the Edinburgh
        Supplement to the Encyclopedia britannica. Together with
        notes explanatory and critical, and a summary of the
        science. By Rev. John M'Vickar... New York, Wilder &
        Campbell, 1825.
        2 p.l., vi, [7]-188 p.   22½ cm.

22840 [McCulloh, James Haines] 1793?-1870.
        Researches on America; being an attempt to settle some
        points relative to the aborigines of America, &c. ...
        By an officer of the United States' army. Baltimore,
        Published by Coale and Maxwell, 1816.
        1 p.l., 130 p., 1 l.   1 illus.   22½ cm.

22841 McCulloh, Richard Sears.
        The proceedings of the late director of the mint, in
        relation to the official misconduct of Franklin Peale,
        esq., chief coiner, and other abuses in the mint.
        Reviewed by Prof. R. S. McCulloh... Princeton, N. J.,
        1853.
        79 p.   23 cm.

22842 McDaniel, Samuel W
        An address delivered at the funeral of Capt. William F.
        Brigham, in Feltonville, Mass., Feb. 18, 1865, by Samuel

W. McDaniel... Feltonville, C. A. Wood, printer, 1865.
19 p.   22½ cm.
Brigham was a captain in the 36th Massachusetts infantry
regiment.

22843 M'Donald, Alexander, L.R.C.S.E.
A narrative of some passages in the history of Eenoolova-
pik, a young Esquimaux, who was brought to Britain in
1839, in the ship "Neptune" of Aberdeen: an account of
the discovery of Hogarth's Sound: remarks on the
northern whale fishery, and suggestions for its improvement, &c., &c. By Alexander M'Donald... Edinburgh,
Fraser & co. [etc.] 1841.
2 p.l., iii, 149 p.   front. (port.) fold. map.,
fold. facsim.   20 cm.

22844 MacDonald, James Madison, 1812-1876.
President Lincoln; his figure in history: a discourse
delivered in the First Presbyterian church, Princeton,
New Jersey, June 1st, 1865. By James M. MacDonald, D.D.
New York, C. Scribner & co., 1865.
23 p.   23½ cm.

22845 MacDonald, James Madison, 1812-1876.
A sketch of the history of the Presbyterian church,
in Jamaica, L. I. By James M. Macdonald... New York,
Leavitt, Trow & co., printers, 1847.
138 p.   19 cm.

22846 M'Dougall, George Frederick.
The eventful voyage of H. M. discovery ship "Resolute"
to the Arctic regions, in search of Sir John Franklin
and the missing crews of H. M. discovery ships "Erebus"
and "Terror," 1852, 1853, 1854... By George F. M'Dougall...
London, Longman, Brown, Green, Longmans, & Roberts, 1857.
xl, 530 p.   col. front., illus., col. plates, fold.
map.   22½ cm.

22847 McDougall, James Alexander, 1817-1867.
French interference in Mexico. Speech of Hon. J. A.
McDougall, of California, in the Senate of the United
States, on Tuesday, February 3d, 1863. Baltimore,
Printed by J. Murphy & co., 1863.
30 p.   23½ cm.

22848 McDowell, Irvin, 1818-1885.
Statement of Major Gen. Irvin McDowell, in review of
the evidence before the court of inquiry, instituted at

his request in special orders, no. 353, headquarters of
the army. Washington, Printed by L. Towers & co., 1863.
cover-title, 64 p.   23 cm.

22849 McDowell, James, 1796-1851.
Address delivered before the Alumni association of the
college of New Jersey. September 26, 1838. By James
M'Dowell... Princeton, J. Bogart [1838]
51 p.   23½ cm.

22850 Macduff, John Ross, 1818-1895.
The soldier's text-book; or, Confidence in time of
war. By J. R. Macduff... Boston, American tract society
186-?
48, 16 p.   13½ cm.
"Hymns": 16 p. at end.

22851 McDuffie, George, 1790-1851.
Defence of a liberal construction of the powers of
Congress, as regards internal improvement, etc. with a
complete refutation of the ultra doctrines respecting
consolidation and state sovereignty. Written by George
M'Duffie, esq. in the year 1821. Over the signature of
"One of the people." To which are prefixed an encomiastic
advertisement of the work by Major (now Governor) Hamilton,
and a preface by the editor... Philadelphia, Printed
by L. R. Bailey, 1831.
1 p.l., 22 p.   21½ cm.

22852 McDuffie, George, 1790-1851.
A eulogy upon the life and character of the late Hon.
Robert Y. Hayne: delivered on the 13th February, 1840,
at the Circular church, by appointment of the citizens
of Charleston. By George M'Duffie... Charleston,
Printed by W. Riley, 1840.
xv, [17]-63 p.   22½ cm.

22853 [McDuffie, George] 1790-1851.
Speech, in the House of representatives of the U.S.
on the woollens' bill. February 7, 1827. Washington,
Gales & Seaton, 1827.
19 p.   18 cm.

22854 McDuffie, George, 1790-1851.
Speech of Mr. McDuffie, on the proposed amendment to
the Constitution of the United States, respecting the
election of president and vice president. In the House
of representatives, Feb. 15, 16, 1826. [Washington,

1826]
43 p.   18 cm.

22855 McDuffie, George, 1790-1851.
       Speech of Mr. M'Duffie, on the proposition to clear the
       galleries during the election of President by the House
       of representatives: maintaining the obligation of the
       representatives: maintaining the obligation of the
       representatives to conform to the will of the people in
       making that election. Washington, Printed at the Columbian
       office, 1825.
       24 p.   24 cm.

22856 McDuffie, George, 1790-1851.
       Speech of Mr. M'Duffie, on the subject of the removal
       of the deposites, December 19, 1833. [Washington, 1833?]
       16 p.   24½ cm.

22857 M'Elhiney, Thomas.
       Life of Martin Van Buren, by Thomas M'Elhiney.
       Pittsburgh, Printed by J. T. Shryock, 1853.
       126 p.   23 cm.

22858 McElligott, James Napoleon, 1812-1866.
       The American debater: being a plain exposition of the
       principles and practice of public debate... By James N.
       McElligott... New York, Ivison & Phinney; Chicago, S. C.
       Griggs & co.; [etc., etc.] 1855.
       viii, [9]-312 p.   front. (port.)   19 cm.

22859 MacEl'rey, Joseph H
       The substance of two discourses, occasioned by the
       national bereavement, the assassination of the President,
       the position, the lesson, and the duty of the nation.
       Delivered in the St. James Episcopal church, Wooster,
       Ohio, Easter day, 1865, by the rector, Rev. J. H.
       MacEl'rey... Wooster, O., Republican steam power press,
       1865.
       24 p.   19½ cm.

22860 McEwen, Abel, 1780-1860.
       A sermon preached at the anniversary election,
       Hartford, May 8, 1817. By Abel McEwen, pastor of a
       church in New London. Hartford, George Goodwin & sons,
       printers, 1817.
       22 p.   23½ cm.

22861 McEwen, Abel, d. 1860.
       A sermon preached at the funeral of Gen. Jedediah

Huntington, of New London, who died September 25, 1818;
aged 75 years. By Abel McEwen... New York, Printed by
D. Fanshaw, 1818.
16 p. 23½ cm.

22862 McEwen, Abel, 1780-1860.
A sermon, preached in the First Congregational church,
New London, Conn., on the day of Thanksgiving, November 28,
1850. By Abel M'Ewen... New London, Daniels & Bacon,
1851.
16 p. 23 cm.
Discusses the Fugitive slave law.

22863 M'Ewen, R   S
The mysteries, miseries, and rascalities of the Ohio
penitentiary, from the 18th of May 1852, to the close of
the administration of J. B. Buttles. By R. S. M'Ewen...
Columbus, J. Geary, son & co., printers, 1856.
75 p. incl. illus., plates.   21½ cm.

22864 M'Ewen, John Alexander.
An address delivered at the laying of the corner stone
of the University of Nashville, on the 7th of April,
1853. By John A. M'Ewen, A.M. Nashville, Tenn.,
J. T. S. Fall, printer, 1853.
32 p. 23 cm.

22865 M'Farland, Asa, 1769-1827.
An oration, pronounced before the society of the Phi
beta kappa, at their anniversary at Hanover, August 25,
1802. By Rev. Asa M'Farland, A.M. Hanover, Printed by
Moses Davis, 1802.
24 p. 18½ cm.

22866 McFarland, Asa, 1769-1827.
A sermon, preached at Concord, before His Excellency
the Governor, the honorable Council, Senate, and House
of representatives, of the state of New-Hampshire,
June 2, 1808. By the Rev. Asa M'Farland, A.M., pastor
of the church in Concord. Concord, Printed by George
Hough, for the honorable General court, 1808.
30 p. 22 cm.

22867 Macfarland, William H
An address on the life, character and public services,
of the late Hon. Benjamin Watkins Leigh, delivered
before the Virginia historical society... By William H.
Macfarland, esq. Pub. by the society. January, 1851.
12 p. 21 cm.

22868   MacFarlane, Charles, 1799-1858.
        The lives and exploits of banditti and robbers in all
        parts of the world. By C. MacFarlane... New York, J. &
        J. Harper, 1833.
        2 v.   21 cm.

22869   [MacFarlane, Robert] 1734-1804.
        The history of the first ten years of the reign of
        George the Third... from his accession to the throne, in
        1760, to the conclusion of the third session of the
        thirteenth Parliament of Great Britain, in 1770; to
        which is prefixed, a review of the war, which was
        terminated by the peace of Paris, in 1763. 2d ed. ...
        London, Printed for the author, and sold by T. Evans,
        1783.
        1 p.l., 402 p.   21½ cm.

22870   Macfarlane, Robert, 1815-1863.
        History of propellers and steam navigation with biogra-
        phical sketches of the early inventors, by Robert Mac-
        farlane. New York, G. P. Putnam, 1851.
        144 p. incl. front., illus.   19½ cm.

22871   McGavock, Randal William, 1826-1863.
        A Tennessean abroad; or, Letters from Europe, Africa,
        and Asia, by Randal W. MacGavock... New York, Redfield,
        1854.
        x, [11]-398 p.   18½ cm.

22872   McGeachy, Edward, d. 1851.
        Suggestions towards a general plan of rapid communica-
        tion by steam navigation and railways: shortening the
        time of transit between the eastern and western hemi-
        spheres. By Edward McGeachy... London, Smith, Elder &
        co., 1846.
        17, [1] p.   2 fold. maps (incl. front.)   23 cm.

22873   McGee, Thomas D'Arcy, 1825-1868.
        Canadian ballads, and occasional verses. By Thomas
        D'Arcy McGee, M.P.P. Montreal, J. Lovell; [etc., etc.]
        1858.
        viii, 9-124 p.   17½ cm.

22874   McGee, Thomas D'Arcy, 1825-1868.
        The Catholic history of North America. Five discourses.
        To which are added two discourses on the relations of
        Ireland and America. By Thomas D'Arcy McGee... Boston,
        P. Donahoe, 1855.
        2 p.l., 3-239 p.   front.   19 cm.

22875 McGee, Thomas D'Arcy, 1825-1868.
A history of the Irish settlers in North America, from
the earliest period to the census of 1850. By Thomas
D'Arey McGee... Boston, Office of the "American Celt",
1851.
vii, [1], [9]-180 p.   20½ cm.

22876 McGee, Thomas D'Arcy, 1825-1868.
The Irish position in British and in republican North
America. A letter to the editors of the Irish press
irrespective of party. By the Hon. Thomas D'Arcy McGee...
Montreal, M. Longmoore & co., 1866.
[1], 36 p.   22 cm.

22877 McGee, Thomas D'Arcy, 1825-1868.
The poems of Thomas D'Arcy McGee. With copious notes.
Also an introduction and biographical sketch, by Mrs. J.
Sadlier... New York, D. & J. Sadlier & co.; Boston,
P. H. Brady; [etc., etc.] 1869.
xii p., 1 l., [15]-612 p.   front. (port.)   20 cm.

22878 McGee, Thomas D'Arcy, 1825-1868.
The present American revolution. The internal condition of the American democracy considered, in a letter
from the Hon. Thomas D'Arcy M'Gee... to the Hon. Charles
Gavan Duffy... London, R. Hardwicke, 1863.
19 p.   19½ cm.

22879 McGee, Thomas D'Arcy, 1825-1868.
Speeches and addresses chiefly on the subject of
British-American union. By the Hon. Thomas D'Arcy
McGee... London, Chapman and Hall, 1865.
viii, 308 p.   20½ cm.

22880 McGill, P   M
The wrongs and rights of labor fully and fairly shown,
and a remedy proposed... Written for the benefit of
labor and capital, proving that the mutual interests of
both demand reciprocal justice. By P. M. McGill...
Washington, Gibson brothers, printers, 1867.
2 p.l., [3]-112 p. incl. tables.   22 cm.

22881 Macgowan, Daniel Jerome, 1815-1893.
Claims of the missionary enterprise on the medical
profession; an address delivered before the Temperance
Society of the College of Physicians and Surgeons of the
University of the State of New York, October 28, 1842.
New York, Printed by W. Osborn, 1842.
24 p.   22 cm.

22882 MacGregor, John, 1797-1857.
         Commercial statistics. A digest of the productive
     resources, commercial legislation, customs tariffs...
     of all nations... By John Macgregor... London, C. Knight
     and co., 1844-50.
         5 v.   25 cm.

22883 Macgregor, John, 1797-1857.
         The history of the British empire, from the accession
     of James the First. To which is prefixed a review of
     the progress of England from the Saxon period to... 1603.
     By John Macgregor... London, Chapman and Hall, 1852.
         2 v.   22 cm.

22884 MacGregor, John, 1797-1857.
         Holland and the Dutch colonies. By John MacGregor,
     M.P. ... London, Whittaker and co., 1848.
         2 p.l., 223 p.   24½ cm.

22885 MacGregor, John, 1797-1857.
         Sketches of the progress of civilization and public
     liberty; with a view of the political condition of Europe
     and America in 1848. By John Macgregor... London,
     Whittaker and co., 1848.
         iv, [5]-72 p.   24 cm.

22886 McGuier, Henry.
         A concise history of High Rock Spring. By Henry
     McGuier. Albany, Printing house of C. Van Benthuysen &
     sons, 1868.
         42 p.   16 cm.

22887 M'Guire, Edward Charles.
         The religious opinions and character of Washington.
     By E. C. M'Guire... 2d ed. New York, Harper & brothers,
     1847.
         xxviii, [29]-414 p.   18 cm.
     First edition, New York, 1836.

22888 McHenry, George.
         The cotton supply of the United States of America. By
     George M'Henry. [Printed for private circulation]
     [2d ed., with additional remarks] London, Spottiswoode &
     co., printers, 1865.
         66 p. incl. tables.   21½ cm.

22889 McHenry, George.
         ... A paper containing a statement of facts relating to

200

the approaching cotton crisis. By George McHenry.
Richmond, Dec. 31, 1864. [Richmond, 1865]
87 p. 22½ cm.

22890 M'Henry, James, 1753-1816.
A letter to the Honourable the speaker of the House of
representatives of the United States, with the accompa-
nying documents; read in that honourable House, on the
28th December, 1802. By James M'Henry... Baltimore,
Printed by John W. Butler, corner of Gay & Water streets,
1803.
91 p. 22½ cm.

22891 McHenry, James, 1785-1845.
Waltham: an American revolutionary tale. In three
cantos. By James M'Henry. New York, E. Bliss & E. White,
1823.
ix p., 1 l., [13]-70 p. 15½ cm.

22892 Machias, Me.
Memorial of the centennial anniversary of the settlement
of Machias. Machias, Printed by C. O. Furbush, 1863.
179, [1] p. 22 cm.

22893 McIlvaine, Charles Pettit, bp., 1799-1873.
Rev. Mr. M'Ilvaine in answer to the Rev. Henry U. Onder-
donk, D.D. Philadelphia, W. Stavely, 1827.
43 p. 21½ cm.

22894 McIlvaine, Charles Pettit, bp., 1799-1873.
The work of preaching Christ. A charge: delivered to
the clergy of the diocese of Ohio, at its forty-sixth
annual convention, in St. Paul's church, Akron, on the
3d of June 1863. By Charles Pettit McIlvaine... 2d ed.
New York, A. D. F. Randolph, 1864.
72 p. 17 cm.

22895 McIntosh, John.
The discovery of America by Christopher Columbus; and
the origin of the North American Indians. By J.
Mackintosh. Toronto, W. J. Coates, 1836.
v, [7]-152 p. 22 cm.

22896 McIntosh, John.
The origin of the North American Indians; with a faithful
description of their manners and customs... their religions, languages, dress, and ornaments: including various
specimens of Indian eloquence, as well as historical and

biographical sketches of almost all the distinguished
nations and celebrated warriors, statesmen and orators,
among the Indians of North America. By John McIntosh.
New ed., improved and enlarged. New York, Cornish,
Lamport & co., 1853.
xxxv, [39]-345 p. incl. col. front.   col. pl.
22½ cm.

22897 McIntosh, Maria Jane, 1803-1878.
Woman in America: her work and her reward. By Maria J.
McIntosh... New York, D. Appleton & company; Philadelphia,
G. S. Appleton, 1850.
3 p.l., [11]-155 p.   20 cm.

22898 [M'Intyre, Archibald] 1772-1858.
A letter to His Excellency, Daniel D. Tompkins, late
governor of the state of New York. Albany. Printed by
Jeremiah Tryon, 22 Hudson-street, 1819.
112, xl p.   23 cm.

22899 McJilton, John Nelson, 1805-1875.
Poems. By J. N. M'Jilton. Boston, Otis, Broaders &
co.; New York, Wiley and Putnam; [etc., etc.] 1840.
xi, [13]-360 p.   19½ cm.

22900 [McJilton, John Nelson] 1805-1875.
Report of the delegate to the educational conventions
of Buffalo and Buston, to the commissioners of public
schools of Baltimore, and address on the teacher's
calling, nationally considered, delivered at Buffalo.
Baltimore, Bull & Tuttle, 1860.
126 p.   22½ cm.

22901 Mack, Ebenezer.
The cat-fight; a mock heroic poem. Supported with
copious extracts from ancient and modern classic authors
... By Doctor Ebenezer Mack... Illustrated with five
engravings, designed and executed by D. C. Johnston,
of Philadelphia, author, from recollection, of "Matthews
at home, In la diligence, Polly Packet", etc. New York,
1824.
276 p.   pl.   18½ cm.

22902 Mack, Ebenezer.
The life of Gilbert Motier de Lafayette... from
numerous and authentick sources. By Eben^r. Mack...
Ithica, N. Y., Mack, Andrus & Woodruff, 1841.
1 p.l., xii, [13]-371 p. incl. plates.   front., illus.
20 cm.

22903 Mack, Robert.
Kyle Stuart; with other poems; by Robert Mack, esq.
Vol. I... Columbia, Tenn., Printed for the author, by
F. K. Zollicoffer, 1834.
xii p., 2 l., 209 p.   16½ cm.

22904 Mack, Robert C   comp.
The Londonderry celebration. Exercises on the 150th
anniversary of the settlement of old Nutfield, comprising
the towns of Londonderry, Derry, Windham, and parts of
Manchester, Hudson and Salem, N. H., June 10, 1869.
Compiled by Robert C. Mack. Manchester, J. B. Clarke,
1870.
124 p., 1 l. incl. illus., facsims.   front., ports.
22½ cm.

22905 Mackay, Alexander, 1808-1852.
The crisis in Canada; or, Vindication of Lord Elgin
and his cabinet as to the course pursued by them in
reference to the rebellion losses bill. By Alexander
Mackay... London, J. Ridgway, 1849.
67 p.   22½ cm.

22906 Mackay, Alexander, 1808-1852.
Die westliche welt. Reise durch die Vereinsstaaten von
Amerika von Alexander McKay. Aus dem englischen über-
setzt von Marie Heine. Nebst einer einleitung und vier
illustrationen von Wilhelm Heine... Leipzig, C. E.
Kollmann, 1861.
4 v. in 2.   fronts.   21½ cm.

22907 Mackay, J
Quebec Hill; or, Canadian scenery. A poem. In two
parts. By J. Mackay... London, Printed by W. Blackader,
for the author; and sold by Elliot & Kay [etc.] 1797.
1 p.l., ii, [3]-34 p.   28 cm.

22908 McKay, Neill.
A centenary sermon, delivered before the presbytery of
Fayetteville, at the Bluff church, the 18th day of
October, 1858. By Rev. Neill McKay. Fayetteville
[N. C.] Printed at the Presbyterian office, 1858.
19 p.   22½ cm.

22909 Mackay, Robert W   Stuart.
The stranger's guide to the cities and principal towns
of Canada, with a glance at the most remarkable cataracts,
falls, rivers, watering places, mineral springs, &c., &c.;

and a geographical & statistical sketch of the province, brought down to 1854... By Robert W. Stuart Mackay... Montreal, C. Bryson [etc.] 1854.
168 p.   illus., fold. maps.   18 cm.

22910   McKaye, James.
The birth and death of nations. A thought for the crisis. By James McKaye. Reprinted from the Rebellion record. New York, G. P. Putnam, 1862.
1 p.l.,   55 -64 p.   24½ cm.

22911   [McKean, Joseph] 1776-1818.
Sermon. The question of war with Great Britain, examined upon moral and Christian principles...   Boston, Printed by Snelling & Simons, 1808.
14 p.   22½ cm.

22912   McKean, Joseph, 1776-1818.
A sermon, delivered at the ordination of the Reverend Nathaniel Langdon Frothingham, A.M., pastor of First church, Boston, XV. March, MDCCCXV. By Joseph McKean... Boston, Printed by Munroe, Francis & Parker, no. 4 Cornhill, 1815.
43 p.   22 cm.

22913   McKee, Samuel, 1833-1898.
Speech of Hon. Samuel McKee, of Kentucky, on reconstruction. Delivered in the House of representatives, March 3, 1866. [Washington, D. C., Printed by L. Towers, 1866]
8 p.   24 cm.

22914   McKee, William H.
The territory of New Mexico, and its resources. By W. H. McKee... New York, Printed at the office of the "American mining index," 1866.
cover-title, 12 p.   fold. map.   23 cm.

22915   McKeehan, J   B
... The crisis of our country; the duty of Republicans. By J. B. McKeehan. Cincinnati, 1860.
16 p.   21 cm.

22916   McKeen, Joseph, 1757-1807.
A sermon preached before the honorable the Council, and the honorable the Senate, and House of representatives of the commonwealth of Massachusetts, May 28, 1800, being the day of general election. By Joseph McKeen...

Boston, Printed by Young & Minns, 1800.
30 p.   20 cm.

22917 McKeen, Joseph, 1757-1807.
A sermon, preached on the public fast in the common-
wealth of Massachusetts, April 11, 1793. By Joseph McKeen
... Salem, Printed by Thomas C. Cushing; sold by William
Carlton, at the Bible and heart, 1793.
22 p.   21½ cm.

22918 Mackellar, Patrick, 1717-1778.
A correct journal of the landing His Majesty's forces
on the island of Cuba; and of the siege and surrender
of the Havannah, August 13, 1762. By Patrick Mackellar,
chief engineer. Pub. by authority. The 2d ed. London
printed; Boston, Re-printed and sold by Green and Russell
in Queen-street, 1762.
19 p.   20½ cm.

22919 MacKellar, Thomas, 1812-1899.
Droppings from the heart; or, Occasional poems. By
Thomas MacKellar. Philadelphia, Sorin & Ball, 1844.
viii, [9]-144 p.   17 cm.

22920 MacKellar, Thomas, 1812-1899.
Tam's fortnight ramble, and other poems. By Thomas
MacKellar... Philadelphia, Carey and Hart, 1847.
ix, [11]-216 p.   19 cm.

22921 McKenney, Thomas Loraine, 1785-1859.
Catalogue of one hundred and fifteen Indian portraits,
representing eighteen different tribes, accompanied by
a few brief remarks on the character &c. of most of them.
More detailed biographies will appear in the great work
on Indian history, by Col. M'Kenney & James Hall...
[Philadelphia, 1836?]
24 p.   22½ cm.

22922 [McKenney, Thomas Loraine] 1785-1859.
Essays on the spirit of Jacksonism, as exemplified in
its deadly hostility to the Bank of the United States...
By Aristides [pseud.]   Philadelphia, J. Harding, printer,
1835.
iv, [5]-151 p.   22 cm.

22923 McKenney, Thomas Loraine, 1785-1859.
Reply to Kosciusko Armstrong's assault upon Col.
McKenney's Narrative of the causes that led to General

Armstrong's resignation of the office of secretary of
war in 1814. By Thomas L. McKenney. New York, W. H.
Graham, 1847.
     28 p.   22 cm.

22924   Mackenzie, Sir Alexander, 1763-1820.
     Tableau historique et politique du commerce des pelle-
teries dans le Canada, depuis 1608 jusqu'à nos jours.
Contenant beaucoup de détails sus les nations sauvages
qui l'habitent, et sur les vastes contrées qui y sont
contiguës; avec un vocabulaire de la langue de plusieurs
peuples de ces vastes contrées. Par Alexandre Mackenzie.
Traduit de l'anglais, par J. Castéra. Orné du portrait
de l'auteur. Paris, Dentu, 1807.
     2 p.l., 310 p., 1 l.   20 cm.

22925   Mackenzie, Alexander Slidell, 1803-1848.
     The American in England. By A. Slidell Mackenzie...
4th ed. New York, Harper & brothers, 1835.
     2 v.   18 cm.

22926   Mackenzie, Alexander Slidell, 1803-1848.
     Case of the Somers' mutiny. Defence of Alexander
Slidell Mackenzie, commander of the U. S. brig Somers,
before the court martial held at the Navy yard,
Brooklyn. New York, Tribune office, 1843.
     30, ii p.   20½ cm.

22927   Mackenzie, Alexander Slidell, 1803-1848.
     The life of Paul Jones. By Alexander Slidell Mackenzie,
U.S.N. Boston, Hilliard, Gray, and company, 1841.
     2 v.   16½ cm.

22928   [Mackenzie, Alexander Slidell] 1803-1848.
     Popular essays on naval subjects. By the author of a
"Year in Spain"... New York, G. Dearborn, 1833.
     2 p.l., [vii]-xiv, [15]-166 p.   15½ cm.

22929   Mackenzie, Alexander Slidell, 1803-1848.
     Proceedings of the naval court martial in the case of
Alexander Slidell Mackenzie, a commander in the navy of
the United States, &c. including the charges and speci-
fications of charges, preferred against him by the
secretary of the navy. To which is annexed, an elaborate
review, by James Fennimore Cooper. New York, H. G.
Langley, 1814.
     2 p.l., 344 p.   21 cm.
     Relates to the execution on the brig "Somers" of three
midshipmen, Philip Spencer, Samuel Cromwell and Elisha
Small, suspected of mutiny.

22930 Mackenzie, Charles, F. R. S.
Notes on Haiti, made during a residence in that
republic. By Charles Mackenzie... London, H. Colburn
and R. Bentley, 1830.
2 v. 2 pl. (incl. front.) fold. map, fold. facsim.,
tables. 19½ cm.

22931 Mackenzie, Henry, 1745-1834.
An answer to Paine's Rights of man. By H. Makenzie,
esq. of Edinborough. To which is added a letter from
P. Porcupine to Citizen John Swanwick, an Englishman,
the son of a British waggon-master, and member of
Congress for the city of Philadelphia. Philadelphia,
Printed for, and sold by, William Cobbett, North Second
street, opposite Christ church, Oct. 1796.
vii, [9]-96 p. 22 cm.

22932 Mackenzie, Robert, 1823-1881.
America and her army. By Robert Mackenzie. London,
New York etc. T. Nelson and sons, 1865.
iv, [5]-60 p. 19 cm.

22933 Mackenzie, Robert, 1823-1881.
The United States of America: a history. By Robert
Mackenzie. London etc. New York, T. Nelson & sons,
1870.
1 p.l., vii, [8]-278 p. 19 cm.

22934 Mackenzie, William Lyon, 1795-1861.
The life and times of Martin Van Buren: the correspondence of his friends, family and pupils; together
with brief notices, sketches, and anecdotes, illustrative
of the public career of James Knox Polk, Benjamin F.
Butler... &c. By William L. Mackenzie... Boston,
Cooke & co., 1846.
xii, 308 p. 23½ cm.

22935 Mackenzie, William Lyon, 1795-1861.
Sketches of Canada and the United States. By William
L. Mackenzie... London, E. Wilson, 1833.
xxiv, 504 p. 20 cm.

22936 McKeon, John, 1808-1883.
The administration reviewed. Speech of the Hon. John
McKeon before the Democratic union association, at
their headquarters... Wednesday, October 29, 1862.
New York, Van Evrie, Horton & co., 1862.
15 p. 22½ cm.

22937 [Mackey, Albert Gallatin] 1807-1881.
        The political record of Senator F. A. Sawyer and
        Congressman C. C. Bowen, of South Carolina. [Charleston?
        1869?]
        23 p.   22 cm.

22938 Mackie, John Milton, 1813-1894.
        From Cape Cod to Dixie and the tropics. By J. Milton
        Mackie... New York, G. P. Putnam, 1864.
        422 p.   19 cm.

22939 McKinney, Mordecai, 1796(ca.)-1867.
        The United States constitutional manual; being a compre-
        hensive compendium of the system of government of the
        country; presenting a view of the general government,
        in its legislative, executive and judical departments;
        and of the governments of the states, particularly...
        Pennsylvania, and their relations... to the Union, and
        to each other; with definitions, constructions of consti-
        tutional provisions, and explanations; in the form of
        questions and answers; designed for academies, schools
        and readers in general. By Mordecai M'Kinney. Harrisburg
        Hickok & Cantine, printers, 1845.
        xv, 304 p.   22½ cm.

22940 McKinnon, Daniel, 1767-1830.
        A tour through the British West Indies, in the years
        1802 and 1803, giving a particular account of the Bahama
        islands. By Daniel McKinne, esq. London, Printed for
        J. White, 1804.
        2 p.l., viii, 272 p.   front. (fold. map)   18½ cm.

22941 Mackinnon, Laughlan Bellingham, 1815-1877.
        Atlantic and transatlantic: sketches afloat and
        ashore. By Captain Mackinnon... New York, Harper &
        brothers, 1852.
        1 p.l., [v]-viii, [9]-324 p.   19½ cm.

22942 Mackinnon, Laughlan Bellingham, 1815-1877.
        Some account of the Falkland Islands, from a six
        months' residence in 1838 and 1839. By L. B. Mackinnon..
        London, A. H. Baily and co., 1840.
        79 p.   front. (fold. map)   21½ cm.

22943 Mackinnon, William Alexander, 1789-1870.
        History of civilisation. By William Alex^r Mackinnon...
        London, Printed for Longman, Brown, Green, and Longmans,
        1846.
        2 v.   22 cm.

22944   Mackinnon, William Alexander, 1789-1870.
        On the rise, progress, and present state of public
        opinion, in Great Britain, and other parts of the world.
        By William Alexander Mackinnon, F.R.S.   2d ed.   London,
        Saunders and Otley, 1828.
        ix, 343, [1] p.   22 cm.

22945   McKinnon, William Charles.
        St. George: or, The Canadian league. By William
        Charles McKinnon...   Halifax, E. G. Fuller, 1852.
        2 v.   19 cm.

22946   McKinstry, Justus, b. 1814.
        Vindication of Brig. Gen. J. McKinstry, formerly
        quartermaster Western department.   [St. Louis, 1862]
        102 p. incl. cover-title.   23 cm.

22947   Mackintosh, Sir James, 1765-1832.
        A discourse on the study of the law of nature and
        nations. By Sir James Mackintosh...   London, H. Goode &
        co., 1828.
        2 p.l., 89 p.   19½ cm.

22948   M'Knight, John, 1754-1823.
        The divine goodness to the United States of America,
        particularly in the course of the last year.   A thanks-
        giving sermon, preached in New York, February 19, 1795.
        By John M'Knight...   New York, Printed by T. Greenleaf,
        1795.
        23, [3] p.   21 cm.

22949   M'Knight, John, 1754-1823.
        God the author of promotion.   A sermon preached in the
        new Presbyterian church, New York, on the 4th July, 1794,
        at the request of the Democratic society and the military
        officers.   By John M'Knight, D.D.   New York, From the
        press of William Durell, no. 208 Pearl-street, 1794.
        1 p.l., [5]-24 p.   21 cm.

22950   Macknight, Thomas, 1829-1899.
        History of the life and times of Edmund Burke.   By
        Thomas Macknight...   London, Chapman and Hall, 1858-60.
        3 v.   2 facsim.   22½ cm.

22951   MacKonochie, [Alexander]
        A summary view of the statistics and existing commerce
        of the principal shores of the Pacific Ocean.   With a
        sketch of the advantages, political and commercial,
        which would result from the establishment of a central

209

free port within its limits; and also of one in the southern Atlantic... By Captain M'Konochie... London, J. M. Richardson; [etc., etc.] 1818.
xxi, 365, [1] p.   front. (fold. map)   23 cm.

22952 Mackrill, Joseph.
The history of the yellow fever, with the most successful method of treatment. By Joseph Mackrill, M.D. ... Baltimore, Printed by John Hayes, in Public-alley, 1796.
3 p.l., 5-26 p.   17 cm.

22953 M'Lain, William, 1806-1873.
Discourse, occasioned by the death of John Coyle. Preached in the First Presbyterian church, Washington city, of which he was an elder. July 8, 1838. By W. M'Lain. Washington city, Printed by J. Gideon, jr., 1838.
27 p.   23 cm.

22954 McLane, [Louis] 1786-1857.
Speech of Mr. McLane, of Delaware, on the admission of Missouri. Delivered in the House of representatives, Dec. 12, 1820. [Washington, 1820]
22 p.   12⁰.

22955 McLane, Robert Milligan, 1815-1898.
Speech of Hon. R. M. McLane of Maryland, on the war with Mexico. Delivered in the House of representatives, January 19, 1848. Washington, Printed at the Congressional globe office, 1848.
8 p.   24½ cm.

22956 [Maclaren, James]
Observations on the effect of the Californian & Australian gold: and on the impossibility of continuing the present standard, in the event of gold becoming seriously depreciated. London, T. Bumpus [etc.] 1852.
32 p.   21 cm.

22957 [McLaughlin, James Fairfax] 1839-1903.
The American Cyclops, the hero of New Orleans, and spoiler of silver spoons. Dubbed LL. D. by Pasquino. Baltimore, Kelly & Piet, 1868.
27 p.   12 pl. (incl. front.)   20 x 16 cm.
In verse. The illustrations are etchings by Dr. A. J. Volck.

22958 M'Lean, Alexander.
An appeal to the public, or, An exposition of the conduct of Rev. Isaac Jennison and others, in Ludlow,

in the months of February and March, 1828. Also, an
address to the local preachers of the Methodist Episcopal
church; with remarks on the government, discipline and
monied system of said church. By Alexander M'Lean...
Belchertown [Mass.] Printed by C. A. Warren, 1828.
56 p.   23 cm.

22959   M'Lean, James.
Seventeen years' history of the life and sufferings of
James M'Lean, an impressed American citizen and seaman.
Embracing but a summary of what he endured, while
detained in the British service, during that long and
eventful period. Written by himself. Hartford,
The author, 1814.
27 p. $17\frac{1}{2}$ cm.

22960   Maclean, John, 1800-1886.
Letters on the elder question. [Princeton, N. J.]
J. T. Robinson, 1844.
55, [1] p.   21 cm.

22961   Macleane, Lauchlin.
An essay on the expediency of inoculation and the seasons
most proper for it. Humbly inscribed to the inhabitants
of Philadelphia, by Lauchlin Macleane... Philadelphia,
Printed by W. Bradford, 1756.
39, [1] p.   19 cm.

22962   McLellan, Isaac, 1806-1899.
The fall of the Indian, with other poems. By Isaac
McLellan, jun. ... Boston, Carter and Hendee, 1830.
99 p.   20 cm.

22963   McLellan, Isaac, 1806-1899.
Mount Auburn, and other poems, by Isaac M'Lellan, jr.
... Boston, W. D. Ticknor, 1843.
3 p.l., [3]-156 p. $16\frac{1}{2}$ cm.

22964   [McLellan, Isaac] 1806-1899.
The year, with other poems. By the author of "The
fall of the Indian," &c. A New Year's gift. Boston,
Carter and Hendee, 1832.
2 p.l., 60 p.   22 cm.

22965   McLeod, Alexander, 1774-1833.
A scriptural view of the character, causes, and
ends of the present war. By Alexander McLeod, D.D.,
pastor of the Reformed Presbyterian church, New York...
New York, Published by Eastburn, Kirk and co.;

211

Whiting and Watson; and Smith and Forman. Paul & Thomas, printers, 1815.
viii, [9]-224 p.   21½ cm.

22966 [McLeod, Daniel]
The rebellion in Tennessee. Observations on Bishop Otey's letter to the Hon. William H. Seward. By a native of Virginia... Washington, McGill, Witherow & co., printers, 1862.
11 p.   21 cm.

22967 McLeod, Donald.
History of Wiskonsan, from its first discovery to the present period. Including a geological and topographical description of the territory, with a correct catalogue of all its plants. By Donald McLeod. Buffalo, Steele's press, 1846.
1 p.l., [vii]-xii, [13]-310 p.   front. (fold. map) IV pl.   18 cm.

22968 [McLeod, Isabella]
Westfield, a view of home life during the American war. Edinburgh, Edmonston and Douglas, 1866.
4 p.l., 222 p.   20 cm.

22969 Macleod, Norman, 1812-1872.
Wee Davie, by Norman Macleod... Richmond, Va., Presbyterian committee of publication, 1864.
52 p.   18½ cm.

22970 M'Mahon, Benjamin.
Jamaica plantership, by Benjamin M'Mahon... London, E. Wilson, 1839.
2 p.l., viii, [9]-304 p.   19½ cm.

22971 MacMahon, Bernard, 1775?-1816.
American gardener's calendar; adapted to the climates and seasons of the United States. Containing a complete account of all the work necessary to be done... for every month in the year; with ample practical directions for performing the same... By Bernard M'Mahon... Philadelphia, Printed by B. Graves, no. 40, North fourth-street, for the author, 1806.
v, [1], 648, 18 p.   fold. tab.   22 cm.

22972 MacMaster, Erasmus Darwin, 1806-1866.
Speech of Mr. MacMaster in the synod of Indiana, October 4, 1844, in relation to Madison university. Madison, Jones & Lodge, 1844.
39 p.   20 cm.

22973 MacMaster, Erasmus Darwin, 1806-1866.
The true life of a nation; an address, delivered at the invitation of the Erodelphian and Eccritean societies of Miami university, the evening preceeding the annual commencement, July 2d, 1856. By E. D. MacMaster. Pub. by request of the societies. New Albany [Ind.?] Printed by Norman, Morrison, & Matthews, 1856.
47 p.   21½ cm.

22974 McMaster, Gilbert, 1778-1854.
The moral character of civil government, considered with reference to the political institutions of the United States, in four letters. By Gilbert McMaster... Albany, W. C. Little; Schenectady, J. C. Magoffin, 1832.
72 p.   22 cm.

22975 McMaster, Guy Humphrey, 1829-1887.
History of the settlement of Steuben county, N. Y. including notices of the old pioneer settlers and their adventures. By Guy H. McMaster. Bath [N. Y.] R. S. Underhill & co., 1853.
iv, 318 p. incl. pl.   19 cm.

22976 McMicken, Charles, 1782-1858.
The will of Charles McMicken, of Cincinnati, Ohio. Probated April 10, 1858. - With an index... Cincinnati, Printed at the office of the "Cincinnatus," 1859.
30 p.   30 cm.

22977 MacMullen, John, 1818-1896.
A lecture on the past, the present, and the future of the New York society library, delivered before the shareholders February 15th, 1856. By John MacMullen, librarian. Printed by order of the committee. New York, J. F. Trow, printer, 1856.
42 p.   23 cm.

22978 MacMullen, John, 1818-1896.
Nathan Hale, a poem, delivered before the Alumni association of Columbia college, October 27, 1858. By John MacMullen, A.M. New York, J. F. Trow, printer, 1859.
31 p.   23 cm.

22979 McMullen, John Mercier, 1820-1907.
The history of Canada, from its first discovery to the present time. By John MacMullen... [2d ed.] Brockville [Ont.] McMullen & co., 1868.
xxxi, 613 p.   23½ cm.

213

22981   McMurray, William, 1783-1835.
        A sermon, preached in behalf of the American coloniza-
        tion society, in the Reformed Dutch church, in Market-
        street, New York, July 10, 1825. By William M'Murray...
        New York, Printed by J. Seymour, 1825.
        28 p.   21 cm.

22981   McNair, John.
        Eighty original poems; secular and sacred, and chiefly
        adapted to the times. By John McNair... Lancaster, Pa.,
        J. E. Barr, 1865.
        263 p.   18 cm.

22982   McNally, William.
        Evils and abuses in the naval and merchant services,
        exposed; with proposals for their remedy and redress.
        By William McNally... Boston, Cassady and March, 1839.
        viii, 201, [1] p.   18½ cm.

22983   Macnamara, Henry Tyrwhitt Jones, 1820-1877.
        Peace, permanent and universal: its practicability,
        value, and consistency with divine revelation. A prize
        essay, by H. T. J. Macnamara. London, Saunders and
        Otley, 1841.
        vii, 354 p.   20½ cm.

22984   McNeile, Hugh, 1795-1879.
        ... A lecture on the life of Dr. Franklin. By the
        Rev. Hugh M'Neile, A.M., as delivered by him at the
        Liverpool Royal amphitheatre... 17th Nov. 1841, with
        the addition of a prefatory note to the reader, by John
        B. Murray... New York, H. Greene; Philadelphia, Carey
        and Hart; [etc., etc.] 1841.
        viii, [9]-46, [2] p.   front. (fold. facsim.) pl.
        21½ cm.

22985   McPhail, Leonard C   d. 1867.
        On the life and services of William Henry Harrison,
        late president of the United States; an eulogium,
        pronounced before the citizens of Eastport, Maine, by
        Dr. Leonard McPhail, U.S.A., April 15, 1841. Boston,
        B. B. Mussey; Eastport, J. Beckford, 1841.
        28 p.   23½ cm.

22986   Macpherson, David, 1746-1816.
        Annals of commerce, manufactures, fisheries and
        navigation, with brief notices of the arts and sciences
        connection with them. Containing the commercial trans-
        actions of the British Empire and other countries,

from the earliest accounts to the meeting of the Union
parliament in January, 1801; and comprehending the most
valuable part of the late Mr. Anderson's History of
commerce... with a large appendix... By David Macpherson... London, Nichols and son; [etc., etc.] 1805.
4 v.   29 cm.

22987   McPherson, Edward, 1830-1895.
The political history of the United States of America
during the period of reconstruction (from April 15, 1865,
to July 15, 1870) including a classified summary of the
legislation of the Thirty-ninth, Fortieth, and Forty-first
congresses. With the votes thereon; together with the
action, congressional and state, on the fourteenth and
fifteenth amendments to the Constitution of the United
States, and the other important executive, legislative,
politico-military, and judicial facts of that period.
By Hon. Edward McPherson... Washington, D.C., Philip &
Solomons, 1871.
v, 6-9, 648 p.   24½ cm.

22988   McPherson, Edward, 1830-1895.
The rebellion. Two speeches of Hon. Edward McPherson,
of Pennsylvania, in the House of representatives,
January 23, 1861, and February 14, 1862. [Washington,
Scammell & co., printer, 1862]
16 p.   25 cm.

22989   McPhetres, Samuel A.
A political manual for the campaign of 1868, for use in
the New England states, containing the population and
latest election returns of every town... By S. A.
McPhetres. Boston, A. Williams and company, 1868.
2 p.l., [7]-96 p.   15 cm.

22990   Macqueen, John Fraser, 1803-1881.
Chief points in the laws of war and neutrality, search
and blockade; with the changes of 1856, and those now
proposed. By John Fraser Macqueen... Richmond [Va.]
West and Johnston, 1863.
x, 102 p.   19½ cm.

22991   McRae, John J   1815-1868.
Speech of Hon. J. J. McRae, of Mississippi, on the
compromise question. Delivered in the Senate of the
United States, January 29, and February 2, 1852.
Washington, Printed at the Congressional globe office,
1852.
24 p.   24 cm.

22992 McRee, Griffith John, 1819-1873.
Life and correspondence of James Iredell, one of the associate justices of the Supreme Court of the United States. New York, Appleton, 1857-58.
2 v. port., facsim. 24 cm.

22993 M'Robert, Patrick.
Tour through part of the north provinces of America: being a series of letters wrote on the spot, in the years 1774, & 1775. To which are annex'd, tables, shewing the roads, the value of coins, rates of stages, &c. By Patrick M'Robert. Edinburgh, Printed for the author, 1776.
64 p. 20½ cm.

22994 McRoberts, Samuel, 1799-1843.
Speech of Mr. Samuel McRoberts, of Illinois, on the title of the United States to the Territory of Oregon, and in favor of the bill for its occupation and settlement: delivered in the United States Senate, December 30, 1842, and January 9, 1843. Washington, Printed at the Globe office, 1843.
13 p. 25 cm.

22995 McSherry, Richard, 1817-1885.
Essays and lectures on: 1. The early history of Maryland: 2. Mexico and Mexican affairs: 3. A Mexican campaign: 4. Homoeopathy: 5. Elements of hygiene: 6. Health and happiness. By Richard McSherry... Baltimore, Kelly, Piet & company, 1869.
2 p.l., [iii]-iv, 125 p. 23 cm.

22996 [MacSparran, James] 1693-1757.
America dissected, being a full and true account of all the American colonies: shewing, the intemperance of the climates; excessive heat and cold... badness of money; danger from enemies; but, above all, the danger to the souls of the poor people that remove thither, from the multifarious wicket and pestilent heresies that prevail in those parts. In several letters, from a rev. divine of the Church of England, missionary to America... Published as a caution to unsteady people who may be tempted to leave their native country. Dublin, Printed and sold by S. Powell, 1753.
1 l., 48 p. 19½ cm.

22997 Mactaggart, John, 1791-1830.
Three years in Canada: an account of the actual state of the country in 1826-7-8. Comprehending its resources,

productions, improvements, and capabilities; and
including sketches of the state of society, advice to
emigrants, &c. By John Mactaggart... London, H.
Colburn, 1829.
2 v.   19½ cm.

22998   McVean, Charles, 1802-1848.
Speech of Mr. McVean of New York, on the bill regu-
lating the deposit of the moneys of the United States
in certain local banks. [Washington? 1834]
7 p.   24 cm.
Delivered in the House of representatives, June 24, 1834.

22999   [McVickar, John] 1787-1868.
Considerations upon the expediency of abolishing
damages on protested bills of exchange, and the effect
of establishing a reciprocal exchange with Europe: to
which are annexed, the Report made to the House of representatives of the United States, March 22, 1826: and an
examination into the nature and operation of bills of
exchange. New York, Elliott and Palmer, printers, 1829.
iv, [5]-67 p.   21 cm.

23000   McVickar, John, 1787-1868.
A domestic narrative of the life of Samuel Bard, M.D.,
LL.D., late president of the College of physicians and
surgeons of the University of the state of New York, &c.
By the Rev. John M'Vickar... New York, The literary
rooms [Columbia college] A. Paul, printer, 1822.
244 p.   front. (port.)   22 cm.

23001   McVickar, John, 1787-1868.
Tribute to the memory of Sir Walter Scott, baronet.
By Rev. M. McVickar, D.D. New York, Printed by G. P.
Scott and co., 1833.
42 p.   22 cm.

23002   Macwhorter, Alexander, 1734-1807.
A funeral sermon, preached in Newark, December 27,
1799. A day of public mourning, observed by that town,
for the universally lamented George Washington, late
president of the United States... to which is subjoined,
his last address, to his beloved countrymen... By
Alexander Macwhorter... Newark, Printed and sold by
Jacob Halsey, 1800.
2 p.l., iv, 44 p.   21 cm.

23003   Macedo, Joaquim Manuel de, 1820-1882.
As victimas-algozes, quadros da escravidão, romances

por Joaquim Manoel de Macedo... Rio de Janeiro, Typ. americana, 1869.
2 v.   18 cm.

23004 Machpelah: a book for the cemetery... New York, A. D. F. Randolph, 1865.
205 p. incl. plates.   14 cm.

23005 Macy, Obed.
The history of Nantucket; being a compendious account of the first settlement of the island by the English, together with the rise and progress of the whale fishery; and other historical facts relative to said island and its inhabitants. In two parts. By Obed Macy... Boston, Hilliard, Gray and co., 1835.
xi, 300 p.   front. (map) pl.   18 cm.

23006 Madden, Richard Robert, 1798-1886.
The shrines and sepulchres of the Old and New world; records of pilgrimages in many lands and researches connected with the history of places remarkable for memorials of the dead, or monuments of a sacred character; including notices of the funeral customs of the principal nations, ancient and modern. By R. R. Madden... London, T. C. Newby, 1851.
2 v.   plates.   22½ cm.

23007 Madden, Richard Robert, 1798-1886.
A twelvemonth's residence in the West Indies, during the transition from slavery to apprenticeship; with incidental notices of the state of society, prospects, and natural resources of Jamaica and other islands. By R. R. Madden... Philadelphia, Carey, Lea and Blanchard 1835.
2 v.   16 cm.

23008 Madden, Samuel 1686-1765.
Memoirs of the twentieth century. Being original letters of state, under George the Sixth: relating to the most important events in Great-Britain and Europe, as to church and state, arts and sciences, trade, taxes, and treaties, peace, and war: and characters of the greatest persons of those times; from the middle of the eighteenth, to the end of the twentieth century, and the world. Received and revealed in the year 1728; and now published, for the instruction of all eminent states-men, churchmen, patriots, politicians, projectors, Papists, and Protestants. In six volumes. Vol. I... London, Osborn and Longman [etc.] 1733.
2 p.l., x, 31, 527 p.   fold port.   20½ cm.

23009   Maddox, Isaac, bp. of Worcester, 1697-1759.
        A sermon preached before His Grace Charles duke of
        Marlborough, president, the vice-presidents and
        governors of the Hospital for the small-pox, and for
        inoculation, at the parish-church of St. Andrew Holborn,
        on Thursday, March 5, 1752. By Isaac lord bishop of
        Worcester. Published at the request of the president,
        vice-presidents, and governors. The 4th ed., with a
        new preface. London, Printed by H. Woodfall, and sold
        by H. Whitridge [etc., 1753?]
            2 p.l., viii, 9-32 p.   21½ x 16½ cm.

23010   Madison, James, bp., 1749-1812.
        An address to the members of the Protestant Episcopal
        Church in Virginia. Richmond, Printed by T. Nicolson,
        1799.
            24 p.   21 cm.

23011   Madison, James pres. U.S., 1751-1836.
        An examination of the British doctrine which subjects
        to capture a neutral trade not open in time of peace.
        The 2d ed. containing a letter from the minister pleni-
        potentiary of the United States, to Lord Mulgrave, late
        secretary of state for foreign affairs. America printed;
        London, Reprinted for J. Johnson and W. J. & J. Richardson,
        1806.
            1 p.l., 200 p.   21½ cm.

23012   Madison, James M
        An exposition of the forms and usages observed in the
        various lodges of the Independent order of Odd fellows,
        as organized in the United States... By James M.
        Madison... New York, For the author, 1848.
            32 p.   front., plates.   21½ cm.

23013   Madison, James, pres. U.S., 1751-1836.
        Jonathan Bull and Mary Bull: by James Madison. An
        inedited manuscript. Printed for presentation by
        J. C. M'Guire. Washington, 1856.
            14 p.   21 cm.
        "Written but not published at the period of the
        Missouri question, 1821."

23014   Madison, James, bp., 1749-1812.
        Manifestations of the beneficence of divine providence
        towards America. A discourse, delivered on Thursday
        the 19th of February, 1795, being the day recommended
        by the President of the United States, for general
        thanksgiving and prayer. By Bishop Madison... Richmond,

Printed by Thomas Nicolson, 1795.
23 p.   18½ cm.

23015   Madison, James, pres. U.S., 1751-1836.
Religious freedom. A memorial and remonstrance, drawn
by His Excellency James Madison, late President of the
United States, against the general assessment, in "A bill
establishing provision for the teachers of the Christian
religion," presented to the General assembly of Virginia,
at the session of 1785... Boston, Printed and sold by
Lincoln & Edmands, 1819.
12 p.   18½ cm.

23016   The madmen's chronicle; exemplified in the conduct of George
the Third, and his ministers towards the United States,
from the conclusion of the treaty of peace to the present
time. To which are annexed, biographical and characteris
tic sketches, of the king, royal family, present and
ex-ministers, etc. Philadelphia, 1807.
24 p.   8⁰.

23017   [Madre de Deus, Manuel da] b. 1724.
Summa triunfal da nova, e grande celebridade do glorios
e invicto martyr s. Gonçalo Garcia: dedicada, e offereci
ao senhor capitãó Jozé Rabello de Vasconcellos, por seu
autor Soterio da Sylva Ribeiro [pseud.]: com huma
colleção de varios folgedos, e danças, oração panegirica,
que ricitou o doutissimo, e reverendissimo padre fr.
Antonio de Santa Maria Jaboatam... na igreja dos pardos
da Senhora do Livramento, em Pernambuco no primeiro de
mayo do anno de 1745. Lisboa, Na Officina de P.
Ferreira, impressor da Augustissima Rainha Nossa Senhora,
1753.
4 p.l., 164 p.   19 cm.

23018   Maffitt, John Newland, 1794-1850.
Pulpit sketches. By Rev. John Newland Maffit...
First series. Louisville, Ky., W. H. Johnston, 1839.
xi, [13]-178 p.   18½ cm.

23019   ... Maga excursion papers. New York, G. P. Putnam & son,
1867.
304 p.   17 cm.   (Putnam's railway classics)
Reprinted from Putnam's monthly magazine)
Contents. - Newport in winter. - From Venice to Vienna.
Sketches in a Parisian café. - Robinson Crusoe's island.
The midnight sun. - A few days in Vienna. - Experiences
in Mount Lebanon. - Acadie, and the birthplace of
Evangeline. - Adventures on a drift-log. - The ghost

of a city. - Hayti and the Haitians. - A glimpse of
Munich. - How they live in Havana. - Wood-notes. -
Forty days in a western hotel.

23020 Magalhães, Domingos José Gonçalves de, visconde de Ara-
guaya, 1811-1882.
A confederação dos Tamoyos; poema. Rio de Janeiro,
Empreza Typog. de P. Brito, 1856.
340, 19 p. 31 cm.

23021 Magalhães de Gandavo, Pedro de.
Histoire de la province de Sancta-Cruz, que nous
nommons ordinairement le Brésil, par Pero de Magalhanes
de Gandavo... Lisbonne, A. Gonsalvez. - 1576. [Paris,
A. Bertrand, 1837]
3 p.l., [3]-159 p. 21 cm.

23022 Magaw, Samuel, 1740-1812.
An oration commemorative of the virtues and greatness
of General Washington; pronounced in the German Lutheran
church, Philadelphia: before the Grand lodge of Pennsylvania, on the twenty-second day of February, 1800.
By Samuel Magaw, D.D. Pub. at the request of the Grand
lodge. Philadelphia, Printed by J. Ormrod, 1800.
45 p. 23 cm.

23023 Magaw, Samuel, 1740-1812.
A sermon delivered in St. Paul's church, on the 4th of
july, 1786... By Samuel Magaw, D.D. Rector of St.
Paul's in Philadelphia, and vice-provost of the University
of Pennsylvania. Philadelphia, Printed by Young and
McCulloch, the corner of Chestnut and Second streets,
1786.
30 p. 19½ cm.

23024 Magie, David, 1795-1865.
A discourse delivered in the Second Presbyterian
church, Elizabeth, N. J., August 6th, 1863, on occasion
of the public thanksgiving appointed by Abraham Lincoln,
president of the United States, to commemorate the
signal victories vouchsafed to the federal arms. By
Rev. David Magie, D.D. New York, Printed by F. Hart &
co., 1863.
28 p. 23 cm.

23025 Magoon, Elias Lyman, 1810-1886.
The eloquence of the colonial and revolutionary times.
With sketches of early American statesmen and patriots.
Delivered before the New England society of Cincinnati.

221

By Rev. E. L. Magoon... Cincinnati, Derby, Bradley &
co., 1847.
96 p.   19 cm.

23026   Magoon, Elias Lyman, 1810-1886.
Westward empire; or, The great drama of human progress.
By E. L. Magoon... New York, Harper & brothers, 1856.
xviii, [19]-445 p.   19½ cm.

23027   Magoun, George Frederic.
Historical sketch of Iowa college, by President Magoun.
[Chicago, 1865]
8 p.   21 cm.

23028   Maguire, John Francis, 1815-1872.
Father Mathew: a biography. By John Francis Maguire...
London, Longman, Green, Longman, Roberts, & Green, 1863.
xv, 557 p.   front. (port.)   19½ cm.

23029   [Maguire, Thomas] 1774-1854.
Observations d'un catholique sur l'Histoire du Canada
par l'honorable William Smith. (Extrait de la Gazette
de Québec du 11 janvier 1827) [n.p., 1827?]
13 p.   22½ cm.

23030   Mahan, Dennis Hart, 1802-1871.
An elementary treatise on advanced-guard, out-post, and
detachment service of troops, and the manner of posting
and handling them in presence of an enemy. Intended
as a supplement to the system of tactics adopted for the
military service of the United States, and especially
for the use of officers of militia and volunteers. By
D. H. Mahan... New Orleans, Bloomfield & Steel, 1861.
143 p.   14½ cm.

23031   Mahan, Dennis Hart, 1802-1871.
Summary of the course of permanent fortification and
of the attack and defence of permanent works, for the
use of the cadets of the U.S. Military academy. By
D. H. Mahan... Richmond, West & Johnston, 1863.
352 p.   illus.   23 cm.

23032   Mahan, Milo, 1819-1870.
Dr. Mahan's speech. [n.p., 1862]
16 p.   21½ cm.
On slavery; apparently spoken in the General convention
of the Protestant Episcopal church, 1862.

23033   Mahony, Dennis A
The four acts of despotism: comprising I. The tax bill,

with all the amendments. II. The finance bill. III.
The conscription act. IV. The indemnity bill. With
introductions and comments. By A. A. Mahony... New
York, Van Evrie, Horton & co., 1863.
160 p.   24 cm.

23034 Mai-jour (translated May-day) General George Barnum
McClellan, militant-homoeopath to the army of the
Confederates. Attacked, after his own mode, through
parallels... London, J. Lee, 1864.
1 p.l., 103-139 p.   17½ cm.

23035 Mailhe, Jean Baptiste, 1754-1839.
Discours qui a remporté le prix à l'Académie des jeux
floraux en 1784, sur la grandeur et l'importance de la
révolution qui vient de l'opérer dans l'Amérique Septentrionale. Par M. Mailhe... Toulouse, De l'imprimerie
de D. Desclassan, 1784.
1 p.l., 40 p.   20 cm.

23036 Maillet, Benoit de 1656-1738.
Telliamed; or, The world explain'd: containing discourses between an Indian philosopher and a missionary,
on the diminution of the sea-the formation of the earth-
the origin of men & animals: and other singular subjects,
relating to natural history & philosophy. A very
curious work. Baltimore, Printed by W. Pechin, no. 15,
Market street - for D. Porter, at the Observatory,
Federal-mill, 1797.
xxix, [31]-268 p.   21 cm.
The title is an anagram of the author's name.

23037 Mailly, Éd[ouard] i.e. Nicolas Édouard, 1810-1891.
Précis de l'histoire de l'astronomie aux États-Unis
d'Amérique, par Ed. Mailly... Bruxelles, Hayez,
imprimeur, 1860.
1 p.l., 88 p.   18 cm.

23038 Main, Thomas.
Directions for the transplantation and management of
young thorn or other hedge plants, preparative to their
being set in hedges. With some practical observations
on the method of plain hedging. By Thomas Main...
City of Washington, A. & G. Way, printers... 1807.
37, [1] p.   19½ cm.

23039 Maine (District) Constitutional convention, 1819.
The debates, resolutions, and other proceedings, of
the convention of delegates, assembled at Portland on

223

the 11th, and continued until the 29th day of October,
1819, for the purpose of forming a constitution for the
state of Maine. To which is prefixed the constitution
taken in convention. By Jeremiah Perley... Portland,
A. Shirley, printer, 1820.
iv, [5]-300 p., 1 l.   19 cm.

23040 Maine. State Library, Augusta.
Catalogue of the Maine state library, 1856. Arranged
and published agreeably to Resolve approved April 4, 1856,
under direction of Caleb B. Ayer, secretary of state.
Augusta, Fuller & Fuller, printers, 1856.
439 p.   23 cm.

23041 Mais, Charles, reporter.
The surprising case of Rachel Baker, who prays and
preaches in her sleep: with specimens of her extraordinary performances taken down accurately in short
hand at the time... The whole authenticated by the
most respectable testimony of living witnesses. By
Charles Mais... stenographer... New York, Printed by
S. Marks, 63 Anthony street, 1814.
34 p.   21 cm.

23042 Major, Richard Henry, 1818-1891.
The life of Prince Henry of Portugal, surnamed the
Navigator; and its results: comprising the discovery,
within one century, of half the world... With... the
history of the naming of America... By Richard Henry
Major... London, A. Asher & co., 1868.
2 p.l., lii, 487 p.   col. front., plates, ports.,
7 maps.   23½ cm.

23043 Major, Richard Henry, 1818-1891.
The true date of the English discovery of the American
continent under John and Sebastian Cabot: a letter
addressed by Richard Henry Major, esq., F.S.A., to
C. S. Perceval, esq. ...
(In Archaeologia: or, Miscellaneous tracts relating to
antiquity... London, 1871. 31 cm. v. 43, p. 17-42)

23044 Makemie, Francis, 1658-1708.
A narrative of a new and unusual American imprisonment
of two Presbyterian ministers: and prosecution of Mr.
Francis Makemie one of them, for preaching one sermon
at the city of New York. By a learner of law, and lover
of liberty. Boston? Printed for the publisher, 1707.
2 p.l., 47 p.   19½ x 15 cm.

23045   Malan, César, 1787-1864.
The Swiss peasant. By the Rev. Cesar Malan, of Geneva
... The one thing needful... Park Hill [Ind. Ter.]
Mission press; E. Archer, printer, 1848.
24 p.   13 cm.
In Cherokee language and characters; title also in
Cherokee.

23046   Malaspina, Alexxandro, 1754-1809.
Tablas de latitudes y longitudes de los principales
puntos del Rio de la Plata, nuevamente arregladas al
meridiano que pasa por lo mas occidental de la Isla de
Ferro; pro D. Alejandro Malaspina... [1789] 1. ed.
Buenos Aires, Imprenta del estado, 1837.
1 p.l., v, [3]-10 p.   33 cm.

23047   [Malcom, Howard] 1799-1879.
A brief memoir of Mrs. Lydia M. Malcom, late of Boston,
Mass., wife of Rev. Howard Malcom... 4th ed. Boston,
W. D. Ticknor, 1835.
1 p.l., 122 p.   15½ cm.

23048   Malcolme, David d. 1748.
An essay on the antiquities of Great Britain and Ireland:
wherein they are placed in a clearer light than hitherto.
Designed as an introduction to a larger work, especially
an attempt to shew an affinity betwixt the languages, &c.
of the ancient Britains and the Americans of the Isthmus
of Darien. In answer to an objection against revealed
religion... Edinburgh, Printed by T. and W. Ruddimans,
and sold by A. Kincaid, 1738.
1 p.l., [256] p.   20½ cm.

23049   Malden, Mass.
Oration, poem, speeches, chronicles, &c., at the
dedication of the Malden town hall on Thursday evening,
October 29th, 1857. Malden [Mass.] C. C. P. Moody, 1857.
52 p.   23½ cm.

23050   Malenfant, Colonel.
Des colonies, particulièrement de celle de Saint-
Domingue; mémoire historique et politique, où l'on trouvera:
1°, Un exposé impartial des causes et un précis historique
des guerres civiles qui ont rendu cette dernière colonie
indépendante; 2°, Des considérations sur l'importance de
la rattacher à la métropole et sur les moyens de le tenter
avec succès, d'y ramener une paix durable, d'en rétablir
et accroître la prospérité. Par le colonel Malenfant...

Paris, Audibert [etc.] 1814.
2 p.l., xii, 334, [2] p., 1 l.   20½ cm.

23051   Malet, Sir Alexander, 2d bart., 1800-1886.
The Canadas: the onerous nature of their existing
connexion with Great Britain state, the discontents of
these colonies discussed, and a remedy proposed; in a
letter to Lord Viscount Howick, under secretary for the
colonial department, &c. &c. &c. By Sir Alexander Malet,
bart. London, J. Ridgway, 1831.
vii, [9]-34 p.   22½ cm.

23052   Malham, John, 1747-1821.
The naval gazetteer; or, Seaman's complete guide. Containing a full and accurate account, alphabetically
arranged, of the several coasts of all the countries
and islands in the known world... Also comprehending
ample directions for sailing into or out of the different
ports, straits, and harbours of the four quarters of the
world... By the Rev. John Malham... Illustrated with a
correct set of charts from the latest and best surveys.
1st American ed. ... Boston, Printed for and sold by
W. Spotswood and J. Nancrede, 1797.
2 v.   17 fold. maps (incl. front.)   22 cm.

23053   Malin, William Gunn.
Some account of the Pennsylvania hospital, its origin,
objects, and present state. By W. G. Malin... Philadelphia, Printed by T. Kite & co., 1832.
46 p.   front.   22½ cm.

23054   Mallary, Rollin Carolus, 1784-1831.
An oration pronounced at Rutland, Fourth July, 1826;
being the fiftieth anniversary of American independence,
and the year of jubilee. By R. C. Mallary... Rutland,
Vt., W. Fay [1826]
24 p.   23 cm.

23055   Mallary, Rollin Carolus, 1784-1831.
Speech of Mr. Mallary, of Vt., on the tariff bill.
In the House of representatives of the United States,
March 3, 1828. Washington, Printed by Gales & Seaton,
1828.
34 p.   18 cm.

23056   Mallet, Alain Manesson, 1630?-1706?
Description de l'univers, contenant des differents
systêmes du monde, les cartes generales & particulieres

226

de la geographie ancienne & moderne: les plans & les
profils des principales villes & des autres lieux plus
considerables de la terre: avec les portraits des
souverains qui y commandent, leurs blasons, titres &
livrees: et les moeurs, religions, gouvernemens & divers
habillemens de chaque nation... Par Allain Manesson
Mallet... Paris, D. Thierry, 1683.
  5 v.   illus. (incl. maps)   plates, ports., plans,
tables.   22 cm.

23057 Mallet, F   fl. 1797.
  Descriptive account of the island of Trinidad: made by
order of Sir Ralph Abercrombie... commander in chief
of the British forces in the West Indies; by F. Mallet,
capt. of the surveying engineers, 1797... London,
Printed for W. Faden, 1802.
  15 p.   front. (fold. map) 2 fold. tab.   26½ cm.

23058 Mallet, John William, 1832-1912.
  Cotton: the chemical, geological, and meteorological
conditions involved in its successful cultivation. With
an account of the actual conditions and practice of
culture in the southern or cotton states of North America.
By Dr. John William Mallet... London, Chapman and Hall,
1862.
  xvi, 183, [1] p.   col. front., fold. map, diagrs.
19 cm.

23059 Malouet, Pierre Victor, baron, 1740-1814.
  Lettre à M. S. D., membre du Parlement, sur l'intérêt
de l'Europe, au salut des colonies de l'Amérique. Par
M. Malouet, député de la colonie de St. Domingue.
Londres, De l'impr. de Baylis, et se trouve chez J.
Deboffe [etc.] 1797.
  2 p.l., 36 p.   23 cm.

23060 Malouet, Pierre Victor, baron, 1740-1814.
  Voyage dans les forêts de la Guyane Française, par
P.-V. Malouet... Nouv. éd. pub. par m. Ferdinand Denis.
Paris, G. Sandré [1853]
  128 p.   12½ cm.

23061 Malte-Brun, Victor Adolphe, 1816-1889.
  La Sonora et ses mines. Esquisse geographique. Par
M. V. A. Malte-Brun... Paris, A. Bertrand, 1864.
  31 p.   fold. map.   22 cm.

23062 Mamiani della Rovere, Ludovico Vincenzo, 1652-1730.
  Arte de grammatica da lingua brasilica de nacam kiriri

227

composta pelo P. Luis Vincencio Mamiani, da Companhia de
Jesu, Missionario nas Aldeas da dita Naçao, Lisboa, na
Officina de Miguel Deslandes, Impressor de Sua Mag.
Anno de 1699. Com todas as licenças necessarias.
8 p.l., 124 p.   14 cm.

23063   Mammoth Vein Consolidated Coal Company.
        ... Report of joint committee and treasurer's circular.
        April 24, 1866. Boston, Printed by A. Mudge & son, 1866.
        cover-title, 13 p.   13½ cm.

23064   Mammoth Vein Consolidated Coal Company.
        ... Reports of the directors, trustees, superintendents,
        engineer, etc. November 25, 1864. Boston, Wright &
        Potter, printers, 1864.
        61 p.   23½ cm.

23065   Man, George Flagg.
        An oration, delivered before the citizens of the county
        of Kent, at Apponaug, Warwick, July 4, 1838. By George F.
        Man. Providence, Knowles, Vose, and company, 1838.
        23 p.   22 cm.

23066   Man, Thomas.
        Picture of a factory village: to which are annexed,
        remarks on lotteries. By Sui Generis: alias, Thomas Man...
        Providence, Printed for the author, 1833.
        144 p.   illus., 2 pl.   19 cm.
        "Picture of a factory village" is in verso; contains
        also several prose pieces.

23067   Man, Thomas.
        A picture of Woonsocket; or, The truth in its nudity;
        to which are added translations from the best French,
        Spanish and Italian writers. By Thomas Man... [n.p.]
        Printed for the author, 1835.
        103 p.   front., pl.   19 cm.

23068   Manasseh ben Joseph ben Israel, 1604-1657.
        The hope of Israel, written by Menasseh ben Israel...
        The 2d ed., corrected and amended. Whereunto are added,
        in this second edition, some discourses upon the point
        of the conversion of the Jewes. By Moses Wall. London,
        Printed by R. I. for L. Chapman, 1652.
        5 p.l., 62 p.   front. (port.)   26½ cm.

23069   Manby, George William, 1765-1854.
        Journal of a voyage to Greenland, in the year 1821.

228

With graphic illustrations. By George William Manby,
esq. London, Printed for G. and W. B. Whittaker, 1822.
viii, 143, [1] p.   illus., plates (1 fold.) fold.
map.   27½ x 22½ cm.

23070 Manchester, N. H. City library.
       Catalogue of the library of the Manchester Atheneum,
       and index of titles and authors, to which is added the
       constitution and by-laws, and a list of the officers
       and proprietors. Manchester, Union steam printing works,
       Campbell & Gilmore, 1853.
       xv, 112 p.   21 cm.

23071 [Mandar-Argeaut, pseud.]
       Quelques éclaircissemens sur les troubles survenus
       dans le Département du Sud de Saint Domingue, en fructidor
       an 4eme (août 1796 vieux style) Hambourg, Impr. de P. F.
       Fauche, 1797.
       3 p.l., [3]-95, 80 p.   22 cm.

23072 [Mandrillon, Joseph] 1743-1794.
       Le spectateur américain. Ou Remarques générales sur
       l'Amérique Septentrionale et sur la république des Treize-
       Etats-Unis. Suivi de Recherches philosophiques sur la
       découverte du Nouveau-monde. Par m. J^h. M*** ...
       Amsterdam, Les héritiers E. van Harrevelt, 1784.
       xvi, 128, 307, [4], [3]-91, [4] p.   fold. map, fold.
       tables.   22 cm.

23073 Manford, Erasmus.
       Twenty-five years in the West. By Erasmus Manford.
       Chicago, E. Manford, 1870.
       359 p.   19 cm.

23074 Manhattan Quartz Mining Company.
       Facts concerning quartz and quartz mining, together
       with the charter of the Manhattan quartz mining company,
       organized December 7th, 1851, under the general incor-
       poration act of California. New York, W. L. Burroughs'
       steam power presses, 1852.
       30, [2] p.   illus.   23 cm.

23075 Manigault, Gabriel, 1809-1888.
       The signs of the times. By G. Manigault, of South-
       Carolina. New York, Blelock & co. [186-]
       60 p.   23 cm.

23076 Manley, James R   1781-1851.
       Anniversary discourse, before the New York academy of

medicine, delivered in the Church of the crucifixion,
November 8th, 1818. By James R. Manley, M.D. Pub. by
order of the academy. New York, H. Ludwig & co.,
printers, 1849.
36 p.   23 cm.

23077   Manley, James R   1781-1851.
Exposition of the conduct and character of Dr. John
Augustine Smith, president of the Coll. of physicians
and surgeons in the city of New York, and professor of
physiology: as exhibited in the session of 1839-40.   By
James R. Manley, M.D., late lecturer on obstetrics.
New York, 1841.
48 p.   22 cm.

23078   Manley, James R   1781-1851.
An inaugural address delivered before the Medical
society of the state of New York, at the capitol in the
city of Albany, on the 8th day of February, 1826.   By
James R. Manley...   New York, Printed by J. Seymour, 1826.
28 p.   21½ cm.

23079   [Manley, James R   ] 1781-1851.
Letters on the College of physicians and surgeons, by
Graviora manent [pseud.]   New York, Printed by A. S.
Gould, 1841.
16 p.   22 cm.
An attack on John Augustine Smith, president of the
college.

23080   Manley, John, comp.
Cattaraugus County: embracing its agricultural
society, newspapers, civil list...   biographies of the
old pioneers...   colonial and state governors of New
York: names of towns and post officers, with the
statistics of each town.   Comp. by John Manley...
Little Valley, N. Y., J. Manley, 1857.
140 p.   ports.   23 cm.

23081   Mann, Cyrus, 1785-1859.
The Clinton family: or, The history of the temperance
reformation.   By Rev. Cyrus Mann...   Written for the
Massachusetts Sabbath school society, and rev. by the
Committee of publication.   Boston, Massachusetts Sabbath
school society, 1833.
vi, [12]-263 p. incl. front., illus.   15 cm.

23082   Mann, Edwin John, b. 1812, comp.
The deaf and dumb: or, A collection of articles relating

230

to the condition of deaf mutes; their education, and
the principal asylums devoted to their instruction. By
Edwin John Mann... Boston, D. K. Hitchcock, 1836.
xii, [13]-312 p. incl. front., plates.   18 cm.

23083 Mann, Horace, 1796-1859.
Answer to the "Rejoinder" of twenty-nine Boston school-
masters, part of the "thirty-one" who published "Remarks"
on the Seventh annual report of the secretary of the
Massachusetts Board of education. By Horace Mann,
secretary of the board. Boston, W. B. Fowle and N. Capen,
1845.
124 p.   23½ cm.

23084 Mann, Horace, 1796-1859.
Dedication of Antioch college, and inaugural address
of its president, Hon. Horace Mann; with other proceedings.
Yellow Springs, O., A. S. Dean; Boston, Crosby & Nichols,
1854.
132 p.   16 cm.

23085 [Mann, Herman] 1772-1833.
The female review: or, Memoirs of an American young
lady, whose life and character are peculiarly distinguished,
being a Continental soldier, for nearly three years, in the
late American war. During which time she performed the
duties of every department, into which she was called,
with punctual exactness, fidelity and honor, and preserved her chastity inviolate by the most artful conceal-
ment of her sex. With an appendix, containing characteristic traits, by different hands; her taste for economy,
principles of domestic education, &c. By a citizen of
Massachusetts. Dedham [Mass.] Printed by Nathaniel and
Benjamin Heaton, for the author, 1797.
xv, 258, [7] p.   port.   18 cm.

23086 Mann, Herman, 1795-1851.
Historical annals of Dedham, from its settlement in
1635, to 1817. By Herman Mann. Dedham, Mass., H. Mann,
1847.
viii, [9]-136 p.   23 cm.

23087 Mann, Horace, 1796-1859.
Lecture on education. By Horace Mann... Boston,
Marsh, Capen, Lyon and Webb, 1840.
62 p.   18½ cm.

23088 Mann, Horace, 1796-1859.
An oration delivered before the authorities of the city

of Boston, July 4, 1842. By Horace Mann. Boston, J. H.
Eastburn, city printer, 1842.
86 p.   21 cm.

23089   Mann, Horace, 1796-1859.
Reply to the "Remarks" of thirty-one Boston school-
masters on the Seventh annual report of the secretary of
the Massachusetts Board of education. By Horace Mann,
secretary of the board. Boston, W. B. Fowle and N. Capen,
1844.
176 p.   23½ cm.

23090   Mann, Horace, 1796-1859.
Report of an educational tour in Germany, and parts of
Great Britain and Ireland, being part of the seventh
annual report of Horace Mann, esq., secretary of the
Board of education, Mass., U.S., 1844, with preface and
notes, by W. B. Hodgson... London, Simpkin, Marshall,
and company; [etc., etc.] 1846.
x, 272 p.   16½ cm.

23091   Mann, Horace, 1796-1859.
Sequel to the so called correspondence between the
Rev. M. H. Smith and Horace Mann, surreptitiously
published by Mr. Smith; containing a letter from Mr.
Mann, suppressed by Mr. Smith, with the reply therein
promised. Boston, W. B. Fowle, 1847.
56 p.   22½ cm.

23092   Mann, Horace, 1796-1859.
Two lectures on intemperance. 1. - The effects of
intemperance on the poor and ignorant. II. - The
effects of intemperance on the rich and educated. By
Horace Mann... Syracuse [N. Y.] Hall, Mills, and
company; Boston, W. J. Reynolds & co., 1852.
127 p.   16 cm.

23093   Mann, James.
The American bird-keeper's manual; or, Directions for
the proper management of American and foreign singing
birds. With particular instructions for the breeding
of canary birds, and the proper treatment of their
young. Together with some remarks upon the diseases
to which birds are liable... By James Mann... Boston,
The author, and sold by Little and Brown [etc.] 1848.
viii, [9]-166 p.   16 cm.

23094   Mann, Joel, 1789-1884.
A discourse delivered in Bristol, December 22, 1820,

on the anniversary of the landing of our ancestors at Plymouth. By Joel Mann... Warren [R. I.] Printed by S. Randall, 1821.
19 p.   20½ cm.

23095   Mann, William Julius, 1819-1892.
Lutheranism in America: an essay on the present condition of the Lutheran church in the United States. By W. J. Mann...   Philadelphia, Lindsay & Blakiston, 1857.
1 p.l., [vii]-xii, [13]-152 p.   19 cm.

23096   Mannequin, Théodore, b. 1819.
Les provinces argentines et Buénos Ayres depuis leur independance jusqu'à nos jours.   Étude historique et économique au point de vue de l'état actuel des choses dans ces contrées. Par m. Th. Mannequin...   Paris, Guiillaumin et co., 1856.
cover-title, 48 p.   25 cm.

23097   Manning, James.
A sketch of the life and writings of the Rev. Micaiah Towgood, by James Manning...   Exeter, Printed for the author, by E. Grigg, 1792.
2 p.l., 191 p.   23½ cm.

23098   Mansfield, Daniel, 1807-1847.
Two sermons, delivered on the second centennial anniversary of the organization of the first church, and the settlement of the first minister in Wenham. By Daniel Mansfield...   Published by request of the church. Andover, Printed by Allen, Morrill and Wardwell, 1845.
72 p.   23½ cm.

23099   Mansfield, Edward Deering, 1801-1880.
American education, its principles and elements. Dedicated to the teachers of the United States.   By Edward D. Mansfield...   New York, A. S. Barnes & co.; Cincinnati, H. W. Derby & co., 1851.
2 p.l., [vii]-viii, [9]-330 p.   20½ cm.

23100   [Mansfield, Edward Deering] 1801-1880.
[Articles on the tariff. Cincinnati, 1865]
16 p.   13 cm.   (Society for encouragement of American industry. [Publications no. 1])

23101   Mansfield, Edward Deering, 1801-1880.
Exposition of the natural position of Mackinaw City, and the climate, soil, and commercial elements of the

surrounding country. By E. D. Mansfield, esq.
Cincinnati, Wrightson & co., printers, 1857.
48, [2] p.   2 fold. maps.   21½ cm.

23102   Mansfield, Edward Deering, 1801-1880.
The legal rights, liabilities and duties of women;
with an introductory history of their legal condition in
the Hebrew, Roman and feudal civil systems. Including
the law of marriage and divorce, the social relations of
husband and wife, parent and child, of guardian and ward,
and of employer and employed. By Edward D. Mansfield...
Salem [Mass.]   J. P. Jewett & co.;   Cincinnati, W. H.
Moore & co., 1845.
369 p.   18 cm.

23103   Mansfield, Edward D[eering]
A letter in regard to the tariff on iron and labor, by
Edward D. Mansfield... Cincinnati, Wrightson & co.,
printers, 1869.
40 p.   22½ cm.

23104   Mansfield, Edward Deering, 1801-1880.
The life of General Winfield Scott. By Edward D.
Mansfield, esq. New York, A. S. Barnes & co., 1846.
x, [11]-366 (i.e. 368) p. incl. illus., maps, plans.
front. (port.) plates.   19½ cm.

23105   Mansfield, Edward Deering, 1801-1880.
The Mexican war: a history of its origin, and a
detailed account of the victories which terminated in
the surrender of the capital; with the official des-
patches of the generals. By Edward D. Mansfield...
New York, A. S. Barnes & co.; Cincinnati, Derby,
Bradley & co., 1848.
iv, [5]-323 p. incl. maps, plans.   front., pl.
20 cm.

23106   Mansfield, Edward Deering, 1801-1880.
On the railway connections of Philadelphia with the
central West. Letters of Prof. Edward D. Mansfield...
to Job R. Tyson... Philadelphia, J. C. Clark,
printer, 1853.
3 p.l., [5]-36 p.   23½ cm.

23107   Mansfield, Edward Deering, 1801-1880.
The political manual: being a complete view of the
theory and practice of the general and state governments
of the United States. Adapted to the use of colleges,
academies, and schools. By Edward D. Mansfield...

New York, A. S. Barnes & co., 1872.
349 p.   19 cm.

23108   Mansfield, Edward Deering, 1801-1880.
The United States Military academy at West Point. By
E. D. Mansfield...   Hartford, H. Barnard; etc., etc.,
1863
1 p.l., p. [17]-48.   23 cm.

23109   Mansfield, Isaac, 1750-1826.
A sermon, preached in the camp at Roxbury, November 23,
1775; being the day appointed by authority for thanksgiving through the province. By Isaac Mansfield, jun.,
A.M. chaplain to General Thomas's regiment, in the Continental army. Published at the request of the officers in
said regiment... Boston, Printed by S. Hall, at his
office in School-street, 1776.
27, [1] p.   20½ cm.

23110   Mansfield, Mrs. Lucy (Langdon) ed.
Memorial of Charles Finney Mansfield, comprising extracts from his diaries, letters, and other papers.
New York, Baker & Godwin, printers, 1866.
viii, [9]-265 p., 1 l.   front. (port.)   24 cm.

23111   Manship, Andrew, 1824-   comp.
National jewels: Washington, Lincoln, and the fathers
of the revolution. By Rev. Andrew Manship... Philadelphia, A. Manship, 1865.
vi p., 1 l., [9]-123 p.   front. (port.)   23½ cm.

23112   Manship, Andrew, 1824-
Thirteen years' experience in the itineracy. By Rev.
Andrew Manship... 2d ed. Philadelphia, Higgins & Per-
kinpine, 1856.
2 p.l., xii, 13-398 p.   front. (port.) plates.
20 cm.
Autobiography.

23113   Mansie, Alexander.
... The apprenticed labourer's manual; or, An essay
on the apprenticeship system, and the duties of the
apprenticed labourers, including several of the
personal and relative duties binding on mankind in
general. By Alexander Mansie... British Guiana,
Society for the instruction of the labouring classes,
1837.
xiii, [1], 215, [2], 13 p.   23 cm.

235

23114   Mantegazza, Carlo.
        Viaggio del cittadino Carlo Mantegazza, Milanese, a
        S. Domingo nell' anno 1802... Milano, Stamperia e
        fonderia del Genio tipografico, 1803.
        3 p.l., 136 p.   20 cm.

23115   The manufacturing interests of the city of Buffalo.
        Including sketches of the history of Buffalo. With
        notices of its principal manufacturing establishments.
        2d ed. Buffalo, C. F. S. Thomas, 1866.
        iv, 99 p.   23 cm.

23116   Manwaring, Christopher, 1774-1832.
        Essays, historical, moral, political and agricultural...
        By Christopher Manwaring... New London, Printed by
        Samuel Green, for the author, 1829.
        204 p., 1 l.   18 cm.

23117   Manzini, Nicolás B   L   1812-1896.
        Histoire de l'inoculation préservative de la fièvre
        jaune, pratiquée par ordre du gouvernement espagnol à
        l'Hôpital militaire de la Havane, rédigée par Nichoas
        B. L. Manzini... Paris, J. B. Baillière et fils;
        New York, H. Ballière; [etc., etc.] 1858.
        xii, 243 p.   21½ cm.

23118   Mapes, James Jay, 1806-1866.
        Inaugural address... Jan. 7, 1845, before the Mechanics
        institute, of the city of New York, by James J. Mapes...
        New York, Institute rooms, 1845.
        23 p.   23 cm.

23119   Maple leaves from Canada, for the grave of Abraham Lincoln:
        being a discourse delivered by Rev. Robert Norton,
        pastor of the First Presbyterian church, and address
        by Rev. Robert F. Burns, pastor of the Canada Presby-
        terian church, at St. Catharines, Canada West, April 23rd,
        1865, together with proceedings of public meetings, &c.
        St. Catharines, Printed at E. S. Leavenworth's book &
        job office, 1865.
        39 p.   21½ cm.

23120   Mapleson, Thomas W   Gwilt.
        A hand-book of heraldry. By G. [!] W. Gwilt Maple-
        son, esq. New York, J. Wiley, 1851.
        57, [5] p.   illus., plates (partly col.)   20 cm.

23121   Marcandier,
        ... An abstract of the most useful parts of a late

treatise on hemp, translated from the French of M.
Marcaudier... Together with some observations upon the
prospect of singular advantage which may be derived to
Great-Britain and her colonies from their early adopting
the method prescribed. To which is added, some account
of the use of the horse-chesnut; and a plan of the Pennsylvania hemp brake. Boston, Printed and sold by Edes &
Gill, in Queen-street, 1766.
2 p.l., 30 p., 1 l.   plan.   19½ cm.

23122 Marcellus, pseud.
Essays on the liberty of the press. By Marcellus.
Originally pub. in the Virginia argus, in December, 1803.
Richmond, Printed by S. Pleasants, jr., 1804.
19 p.   17½ cm.

23123 Marcellus, pseud.
Marcellus; pub. in the Virginia gazette, November and
December, 1794. [Richmond, 1794?]
36 p.   22½ cm.

23124 March, Alden, 1795-1869.
Semi-centennial address delivered before the medical
society of the state of New York, and members of the
Legislature, in the capitol at Albany, Feb. 4, 1857.
By Alden March, M.D., president of the society.   Albany,
C. Van Benthuysen, printer, 1857.
20 p.   23 cm.

23125 March, Charles Wainwright, 1815-1864.
Reminiscences of Congress. By Charles W. March.   New
York, Baker and Scribner, 1850.
viii, 295 p.   front. (port.)   19 cm.

23126 March, Daniel, 1816-1909.
Yankee land and the Yankee. By Daniel March. Hartford, Printed by Case, Tiffany and Burnham, 1840.
33 p.   19½ cm.
Contains also: The iron horse (p. [23]-33)

23127 [Marchmont, Hugh Hume, 3d earl of] 1708-1794.
A state of the rise and progress of our disputes with
Spain, and of the conduct of our ministers relating
thereto. London, Printed for T. Cooper, 1739.
1 p.l., 76 p.   19½ cm.

23128 Marckmann, Jørgen Wilhelm, 1804-1861.
Bogtrykkeren Benjamin Franklins liv og levnet. Af

237

J. W. Marckmann... Udgivet af Selskabet for trykke-
frihedens rette brug... Kjøbenhavn, Trykt i det Ber-
lingske bogtrykkeri, 1837.
iv, 159, [1] p.   16½ cm.

23129 Marcou, Jules, 1824-1898.
       The taconie and Lower Silurian rocks of Vermont and
       Canada. By Jules Marcou... Boston, Press of G. C. Rand
       & Avery, 1862.
       cover-title, p. 239-253.   22½ cm.

23130 Mariátegui, Francisco Javier.
       Reseña histórica de los principales concordatos cele-
       brados con Roma, y breves reflexiones sobre el último
       habido entre Pio IX y el gobierno de Bolivia. Por F. J.
       Mariátegui... Lima, Impreso por J. Mira, 1856.
       4 p.l., 286, 2 p.   20½ cm.

23131 Mariz, Pedro de, d. 1615.
       Dialogos de varia historia, em qve se referem as vidas
       dos senhores reyes de Portugal. Com os mais verdadeiros
       retratos que se puderam achar. Com as noticias de nossos
       reynos, & conquistas, & successos do mundo. Autor,
       Pedro de Mariz: acrecentados por Antonio Craesbeeck de
       Mello, impressor de Sua Alteza. Te a vida do senhor rey
       dom Ioam o IV. de boa memoria. E na sua officina
       impressos. [Lisboa] 1674.
       5 p.l., 560 p.   ports.   21 cm.

23132 Marke, Desdemona.
       An appeal to the women of America, by Desdemona Marke...
       Philadelphia, W. S. Young, printer, 1858.
       cover-title, 8 p.   23½ cm.
       In favor of a protective tariff.

23133 Markham, Sir Clements Robert, 1830-1916.
       Travels in Peru and India while superintending the
       collection of chinchona plants and seeds in South America,
       and their introduction into India. By Clements R.
       Markham... London, J. Murray, 1862.
       xviii, 572 p.   front., illus., plates, fold. maps,
       fold. tab.   22 cm.

23134 Markham, William, abp. of York, 1719-1807.
       A sermon preached before the incorporated Society for
       the propagation of the gospel in foreign parts; at their
       anniversary meeting in the... church of St. Mary-le-Bow,
       on... February 21, 1777. By the Most Reverend Father

in God, William, lord archbishop of York. London,
Printed by T. Harrison and S. Brooke, 1777.
xxv, 27-104 p., 1 l.   22½ cm.

23135   [Markoe, Peter] 1753?-1792.
The times; a poem... Philadelphia, Printed by William
Spotswood, 1788.
2 p.l., 22 p.   23 cm.

23136   Marks, David, 1805-1845.
Memoirs of the life of David Marks, minister of the
gospel; edited by Mrs. Marilla Marks... Dover, N. H.,
Free-will Baptist printing establishment, 1846.
xi, [13]-516 p.   front. (port.)   20½ cm.

23137   Marly; or, The life of a planter in Jamaica: comprehending
characteristic sketches of the present state of society
and manners in the British West Indies. And an impartial
review of the leading questions relative to colonial
policy. 2d ed. Glasgow, Printed for Griffin & co.;
[etc., etc.] 1828.
2 p.l., ii, 363, [1] p.   21½ cm.

23138   Marmier, Xavier, 1809-1892.
Cartas sobre la America, por X. Marmier. Traducidas
para el Universal... Mexico, Impr. del Universal [185-]
2 v.   20 cm.
Travels in Canada, the United States, Cuba, and South
America.

23139   Marmont, Auguste Frédéric Louis Viesse de, duc de Ragase,
1774-1852.
The spirit of military institutions, by Marshal Marmont,
duke of Ragusa. Tr. from the last Paris ed. (1859), and
augm. by Biographical, historical, topographical, and
military notes; with a new version of General Jomini's
celebrated thirty-fifth chapter, of part 1, of Treatise
on grand military operations. By Frank Schaller...
Columbia, S. C., Evans and Cogswell, 1864.
278 p.   18 cm.

23140   Márquez, José Arnaldo.
El Perú y la España moderna, por J. Arnaldo Márquez.
Lima, Impr. de "El Nacional" [etc.] 1866.
2 v.   26 cm.

23141   Márquez, José Arnaldo, 1830-1904.
Recuerdos de viaje a los Estados-Unidos de la América

239

del norte (1857-1861) por José Arnaldo Márquez. Lima,
Imprenta del "Comercio" pop [!] J. M. Monterola, 1862.
3 p.l., 135 p., 1 l.   20½ cm.

23142   Marr, Wilhelm, b. 1819.
        Reise nach Central-Amerika. Von Wilhelm Marr...
        Hamburg, O. Meissner, 1863.
        2 v.   21 cm.

23143   Marrant, John, bl 1755.
        A narrative of the life of John Marrant, of New York,
        in North America: giving an account of his conversion
        when only fourteen years of age: his leaving his mother's
        house from religious motives, wandering several days in
        the desert without food, and being at last taken by an
        Indian hunter among the Cherokees, where he was condemned
        to die. With an account of the conversion of the king of
        the Cherokees and his daughter, &c. &c. &c. The whole
        authenticated by the Reverend W. Aldridge. Leeds,
        Printed by Davies and co., 1810.
        iv, [5]-24 p.   21½ cm.

23144   Marriott, Sir James, bart. 1730?-1803.
        The case of the Dutch ships, considered. London,
        Printed for R. and J. Dodsley, and sold by M. Cooper,
        1758.
        2 p.l., 59 p.   21 cm.

23145   [Marriott, Sir James, bart.] 1730?-1803.
        Memoire justificatif de la conduite de la Grande
        Bretagne, en arrêtant les navires étrangers et les
        munitions de guerre, destinées aux insurgens de l'Amérique
        London, Imprimé par T. Harrison et S. Brooke, 1779.
        vii, 60 p.   24 cm.

23146   Marriott, John, 1762-1797.
        Poems, by John Marriott. To which is prefixed a short
        account of the author, including extracts from some of
        his letters. Printed in England, 1803. New-Bedford,
        Re-printed by A. Shearman, jun., 1805.
        xlii p., 1 l., 141 p.   16½ cm.

23147   [Marryat, Joseph] 1757-1824.
        Concessions to America the bane of Britain; or, The
        cause of the present distressed situation of the British
        colonial and shipping interests explained, and the proper
        remedy suggested... London, W. J. & J. Richardson [etc.]
        1807.
        63 p.   21 cm.

23148   Marryat, Joseph, 1757-1824.
        Speech of Joseph Marryat, esq., in the House of commons,
        on Monday, June 5, 1820, upon the petition of the ship
        owners of the port of London, against any alteration in
        the duties on timber... 2d ed. The Pamphleteer. London,
        1820. 22½ cm. v. 17, p. [57]-72.

23149   Marsden, Joshua, b. 1777.
        Grace displayed: an interesting narrative of the life,
        conversion, Christian experience, ministry, and missionary
        labours of Joshua Marsden... New York, Published for,
        and sold by, the author, corner of Rivington and sixth-
        street; sold also by Griffin and Rudd, Eastburn, Kirk,
        and co., and John C. Totten. Paul and Thomas, printers,
        1813.
        2 p.l., 240 p.   19 cm.
        Including an account of his journey to, and missionary
        work in Nova Scotia, New Brunswick, and the Bermudas.

23150   Marsden, Joshua, 1777-1837.
        The narrative of a mission to Nova Scotia, New Brunswick,
        and the Somers islands; with a tour to lake Ontario.
        To which is added, The mission, an original poem, with
        copious notes. Also, a brief account of missionary
        societies, and much interesting information on missions
        in general. By Joshua Marsden late missionary to Nova
        Scotia, New Brunswick, and the Bermudas... Plymouth-
        Dock, Printed and sold by J. Johns, 53 St. Aubyn-street;
        sold also by Thomas Kayne, 42 Castle-street, Liverpool;
        Baynes, Pater-noster-row; Williams and son, Stationer's
        court; Burton and Briggs, 156 Leadenhall-street; Booth,
        Duke-street Manchester-square; Blanchard, City-road,
        London; and at all the Methodist preaching houses in
        town and country, 1816.
        xiv, 289 p.   front. (port.) 2 fold. tab.   21½ cm.

23151   [Marsh, Catherine] 1818-1912.
        The brave and happy soldier. By the author of "The
        memorials of Captain Hedley Vicars." Boston, American
        tract society [186-?]
        16 p.   13½ cm.

23152   [Marsh, Catherine] 1818-1912.
        The life of the Rev. William Marsh, D.D., by his
        daughter... New York, R. Carter and brothers, 1867.
        2 v.   fronts. (v. 1, port.) 1 illus., plates.
        20 cm.

241

23153 Marsh, George P erkins 1801-1882.
       Report made under authority of the legislature of
Vermont, on the artificial propagation of fish, by
George P. Marsh. Burlington, Free press print, 1857.
52, 62, 2 p.   23 cm.
"Artificial fish-breeding. Abridged from an essay by
Professor Karl Vogt, of Geneva, Switzerland": p. 22-52.
The Appendix includes "Pisciculture," signed Jules
Haime, Revue des deux mondes, June 1854, and "Extracts
from the Transactions of the Connecticut state agricul-
tural society for the year 1856," containing "Experiments
in artificial fish-breeding, by E. C. Kellogg," etc., etc.

23154 Marsh, George Perkins, 1801-1882.
       Speech of Mr. G. P. Marsh, of Vermont, on the Mexican
war, delivered in the House of representatives of the
U. S., February 10, 1848. Washington, Printed by
J. & G. S. Gideon, 1848.
16 p.   24 cm.

23155 Marsh, George Perkins, 1801-1882.
       Speech of Mr. George P. Marsh, of Vermont, on the
tariff bill. Delivered in the House of representatives
of the United States on the 30th of April, 1844. St.
Albans, Vt., Printed by E. B. Whiting, 1844.
15 p.   24½ cm.

23156 Marsh, James, 1794-1842.
       The remains of the Rev. James Marsh, D.D., late
president and professor of moral and intellectual
philosophy, in the University of Vermont; with a memoir
of his life... Boston, Crocker and Brewster, 1843.
xii, [3]-642 p.   24½ cm.

23157 Marsh, James W
       Washington's prophecy; or, Facts concerning the
rebellion. By James W. Marsh... Louisville [Ky.]
Bradley & Gilbert, 1866.
146 p.   illus. (port.)   22 cm.

23158 Marsh, John, 1743-1821.
       A discourse delivered at Wethersfield, December 11th,
1783. Being a day of public thanksgiving, throughout
the United States of America. By John Marsh, A.M.,
pastor of the First church and society in Wethersfield.
Published at the desire and expence of said society.
Hartford, Printed by Hudson and Goodwin [1783?]
22 p.   24½ cm.

23159   Marsh, John, 1743-1821.
A discourse, delivered in Wethersfield, at the funeral
of the Honourable John Chester, esq. who died November 4th,
1809, in the 61st year of his age. By John Marsh, D.D.,
pastor of the First church in Wethersfield... Hartford,
Printed by Hudson and Goodwin, 1809.
24 p.   21 cm.

23160   Marsh, John, 1743?-1821.
A sermon, preached before His Honor Oliver Wolcott, esq.,
L.L.D., lieutenant-governor and commander in chief, and
the honorable the General assembly of the state of
Connecticut, convened at Hartford, on the day of the
anniversary election, May 12th, 1796. By John Marsh,
A.M., pastor of the First church in Wethersfield.
Hartford, Printed by Hudson and Goodwin, 1796.
34 p.   21 cm.

23161   Marsh, John, 1788-1868.
A discourse on the extent and evils of the Sunday
liquor traffic in cities. Delivered before the New York
Tenth ward temperance society, and in several churches
in the city. By Rev. John Marsh... New York, American
temperance union, 1848.
24 p.   22 cm.

23162   Marsh, John, 1788-1868.
A half century tribute to the cause of temperance.
An address delivered at New Paltz, before the Ulster
County temperance society, January 8, 1851, by Rev. John
Marsh... New York, American temperance union, 1851.
32 p.   22½ cm.

23163   Marsh, John, 1788-1868.
The temperance battle not man's but God's. Written and
published for the instruction and encouragement of the
friends of temperance throughout the United States, by
Rev. John Marsh... New York, American temperance union,
1858.
23, [1] p.   22½ cm.

23164   Marsh, John, 1788-1868.
Temperance recollections. Labors, defeats, triumphs.
An autobiography. By John Marsh... New York, C.
Scribner & co., 1866.
6, vii, [7]-373 p.   20 cm.

23165   Marsh, John, 1788-1868.
The triumphs of temperance, a discourse, by Rev. John

Marsh... New York, J. P. Prall, printer, 1855.
16 p.   22½ cm.

23166 [Marsh, Leonard] 1800-1870.
The apocatastasis; or, Progress backwards. A new "Tract
for the times"... By the author. Burlington Vt.
C. Goodrich, 1854.
202 p., 1 l.   24 cm.

23167 Marsh, Othniel Charles, 1831-1899.
Description of an ancient sepulchral mound near Newark,
Ohio. By O. C. Marsh, F.G.S. [New Haven? 1866]
cover-title, 11 p.   22½ cm.

23168 Marsh, Roswell.
Important correspondence. Friendly discussion of party
politics in 1860-1. Letters of Hon. Roswell Marsh, of
Steubenville, Ohio, and Hon. Chas. Reemelin, of Cincinnati.
[n.p., 1865?]
51 p.   23½ cm.

23169 Marshall, Christopher, 1709-1797.
Extracts from the diary of Christopher Marshall, kept in
Philadelphia and Lancaster, during the American revolution,
1774-1781. Ed. by William Duane... Albany, J. Munsell,
1877.
iv, [5]-330 p.   21 cm.

23170 Marshall, Edward Chauncey, 1824-
History of the United States Naval academy, with
biographical sketches, and the names of all the superin-
tendents, professors and graduates, to which is added a
record of some of the earliest votes by Congress, of
thanks, medals, and swords to naval officers. By Edward
Chauncey Marshall... New York, D. Van Nostrand, 1862.
156 p.   front., pl.   18½ cm.

23171 Marshall, James, 1834-1896.
The nation's grief: death of Abraham Lincoln. A discourse delivered in the chapel of the officers' division
of the United States general hospital, near Fort Monroe,
Va., Sunday, April 29th, 1865, and repeated by special
request in St. Paul's church, Norfolk, Va., by James
Marshall... Pub. by Battery 'F' 3d Pa. H. artillery.
Syracuse, N. Y., The Daily journal steam book and job
printing office, 1865.
40 p.   22 cm.

23172   Marshall, James, 1834-1896.
        The nation's prospects of peace. A discourse delivered
        at the Officers' general hospital, and repeated at the
        Hampton hospital, near Fort Monroe, Va., on Thanksgiving
        day, September 11, 1864. By James Marshall. Published
        by the patients in the hospital. Philadelphia, King &
        Baird, printers, 1864.
            32 p.   23½ cm.

23173   Marshall, James V
        The United States manual of biography and history:
        comprising lives of the presidents and vice presidents of
        the United States, and the cabinet-officers, from the
        adoption of the Constitution to the present day. Also,
        lives of the signers of the Declaration of independence,
        and of the old Articles of confederation, of the framers
        of the Constitution of the United States, and of the
        chief justices of the Supreme court of the United States.
        With authentic copies of the Declaration of independence,
        the Articles of confederation, and the Constitution of
        the United States. To which is prefixed an introductory
        history of the United States. By James V. Marshall...
        Philadelphia, J. B. Smith & co., 1856.
            712 p.   front., plates, ports.   24 cm.

23174   Marshall, John, 1755-1835.
        A history of the colonies planted by the English on the
        continent of North America, from their settlement, to
        the commencement of that war which terminated in their
        independence. By John Marshall. Philadelphia, A.
        Small, 1821.
            xv, [9]-486 p.   23 cm.
        Originally published as an introduction to the author's
        Life of George Washington.

23175   Marshall, John, 1755-1835.
        Opinions of the late Chief Justice of the United
        States (John Marshall) concerning freemasonry. [Boston?
        1840]
            4 p.   22 cm.

23176   Marshall, John, 1755-1835.
        The writings of John Marshall, late chief justice of
        the United States, upon the federal Constitution...
        Boston, J. Monroe and company, 1839.
            xvii p., 1 l., 728 p.   22½ cm.
        A collection of Marshall's constitutional opinions.

23177 Marshall, John, 1784?-1837.
Royal naval biography; or, Memoirs of the services of
all the flag-officers, superannuated rear-admirals,
retired-captains, post-captains, and commanders, whose
names appeared on the Admiralty list of sea officers at
the commencement of the present year, or who have since
been promoted; illustrated by a series of historical
and explanatory notes... With copious addenda. By John
Marshall... London, Printed for Longman, Hurst, Rees,
Orme, and Brown, 1823-35.
4 v. in 8.   22½ cm.

23178 Marshall, John A
American bastile. A history of the illegal arrests
and imprisonment of American citizens during the late
civil war. By John A. Marshall... 4th ed. Philadelphia,
Evans, Stoddart & co., 1870.
lxx, 71-728 p.   front., 1 illus., plates.   23½ cm.

23179 Marshall, Josiah T
The dignity of the agricultural occupation. An address,
delivered before an agricultural meeting at Plessis,
Jefferson County, N. Y., on the 26th September, 1838. By
Josiah T. Marshall. Watertown [N. Y.] Printed by Knowlton
& Rice, 1838.
15 p.   19 cm.

23180 Marsillac, Jean.
La vie de Guillaume Penn, fondateur de la Pensylvanie;
premier législateur connu des États-Unis de l'Amérique.
Ouvrage contenant l'historique des premiers fondemens
de Philadelphie, des loix et de la constitution des
États-Unis de l'Amérique, des principes et actions de la
Société des amis (vulgairement connus sous le nom de
Quakers, etc.)... Par J. Marsillac... Paris, De l'
imprimerie du Cercle social, 1791.
2 v.   20½ cm.

23181 Martens, Georg Friedrich von, 1756-1821, ed.
Nouveaux supplémens au Recueil de traités... depuis
1761 jusqu'à présent; fondé par George Frédéric de
Martens. Suivis d'un appendice contenant des traités
et actes publics importans d'une date antérieure...
Par Frédéric Murhard... Goettingue, Dieterich, 1839-42.
3 v.   20½ cm.

23182 The Martial achievements of Great Britain and her allies;
from 1799 to 1815. London, Printed for J. Jenkins, by

246

L. Harrison & J. C. Leigh [1815]
3 p.l., viii, [122] p.   51 col. pl. (incl. front.)
35 x 29½ cm.

23183   Martin, Benjamin Ellis, d. 1909.
In memoriam; Joseph Gilbert Totten. By Benjamin Ellis
Martin... New York, C. B. Richardson, 1866.
8 p.   23 cm.

23184   Martin, Ennalls, 1758-1834.
An essay on the epidemics of the winters of 1813 and
1814, in Talbot & Queen-Anne's counties in the state of
Maryland. By Ennalls Martin... Baltimore, Printed by
Joseph Robinson, 1815.
vii (i.e. viii), [9]-78 p.   22 cm.

23185   Martin, François Xavier, 1762?-1846.
The history of Louisiana, from the earliest period.
By François-Xavier Martin... New Orleans, Printed by
Lyman and Beardslee, 1827-29.
2 v.   22 cm.

23186   Martin, François Xavier, 1762?-1846.
The history of North Carolina, from the earliest period.
By François-Xavier Martin... New Orleans, Printed by
A. T. Penniman & co., 1829.
2 v.   21½ cm.

23187   Martin, Frederick, 1830-1883.
Handbook of contemporary biography. By Frederick Martin
... London, Macmillan and co., 1870.
3 p.l., 287, [1] p.   17½ cm.

23188   Martin, Henry, of Baltimore.
Letter of Henry Martin, esq., president of the Baltimore
copper company, to the Senate of the United States, in
opposition to the bill increasing the duty on imported
copper ores. Baltimore, Sun printing establishment,
1869.
12 p.   12½ cm.

23189   Martin, John, 1741-1820.
Familiar dialogues between Americans and Britannicus;
in which the right of private judgment; the exploded
doctrines of infallibility, passive obedience, and non-
resistance; with the leading sentiments of Dr. Price, on
the nature of civil liberty, &c. are particularly
considered. By John Martin... London, Printed for

247

J. Wilkie [etc.] 1776.
iv, 74 p., 1 1.   21 cm.

23190   Martin, Leopold Charles, 1817-1889.
The current gold and silver coins of all countries,
their weight and fineness, and their intrinsic value in
English money. With facsimiles of the coins. By
Leopold C. Martin... and Charles Trübner. London,
Trübner & co., 1863.
xx p., 1 1., 140 pl.   24½ cm.

23191   Martin, Michael, 1795-1821.
Confession of Michael Martin, or Captain Lightfoot,
who was hung at Cambridge, Massachusetts in the year
1821, for the robbery of Maj. Bray. Also an account of
Dr. John Wilson, who recently died at Brattleboro',
Vt., believed by many to be the notorious Captain
Thunderbolt. Brattleboro', Vt., J. B. Miner, 1847.
30, 12 p.   23½ cm.

23192   Martin, Morgan Lewis, 1805-1887.
Address delivered before the State historical society
of Wisconsin, at Madison, January 21, 1851. By M. L.
Martin. Green Bay, Robinson & brothers, printers, 1851.
48 p.   19 cm.

23193   Martin, Robert Montgomery, 1803?-1868.
History of Nova Scotia, Cape Breton, The Sable
Islands, New Brunswick, Prince Edward Island, the
Bermudas, Newfoundland, &c. &c. By R. Montgomery
Martin, F.S.S. London, Whittaker & co., 1837.
viii, 363, [1] p. incl. tables.   2 fold. maps.
18 cm.

23194   Martin, Robert Montgomery, 1803?-1868.
Taxation of the British empire. By R. Montgomery
Martin... London, E. Wilson, 1833.
xxvi, [2], 264 p. incl. tables.   16½ cm.

23195   Martin, William Charles Linnaeus, 1798-1864.
A general history of humming-birds, or the Trochilidae:
with especial reference to the collection of J. Gould...
now exhibiting in the gardens of the Zoological society
of London. By W. C. L. Martin... London, H. G. Bohn,
1852.
vii p., 1 1., 232 p.   col. front., 14 (i.e. 15) col.
pl.   17 cm.

23196 Martin, William T   1788-1866.
History of Franklin County Ohio : a collection of
reminiscences of the early settlement of the county;
with biographical sketches; and a complete history of
the county to the present time. By William T. Martin.
Columbus, Follett, Foster & Company, 1858.
v, 449, [1] p.   front., plates.   23 cm.

23197 Martindale, Joseph C
A history of the townships of Byberry and Moreland,
in Philadelphia, Pa., from their earliest settlement
by the whites to the present time. By Joseph C. Martindale... Philadelphia, T. E. Zell, 1867.
xii, [13]-379 p.   19½ cm.

23198 Martineau, Harriet, 1802-1876.
A history of the American compromises. Reprinted,
with additions, from the Daily news. By Harriet Martineau. London, J. Chapman, 1856.
35 p.   21½ cm.

23199 Martínez de la Puente, José, fl. 1681.
Compendio de las historias de los descvbrimientos,
conqvistas, y gverras de la India Oriental, y sus islas,
desde los tiempos del infante don Enrique de Portugal
su inventor... hasta los del rey d. Felipe II. de
Portugal, y III. de Castilla. Y la introdvccion del
comercio portugues en las Malucas, y sus operaciones
politicas, y militares en ellas. Hecho, y añadida vna
descripcion de la India, y sus islas y de las costas
de Africa, por donde se començó la nauegacion del mar
del Sur; sus riquezas, costumbres de sus gentes, y otras
cosas notables... Por D. Ioseph Martinez de la Pvente...
Madrid, Viuda de I. Fernandez de Buendia, 1681.
8 p.l., 380, [34] p.   21 cm.

23200 Martius, Karl Friedrich Philipp von, 1794-1868.
Catalogue de la bibliothèque américaine de Mr. de
Martius. Munich, 1848.
1 p.l., 66 p.   29 x 23 cm.

23201 Martius, Karl Friedrich Philipp von, 1794-1868.
Systema materiae medicae vegetabilis brasiliensis.
Composuit Car. Frid. Phil. de Martius. Lipsiae, apud
F. Fleischer; Vindobonae, apud F. Beck in comm., 1843.
4 p.l., [vii]-xxvi, 155, [1] p.   22 cm.

23202 [Martyn, Benjamin] 1699-1763.
Reasons for establishing the colony of Georgia, with

regard to the trade of Great Britain, the increase of
our people, and the employment and support it will
afford to great numbers of our own poor, as well as
foreign persecuted Protestants. With some account of
the country, and the design of the trustees... London,
Printed for W. Meadows, at the Angel in Cornhill, 1733.
48 p.   front., map.   25½ x 20½ cm.

23203   Marure, Alexandro, 1809-1851.
Memoria historica sobre el canal de Nicaragua, seguida
de algunas observaciones inéditas de Mr. J. Baily sobre
el mismo asunto. Escrita por Alejandro Marure...
Guatemala, Imprenta de la Paz, 1845.
1 p.l., 47 p., 1 l.   24½ cm.

23204   Marvin, Abijah Perkins.
History of Worcester in the war of the rebellion. By
Abijah P. Marvin... Worcester [Mass.] The author, 1870.
582 p.   front., ports., plan.   23½ cm.

23205   Marvin, Dudley, 1786-1856.
Letter of the Hon. Dudley Marvin, of New York.
[Washington, J. & G. S. Gideon, printers, 1846]
8 p.   22½ cm.

23206   Marvin, Henry.
A complete history of Lake George, embracing a great
variety of information and compiled with an especial
reference to meet the wants of the traveling community;
intended as a descriptive guide: togehter with a
complete history and present appearance of Ticonderoga.
By Henry Marvin. New York, Sibells & Maigne, printers,
1853.
vi, [7]-102 p.   front. (fold. map)   15 cm.

23207   Marvin, Theophilus-Rogers, 1796-1882.
Genealogical sketch of the descendants of Reinold
and Matthew Marvin, who came to New England in 1635.
Comp. from authentic sources, by T. R. Marvin. Boston,
1848.
56 p.   19½ cm.

23208   Maryland (Colony)
A collection of the governor's several speeches,
and the addresses of each house; together with several
messages and answers thereto, which passed between
each house, at a convention of an assembly, begun the
first of May, 1739. To which is added, the copy of an

order of Council, made on occasion of some members
being stiled, and acting after the prorogation of the
assembly, as a committee of the House of delegates.
[Annapolis, Printed by J. Green, 1739]
1 p.l., 37, xxxviii-xli, 38-80 p.   31½ cm.

23209 Maryland. Constitution.
The constitution of the state of Maryland, reported
and adopted by the Convention of delegates assembled
at Annapolis, November 4th, 1850, and submitted to the
voters of the state for their adoption or rejection,
on the first Wednesday of June, 1851. Correct ed.
Published by authority. Baltimore, J. Murphy & co.,
1851.
70 p., 1 l.   22½ cm.
"The declaration of rights": p. [9]-17.

23210 Maryland. Constitutional convention, 1864.
Proceedings of the State convention of Maryland to
frame a new constitution. Commenced at Annapolis,
April 27, 1864. Annapolis, R. P. Bayly, 1864.
856 p.   22½ cm.

23211 Maryland (Colony) Convention, 1775.
At a meeting of the delegates appointed by the several
counties of the province of Maryland, at the city of
Annapolis, on Wednesday the 26th of July, 1775, and
continued till the 14th day of August, in the same year
... [Annapolis, Frederick Green? 1775]
4 p.   41 cm.

23212 Maryland. General assembly, 1787. House of delegates.
The present state of Maryland. By the delegates of
the people. Baltimore printed: London reprinted; for
John Stockdale, opposite Burlington house, Piccadilly,
1787.
28 p.   20 cm.

23213 Maryland. General assembly. House of delegates. Committee
on federal relations.
... Report of the Committee on federal relations in
regard to the calling of a sovereign convention. Frederick, Md., E. S. Riley, printer, 1861.
22 p.   22½ cm.   ([Document F])

23214 Maryland. General assembly. House of delegates. Committee
on federal relations.
... Report of the Committee on federal relations upon
the messages of the governor, in regard to the arbitrary

proceedings of the United States authorities, and the governor's correspondence with the United States government. Frederick, E. S. Riley, 1861.
8 p. 24½ cm. (Document [H])

23215 Maryland. General assembly. House of delegates. Committee on federal relations.
... Resolutions of the Committee on federal relations of the House of delegates of Maryland, with Senate amendments. Extra session, 1861. Frederick, B. H. Richardson, printer, 1861.
4 p. 23½ cm. [Document E]

23216 Maryland. General assembly. House of delegates. Select committee on the resources of Maryland.
... Report of the Select committee appointed to prepare a statement in relation to the resources of Maryland. Annapolis, R. P. Bayly, printer, 1865.
51 p. 22 cm. ([Document EE])

23217 Maryland. Governor, 1865-1869 (Thomas Swann)
Record of proceedings of the investigation before His Excellency Thomas Swann, governor of Maryland, in the case of Samuel Hindes and Nicholas L. Wood, commissioners of the Board of police of the city of Baltimore, upon charges preferred against them for official misconduct. Baltimore, W. K. Boyle, printer, 1866.
lxx, 201 p. 23 cm.

23218 Maryland. Laws, statutes, etc.
A bill, entitled. An act for the promotion of internal improvement. [Annapolis? 1836]
13 p. 23½ cm.

23219 Maryland. Laws, statutes, etc.
Election laws of the state of Maryland, now in force: with such portions of the constitution as relate to the elective franchise. Baltimore, G. W. Bowen & co., city printers, 1856.
45 p. 23 cm.

23220 Maryland. Laws, statutes, etc.
The Maryland code... Compiled by Otho Scott, and Hiram M'Cullough, commissioners; adopted by the legislature of Maryland, January session, 1860: the acts of that session being therewith incorporated: with an index to each article and section, by Henry C. Mackall... By authority of the state of Maryland. Baltimore, J. Murphy & co., 1860.
2 v. 23 cm.

23221 Maryland. Susquehanna canal commissioners.
Report by the Maryland commissioners on a proposed
canal from Baltimore to Conewago... Baltimore, F.
Lucas, jun., 1823.
84 p., 1 l.   illus., 2 fold. maps (incl. front.)
22 cm.
Signed: Theodorick Bland, George Winchester, John
Patterson, commissioners of Susquehanna canal.

23222 Maseres, Francis, 1731-1824, comp.
A collection of several commissions, and other public
instruments, proceeding from His Majesty's royal authority,
and other papers, relating to the state of the province
in Quebec in North America, since the conquest of it
by the British arms in 1760. Collected by Francis
Maseres... London, Printed by W. and J. Richardson,
1772.
xv, 311 p.   25½ x 21½ cm.

23223 [Maseres, Francis] 1731-1824.
Considerations on the expediency of admitting representatives from the American colonies into the British
House of commons. London, Printed for B. White, 1770.
2 p.l., 3-41 p.   20 cm.

23224 [Maseres, Francis] 1731-1824.
A draught of an act of Parliament for tolerating the
Roman Catholick religion in the province of Quebec, and
for encouraging and introducing the Protestant religion
into the said province, and for vesting the lands
belonging to certain religious houses in the said province
in the crown of this kingdom, for the support of the
civil government of the said province; and for other
purposes. [London? 1772?]
55 p.   32 cm.

23225 [Maseres, Francis] 1731-1824, ed.
Occasional essays on various subjects, chiefly political
and historical; extracted partly from the publick newspapers, during the present reign, and partly from
tracts published in the reigns of Queen Elizabeth,
King Charles I., King Charles II., and from Bishop
Burnet's history of his own times. London, Printed by
R. Wilks, 1809.
xvi, 607 p.   21½ cm.

23226 Masias, Felipe.
Curso elemental de economia politica, por Felipe Masias...
Lima, Impr. de J. M. Masias, 1860.
2 p.l., 347, v p.   20½ cm.

23227 Mason, Benjamin, Quaker.
Light rising out of obscurity. Or, a reply to
Francis Herr's pamphlet, intitled, A short explication
of the written Word of God; likewise, of the Christian
baptism, and the peaceable kingdom of Christ, against
the people called Quakers. By Benjamin Mason... Philadelphia, Printed by Joseph Crukshank, in Market-street,
between Second and Third-streets, 1790.
46 p.   20½ cm.

23228 Mason, Cyrus.
The oration on the thirteenth anniversary of the
American institute, delivered by Cyrus Mason, at the
Broadway tabernacle, October 15th, 1840. 2d ed. New
York, D. Appleton & co., 1840.
38 p.   22½ cm.

23229 Mason, Ebenezer, defendant.
Impartial account of the trial of Ebenezer Mason, on
an indictment for the murder of William Pitt Allen. At
the Supreme judicial court, holden at Dedham, in the
county of Norfolk, and commonwealth of Massachusetts, on
Thursday the sixty day of August, 1802... Dedham [Mass.]
Printed by H. Mann, 1802.
v, 6-28 p.   18½ cm.

23230 Mason, Erskine, 1805-1851.
An evangelical ministry, the security of a nation:
a sermon, preached in behalf of the American home
missionary society, in the Bleecker street church, New
York, January 2, 1848. By Rev. Erskine Mason... New
York, Printed by W. Osborn, 1848.
24 p.   22½ cm.

23231 Mason, Erskine, 1805-1851.
God's hand in human events. A sermon, preached in
the Bleecker street church on the 14th July, 1850. In
reference to the death of President Taylor. By Erskine
Mason, D.D. New York, R. Craighead, printer, 1850.
19 p.   23½ cm.

23232 Mason, Francis, 1799-1874.
The story of a working man's life: with sketches of
travel in Europe, Asia, Africa, and America, as related
by himself. By Francis Mason, D.D. With an introduction, by William R. Williams... New York, Oakley,
Mason & co., 1870.
xxvii, [1], 462 p.   4 pl. (incl. front.)   20 cm.

23233   [Mason, George Champlin] 1820-1894.
        Newport illustrated, in a series of pen & pencil
        sketches. By the editor of the Newport Mercury...
        New York, D. Appleton & co. [c1854]
        110 p.   front., illus., plates.   18½ cm.

23234   Mason, George Champlin, 1820-1894.
        Re-union of the sons and daughters of Newport, R. I.,
        August 23, 1859. By George C. Mason. Comp. and printed
        by order of the general committee of arrangements.
        Newport, R. I., F. A. Pratt & co., city printers, 1859.
        vi, [7]-297, 1 p.   illus.   20 cm.

23235   [Mason, John] 1586?-1635.
        A briefe discourse of the Nevv-found-land, with the
        situation, temperature, and commodities thereof, inciting
        our nation to goe forward in that hopefull plantation
        begunne... Edinbvrgh, Printed bv A. Hart, 1620.
        [Edinburgh, 1869]
        [14] p.   27 x 21½ cm.

23236   Mason, John, 1600-1672.
        A brief history of the Pequot war: especially of the
        memorable taking of their fort at Mistick in Connecticut
        in 1637: written by Major John Mason... With an intro-
        duction and some explanatory notes bv the Reverend Mr.
        Thomas Prince... Boston, Printed & sold by S. Kneeland
        & T. Green, 1736.
        1 p.l., vi, x, 22 p.   16½ cm.

23237   Mason, John Mitchell, 1770-1829.
        A funeral oration delivered in the Brick Presbyterian
        church in the city of New York, on the 22d day of February,
        1800, being the day recommended by Congress to the
        citizens of the United States, publicly to testify their
        grief for the death of Gen. Washington: by appointment
        of a number of the clergy of New York, and pub. at their
        request. By John M. Mason... New York, Printed and
        sold by G. F. Hopkins, 1800.
        23 p.   21 cm.

23238   Mason, John Mitchell, 1770-1829.
        Living faith: a sermon; preached before the Society
        for the relief of the destitute sick, on the evening of
        Sabbath, the 1st of November, 1801. In Bristo-street
        meeting-house, Edinburgh. By John M. Mason, A. M.
        pastor of the Associate-Reformed church in the city of
        New York. New York, Printed by Isaac Collins and son,
        for Cornelius Davis, no. 167, Water-street, 1802.
        35, [1] p.   24 cm.

23239   Mason, John Young, 1799-1859.
        Address before the Alumni association of the University
        of North Carolina, delivered in Gerard hall, June 2,
        1847, (the evening preceding commencement day,) by
        Hon. John Y. Mason, LL.D. Washington, Printed by J. and
        G. S. Gideon, 1847.
        24 p.   22½ cm.

23240   Mason, Samson.
        Speech of Mr. S. Mason, of Ohio, on the objections of
        the President to the bill to establish a fiscal corpora-
        tion. Delivered in the House of representatives,
        September 10, 1841. Washington, Printed at the National
        intelligencer office, 1841.
        16 p.   24½ cm.

23241   Mason, William, 1725-1797.
        An occasional discourse, preached in the Cathedral of
        St. Peter in York, January 27, 1788, on the subject of
        the African slave-trade. York, Printed by A. Ward for
        the author, 1788.
        27 p.   25 cm.

23242   Mason, William Powell, 1791-1867.
        An oration delivered Wednesday, July 4, 1827, in
        commemoration of American independence, before the supreme
        executive of the commonwealth, and the City council and
        inhabitants of the city of Boston. By William Powell
        Mason. Printed by order of the City council. Boston,
        From the press of N. Hale, city printer, 1827.
        31 p.   22½ cm.

23243   The Masonic union: a monthly magazine... v. 1-
        June 1850-   Auburn, N. Y., Printed at the office of
        the Cayuga new era= [etc., etc.] 1850-
            v.   22 cm.
        F. M. King, editor.

23244   Massachusetts, pseud.
        The new states; or, A comparison of the wealth, strength,
        and population of the northern and southern states; as
        also of their respective powers in Congress; with a view
        to expose the injustice of erecting new states at the
        South. By Massachusetts. Boston, J. Belcher, printer,
        1813.
        36 p.   22½ cm.

23245   Massachusetts (Colony) Charters.
        The explanatory charter granted by His Majesty King

George to the province of the Massachusetts-Bay in
New England. Accepted by the General court, Jan. 15th.
Anno 1725. [Boston, 1725] [Boston, 1940]
facsim.: 8 p.   21 cm.   Photostat Americana.
Second series... [Photostated at the Massachusetts
historical society. No. 116]

23246 Massachusetts (Colony) Provincial congress.
The journals of each Provincial congress of Massachusetts
in 1774 and 1775, and of the Committee of safety, with an
appendix, containing the proceedings of the county conventions - narratives of the events of the nineteenth of
April, 1775 - papers relating to Ticonderoga and Crown
Point, and other documents, illustrative of the early
history of the American revolution. Pub. agreeably to a
resolve passed March 10, 1837, under the supervision of
William Lincoln... Boston, Dutton and Wentworth, printers
to the state, 1838.
2 p.l., lix, 778 p.   24½ cm.

23247 Massachusetts (Colony) Provincial congress, Oct.-Dec. 1774.
Extracts from the records of the late Provincial
congress, held at Cambridge in the months of October,
November and December, A.D. 1774. Also extracts from
the minutes of the proceedings of the Congress, held at
Cambridge, February A.D. 1775. Pub. by their order.
Boston, Printed by Edes and Gill, 1775.
14 p.   21 cm.

23248 Massachusetts (Colony) Provincial congress, Feb.-May, 1775.
... Rules and regulations for the Massachusetts army.
Pub. by order. Salem, Printed by Samuel and Ebenezer
Hall, 1775.
(In Boston. A memorial of the American patriots who
fell at the battle of Bunker Hill... Boston, 1889. 28 cm.
p. 263-274)

23249 Massachusetts. Astronomical and trigonometrical survey.
Tables of bearings, distances, latitudes, longitudes,
&c. ascertained by the Astronomical and trigonometrical
survey of Massachusetts. Published agreeably to a
resolve of the General court, by John G. Palfrey...
Boston, Dutton and Wentworth, 1846.
2 p.l., xxxviii p., 1 l., 73 p.   27½ cm.

23250 Massachusetts. Board of internal improvements.
Report of the Board of commissioners, of internal
improvement in relation to the examination of sundry
routes for a railway from Boston to Providence. With

a memoir of the survey. Boston, Dutton & Wentworth,
printers to the state, 1828.
72 p.   23½ cm.

23251 Massachusetts. Board of internal improvements.
Report of the Board of directors of internal improvements of the state of Massachusetts, on the practicability
and expediency of a rail-road from Boston to the Hudson
River, and from Boston to Providence. Submitted to
the General court, January 16, 1829. To which are
annexed, the reports of the engineers... With plans and
profiles of the routes. Boston, Press of the Boston
daily advertiser, 1829.
76, 119 p.   6 fold. maps, tables.   22½ cm.

23252 Massachusetts. Commissioners on flats in Boston harbor.
... Report of the Commissioners in relation to the
flats in Boston harbor. January, 1850. [Boston, 1850]
72 p.   2 fold. plans.   24½ cm.   ([General court,
1850] Senate. [Dec.] 3)

23253 Massachusetts. Commissioners on pauper system.
... Report of the commissioners appointed by an order
of the House of representatives, Feb. 29, 1832, on the
subject of the pauper system of the commonwealth of
Massachusetts. Boston, Dutton and Wentworth, state
printers, 1833.
97 p.   III fold. tab.   22 cm.
House document no. 6. W. B. Calhoun, chairman.

23254 Massachusetts. Constitutional convention, 1779-1780.
Journal of the Convention for framing a constitution
of government for the state of Massachusetts Bay, from
the commencement of their first session, September 1,
1779, to the close of their last session, June 16, 1780...
Pub. by order of the legislature. Boston, Dutton and
Wentworth, printers to the state, 1832.
264 p.   23 cm.

23255 Massachusetts. Constitutional convention, 1820-1821.
Journal of debates and proceedings in the Convention
of delegates, chosen to revise the constitution of
Massachusetts, begun and holden at Boston, November 15,
1820, and continued by adjournment to January 9, 1821.
Reported for the Boston daily advertiser. Boston, Pub.
at the office of the Daily advertiser, 1821.
292 p.   24 cm.

23256 Massachusetts. General court, 1809.
The patriotick proceedings of the legislature of

Massachusetts, during their session from Jan. 26, to
March 4, 1809. Consisting of the lieutenant governour's
speech, answer of both houses, report of the Joint
committee on petitions, Gore's report on Crowninshield's
resolutions, report on the lieutenant governour's military
orders, with three speeches, memorial to Congress,
address to the people. Boston, Printed by J. Cushing,
1809.
2 p.l., 130 p., 1 l.   22½ cm.

23257 Massachusetts. General Court. House of representatives.
Report of a committee of the House of representatives,
respecting certain military orders issued by His Honour
Levi Lincoln, lieutenant-governor... with the documents
referred to in the same. [n.p., 1809]
11, [1] p.   21½ cm.

23258 Massachusetts. General court. House of representatives.
Committee on admission into the state of free negroes
and mulattoes.
Free negroes and mulattoes... Report... [Boston,
1822]
16 p.   22 cm.
Report dated: January 16, 1822; signed: For the
Committee, Theodore Lyman, jr.

23259 Massachusetts. General court. House of representatives.
Committee on capital punishment.
... Report relating to capital punishment... [Boston,
1836]
96 p.   24 cm.   (House [doc.] no. 32)
Robert Rantoul, jr., chairman.

23260 Massachusetts. General court. House of representatives.
Committee on ventilation of the representatives' hall.
[Report of the Committee appointed at the session of
the legislature of 1864 "to improve the ventilation of
the representatives' hall". Boston, 1865]
106 p.   illus.   25½ cm.   ([General court, 1865]
House. [Doc.] 5)
Moses Kimball, chairman.

23261 Massachusetts. General court. Joint committee on ship
canal to connect Barnstable bay and Buzzard's bay.
... Report of the Joint committee of 1860 upon the
proposed canal to unite Barnstable and Buzzard's bays,
under the resolve of April 4, 1860, and subsequent
resolves and votes of the legislature. Boston, Wright &
Potter, state printers, 1864.

165 p.   fold. maps, fold. profiles.   23 cm.
At head of title: Public document no. 41.

23262 Massachusetts. General court. Joint special committee
on laws relating to registration of births, marriages,
and deaths.
... Report of the Joint special committee of the
legislature of Massachusetts appointed to consider the
expediency of modifying the laws relating to the
registration of births, marriages, and deaths, presented
March 3, 1849. Boston, Dutton and Wentworth, state
printers, 1849.
57 p.   25 cm.
At head of title: House. no. 65.

23263 Massachusetts. General court. Joint special committee on
petition of Geo. R. M. Withington and others.
Proceedings of the Senate and House of representatives
upon the petition of George R. M. Withington and others,
praying that James G. Carter be removed from his office
of justice of the peace for the county of Worcester,
with the opening remarks of Hon. Rufus Choate, upon the
constitutional tenure of the office of justice of peace,
and the public character and services of Mr. Carter.
The answer of Mr. Carter to the allegations of the
petitioners. The closing argument of Hon. Pliny Merrick,
upon the allegations of the petitioners, and the evidence
adduced by them in support thereof, with the report of
the Joint special committee of the Senate and House of
representatives, giving the petitioners leave to withdraw
their petition. Boston, G. C. Rand & co., printers,
1849.
     cover-title, 74 p.   22½ cm.
A. H. Nelson, chairman.

23264 Massachusetts. General court, 1814. Senate.
Synopsis of debates, in the Massachusetts legislature.
Boston, 1814
23 p.   21½ cm.

23265 Massachusetts. Geological survey.
Report on the geology, mineralogy, botany, and zoology
of Massachusetts. Made and published by order of the
government of that state: in four parts: pt. I.
Economical geology. pt. II. Topographical geology.
pt. III. Scientific geology. pt. IV. Catalogues of
animals and plants. With a descriptive list of the
specimens of rocks and minerals collected for the

government... By Edward Hitchcock... Amherst, Press
of J. S. and C. Adams, 1833.
  xii, 700 p.   illus.   23 cm.   and atlas of 19 pl.
(incl. fold. map, fold. tab.)   23½ x 30 cm.

23266 Massachusetts. Governor, 1812-1816 (Caleb Strong)
  The speech of His Excellency Governor Strong, delivered
before the legislature of Massachusetts, October 16,
1812. With the documents, which accompanied the same.
Printed by order of the House of representatives. Boston,
Printed by Russell and Cutler, 1812.
  36 p.   21 cm.
Concerning request of secretary of war for militia of
Massachusetts to defend the sea-coast, action of Governor
Strong in the matter, etc.

23267 Massachusetts. Secretary of the commonwealth.
  Abstract of the census of the commonwealth of Massachusetts, taken with reference to facts existing on the first
day of June, 1855. With remarks on the same. Prepared
under the direction of Francis DeWitt, secretary of the
commonwealth. Boston, W. White, printer to the state,
1857.
  xiii, 252 p., 1 l.   24 cm.

23268 Massachusetts. Secretary of the commonwealth.
  Statistical information relating to certain branches
of industry in Massachusetts, for the year ending May 1,
1865. Prepared from official returns, by Oliver Warner,
secretary of the commonwealth. Boston, Wright & Potter,
state printers, 1866.
  xxv, 805 p.   fold. tab.   23½ cm.

23269 Massachusetts general hospital, Boston.
  ... Acts, resolves, by-laws, and rules and regulations.
Boston, Eastburn's press, 1846.
  58 p.   24 cm.

23270 Massachusetts general hospital, Boston.
  Address of the Board of trustees of the Massachusetts
general hospital to the public... Boston, Printed by
J. Belcher, 1814.
  14 p.   20½ cm.

23271 Massachusetts general hospital, Boston.
  Address of the trustees of the Massachusetts general
hospital, to the subscribers and to the public. [Boston,
1822]
  34 p.   24 cm.

23272 Massachusetts historical society, Boston.
The act of incorporation, with the additional acts and
by-laws of the Massachusetts historical society; with a
list of officers and resident members. Boston, Printed
for the Society, 1882.
23 p.   22 cm.

23273 Massachusetts historical society, Boston. Library.
Catalogue of books in the Massachusetts historical
library. Boston, Printed by S. Hall, no. 53, Cornhill,
1796.
40 p.   23 cm.

23274 Massachusetts historical society, Boston. Library.
Catalogue of the books, pamphlets, newspapers, maps,
charts, manuscripts &c., in the library of the Massachusetts historical society. Boston, From the press of
J. Eliot, jun., 1811.
vi p., 1 l., 96 p.   23 cm.

23275 Massachusetts historical society, Boston. Library.
Catalogue of the library of the Massachusetts
historical society... Boston, Printed for the Society,
1859-60.
2 v.   23 cm.
Third catalogue of the library (1st issued 1796; 2d,
1811) Prepared by the assistant librarian, John Appleton,
M.D., under the supervision and direction of the standing
committee (select committee: Chandler Robbins, Charles
Deane) The Dowse library of 5,000 vols., which is
separately cataloged, is not included here.

23276 Massachusetts historical society, Boston. Library.
Catalogue of the private library of Thomas Dowse, of
Cambridge, Mass., presented to the Massachusetts
historical society, July 30, 1856. Boston, Printed by
J. Wilson & son, 1870.
1 p.l., 214 p.   26 cm.

23277 Massachusetts historical society, Boston.
Lectures delivered in a course before the Lowell
institute, in Boston, by members of the Massachusetts
historical society, on subjects relating to the early
history of Massachusetts. Boston, The Society, 1869.
viii, 498 p.   24 cm.

23278 Massachusetts historical society, Boston.
Proceedings of the Massachusetts historical society

in respect to the memory of William Hickling Prescott, February 1, 1859. Boston, Massachusetts historical society, 1859.
53 p.   23 cm.

23279 Massachusetts historical society, Boston.
Report of a committee appointed by the Massachusetts historical society on exchanges of prisoners during the American revolutionary war. Presented Dec. 19, 1861. Boston, Printed for the Society, 1861.
26 p.   23½ cm.

23280 Massachusetts historical society, Boston.
Tribute of the Massachusetts historical society to the memory of Josiah Quincy, July 14, 1864. Boston, Massachusetts historical society, 1864.
32 p.   24 cm.

23281 Massachusetts horticultural society.
Properties of plants and flowers, compiled by the Flower committee of the Massachusetts horticultural society and approved by the society as the standard for judging plants and flowers. Boston, The Society, 1862.
33 p., 1 l.   20 cm.

23282 Massachusetts horticultural society.
Report of the transactions of the... society, for the year 1837-8 [10th anniversary... Sept. 1838] with preliminary observations. By John Lewis Russell... Boston, Tuttle, Dennett & Chisholm, 1839.
116 p.   22 cm.

23283 Massachusetts horticultural society.
Report of the twentieth annual exhibition of the Massachusetts horticultural society, and third triennial festival... Sept. 19, 20, 21, 22, 1848. Boston, Printed by Tuttle & Dennett, 1848.
61 p.   21½ cm.

23284 Massachusetts medical society.
Address of the counsellors to the fellows of the Massachusetts medical society. Boston, Printed by J. Eliot, jun., 1813.
11 p.   22½ cm.

23285 Massachusetts medical society.
Fellows of the Massachusetts medical society, 1787-1854. Alphabetically arranged. Boston, Printed by J. Wilson

263

and son, 1855.
1 p.l., [5]-50 p.   23½ cm.

23286   Massachusetts medical society. Library.
A catalogue of books, belonging to the Massachusetts
medical society.   17th June, 1822.   [Boston? 1822]
12 p.   21½ cm.

23287   Massachusetts peace society (Founded 1815)
A catalogue of the officers and members of the Massachusetts peace society.   Cambridge, Printed by Hilliard
& Metcalf.
v.   22½ cm.

23288   Massachusetts school of agriculture.
... Circular, explaining the design of the association
and appealing to the community for funds. List of
officers, act of incorporation, by-laws, etc.   Boston,
J. H. Eastburn's press, 1858.
8 p.   24½ cm.

23289   Massachusetts society for promoting agriculture.
Papers on agriculture, consisting of communications
made to the Massachusetts society for promoting agriculture, with extracts from various publications; recommended to the attention of farmers, by the trustees of
the society.   Boston, Printed by Young and Minns,
printers, 1799.
103 p.   21 cm.

23290   Massachusetts temperance convention, Worcester, 1833.
Journal of the proceedings of the Massachusetts
temperance convention, begun and held at Worcester, on
Wednesday, September 18, 1833.   Boston, Ford and
Damrell, 1833.
36 p.   22 cm.

23291   Massachusetts temperance society.
... Doings of the council of the Massachusetts
temperance society.   Published by the council of the
Massachusetts temperance society.   Boston, Ford and
Damrell, 1834.
24 p.   17 cm.

23292   Masse, Étienne Michel, b. 1778.
L'isle de Cuba et la Havane, ou, Histoire, topographie,
statistique, moeurs, usages, commerce et situation
politique de cette colonie, d'après un journal écrit sur

264

les lieux. Par E.-M. Masse. Paris, Lebegue [etc.]
1825.
    3 p.l., [5]-410 p.   21 cm.

23293 Massie, Joseph, d. 1784.
    A state of the British sugar-colony trade; shewing
that an additional duty of twelve shillings per 112
pounds weight may be laid upon brown or muscovado sugar
(and proportionably higher duties upon sugar refined
before imported) without making sugar dearer in this
kingdom than it hath been of late years, and without
distressing the British sugar-planters... Submitted to
the consideration of the honourable House of commons.
By J. Massie. London, T. Payne, 1759.
    1 p.l., 40 p.   23½ cm.

23294
    A sermon against the dangerous and sinful practice of
inoculation. Preach'd at St. Andrew's Holborn, on
Sunday, July the 8th, 1722. By Edmund Massey... From
the 3d ed. London, printed. Boston, Re-printed for
B. Indicott, 1730.
    32 p.   18½ cm.

23295 [Mather, Cotton] 1663-1728.
    An advice to the churches of the faithful: briefly
reporting, the present state of the church, throughout
the world; and bespeaking, that fervent prayer for the
church, which this time calleth for... Boston, Printed
by B. Green, & J. Allen, 1702.
    16 p.   14½ cm.

23296 [Mather, Cotton] 1663-1728.
    Agricola. Or, The religious husbandman: the main
intentions of religion, served in the business and
language of husbandry. A work adapted unto the grand
purposes of piety: and commended therefore by a number
of ministers, to be entertained in the families of the
countrey... Boston, Printed by T. Fleet, for D.
Henchman, overagainst the Brick meeting-house in Cornhil,
1727.
    3 p.l., 221, [1] p.   18½ cm.

23297 [Mather, Cotton] 1663-1728.
    Another tongue brought in, to confess the great Saviour
of the world. Or, Some communications of Christianity,
put into a tongue used among the Iroquois Indians, in
America. And, put into the hands of the English and
the Dutch traders: to accomodate the great intention

265

of communicating the Christian religion, unto the
salvages, among whom they may find anything of this
language to be intelligible... Boston, Printed by
B. Green, 1707. [Boston, 1940]
facsim.: 16 p. 21 cm. Photostat Americana.
Second series... [Photostated at the Massachusetts
historical society. No. 109]

23298 [Mather, Cotton] 1663-1728.
The balance of the sanctuary. A short and plain essay;
declaring, the true balance wherein every thing should
be weighed, and, detecting, the false balance wherein
many things are weighed, among the children of men.
A lecture; in the audience of the General assembly at
Boston. Oct. 5, 1727... Boston, Printed and sold by
T. Fleet, in Pudding-lane, near the Town-house, 1727.
1 p.l., 24 p. 15½ cm.

23299 [Mather, Cotton] 1663-1728.
Bonifacivs. An essay upon the good, that is to be
devised and designed, by those who desire to answer the
great end of life, and to do good while they live. A
book offered, first, in general, unto all Christians,
in a personal capacity, or in a relative. Then more
particularly. Unto magistrates, unto ministers, unto
physicians, unto lawyers, unto scholemasters, unto wealthy
gentlemen, unto several sorts of officers, unto churches,
and unto all societies of a religious character and
intention. With humble proposals, of unexceptionable
methods, to do good in the world... Boston, Printed by
B. Green, for Samuel Gerrish at his shop in Cornhill,
1710.
1 p.l., xviii, 19-206 p. 15½ cm.

23300 [Mather, Cotton] 1663-1728.
Baptismal piety. Two brief essays. I. The angel of
the waters. Instructing the spectators of the sacred
baptism, administered in our assemblies, how to make it
a most profitable spectacle. II. The angel of the
little ones directing the aims and the frames wherewith
parents are to bring their infants unto the holy baptism...
Boston, Printed in the year 1727.
48 p. 18 cm.

23301 Mather, Cotton, 1663-1728.
The fisher-mans calling. A brief essay, to serve the
great interests of religion among our fisher-men; and
set before them the calls of their Saviour, whereof
they should be sensible, in the employments of their

fishery. By Cotton Mather... Boston in N. E., Printed:
Sold by T. Green, 1712. [Boston, 1941]
    facsim.: 1 p.l., iv, 49, [1] p.   21½ cm.   [Photostat
Americana. Second series... Photostated at the
Massachusetts historical society. No. 141]

23302 [Mather, Cotton] 1663-1728.
    The good old way. Or, Christianity described, from
the glorious lustre of it, appearing in the lives of the
primitive Christians. An essay tending, from illustrious
examples of a sober, & a righteous, and a godly life,
occurring in the ancient church history, to revive the
languishing interests of genuine and practical Christianity
... Boston, Printed by B. Green, for Benj. Eliot at his
shop under the west-end of the townhouse, 1706.
    1 p.l., 94 p.   14 cm.

23303 [Mather, Cotton] 1663-1728.
    The greatest concern in the world. A short and plain
essay, to answer that most concerning and all concerning
inquiry, What must I do to be saved? now published with
a design to assist the addresses of good men unto their
neighbours, whom they press to mind the one thing needful.
4th ed. New Haven, Printed for and sold by R. Sherman
and B. Mecom, 1765.
    20 p.   21½ cm.

23304 [Mather, Cotton] 1663-1728.
    Instructions to the living, from the condition of the
dead. A brief relation of remarkables in the shipwreck
of above one hundred pirates, who were cast away in the
ship Whido, on the coast of New England, April 26, 1717.
And in the death of six, who after a fair trial at Boston,
were convicted & condemned, October 22. And executed,
November 1717. With some account of the discourse had
with them on the way to their execution. And a sermon
preached on their occasion. Boston, Printed by John
Allen, for Nicholas Boone, at the sign of the Bible in
Cornhill, 1717. [Boston, 1941]
    facsim.: 64 p.   19 cm.   [Photostat Americana.
Second series... Photostated at the Massachusetts
historical society. No. 134]

23305 Mather, Cotton, 1663-1728.
    Magnalia Christi americana: or, The ecclesiastical
history of New-England, from its first planting in the
year 1620, unto the year of Our Lord, 1698. In seven
books. By the reverend and learned Cotton Mather...
1st American ed., from the London edition of 1702.

Hartford, Published by Silas Andrus, Roberts & Burr, Printers, 1820.
2 v.   23 cm.

23306   [Mather, Cotton] 1663-1728.
Memoirs of the life of the late Reverend Increase Mather, D.D., who died August 23, 1723. With a preface by the Reverend Edmund Calamy, D.D. London, J. Clark & R. Hett, 1725.
4 p.l., 88 p.   front. (port.   20 cm.

23307   [Mather, Cotton] 1663-1728.
A monitory, and hortatory letter, to those English, who debauch the Indians, by selling strong drink to them. Written at the desire of some Christians, to whom the mischiefs arising from that vile trade, are matters of much apprehension and lamentation... Boston, N. E., Printed in the year 1700.
16 p.   15 cm.

23308   Mather, Cotton 1663-1728.
Parentator. Memoirs of remarkables in the life and the death of an ever-memorable Dr. Increase Mather. Who expired, August 23, 1723... Boston, Printed by B. Green, for Nathaniel Belknap, at the corner of Scarlets-Wharff, 1724.
1 p.l., x, xiv, 239, [5] p., 1 l.   17½ cm.

23309   [Mather, Cotton] 1663-1728.
Pietas in patriam: the life of His Excellency Sir William Phips, knt. Late captain general, and governour in chief of the province of the Massachuset-bay, New England. Containing the memorable changes undergone, and actions performed by him. Written by one intimately acquainted with him. London, Printed by S. Bridge for N. Hiller, 1697.
6 p.l., 110, [6] p.   26 cm.

23310   [Mather, Cotton] 1663-1728.
Right thoughts in said hours, representing the comforts and the duties of good men under all their afflictions; and particularly, that one, the untimely death of children: in a sermon delivered at Charls-town, New-England; under a fresh experience of that calamity... London, Printed by James Astwood, 1689.
3 p.l., 54, [2] p.   15½ cm.

23311   [Mather, Cotton] 1663-1728.
The right way to shake off a viper. An essay, upon a

case too commonly calling for consideration; what shall
good men do, when they are evil spoken of? With a
preface of Dr. Increase Mather, The second impression...
Boston, Printed by S. Kneeland, for S. Gerrish, 1720.
1 p.l., xiv, 64 p.   15½ cm.

23312 Mather, Cotton, 1663-1728.
       Seasonable thoughts upon mortality. A sermon occasioned
by the raging of a mortal sickness in the colony of
Connecticut, and the many deaths of our brethren there.
Delivered at Boston-lecture, 24. d. 11. m. 1711, 12.
By Cotton Mather, D.D. ... Boston Printed: Sold by T.
Green, 1712.
       1 p.l., 56, [2] p.   13 cm.

23313 Mather, Cotton, 1663-1728.
       Shaking dispensations. An essay upon the mighty shakes,
which the hand of heaven, hath given, and is giving,
to the world. With some useful remarks on the death
of the French king, who left off to make the world a
wilderness, and to destroy the cities thereof; on the
twenty-first of August 1715. In a sermon on that great
occasion, at Boston, New England. 13 d. VIII m. 1715.
By Cotton Mather... Boston, Printed by B. Green.
Sold by S. Gerrish, at his shop at the n. side of the T.
house, 1715.
       1 p.l., 50 p.   14½ cm.

23314 Mather, Cotton, 1663-1728.
       Souldiers counselled and comforted. A discourse
delivered unto some part of the forces engaged in the
just war of New-England against the northern & eastern
Indians. September 1689. By Cotton Mather minister of
the gospel in Boston... Boston, Printed by Samuel
Green, 1689.
       5 p.l., 38 p.   14½ cm.

23315 Mather, Cotton, 1663-1728.
       Strange phenomena of New England: in the seventeenth
century: including the "Salem witchcraft," "1692."
From the writings of "the Rev. Cotton Mather, D.D."...
Collected and arranged for re-publication by Henry
Jones... New York, Piercy and Reed, 1846.
       iv, [5]-54 p.   23 cm.

23316 Mather, Cotton, 1663-1728.
       The valley of Baca. The divine sov'reignty, displayed
& adored; more particularly, in bereaving dispensations,
of the Divine Providence. A sermon preached on the

death of Mrs. Hannah Sewall, the religious & honourable
consort of Samuel Sewall, esq; which befell us, on the
19 d. VIII m. 1717. In the sixtieth year of her age.
By Cotton Mather... Boston, Printed by B. Green, 1717.
1 p.l., 4, 28 p.   15 cm.

23317 [Mather, Cotton] 1663-1728.
The vial poured out upon the sea. A remarkable relation
of certain pirates brought unto a tragical and untimely
end. Some conferences with them, after their condemnation
Their behaviour at their execution. And a sermon
preached on that occasion... Boston, Printed by T. Fleet,
for N. Belknap, and sold at his shop near Scarlet's wharf,
1726.
1 p.l., 51 p.   17 cm.

23318 Mather, Cotton, 1663-1728.
The wonders of the invisible world: being an account
of the tryals of several vvitches, lately excuted [!]
in New England: and of several remarkable curiosities
therein occurring. Together with, I. Observations upon
the nature, the number, and the operations of the devils.
II. A short narrative of a late outrage committed by a
knot of witches in Swede-land, very much resembling, and
so far explaining, that under which New-England has
laboured. III. Some councels directing a due improvement
of the terrible things lately done by the unusual and
amazing range of evil spirits in New-England. IV. A
brief discourse upon those temptations which are the
more ordinary devices of Satan. By Cotton Mather.
Published by the special command of his excellency the
governour [!] of the province of the Massachusetts-Bay
in New England. Printed first, at Bostun [!] in New
England; and reprinted at London, for John Dunton, 1693.
2 p.l., [1]-98 (i.e. 106) p., 1 l.   21 cm.

23319 Mather, Increase, 1639-1723.
A brief history of the vvar with the Indians in Nevv-
England, (from June 24, 1675, when the first Englishman
was murdered by the Indians, to August 12, 1676, when
Philip, alias Metacomet, the principal author and
beginner of the warr, was slain.) Wherein the grounds,
beginning, and progress of the warr, is summarily express
Together with a serious exhortation to the inhabitants
of that land, by Increase Mather... Boston, Printed
and sold by John Foster over against the Sign of the
Dove, 1676.
3 p.l., 51, 8, [4], 26 p.   19½ x 14½ cm.

23320 [Mather, Increase] 1639-1723, supposed author.
A brief relation of the state of New England, from
the beginning of that plantation to this present year,
1689. In a letter to a person of quality. Licenced,
July 30th, 1689. London, Printed by Richard Baldwine,
near the Black Bull in the Old-Bailey, 1689.
18, [2] p.   19 cm.
The "Brief relation" includes the 12th article of the
Declaration of the gentlemen, merchants and inhabitants
of Boston, Apr. 18, 1689 (believed to have been written
by Mather); Abraham Kick's letter to the Princess of
Orange, Feb. 1, 1689 n.s., and a translation of Mather's
"De successu evangelij apud Indios in Nova-Anglia epistola.
Ad... Johannem Leusaenum." It was reprinted in Force's
Tracts, v. 4, no. 11, and Andros tracts, v. 2, p. 147-
170; the latter containing a discussion of the authorship.

23321 Mather, Increase, 1639-1723.
Burnings bewailed: in a sermon, occasioned by the
lamentable fire which was in Boston, October 2, 1711.
In which the sins which provoke the Lord to kindle fires,
are enquired into. By Increase Mather, D.D. ...
Boston printed: Sold by Timothy Green, 1711.
2 p.l., 36 p.   16 cm.

23322 Mather, Increase, 1639-1723.
Cases of conscience concerning evil spirits personating
men, witchcrafts, infallible proofs of guilt in such
as are accused with that crime; all considered according
to the Scriptures, history, experience, and the judgment
of many learned men. Boston, B. Harris, 1693.
67 p.   port.   16 cm.

23323 Mather, Increase, 1639-1723.
David serving his generation; or, A sermon shewing
what is to be done in order to our so serving our
generation, as that when we dy, we shall enter into a
blessed rest (wherein some account is given concerning
many eminent ministers of Christ at London, as well as
in N. E. lately gone to their rest.) Occasioned by the
death, of the Reverend Mr. John Baily, who deceased at
Boston in New-England, December 12th, 1697. By Increase
Mather president of Harvard college... Boston, Printed
by B. Green & J. Allen, 1698.
39 p.   15 cm.

23324 Mather, Increase, 1639-1723.
A discourse concerning the maintenance due to those

271

that preach the gospel: in which, that question whether tithes are by the divine law the ministers due, is considered, and the negative proved. By I. Mather... Boston, N. E. Printed by B. Green, 1706.
1 p.l., 60 p.   14 cm.

23325 Mather, Increase, 1639-1723.
Early history of New England; being a relation of hostile passages between the Indians and European voyagers and first settlers: and a full narrative of hostilities, to the close of the war with the Pequots, in the year 1637; also a detailed account of the origin of the war with King Philip. By Increase Mather. With an introduction and notes, by S. G. Drake. Albany, N. Y., J. Munsell, 1864.
xxxviii, [39]-309 p. $22\frac{1}{2}$ x 19 cm.

23326 Mather, Increase, 1639-1723.
A further account of the tryals of the New England witches. With the observations of a person who was upon the place several days when the suspected witches were first taken into examination. To which is added, Cases of conscience concerning witchcrafts and evil spirits personating men. Written at the request of the ministers of New England. By Increase Mather, president of Harvard college... Licensed and entred according to Order. London, Printed for J. Dunton, at the Raven in the Poultry, 1693.
1 p.l., 10 p., 1 l., [2], 39, [5] p.   20 cm.

23327 Mather, Increase, 1639-1723.
Ichabod. Or, A discourse, shewing what cause there is to fear that the glory of the Lord, is departing from New England. Delivered in two sermons, by Increase Mather... Boston, Printed by Timothy Green, sold by the book-sellers, 1702.
122 p. $13\frac{1}{2}$ x $7\frac{1}{2}$ cm.

23328 [Mather, Increase] 1639-1723.
The life and death of that reverend man of God, Mr. Richard Mather, teacher of the church in Dorchester in New England... Cambridge Mass. : Printed by S[amuel] G[reen] and M[armaduke] J[ohnson] 1670.
2 p.l., 38 p. $17\frac{1}{2}$ cm.

23329 Mather, Increase, 1639-1723.
The wicked mans portion. Or a sermon (preached at the lecture in Boston in New England the 18th day of the I month 1674. when two men were executed, who had murthere(

their master.) Wherein is shewed that excesse in
wickedness doth bring untimely death. By Increase
Mather, teacher of a church of Christ... Boston,
Printed by John Foster, 1675.
2 p.l., 25 p.   18 cm.

23330 [Mather, John] 1780-1858.
Genealogy of the Mather family, from about 1500 to
1847; with sundry biographical notices... Hartford,
Press of E. Geer, 1848.
vi, [7]-76 p. incl. front. (coat of arms)   17 cm.

23331 Mather, Joseph H
Geography of the state of New York. Embracing its
physical features, climate, geology, mineralogy, botany,
zoology, history, pursuits of the people, government,
education, internal improvements, &c. With statistical
tables, and a separate description and map of each
county... By J. H. Mather... and L. P. Brocket...
Hartford, J. H. Mather & co.; New York, M. H. Newman &
co.; [etc., etc.] 1847.
xii, [13]-432 p. incl. front., illus. (maps.)   19½ cm.

23332 Mather, Moses, 1749-1806.
The visible church, in covenant with God: or, An
inquiry into the constitution of the visible church of
Christ. Wherein the divine right of infant baptism
is defended; and, the admission of adults to compleat
standing in the visible church, though destitute of a
saving faith, shown to be agreeable to the revealed
will of God. By Moses Mather... New York, Printed by
H. Gaine, at the Bible and crown, in Hanoversquare,
1759.
60 p.   20½ cm.

23333 Mather, Nathanael, 1631-1697.
A discussion of the lawfulness of a pastor's acting
as an officer in other churches besides that which he is
specially called to take the oversight of. By the
late Reverend Nathanael Mather. Boston, reprinted and
sold by Thomas Fleet, 1730.
1 p.l., x, 84 p.   14½ cm.

23334 Mather, Richard, 1596-1669.
A farewel-exhortation to the church and people of
Dorchester in New England. But not unusefull to any
others, that shall heedfully read and improve the same,
as containing Christian and serious incitements, and
perswasions to the study and practise of seven principal

dutyes of great importance for the glory of God, and
the salvation of the soul, and therefore needfull to be
seriously considered of all in these declining times.
By Richard Mather, teacher to the church above mentioned
... Printed by Samuel Green at Cambridge in New-
England, 1657.
2 p.l., 27 p.   18 x 14 cm.

23335 Mather, Samuel, 1626-1671.
The figures of types of the Old Testament, by which
Christ and the heavenly things of the gospel were
preached and shadowed to the people of God of old.
Explain'd and improv'd in sundry sermons. By Samuel
Mather, sometime pastor of a church in Dublin. The
2d ed., to which is annex'd, (more than was in the
former edition) a scheme and table of the whole, whereby
the reader may readily turn to any subject treated of
in this book. London, Printed for N. Hillier, 1705.
vii, [5], 540, [12] p.   21½ cm.
Edited by the author's brother, Nathaniel Mather.

23336 [Mather, Samuel] 1706-1785.
An attempt to shew, that America must be known to the
ancients; made at the request, and to gratify the
curiosity, of an inquisitive gentleman: to which is
added an appendix, concerning the American colonies,
and some modern managements against them. By an American
Englishman... Boston, New England: Printed by J. Kneeland, in Milk-Street, for T. Leverett, and H. Knox,
in Cornhill, 1773.
35 p.   21½ cm.

23337 [Mather, Samuel] 1706-1785.
The dying legacy of an aged minister of the ever-
lasting gospel, to the United States of North America...
Boston, Printed by Benjamin Edes and Sons, in Cornhill,
1783.
2 p.l., ii, [7]-29 p.   20 cm.

23338 Mather, Samuel, 1706-1785.
The fall of the mighty lamented. A funeral discourse
upon the death of Her most excellent Majesty Wilhelmina
Dorothea Carolina, queen-consort to His Majesty of
Great-Britain, France and Ireland: preach'd on March 23
1737, 8, in the audience of His Excellency the governour
the Honourable the lieutenant-governour, and the
Honourable His Majesty's council, at the Thursday-lectur
in Boston, New England. By Samuel Mather, M.A. pastor
of a church in Boston... Boston, in New England,

Printed by J. Draper, printer to His Excellency the
governour and council. Sold by D. Henchman and N.
Procter, booksellers, 1738.
1 p.l., 33 p.   19½ cm.

23339   Mather, William Williams, 1804-1859.
Report on the State house artesian well at Columbus,
Ohio. By W. W. Mather. Columbus, Nevins' printing
house, 1859.
cover-title, 41 p.   22½ cm.

23340   Mather, William W[illiams] 1804-1859.
Sketch of the geology and mineralogy of New-London
and Windham counties, in Connecticut. By Wm. W. Mather
... Norwich, W. Lester, jr., 1834.
36 p.   front. (fold. map)   21½ cm.

23341   Mathers, William.
The rise, progress and downfall of aristocracy. Taken
from ancient and modern history, sacred and profane;
together with a comment on the two witnesses (Rev. XI)
the three "Unclean spirits like frogs, which go forth
to the kings of the earth..." the great earthquake which
will convulse the world... and the certain deliverance
of the family of man from the cruel oppression and mis-
rule of kings-craft, priestcraft and aristocracy...
By William Mathers. Wheeling, The author, 1831.
viii, [9]-200 p.   21 cm.

23342   Mathews, Mrs. Anne (Jackson) 1782?-1869.
Memoirs of Charles Mathews, comedian. By Mrs. Mathews
... London, R. Bentley, 1838-39.
4 v.   fronts., ports.   22 cm.

23343   Mathews, Cornelius, 1817-1889.
The better interests of the country, in connexion
with international copy-right... By Cornelius Mathews.
New-York and London, Wiley & Putnam, 1843.
30 p.   19 cm.
(A lecture delivered at the lecture-room of the
Society library, Feb. 2, 1843.)

23344   Mathews, Cornelius, 1817-1889.
A pen-and-ink panorama of New-York city. By Cornelius
Mathews. New York, J. S. Taylor, 1853.
iv, [5]-209 p.   14½ cm.

23345   Mathews, Cornelius, 1817-1889.
The politicians: a comedy, in five acts. By Cornelius

Mathews... New York, B. G. Trevett [etc.] 1840.
118 p.   18½ cm.

23346 [Mathews, Cornelius] 1817-1889.
Wakondah; the master of life. A poem. New York,
G. L. Curry & co., 1841.
24 p.   20½ cm.

23347 Mathews, Cornelius, 1817-1889.
Withcraft: a tragedy, in five acts. By Cornelius
Mathews. New York, S. French, 1852.
3 p.l., [9]-99 p.   16½ cm.

23348 Matlack, Timothy, 1736-1829.
An oration, delivered March 16, 1780, before the patron,
vice-presidents and members of the American philosophical
society, held at Philadelphia, for promoting useful
knowledge. By Timothy Matlack, esquire, a member of
said society and secretary of the Supreme executive
council of the state of Pennsylvania. Philadelphia,
Printed by Styner and Cist, in Second-street, 1780.
27 p.   26½ x 20 cm.

23349 Matrimonial brokerage in the metropolis... By a reporter
of the New York press. New York, Thatcher & Hutchinson,
1859.
x, 11-355 p.   front., plates.   19 cm.

23350 Matson, Nehemiah, 1816-1883.
French and Indians of Illinois river. By N. Matson...
Princeton, Ill., Republican job printing establishment,
1874.
4 p.l., [13]-260 p.   front. (port.)   18 cm.

23351 Matteson, Mrs. Frances F
The fragment; or, Letters & poems, by Mrs. Frances F.
Matteson... Rome, N. Y., A. Sandford, printer, 1855.
144 p.   front. (port.)   15½ cm.

23352 Matteson, Orsamus B   1805-1889.
Speech of Hon. O. B. Matteson, of New York, on the
cheap postage bill. Delivered in the House of representatives, January 11, 1851. Washington, Buell &
Blanchard, 1851.
15 p.   22½ cm.

23353 [Matthews, John, R.N.]
Twenty-one plans, with explanations, of different
actions in the West Indies, during the late war: by an

officer of the Royal navy, who was present. Chester [Eng.] Printed by J. Fletcher, for the author, 1784.
24 p.   21 fold. col. plans.   20½ x 16 cm.

23354 Matthews, Lyman, 1801-1866.
History of the town of Cornwall, Vermont, by Rev. Lyman Matthews... Middlebury, Mead and Fuller, Register book and job office, 1862.
xii, [13]-356 p.   1 illus., pl., 7 port. (incl. front.) 23 cm.

23355 Matthews, Lyman, 1801-1866.
Memoir of the life and character of Ebenezer Porter, D.D., late present of the Theological seminary, Andover. By Lyman Matthews... Boston, Perkins & Marvin; Philadelphia, H. Perkins, 1837.
396 p.   front. (port.)   19½ cm.

23356 Matthias, Benjamin.
The politician's register; containing a brief sketch of the executive, legislative and judicial departments of the federal and state governments... Also, returns of the votes cast in the last elections for presidential electors, members of Congress, and governors of the several states. By Benjamin Matthias. Philadelphia, Key and Biddle, 1835.
2 p.l., 104 p.   18½ cm.

23357 Mattison, Hiram, 1811-1868.
Spirit rapping unveiled! An exposé of the origin, history, theology and philosophy of certain alleged communications from the spirit world, by means of "spirit rapping," "medium writing," "physical demonstrations," etc. ... By Rev. H. Mattison... New York, Mason brothers, 1853.
192 p.   illus.   18 cm.

23358 Maubert de Gouvest, Jean Henry, 1721-1767.
Lettres iroquoises. A Irocopolis, Chez les Venerables. MDCCLII. [Lausanne, 1752]
2 v. in 1.   16 cm.

23359 Mauduit, Israel, 1708-1787.
The case of the dissenting ministers. Addressed to the lords spiritual and temporal. By Israel Mauduit. To which is added, a copy of the bill proposed for their relief. 3d ed. London, Printed for J. Wilkie, 1772.
2 p.l., [3]-65 p.   21 cm.

23360   [Mauduit, Israel] 1708-1787.
        Considerations on the present German war.   3d ed.
        London, Printed for J. Wilkie, 1760.
            144 p.   19 cm.

23361   [Mauduit, Israel] 1708-1787.
        Strictures on the Philadelphia mischianza or triumph
        upon leaving America unconquered. With extracts, con-
        taining the principal part of a letter, published in the
        "American crisis." In order to shew how far the King's
        enemies think his general deserving of public honours...
        London, Printed for J. Bew, 1779.
            2 p.l., 42 p.   21 cm.

23362   [Mauduit, Israel] 1708-1787.
        Three letters to Lieut.-General Sir William Howe.
        With an appendix. London, Printed for G. Wilkie, 1781.
            2 p.l., 48 p.   front. (fold. map)   21 cm.

23363   Mauduit, Jasper.
        The legislative authority of the British Parliament,
        with respect to North America, and the privileges of the
        assemblies there, briefly considered. By J. M. of the
        Inner-Temple. London, Printed for W. Nicoll, 1766.
            20 p.   20½ cm.

23364   [Maule, Thomas] 1645-1724.
        An abstract of a letter to Cotton Mather of Boston in
        New-England. By T. M. [New York] Printed [by William
        Bradford] in the year 1701. [Boston, 1936]
            facsim.: 19 p.   23 cm.   [Photostat Americana.
        Second series... Photostated at the Massachusetts
        historical society. no. 10]

23365   Maule, Joseph E
        A serious review, affectionately recommended to the
        careful examination of Friends. By Joseph E. Maule.
        Philadelphia, W. S. Young, printer, 1860.
            31 p.   19½ cm.

23366   Maull, D   W
        The life and military service of the late Brigadier
        General Thomas A. Smyth. By D. W. Maull... Wilmington,
        Del., H. & E. F. James, printers, 1870.
            50 p.   front. (port.)   23 cm.

23367   Maunder, Samuel, 1785-1849.
        The history of the world: comprising a general history

278

both ancient and modern, of all the principal nations of
the globe, their rise, progress, present condition, etc.
By Samuel Maunder... Including a complete history of
the United States to the present time, also the late war
with Mexico, California, etc. Ed. by John Inman...
New York, H. Bill, 1852.
2 v.   front., plates (part fold.) ports.   23½ cm.

23368 [Maupertuis, Pierre Louis Moreau de] 1698-1759.
Dissertation physique à la'occasion du nègre blanc...
Leyde, 1744.
6 p.l., 132 p.   18 cm.

23369 Mauran, Joseph, 1796-1873.
An address delivered before the Alumni association of
the College of physicians and surgeons, Medical department
of Columbia college, New York, at the spring commencement,
March 10, 1864. By J. Mauran... New York, F. Hart & co.,
printers, 1864.
25 p.   24 cm.

23370 Mauran, Joseph 1796-1873.
Remarks on the cholera, embracing facts and observations
collected at New York, during a visit to the city
expressly for that purpose. 2d ed. Providence, W.
Marshall and co. printers, 1832.
34 p.   21½ cm.

23371 Maurice, Frederick Denison, 1805-1872.
The religions of the world and their relations to
Christianity, considered in eight lectures founded by
the Right Hon. Robert Boyle. By Frederick Dennison
Maurice... London, J. W. Parker, 1847.
xx, 257 p.   22½ cm.

23372 Maury, Abraham Poindexter, 1801-1848.
Address of the Honorable Abram P. Maury, on the life
and character of Hugh Lawson White, delivered at
Franklin, May 9, 1840... Franklin Tenn. Printed at
the Review office, 1840.
15 p.   23½ cm.

23373 Maury, Matthew Fontaine, 1806-1873.
The Amazon, and the Atlantic Slopes of South America.
A series of letters published in the National intelli-
gencer and Union newspapers, under the signature of
"Inca," by M. F. Maury... Rev. and cor. by the author.
Washington, F. Taylor, 1853.
63 p.   front. (map)   25 cm.

23374 Maury, Matthew Fontaine, 1806-1873.
       Maury's wind and current charts. Gales in the Atlantic.
       Washington, 1857.
       [3] p.   24 col. maps.   29 x 23½ cm.

23375 Maury, Matthew Fontaine, 1806-1873.
       The petition of M. F. Maury to the Senate and House of
       representatives in Congress assembled... [Washington,
       1856]
       17, 18 p.   23 cm.

23376 Maury, Matthew Fontaine, 1806-1873.
       ... Sailing directions from sea to Sandy Hook. Pub.
       separately by authority of Hon. J. C. Dobbin, secretary
       of navy. May, 1855. Philadelphia, E. C. & J. Biddle,
       1855.
       cover-title, 8 p.   double chart.   28 x 23 cm.

23377 Maury, Matthew Fontaine 1806-1873.
       ... The world we live in. [Intermediate] New York,
       Richardson and company; New Orleans, D. H. Maury;
       [etc., etc.] 1868.
       104 p.   illus.   26½ cm.

23378 Mavor, William Fordyce, 1758-1837.
       Historical account of the most celebrated voyages,
       travels, and discoveries, from the time of Columbus to
       the present period... By William Mavor... London,
       E. Nerbery, 1796-97.
       25 v.   front. (port.) plates (part fold.) fold.
       map, fold. tab.   14½ cm.

23379 Mavor, William Fordyce, 1758-1837.
       Universal history, ancient and modern; from the
       earliest records of time, to the general peace of 1801...
       By William Mavor... London, Printed for R. Phillips,
       1802-04.
       20 v.   front., fold. maps.   16 cm.

23380 Mawe, John, 1764-1829.
       Travels in the interior of Brazil; with notices on its
       climate, agriculture, commerce, population, mines,
       manners, and customs: and a particular account of the
       gold and diamond districts. Including a voyage to the
       Rio de la Plata. By John Mawe. 2d ed. ... London,
       Longman, Hurst, Rees, Orme, and Brown, 1822.
       x p., 1 l., 493, [1] p. incl. col. front.   col. plates
       map.   22 cm.

23381 Mayer, Brantz, 1809-1879.
Memoir of Jared Sparks, LL.D. By Brantz Mayer, president
of the Maryland historical society: prepared at the
request of the Society, and read before its annual meeting,
on Thursday evening, February 7, 1867. [Baltimore, Printed
for the author, by J. Murphy, 1867]
36 p.   front. (port.)   30½ x 24 cm.

23382 Maxcy, Jonathan, 1768-1820.
Funeral sermon, delivered on Lord's day, December 17,
1817, in the Representatives' chamber before both
branches of the legislature of the state of South Carolina.
By Jonathan Maxcy... Columbia, S. C., Printed at the
Telescope press, 1818.
50 p.   18½ cm.

23383 Maxcy, Jonathan, 1768-1820.
An oration, delivered in the Baptist meeting-house
in Providence, July 4, A.D. 1795, at the celebration of
the nineteenth anniversary of American independence. By
Jonathan Maxcy, A.M., president of the Rhode-Island
college. Published at the request of the town. Providence,
Printed by Carter and Wilkinson, and sold at their book-
store, 1795.
20 p.   19½ cm.

23384 Maxcy, Jonathan, 1768-1820.
An oration, delivered in the First Congregational meeting-
house, in Providence, on the fourth of July, 1799. By
Jonathan Maxcy... Providence, Printed by John Carter,
jun. at the New Printing-Office, Market-S reet, 1799.
16 p.   19½ x 15 cm.

23385 Maxcy, Jonathan, 1768-1820.
A sermon delivered in the chapel of Rhode-Island college,
to the senior class, on the Sunday preceding the anniversary commencement, September 3d, 1800. By Jonathan Maxcy...
Printed at Providence, by Bennett Wheeler, 1801.
14 p., 1 l.   21 cm.

23386 Maxcy, Virgil, 1785-1844.
Address to the Agricultural society of Maryland.
Delivered at their anniversary meeting... at Annapolis...
the 15th December, 1819. By the Hon. Virgil Maxcy...
Annapolis, Printed by J. Green, 1820.
19 p.   20½ cm.

23387 Maxcy, Virgil, 1785-1844.
A discourse before the Phi Beta Kappa society of Brown

university. Delivered September fourth, 1833. By
Virgil Maxcy. Boston, Lilly, Wait, Colman, and Holden,
1833.
31 p.   22½ cm.

23388 [Maxcy, Virgil] 1785-1844.
The Maryland resolutions, and the objections to them
considered. By a citizen of Maryland. Baltimore, E. J.
Coale & co., 1822.
39 p.   23 cm.
"Maryland resolutions in favour of the appropriation
of public land for the purposes of education."

23389 Maxson, Edwin R
Hospitals, British, French, and American. To which is
appended, A glance at the British Islands, France, and
America. Ethnological, climatic, and general. By Edwin
R. Maxson... Philadelphia, Pub. for the author, 1868.
122 p.   16 cm.

23390 Maxwell, Wright & co., Rio de Janeiro.
Commercial formalities of Rio de Janeiro. By Maxwell,
Wright & co. Baltimore, Printed by B. Edes, 1830.
77 p., 1 l. incl. tables.   17½ cm.

23391 May, Sir Thomas Erskine, baron Farnborough, 1815-1886.
The constitutional history of England since the
accession of George Third, 1760-1860; by Thomas Erskine
May... Boston, Crosby and Nichols, 1863.
2 v.   19½ cm.

23392 Mayall, Samuel.
Speech of Hon. S. Mayall, of Maine, on the financial
and territorial policy of the administration. Delivered
in the House of representatives, January 2, 1855.
Washington, Printed at the Congressional globe office,
1855.
8 p.   23 cm.

23393 Maycock, James Dottin.
Flora barbadensis: a catalogue of plants, indigenous,
naturalized, and cultivated, in Barbados. To which is
prefixed, a geological description of the island. By
James Dottin Maycock... London, J. Ridgway, 1830.
1 p.l., xx, 446, [3] p.   front. (map) 1 pl.   23 cm.

23394 Mayhew, Experience, 1673-1758.
Indian converts: or, Some account of the lives and dying

speeches of a considerable number of the Christianized
Indians of Martha's Vineyard, in New-England... By
Experience Mayhew... To which is added, Some account of
those English ministers who have successively presided
over the Indian work in that and the adjacent islands.
By Mr. Prince... London, Printed for S. Gerrish, bookseller in Boston in New-England; and sold by J. Osborn
[etc.] 1727.
7, ix-xxiv, 310 p. 19 cm.

23395 Mayhew, Jonathan, 1720-1766.
The expected dissolution of all things, a motive to universal holiness. Two sermons preached in Boston, N. E.,
on the Lord's day, Nov. 23, 1755; occasioned by the earthquakes which happened on the Tuesday morning, and
Saturday evening preceeding. By Jonathan Mayhew...
Boston, N. E., Printed by Edes & Gill, and sold at their
printing-office; and by R. Draper, 1755.
76, 5 p. 18 cm.

23396 Mayhew, Jonathan, 1720-1766.
God's hand and providence to be religiously acknowledged
in public calamities. A sermon occasioned by the great
fire in Boston, New-England, Thursday, March 20, 1760.
And preached on the Lord's day following. By Jonathan
Mayhew... Boston, Printed by Richard Draper, in Newbury-
Street, Edes and Gill, in Queen-Street, and Thomas and
John Fleet, in Cornhill, 1760.
38 p., 1 l. 21 cm.

23397 Mayhew, Jonathan, 1720-1766.
Observations on the charter and conduct of the Society
for the propagation of the gospel in foreign parts;
designed to shew their non-conformity to each other.
With remarks on the mistakes of East Apthorp, M.A.,
missionary at Cambridge, in quoting, and representing
the sense of said chapter, &c. As also various incidental
reflections relative to the Church of England, and the
state of religion in North-America, particularly in New-
England. By Jonathan Mayhew, D.D., pastor of the West-
church in Boston... Boston, New England: Printed by
Richard and Samuel Draper, in Newbury-street, Edes and
Gill, in Queen-street, and Thomas and John Fleet at the
Heart and crown in Cornhill, 1763.
176 p. 23 cm.

23398 Mayhew, Jonathan, 1720-1766.
Practical discourses delivered on occasion of the

earthquakes in November, 1755. Wherein is particularly
shown, by a variety of arguments, the great importance of
turning our feet unto God's testimonies, and of making
haste to keep his Commandments; together with the reason-
ableness, the necessity, and great advantage, of a
serious consideration of our ways. By Jonathan Mayhew...
Boston, Printed and sold by Richard Draper, in Newbury-
street, and Edes and Gill, in Queen-street, 1760.
1 p.l., [4], 377, [1] p., 1 l.   19 cm.

23399   Mayhew, Jonathan, 1720-1766.
A sermon preached at Boston in New-England, May 26,
1751. Occasioned by the much-lamented death of His Royal
Highness Frederick, prince of Wales, &c. &c. &c. By
Jonathan Mayhew, D.D., pastor of the West-church in
Boston. Boston, Printed and sold by Richard Draper,
in Newbury-street, and Daniel Gookin, in Marlborough-
street, 1751.
39 p.   20½ cm.

23400   Mayhew, Jonathan, 1720-1766.
The snare broken. A thanksgiving discourse, preached
at the desire of the West church in Boston, N. E. Friday
May 23, 1766. Occasioned by the repeal of the Stamp-act.
By Jonathan Mayhew, D.D. pastor of said church...
Boston, Printed and sold by R. & S. Draper, in Newbury-
Street; Edes and Gill, in Queen-Street; and T. & J. Fleet,
in Cornhill, 1766.
viii, 44 p.   22 cm.

23401   Maynard, Charles Johnson, 1845-
The naturalist's guide in collecting and preserving
objects of natural history, with a complete catalogue of
the birds of the eastern Massachusetts. By C. J. Maynard.
With illustrations by E. L. Weeks. Boston, Fields,
Osgood & co., 1870.
ix, 170 p.   front., illus.   20 cm.

23402   Maynard, Horace, 1814-1882.
A discourse, commemorating the life and services of
Daniel Webster: delivered in the Methodist Episcopal
church, Knoxville, January 1st, 1853, at the request of
the citizens. By Horace Maynard. Knoxville, Tenn.,
A. Blackburn & co., 1853.
47, [1] p.   20 cm.

23403   Maynard, John W
... Extract from the charge of Judge Maynard to the
grand jury of Northampton County, at the opening of the

court, January term, 1863.   Philadelphia, H. B. Ashmead,
1863
3, [1] p.   22 cm.   [Philadelphia. Union league.
Pamphlets. v. 1, no. 9]

23404   Maynarde, Thomas, fl. 1595.
Sir Francis Drake his voyage, 1595. By Thomas Maynarde,
together with the Spanish account of Drake's attack on
Puerto Rico. Ed., from the original manuscripts, by
W. D. Cooley. London, Printed for the Hakluyt society,
1849.
3 p.l., [v]-viii, 65 p.   21½ cm.

23405   Mayne, F[anny] ed.
Voyages and discoveries in the Arctic regions. Ed. by
F. Mayne... London, Longman, Brown, Green, and Longmans,
1855.
2 p.l., 140 p.   17½ cm.   [The traveller's library,
vol. 73]

23406   Mayne, Richard Charles, 1835-1892.
Four years in British Columbia and Vancouver Island.
An account of their forests, rivers, coasts, gold fields
and resources for colonisation. By Commander R. C.
Mayne... London, J. Murray, 1862.
xi, 468 p. incl. front.   plates, 2 maps (1 fold.)
22 cm.

23407   Meacham, Henry H
The empty sleeve: or, The life and hardships of Henry
H. Meacham, in the Union army. By himself. Springfield,
Mass., Sold for the benefit of the author [1869?]
32 p.   18½ cm.

23408   [Mead, Asa] 1792-1831.
Memoir of John Mooney Mead, who died at East Hartford,
Conn., April 8, 1831, aged 4 years, 11 months, and 4 days
... New York, American tract society [1832]

23409   Mead, Charles.
American minstrel, consisting of poetical essays on
various subjects. By Charles Mead. Philadelphia, J.
Mortimer, 1828.
1 p.l., xi, [13]-174 p., 1 l.   14 cm.

23410   Mead, Daniel M
A history of the town of Greenwich, Fairfield county,
Conn., with many important statistics. By Daniel M. Mead
... New York, Baker & Godwin, printers, 1857.
318 p.   19½ cm.

23411 Mead, Samuel, 1764-1818.
   A sermon, delivered December 29, 1799; occasioned by
the death of General George Washington, who died
December 14th, 1799, in his 68th year. By Samuel Mead,
A.M., pastor of a church in Danvers... Published by
desire. Printed by Joshua Cushing, County street, Salem,
1800.
       24 p.   21½ cm.

23412 Meade, Richard Worsam, 1778-1828.
   The case of Richard W. Meade, esq., a citizen of Pennsylvania, U.S.A., seized and imprisoned, 2d of May, 1816, by
the government of Spain, and still detained. Cadiz,
November 27th, 1817. [Washington? 1817?]
       25 p.   22 cm.

23413 Meade, Richard Worsam, 1807-1870, defendant.
   Defense of Capt. Richard W. Meade, tried for the loss of
the United States steamer San Jacinto, on the Bahama
banks, January 1, 1865. Read by his counsel, John W.
Ashmead, on the eighth day of February, 1866, before a
naval court-martial, convened at the Navy yard, in the
city of Philadlephia. New York, Press of Wynkoop & Hallen-
beck, 1866.
       65 p.   23 cm.

23414 Meade, William.
   An experimental enquiry into the chemical properties
and medicinal qualities of the principal mineral waters
of Ballston and Saratoga, in the state of New York.
With directions for the use of those waters in the various
diseases to which they are applicable; and observations on
diet and regimen. To which is added an appendix, containir
a chemical analysis of the Lebanon spring in the state
of New York. By William Meade... Philadelphia, H. Hall,
1817.
       2 p.l., [vii]-xv, 195 p.   illus., plates.   23 cm.

23415 Meade, Willaim, bp., 1789-1862.
   A sermon preached in Christ church, Alexandria, on
Sunday the 18th of Sept. 1825, by the Rev. Wm. Meade,
on the occasion of the death of the Rev. Oliver Norris,
and published by the vestry, for the benefit of his
bereaved congregation. Alexandria, Printed by S. Snowden
and W. F. Thornton, 1825.
       23, 6 p.   23 cm.

23416 Meader, J   W
   The Merrimack River; its source and its tributaries.

Embracing a history of manufactures, and of the towns
along its course; their geography, topography, and
products, with a description of the magnificent natural
scenery about its upper waters. By J. W. Meader. Boston,
B. B. Russell, 1869.
viii, 9-307 p.   front. (fold. map)   23½ cm.

23417   The Mechanics' magazine, and journal of public internal
improvement; devoted to the useful arts, and the recording
of projects, inventions, and discoveries of the age. v. 1;
Feb. 1830-Jan. 1831. Boston, S. N. Dickinson, 1830.
x, 384 p.   illus., plates, diagrs.   26 cm.   monthly.
No more published.

23418   Medford, Macall.
Oil without vinegar, and dignity without pride; or,
British, American, and West-India interests considered.
By Macall Medford, esq. London, Printed for W. J. and
J. Richardson, Cornhill: and Thomas Dobson, Philadelphia,
1807.
87, [15] p.   21½ cm.

23419   ... The mediator between North and South: or, The seven
pointers of the North star. Thoughts of an American in
the wilderness... [4th rev. ed.] Baltimore, 1862.
cover-title, 4 p.   23 cm.

23420   ... The Medical and agricultural register, for the years
1806 and 1807. Containing practical information on
husbandry; cautions and directions for the preservation
of health, management of the sick, &c. Designed for the
use of families. Edited by Daniel Adams, M.B. ...
[v. 1; Jan. 1806-Dec. 1807] Boston, Printed by Manning
& Loring... [1806-07]
2 p.l., 378, [6] p.   22 cm.

23421   Medill, William, 1805-1865.
Speech of Mr. William Medill, of Ohio, on the appropriation bill. In the House... April 5, 1842.
[Washington, 1842]
8 p.   24½ cm.

23422   Medina, Baltasar, de, d. 1697.
Chronica de la santa provincia de San Diego de Mexico,
de religiosos descalços de n. s. p. s. Francisco en la
Nueva España. Vidas de ilvstres, y venerables varones,
que la han edificado con excelentes virtudes. Escrivelas,
y consagralas al glorioso san Diego de Alcala, patron y
tutelar de la misma provincia, F. Balthassar de Medina...

287

Mexico, J. de Ribera, 1682.
23 p.l., 259 numb., [21] p.   map.   30 cm.

23423   Medina, Baltasar de. d. 1697.
Vida, martyrio, y beatificacion del invicto proto-martyr
de el Japon, san Felipe de Jesus, patron de Mexico, su
patria, imperial corte de Nueva España, en el nuevo
mundo: que escrivió fray Balthasar de Medina... 2. impression. A expensas de la devota, noble, y generosa platería
de Mexico... En Madrid, En la imprenta de los herederos
de la viuda de Juan Garcia Infanzon, Año de 1751.
14 p.l., 176 p.   1 illus., pl.   20 cm.

23424   Meek, Fielding Bradford, 1817-1876.
Descriptions of new organic remains from north-eastern
Kansas, indicating the existence of Permian rocks in
that territory. By F. B. Meek and F. W. Hayden, M.D.
[Albany, 1858]
16 p.   23 cm.

23425   Meginness, John Franklin, 1827-1899.
Otzinachson; or, A history of the West Branch valley of
the Susquehanna: embracing a full account of its settlement -- trials and privations endured by the first
pioneers -- full accounts of the Indian wars, predatory
incursions, abductions, massacres, &c., together with an
account of the fair play system; and the trying scenes
of the big runaway; interspersed with biographical
sketches of some of the leading settlers, families, etc.,
together with pertinent anecdotes, statistics, and much
valuable matter entirely new. By J. F. Meginness.
Philadelphia H. B. Ashmead, 1857.
xvi, [17]-518 p.   front., plates.   23½ cm.

23426   Meigs, Charles D[elucena] 1792-1869
A memoir of Samuel George Morton, M.D., late president
of the Academy of natural sciences of Philadelphia. By
Charles D. Meigs, M.D. Read November 6, 1851, and
published by direction of the academy. Philadelphia,
T. K. and P. G. Collins, printers, 1851.
48 p.   front. (port.)   23½ cm.

23427   Meigs, James Aitken, 1829-1879.
Catalogue of human crania, in the collection of the
Academy of natural sciences of Philadephia: based upon
the third edition of Dr. Morton's "Catalogue of skulls,"
&c. By J. Aitken Meigs... Philadelphia, J. B. Lippincott
& co., 1857.
112 p.   illus.   23 cm.

23428   Meigs, Josiah, 1757-1822.
        An oration pronounced before a public assembly in
        New-Haven, on the 5th day of November, 1781, at the cele-
        bration of the glorious victory over Lieutenant-General
        Earl Cornwallis, at York-Town in Virginia, on the 19th
        day of October, 1781. By Josiah Meigs, A. M. New-Haven,
        Printed by Thomas and Samuel Green, 1782.
        14 p.   20½ x 15½ cm.

23429   Meigs, Montgomery Cunningham, 1816-1892.
        The three days' battle of Chattanooga, 23d, 24th, 25th
        November, 1864 [!] An unofficial dispatch from General
        Meigs... to the Hon. E. M. Stanton, secretary of war.
        Now first correctly printed.   Washington, D. C., McGill
        & Witherow, printers, 1864.
        8 p.   23 cm.

23430   [Mein, John]
        Sagittarius's letters and political speculations,
        extracted from the Public ledger. Humbly inscribed to
        the very loyal and truly pious Doctor Samuel Cooper,
        pastor of the Congregational church in Brattle street...
        Boston, Printed: by order of the Select men and sold at
        Donation hall, for the benefit of the distressed patriots,
        1775.
        1 p.l., 127 p.   18 cm.

23431   Memoirs of the principal transactions of the last war between
        the English and French in North America. From the
        commencement of it in 1744, to the conclusion of the
        treaty of Aix la Chapelle. Containing in particular
        an account of the importance of Nova Scotia or Acadie
        and the island of Cape Breton to both nations. London,
        Printed for R. and J. Dodsley, 1757.
        viii, 102 p.   10½ cm.

23432   The middle line: or, An attempt to furnish some hints for
        ending the differences subsisting between Great-Britain
        and the colonies. Philadelphia, Printed and sold by
        Joseph Crukshank, in Market-street, 1775.
        48 p.   17 cm.

23433   Minot, George Richards, 1758-1802.
        Continuation of the history of the province of Massa-
        chusetts bay, from the year 1748 [to 1765] With an intro-
        ductory sketch of events from its original settlement.
        By George Richards Minot... Boston, Printed by Manning &
        Loring, Feb., 1798-June, 1803.
        2 v.   22½ cm.

23434 Minot, George Richards, 1758-1802.
The history of the insurrections, in Massachusetts,
in the year 1786, and the rebellion consequent thereon.
By George Richards Minot, A.M. Printed at Worcester,
Massachusetts, by Isaiah Thomas, 1788.
iv, [5]-192 p.   21 cm.

23435 Mirabeau, Honoré Gabriel Riquetti, comte de, 1749-1791.
Considerations on the order of Cincinnatus; to which are
added, as well several original papers relative to that
institution, as also a letter from the late M. Turgot...
to Dr. Price, on the constitutions of America; and an
abstract of Dr. Price's Observations on the importance
of the American revolution: with notes and reflections
upon that work. Tr. from the French of the Count de
Mirabeau... London, Printed for J. Johnson, 1785.
xii, 284 p.   21½ cm.
Translated by Sir Samuel Romilly.

23436 Mirabeau, Honoré Gabriel Riquetti, comte de, 1749-1791.
Reflections on the Observations on the importance of
the American revolution, and the means of making it a
benefit to the world. By Richard Price... Tr. from the
French of the Count de Mirabeau. A new edition with
considerable corrections. Philadelphia, Printed by T.
Seddon, in Market-street, and W. Spotswood, in Front-
street, 1786.
1 p.l., [2]-19 p.   21½ cm.

23437 Missouri. Constitution.
... Constitution of the state of Missouri. November
16, 1820. Read, and referred to a select committee.
Washington, Printed by Gales & Seaton, 1820.
25 p.   22 cm.   ([U.S. 16th Cong., 2d sess. House.
Doc.] 2)

23438 [Mitchell, John] d. 1768.
The contest in America between Great Britain and
France, with its consequences and importance; giving an
account of the views and designs of the French, with the
interests of Great Britain, and the situation of the
British and French colonies, in all parts of America:
in which a proper barrier between the nations in North
America is pointed out, with a method to prosecute the
war, so as to obtain that necessary security for our
colonies. By an impartial hand... London, Printed for
A. Millar, 1757.
2 p.l., iii-xlix, [1], [17]-244 (i.e. 260) p.   21 cm.

23439 Mitchell, Joseph.
       The missionary pioneer; or, A brief memoir of the life,
       labours, and death of John Stewart, (man of colour)
       founder, under God, of the misssion among the Wyandotts,
       at Upper Sandusky, Ohio. Pub. by Joseph Mitchell. New
       York, Printed by J. C. Totten, 1827.
       viii, [9]-96 p.   14½ cm.

23440 Mitchell, W   H
       Dakota County. Its past and present, geographical,
       statistical and historical, together with a general view
       of the state, by W. H. Mitchell. Minneapolis, Tribune
       printing company, 1868.
       vi, 161, [1] p.   front. (port.) illus.   18½ cm.

23441 Monardes, Nicolás, 1493-1588.
       Ioyfvll newes out of the new-found vvorlde. Wherein are
       declared, the rare and singuler vertues of diuers herbs,
       trees, plantes, oyles & stones, with their applications,
       as well as to the vse of phisicke, as of chirurgery...
       Also the portrature of the said hearbs, verie aptly
       described: Englished by John Frampton, marchant. Newly
       cor. ... Whervnto are added three other bookes treating
       of the bezaar stone, the herb escuerconera, the properties
       of iron and steele in medicine, and the benefit of snow.
       London, Printed by E. Allde, by the assigne of B. Norton,
       1596.
       3 p.l., 187 (i.e. 180) numb. l.   illus.   19 cm.

23442 Monroe, James, Pres. U. S., 1758-1831.
       The memoir of James Monroe, esq. relating to his unsettled
       claims upon the people and government of the United States.
       Charlottesville, Va., Gilmer, Davis and co., 1828.
       60 p.   22½ cm.

23443 Monroe, James, pres. U. S., 1758-1831.
       ... Mr. Monroe's letter on the rejected treaty, between
       the United States and Great Britain; concluded by Messrs.
       Monroe and Pinkney. Also, the treaty itself, and
       documents connected with it. Portland, From the Gazette
       press, 1813.
       52 p.   22½ cm.

23444 Montague, E   J
       A directory, business mirror, and historical sketches
       of Randolph county... containing... also... brief notes
       of the pioneer settlers... By E. J. Montague. Alton,
       Ill., Courier steam book and job printing house, 1859.
       246 p.   19 cm.

23445 Montesinos, Fernando, 17th cent.
... Mémoires historiques sur l'ancien Pérou, par le
licencié Fernando Montesinos. Inédits. Paris, A.
Bertrand, 1840.
xv, 235 p.   21 cm.   (Voyages, relations et mémoires
originaux pour servir à l'histoire de la découverte de
l'Amérique. Pub. ... par H. Ternaux-Compans. [t. 17])
A translation from a copy made by J. B. Muñoz of a ms.
preserved in the convent of San José de Mercedarios des-
calzos in Seville.

23446 Montgomery, Elizabeth.
Reminiscences of Wilmington, in familiar village tales,
ancient and new. By Elizabeth Montgomery... Philadelphia,
T. K. Collins, jr., 1851.
xii, [7]-367 p.   front. (port.) plates.   23 cm.

23447 The Monthly anthology, and Boston review. Containing sketches
and reports of philosophy, religion, history, arts, and
manners... v. 1-10; Nov. 1803-June 1811. Boston, Munroe
& Francis [etc.] 1804-11.
10 v.   22½ cm.
Edited by D. P. Adams (Sylvanus Per-se, pseud.) Nov.
1803-Apr. 1804; from May 1804 by William Emerson, later
by S. C. Thacher and other members of the Anthology club.
cf. Mass. hist. soc., Proc., v. 2, p. 387-389.

23448 The Monthly magazine, and American review... v. 1-3;
Apr. 1799-Dec. 1800. New York, Printed by T. & J. Swords,
1800.
3 v.   21½ cm.
Charles Brockden Brown, editor.

23449 [Montúfar, Manuel] 1791-1844.
Memorias para la historia de la revolucion de Centro-
America. Por un Guatemalteco. Jalapa [Guatemala]
Impreso por Aburto y Blanco, en la oficina del gobierno,
1832.
xxxii, 257 p.   16½ cm.
A history of the period from 1820 to 1831.

23450 A monumental inscription of the fifty of March. Together
with a few lines on the enlargement of Ebenezer Richardson
convicted of murder. [Boston, Isaiah Thomas, 1772]
broadside.   49 x 29 cm.
Poetry.
On shooting of Christoph Spider, 11, by Richardson,
Boston Custom House officer, on 22 February 1770.

23451   [Moore, Clement Clarke] 1779-1863.
        Observations upon certain passages in Mr. Jefferson's
        Notes on Virginia, which appear to have a tendency to
        subvert religion, and establish a false philosophy.
        New York, 1804.
        32 p.   22½ cm.

23452   Moore, David N
        Proceedings of the centennial reunion of the Moore
        family, held at Belleville, Ill., May 31 and June 1,
        1882. Arranged and pub. by Dr. D. N. Moore & McCabe
        Moore... St. Louis, Mo., A. R. Fleming, printer, 1882.
        82 p.   21½ cm.

23453   Moore, Frank, 1828-1904.
        Diary of the American revolution. From newspapers and
        original documents. By Frank Moore. New York, C. Scribner;
        London, S. Low, son & company, 1860, '59.
        2 v.   fronts., plates, ports., maps (part fold.)
        23 cm.

23454   Moore, Frank, 1828-1904, ed.
        Materials for history, printed from original manuscripts.
        With notes and illustrations. By Frank Moore... First
        series. New York, Printed for the Zenger club, 1861.
        3 p.l., [15]-240 p.   port.   26 x 20½ cm.

23455   [Moore, Frank] 1828-1904, ed.
        The patriot preachers of the American revolution. With
        biographical sketches. 1766-1783. [New York] Printed
        for the subscribers, 1860.
        vi, [7]-368 p.   20 cm.

23456   [Moreau, Jacob Nicolas] 1717-1804.
        A memorial, containing a summary view of facts, with
        their authorities, in answer to the Observations sent
        by the English ministry to the courts of Europe. Trans-
        lated from the French. Philadelphia, Printed by James
        Chattin, 1757.
        iv, 338 p.   20 cm.
        The French original (Mémoire contenant le précis des
        faits [etc.]) was published at Paris by the French govern-
        ment in 1756 as a justification of the war with England.
        In it were included documents captured from the British
        at Fort Necessity and at Braddock's defeat.

23457   [Moreau, Jacob Nicolas] 1717-1804, comp.
        The mystery reveal'd; or, Truth brought to light.
        Being a discovery of some facts, in relation to the

conduct of the late m---y, which however extraordinary
they may appear, are yet supported by such testimonies
of authentick papers and memoirs: as neither confidence,
can outbrave; nor cunning invalidate. By a patriot...
London, Printed for and sold by W. Cater [etc.] 1759.
1 p.l., 319 p.   21½ cm.

23458 Morse, Jedidiah, 1761-1826.
       Annals of the American revolution; or, A record of the
causes and events which produced, and terminated in the
establishment and independence of the American republic...
To which is prefixed a summary account of the first
settlement of the country, and some of the principal
Indian wars... To which is added... an appendix, containing a biography of the principal military officers,
who were instrumental in achieving our independence...
Hartford, 1824.
       2 p.l., 400, 50 p.   front., plates (1 fold.)   22 cm.

23459 Morse, Jedidiah, 1761-1826.
       A sermon, preached at Charlestown, November 29, 1798, on
the anniversary Thanksgiving in Massachusetts. With an
appendix, designed to illustrate some parts of the
discourse; exhibiting proofs of the early existence,
progress, and deleterious effects of French intrigue and
influence in the United States. By Jedidiah Morse...
Boston, Printed by Samuel Hall, December, 1798.
       74 p.   22 cm.

23460 [Mott, M   H   ]
       History of the Regulators of northern Indians. Pub. by
order of the central committee. Indianapolis, Indianapolis
journal company, printers, 1859.
       67 p.   22½ cm.

23461 Mourelle, Francisco Antonio, 1755-1820.
       Voyage of the Sonora in the second Bucareli expedition
to explore the Northwest Coast, survey the port of San
Francisco, and found Franciscan missions and a presidio
and pueblo at that port: the journal kept in 1775 on the
Sonora, by Don Francisco Antonio Mourelle, the second
pilot of the fleet constituting the sea division of the
expedition; tr. by the Hon. Daines Barrington from the
original Spanish manuscript; reprinted line for line and
page for page from Barrington's Miscellanies published
in London in 1781, with concise notes showing the voyages
of the earliest explorers on the coast, the sea and land
expeditions of Galvez and of Bucareli for settling
California and for founding missions, and many other

interesting notes as well as an entire new index to both
text & notes, by Thomas C. Russell; together with a
reproduction of the de la Bodega Spanish Carta general
showing Spanish discoveries, etc., on the coast up to 1791
and also a portrait of Sir Daines Barrington. San Francisco,
T. C. Russell, 1920.
    xii, 120 p., 1 l. incl. tables.   front. (port.)
2 maps (1 fold.)   29 cm.

23462 Murray, James, 1732-1782.
    An impartial history of the present war in America:
containing an account of its rise and progress, the political springs thereof, with its various successes and
disappointments, on both sides. By the Rev. James
Murray... London, Printed for R. Baldwin; [etc., etc.,
1778-80]
    3 v.   fronts., ports., fold. plan.   21½ cm.

                      N

23463 A narrative of the life and sufferings of Mrs. Jane Johns,
who was barbarously wounded and scalped by Seminole
Indians, in East Florida... Published exclusively for
her benefit. Charleston, Printed by Burke & Giles...
1837.
    29 p.   22½ cm.

23464 The National atlas and Tuesday morning mail. A weekly
periodical for the parlour. v. 1-3. July 31, 1836 -
January 1, 1838. Philadelphia, S. C. Atkinson, 1836-
1838.
    v.   illus., maps.   29½ cm.

23465 Neill, Edward Duffield, 1823-1893.
    Dahkotah land and Dahkotah life, with the history of
the fur traders of the extreme Northwest during the
French and British dominions. By Edw. D. Neill...
Philadelphia, J. B. Lippincott & co.; Chicago, S. C.
Griggs & co., 1859.
    2 p.l., 49-239 p.   22 cm.

23466 New England a degenerate plant. Who having forgot their
former sufferings, and lost their ancient tenderness,
are now become famous among the nations in bringing
forth the fruits of cruelty, wherein they have far
outstript their persecutors the bishops, as by these
their ensuing laws you may plainly see. Published for

the information of all sober people who desire to know
how the state of New-England now stands, and upon what
foundation the New-England churches are built, and by
whose strength they are upholded now they are degenerated
and have forsaken the Lord. The truth of which we are
witnesses, (who by their cruel hands have suffered)
Iohn Rous Iohn Copeland, strangers, Samuel Shattock
Nicholas Phelps Iosiah Southwick inhabitants. Whereunto
is annexed a copy of a letter which came from one who
hath been a magistrate among them, to a friend of his in
London, wherein he gives an account of some of the cruel
suffering of the people of God in those parts under the
rulers of New England, and their unrighteous laws.
London, Printed in the year 1659.
    20 p.   17½ cm.

23467 New Hampshire. Constitution.
    In Congress at Exeter, January 5th, 1776. We the
members of the Congress of the Colony of New Hampshire,
chosen... to establish some form of government...
Portsmouth, N. H., Daniel Fowle, 1776.
    broadside, printed on both sides.   30½ x 19 cm.
    First printing of first New Hampshire constitution;
first constitution of any of the colonies.

23468 New Hampshire. Laws, statutes, etc.
    State of New Hampshire. In the year of Our Lord, one
thousand, seven hundred, and seventy-eight. An act to
prevent the return to the state of certain persons
therein named, and others who have left, or shall leave
this state, or either of the United States of America,
and have joined, or shall join the enemies thereof.
Exeter, N. H., Printed by Zachariah Fowler, 1778.
    broadside. 34 x 34 cm.

23469 The New-York review, and Atheneum magazine. v. 1-2;
    June 1825-May 1826. New-York, E. Bliss & E. White,
    1825-26.
    2 v.   22½-23½ cm.   monthly.
    Library has v. 1, May-Nov. 1825. Each number is in
2 parts: The New-York review, The Atheneum magazine.
R. C. Sands, W. C. Bryant, editors. Preceded by the
Atlantic magazine. In July 1826 merged into the United
States literary gazette, which continued in October 1826
as the United States review and literary gazette.

23470 [Nicola, Lewis] 1717-1807.
    A treatise of military exercise, calculated for the
use of the Americans. In which every thing that is

supposed can be of use to them, is retained, and such manoeuvres, as are only for shew and parade, omitted. To which is added some directions on the other points of discipline. Philadelphia, Printed by Styner and Cist, 1776.
viii, 91, [1] p.   9 fold. pl.   16½ cm.

23471 Noyes, Nicholas, 1647-1717.
... Mr. James Bayley, living (if living) in Roxbury. A poem. [Cambridge, before 1707]
broadside.   22 x 36 cm.

23472 Noyes, Nichoas, 1647-1717.
Upon the much lamented death; of that pious and hopeful young gentlewoman, Mrs. Mary Gerrish, wife of Mr. Samuel Gerrish, the daughter of the Honourable Samuel Sewall Esqr. who departed this life November 17th 1710. [Boston? 1710?]
broadside.   22½ x 32 cm.

O

23473 O'Bryan, William, 1778-1868.
A narrative of travels in the United States of America, with some account of American manners and polity, and advice to emigrants and travellers going to that interesting country. By Wm. O'Bryan. London, Pub. for the author, 1836.
xi, [13]-419 p. incl. 1 illus., pl.   front. (port.) 18½ cm.

23474 The Olden time; a monthly publication devoted to the preservation of documents and other authentic information in relation to the early explorations and the settlement and improvement of the country around the head of the Ohio... Ed. by Neville B. Craig, esq. Pittsburgh, Dumars & co. [etc.] 1846-48; Cincinnati, Reprinted by R. Clarke & co., 1876.
2 v.   24½ cm.

23475 Oldroyd, Osborn Hamiline, 1842-1930.
The assassination of Abraham Lincoln; flight, pursuit, capture, and punishment of the conspirators, by Osborn H. Oldroyd... with an introduction by T. M. Harris... Washington, D. C., O. H. Oldroyd, 1901.
xviii, 305 p. incl. illus., plates, plans, facsim. front., port., fold. map.   20½ cm.

23476 Oliphant, Laurence, 1829-1888.
Minnesota and the far West; by Laurence Oliphant...
Edinburgh and London, W. Blackwood and sons, 1855.
xiii, [1], 306 p. incl. front., illus.   plates, fold.
map.   22 cm.

23477 On the death of five young men who was murthered, March 5th
1770. By the 29th regiment. [Boston? Edes and Gill?
1770?]
broadside.   15 x 31 cm.

23478 Only authentic life of Geo. Brinton McClellan, alias Little
Mac... With an account of his numerous victories from
Philippi to Antietam. [New York] American news co.
[1864?]
cover-title, 16 p.   illus.   14½ cm.

23479 Onstot, Thompson Gains, 1829-
Pioneers of Menard and Mason counties; made up of
personal reminiscences of an early life in Menard county,
which we gathered in a Salem life from 1830 to 1840, and
a Petersburgh life from 1840 to 1850; including personal
reminiscences of Abraham Lincoln and Peter Cartright [!]
By T. G. Onstot. Forest City, Ill, T. G. Onstot, 1902.
7 p.l., [17]-400 p.   front., illus. (incl. ports,
plan)   22½ cm.

23480 [Ortega, José de] 1700-1768.
Apostolicos afanes de la Compañia de Jesus, escritos por
un padre de la misma sagrada religion de su provincia de
Mexico. Barcelona, P. Nadal, 1754.
6 p.l., 452, [7] p., 1 l.   20 cm.
Edited by F. X. Fluvia.

23481 [Overton, John] 1766-1833.
A vindication of the measures of the President and his
commanding generals, in the commencement and termination
of the Seminole war. By a citizen of the state of
Tennessee. Washington, Printed by Gales & Seaton, 1819.
133 p.   22 cm.

P

23482 Pacific railroad convention, Lacon, Ill., 1853.
Proceedings of a Pacific railroad convention, at Lacon,
Illinois: with the address of Col. Samuel R. Curtis.
Cincinnati, Printed by J. D. Thorpe, 1853.
16 p.   22 cm.

23483 Paine, Thomas, 1737-1809.
Public good, being an examination into the claim of
Virginia to be the vacant western territory, and of the
right of the United States to the same: to which are
added, proposals for laying off a new state, to be
applied as a fund for carrying on the war, or redeeming
the national debt. Written in the year 1780. By
Thomas Paine. London, Printed by W. T. Sherin, 1817.
35 p. front. (port.) 22 cm.

23484 [Painter, Henry M]
Brief narrative of incidents in the war in Missouri,
and of the personal experience of one who has suffered.
Boston, Press of the Daily courier, 1863.
23 p. 24 cm.

23485 Patterson, A W
History of the backwoods; or, the region of the Ohio;
authentic, from the earliest accounts. Embracing many
events, notices of prominent pioneers, sketches of early
settlements, etc., etc. Not heretofore published... By
A. W. Patterson. Pittsburgh, The author, 1843.
x, [5]-311 p. front. (fold. map) 22 cm.

23486 [Paulding, James Kirke] 1778-1860.
... The Dutchman's fireside. A tale. By the author of
"Letters from the South," "The backwoodsman," "John Bull
in America," &c. &c.... In two volumes. New-York, J. &
J. Harper, 1839.
2 v. 17½ cm.

23487 [Peck, John Mason] 1789-1858.
"Father Clark," or, The pioneer preacher. Sketches and
incidents of Rev. John Clark, by an old pioneer. New York,
Sheldon, Lamport & Blakeman, 1855.
viii, [9]-287 p. front. 17 cm.

23488 Peck, John Mason, 1789-1858.
A gazetteer of Illinois: in three parts: containing a
general view of the state; a general view of each county;
and a particular description of each town, settlement...
etc. - alphabetically arranged. By J. M. Peck... Jackson-
ville, R. Goudy, 1834.
viii, 376 p. 16 cm.

23489 Perkins, James Handasyd, 1810-1849.
The memoir and writings of James Handasyd Perkins. Ed.
by William Henry Channing... Cincinnati, Trueman &
Spofford; Boston, W. Crosby and H. P. Nichols, 1851.
2 v. front. (port.) 20 cm.

23490 [Perreau, Jean André] 1749-1813.
   Lettres illinoises, par J. A. P., auteur de Clarisse.
   A Londres et se trouve à Paris, chez Merlin, 1772.
   326 p., 1 l.   17½ cm.

23491 Perrot, Nicolas, 1644-1718.
   Mémoire sur les moeurs, coustumes et relligion [!] des
   sauvages de l'Amérique Septentrionale, par Nicolas Perrot;
   publié pour la première fois par le R. P. J. Tailhan...
   Leipzig & Paris, A. Franck, 1864.
   viii, xliii, 341, [1] p.   19½ cm.

23492 Perry, William Stevens, bp., 1832-1898.
   The centenary of the British colonial episcopate. A
   sermon preached in St. Paul's cathedral. London,
   Wednesday, June 22, 1887, on occasion of the 186th anniversary of the Society for the propagation of the gospel
   in foreign parts, by William Stevens Perry, bishop of
   Iowa. Grinnell, Ia., Published for S. Paul's church, 1887.
   22 p.   20 cm.

23493 Peyton, John Lewis, 1824-1896.
   The adventures of my grandfather. With extracts from
   his letters, and other family documents, prepared for the
   press with notes and biographical sketches of himself and
   his son John Howe Peyton, esq., by John Lewis Peyton...
   London, J. Wilson, 1867.
   x, 249 p.   22 cm.

23494 [Phelps, William D   ]
   Fore and aft; or, Leaves from the life of an old sailor.
   By "Webfoot" [pseud.] With illustrations by Hammatt
   Billings. Boston, Nichols & Hall, 1871.
   vi, [7]-359 p.   front., plates.   18 cm.

23495 Phillippo, James M[ursell]
   Jamaica: its past and present state. By James M.
   Phillippo. Philadelphia, J. M. Campbell & co.; New York,
   Saxton & Miles, 1843.
   viii, [9]-176 p.   front., illus.   8°.

23496 Phillis.
   An elegiac poem, on the death of that celebrated divine,
   and eminent servant of Jesus Christ, the late reverend,
   and pious George Whitefield. [Boston, Sold by Ezekiel
   Russell in Queen-Street, and John Byles, in Marlboro-
   Street, 1770]
   broadside.   25½ x 42 cm.

300

23497   Pickard, Samuel, b. 1820.
        Autobiography of a pioneer: or, The nativity, experience,
        travels, and ministerial labors of Rev. Samuel Pickard,
        the "converted Quaker", containing stirring incidents
        and practical thoughts; with sermons by the author, and
        some account of the labors of Elder Jacob Knapp...
        Edited by O. T. Conger... Chicago, Church & Goodman,
        1866.
        xii, [13]-403 p. incl. illus., plates.   19 cm.

23498   Pinkerton, John, 1758-1826.
        Modern geography. A description of the empires, king-
        doms, states, and colonies; with the oceans, seas, and
        isles; in all parts of the world: including the most
        recent discoveries, and political alterations. Digested
        on a new plan. By John Pinkerton. The astronomical
        introduction by the Rev. S. Vince... The article America,
        corrected and considerably enlarged, by Dr. Barton, of
        Philadelphia. With numerous maps, drawn under the
        direction and with the latest improvements, of Arrowsmith,
        and engraved by the first American artists. To the whole
        are added, a catalogue of the best maps, and books of
        travels and voyages, in all languages: and an ample index...
        Philadelphia, J. Conrad, & co.; [etc., etc.] 1804.
        2 v.   diagrs. $23\frac{1}{2}$ cm. and atlas of 65 pl.   28 cm.

23499   Pitcher, Nathaniel, 1685-1723.
        Words of consolation to Mr. Robert Stetson and Mrs.
        Mary Stetson, his wife, on the death of their son Isaac
        Stetson, who perished in the mighty waters, November 7th,
        1718. Aged 22. [n.p., 1718?]
        broadside.   illus.   21 x $26\frac{1}{2}$ cm.

23500   A plain and seasonable address to the freeholders of Great-
        Britain on the present posture of affairs in America...
        London, Printed for Richardson and Urquhart, 1766.
        1 p.l., 21 p.   22 cm.

23501   Plumbe, John.
        Sketches of Iowa and Wisconsin, taken during a residence
        of three years in those territories. By John Plumbe, jr.
        St. Louis, Chambers, Harris & Knapp, 1839.
        3 p.l., [5]-103 p.   fold. map.   19 cm.

23502   A poem, in memory of the fifth of March, 1770. [Boston,
        1770]
        broadside. $33\frac{1}{2}$ x $20\frac{1}{2}$ cm.

23503   Post, Christian Frederick, 1710-1785.
        The second journal of Christian Frederick Post, on a

message from the governor of Pensilvania to the Indians on the Ohio. London, Printed for J. Wilkie, 1759.
v, [7]-67 p. 19½ cm.

23504 Potter, Israel Ralph, 1744-1826?
Life and remarkable adventures of Israel R. Potter, (a native of Cranston, Rhode-Island) who was a soldier in the American revolution... after which he was taken prisoner by the British, conveyed to England, where for 30 years he obtained a livelihood... by crying "Old chairs to mend"... Providence [R.I.] Printed by J. Howard, for I. R. Potter, 1824.
108 p. incl. front. 16½ cm.

23505 Power, John Carroll, 1819-1894.
History of the early settlers of Sangamon county, Illinois. "Centennial record." By John Carroll Power, assisted by his wife, Mrs. S. A. Power. Under the auspices of the Old settlers' society. Springfield, Ill., E. A. Wilson & co., 1876.
797, [1] p. 2 port. (incl. front.) double map.
24½ x 17½ cm.

23506 Powers, Stephen.
A foot and alone; a walk from sea to sea by the southern route. Adventures and observations in southern California, New Mexico, Arizona, Texas, etc. By Stephen Powers... Hartford, Conn., Columbian book company, 1872.
2 p.l., [xi]-xvi, [17]-327 p. front., illus., plates. 20½ cm.

23507 Pratt, Parley Parker, 1807-1857.
A voice of warning, and instruction to all people, or, An introduction to the faith and doctrine of the Church of Jesus Christ, of latter day saints. By Parley P. Pratt... 3d American ed. Nauvoo [Ill.] Printed by J. Taylor, 1844.
x, [11]-284 p. 13 cm.

23508 Prescott, William Hickling, 1796-1859.
History of the conquest of Mexico, with a preliminary view of the ancient Mexican civilization, and the life of the conqueror, Hernando Cortés. By William H. Prescott... New York, Harper and brothers, 1843.
3 v. front. (port.) fold. maps, facsim. 23 cm.

23509 Prescott, William Hickling, 1796-1859.
History of the conquest of Peru, with a preliminary view

302

of the civilization of the Incas. By William H. Prescott...
New York, Harper and brothers, 1847.
2 v.   fronts. (ports.)   map, facsim.   23 cm.

23510 The present state of the country and inhabitants, Europeans
and Indians, of Louisiana, on the north continent of
America. By an officer at New Orleans to his friend at
Paris. Containing the garrisons, forts and forces, price
of all manner of provisions... to which are added, letters
from the governor of that province on the trade of the
French and English with the natives... London, Printed
for J. Millan, 1744.
55 p.   19 cm.

23511 [Prince, Thomas] 1687-1758.
The vade mecum for America: or, A companion for traders
and travellers... Boston, Printed by S. Kneeland, and
T. Green for D. Henchman & T. Hancock, 1732.
1 p.l., iv, [2], 220 p.   19 x 7½ cm.

Q

23512 Quackenbos, George Payn.
Primary history of the United States: made easy and
interesting for beginners. By B. G. P. Quackenbos...
New York, D. Appleton & co., 1860.
192 p.   illus.   17½ x 14½ cm.

23513 The Quadrat. Indispensable in every printing office.
Devoted to the interests of the craft. v. 1-8, Feb. 1873-
Feb. 1880. Pittsburgh, A. C. Bakewell & Co., 1873-1880.
8 v.   illus.   25 cm.

23514 The Quaker vindicated; or, Observations on a late pamphlet,
entitled, The Quaker unmask'd, or, Plain truth...
[Philadelphia] Printed by A. Steuart in the Year 1764.
16 p.   20½ cm.

23515 The Quakers Farewel to England, or Their Voyage to New
Jersey, Scituate on the Continent of Virginia, and
bordering upon New England. To the Tune of, The Inde-
pendents Voyage to New England. London, Printed for
J. G., 1675. [Boston, 1928]
facsim.: broadside. 42 x 30½ cm. fold. to 22 x 16½ cm.
[American series: photostat reproductions by the Massachusetts historical society, no. 213]

23516 Quandary, Christopher, pseud.
Some serious considerations on the present state of parties, with regard to the presidential election; with the author's own case fairly stated, and submitted to all candid and compassionate men. By Christopher Quandry. Richmond, Printed by T. W. White, 1827.
24 p.   21 cm.

23517 [Quandt, Christlieb] 1740-
Nachricht von Suriname und seinen einwohnern; sonderlich den Arawacken, Warauen und Karaiben, von den nuzlichsten gewachsen und thieren des landes, den geschaften der dortigen missionarien der Brüderunität und der sprache der Arawacken. Nebst einer charte und zwey kupfern. Görlitz, Gedruckt bey J. G. Burghart, zu finden bey dem verfasser [etc., 1807]
xiv, [2], 316 p., 1 l.   3 fold. pl. (incl. map, plan)
18 cm.

23518 The Quarterly Christian spectator. Conducted by an association of gentlemen... v. 1-[8], 1819-26; new ser. v. 1-2, 1827-28; [3d ser.] v. 1-10, 1829-38. New Haven [etc., 1819-38]
20 v.   22-23 cm.
Title varies: 1819-28, The Christian spectator monthly ; 1829-38, The Quarterly Christian spectator. Merged into the American Biblical repository.

23519 [Quélus, D   de]
Histoire naturelle du cacao, et du sucre, divisée en deux traités, qui contiennent plusieurs faits nouveaux, & beaucoup d'observations également curieuses & utiles. Paris, L. d'Honry, 1719.
4 p.l., 227, [10] p.   6 pl. (4 fold.)   16½ cm.

23520 [Quen, Jean de] 1603-1659.
Relation de ce qvi s'est passé en la Mission des Peres de la Compagnie de Iesvs, av pays de la Novvelle France, és Années 1655 & 1656. Enuoyée au R. P. Lovys Cellot, Prouncian de la Compagnie de Iesvs, en la Prouince de France. A Paris. Chez Sebastien Cramoisy, Imprimeur ordinaire du Roy, & de la Reyne, et Gabriel Cramoisy, M.DC.LVII.
3 p.l., 168 p.   17½ cm.

23521 The querist: or, A letter to a member of the General assembl. of the colony of New York. Containing a variety of important questions occasioned by the charter lately

granted for the establishment of a college. [New York]
1754.
    14 p.   28 cm.

23522 The querists, part III, or, An extract of sundry passages
       taken out of Mr. G. Tennent's sermon preached at Nottingham,
       of the danger of an unconverted ministry. Together with
       some scruples props'd in proper queries raised on each
       remark. By the same hands with the former. [Five lines
       of quotation] Philadelphia, Printed by B. Franklin in
       Market-street, 1741.
           150 p.   16 cm.

23523 [Quiner, Edwin Bentlee] d. 1868.
           City of Watertown, Wisconsin: its manufacturing &
       railroad advantages, and business statistics. Watertown,
       Published by order of City council, 1856.
           24 p.   front. (fold. map)   18½ cm.

                              R

23524 Reasons humbly offered to prove that the letter printed at
       the end of the French memorial of justification is a
       French forgery, and falsely ascribed to His R--1
       H-----ss... London, Printed for M. Collyer, 1756.
           1 p.l., 61 p.   20½ cm.

23525 The rebuke of secession doctrines. By southern statesmen.
       Philadelphia, Printed for gratuitous distribution, 1863.
           16 p.   22 cm.

23526 Redmond, Patrick H
           History of Quincy and its men of mark; or, Facts and
       figures exhibiting its advantages and resources, manu-
       factures and commerce. By Pat. H. Redmond. Quincy,
       Ill., Heirs & Russell, printers, 1869.
           302 p.   17½ cm.

23527 Reid, Thomas Mayne, 1818-1883.
           The forest exiles; or, The perils of a Peruvian family
       amid the wilds of the Amazon, by Captain Mayne Reid...
       With twelve illustrations. Boston, Ticknor and Fields,
       1860.
           360 p.   illus.   17½ cm.

23528 Reynolds, John, 1788-1865.
           The pioneer history of Illinois, containing the

                              305

discovery, in 1673, and the history of the country to the year eighteen hundred and eighteen, when the state government was organized. By John Reynolds. Belleville, N. A. Randall, 1852.
348 p.   19 cm.

23529   Reynolds, John, 1789-1865.
Sketches of the country, on the northern route from Belleville, Illinois, to the city of New York, and back by the Ohio Valley; together with a glance at the Crystal palace. By John Reynolds. Belleville, Printed by J. A. Willis [and C. Johnson] 1854.
264 p.   17½ cm.

23530   Rice, John Asaph, 1829-1888.
Catalogue of Mr. John A. Rice's library, to be sold by auction on Monday, March 21st, 1870, and five following days by Bangs, Merwin & co. ... New York, J. Sabin & sons, printers and compilers of the catalogue, 1870.
xvi, 556 p.   23 cm.

23531   Richmond, C   W
A history of the county of Du Page, Illinois; containing an account of its early settlement and present advantages, a separate history of the several towns, including notices of religious organizations, education, agriculture and manufactures, with the names and some account of the first settlers in each township... By C. W. Richmond & H. F. Vallette.   Chicago, Steam presses of Scripps, Bross & Spears, 1857.
iv, [5]-212 p. incl. pl.   18½ cm.

23532   Richmond, Legh, 1772-1827.
The dairyman's daughter: by Rev. Legh Richmond... Bob the sailor boy. By Rev. G. C. Smith... Park Hill [Ind. Ter.] Mission press: J. Candy & E. Archer, 1847.
67 p.   13 cm.

23533   Rickman, John
An authentic narrative of a voyage to the Pacific ocean; performed by Captain Cook, and Captain Clerke, in His Britannic Majesty's ships, the Resolution, and Discovery, in the years 1776, 1777, 1778, 1779, and 1780... Also a large introduction, exhibiting, an account of the several voyages round the globe; with an abstract of the principal expeditions to Hudson's bay, for the discovery of a north-west passage. By an officer on board the Discovery...   Philadelphia, Printed and sold by Robert

Bell in Third-street.   Price two thirds of a dollar, 1783.
2 v. in 1.   21½ cm.

23534   Riedesel, Friederike Charlotte Luise (von Massow) Freifrau
von, 1746-1808.
Letters and journals relating to the war of the American
revolution, and the capture of the German troops at Saratoga. By Mrs. General Riedesel. Tr. from the original
German, by William L. Stone... Albany, J. Munsell, 1867.
235 p.   front. (port.)   plates.   22½ cm.

23535   Riggs, Stephen Return, 1812-1883.
The Dakota first reading book, prepared by Stephen R.
Riggs, and Gideon H. Pond... Printed for the American
board of commissioners for foreign missions. Cincinnati,
Kendall and Henry, printers, 1839.
39, [1] p.   illus.   14½ cm.

23536   The rights of Parliament vindicated, on occasion of the
late stamp-act. In which is exposed the conduct of the
American colonists. Addressed to all the people of Great
Britain... London, Printed for J. Almon, 1766.
44 p.   21 cm.

23537   Ringwalt, John Luther, ed.
American encyclopaedia of printing. Ed. by J. Luther
Ringwalt. Philadelphia, Menamin & Ringwalt [etc.] 1871.
1 p.l., vii-xv, [17]-512 p.   col. front., illus.,
plates (part col.) ports., facsims. (part col.)   tab.
27 cm.

23538   Rio, Antonio del.
Description of the ruins of an ancient city, discovered
near Palenque, in the kingdom of Guatemala... translated
from the original manuscript report of Captain Don Antonio
del Rio: followed by Teatro critico americano; or,
A critical investigation and research into the history
of the Americans, by Doctor Paul Felix Cabrera... London,
H. Berthoud, and Suttaby, Evance and Fox, 1822.
[v]-xiii p., 1 l., 128 p.   16 pl.   27½ x 22 cm.

23539   [Rivers, William James] 1822-
A sketch of the history of South Carolina to the close
of the proprietary government by the revolution of 1719.
With an appendix containing many valuable records hitherto
unpublished. Charleston, McCarter & co., 1856.
470 p.   22½ cm.

23540   Robbins, Chandler, 1738-1799.
A sermon. Preached before His Excellency Jonh [!]
Hancock, esq., governour; His Honor Samuel Adams... the
honorable the Council and the honourable the Senate and
House of representatives, of the commonwealth of Massachusetts, May 25, 1791. Being the day of general election.
By Chandler Robbins... Boston, Massachusetts: Printed
by Thomas Adams, Printer to the honourable the General
court, 1791.
51 p.   22½ cm.

23541   Robinson, Conway, 1805-1884.
An account of the discoveries in the West until 1519, and
of voyages to and along the Atlantic coast of North
America, from 1520 to 1573. Prepared for "The Virginia
historical and philosophical society." By Conway Robinson,
chairman of its executive committee, and published by the
Society. Richmond, Printed by Shepherd and Colin, 1848.
xv, 491 p.   21½ cm.

23542   Robinson, William Davis.
A cursory view of Spanish America, particularly the
neighbouring vice-royalties of Mexico and New-Granada,
chiefly intended to elucidate the policy of an early
connection between the United States and those countries.
By William D. Robinson. Georgetown, D. C., Richards and
Mallory, 1815.
41, [1] p.   20 cm.

23543   Robson, Joseph.
An account of six years residence in Hudson's-bay from
1733 to 1736, and 1744 to 1747. By Joseph Robson...
Containing a variety of facts, observations, and discoveries about Hudson's-bay to Great Britain... And, II.
The interested views of the Hudson's bay company; and the
absolute necessity of laying open the trade... To which
is added an appendix... London, Printed for J. Payne
and J. Bouquet; [etc., etc.] 1752.
1 p.l., vi, 84, 95 p.   3 fold. maps.   22 cm.

23544   Roche, Richard W
Catalogue of the private library of Mr. Richard W. Roche
New York, Bradstreet press, 1867.
4 p.l., [3]-251 p.   24½ cm.
Cover-title: Bibliotheca americana. "Catalogue of the
library belonging to Mr. Richard W. Roche... to be sold
at auction... October 28th, 1867, and four following days.

23545 Rodgers, John, 1727-1811.
The divine goodness displayed, in the American revolution: a sermon preached in New York, December 11th, 1783,
appointed by Congress as a day of public thanksgiving,
throughout the United States; by John Rodgers, D.D.
New York, Printed by Samuel Loudon, 1784.
42 p.   19 cm.

23546 Roebuck, John, 1718-1794.
An enquiry whether the guilt of the present civil war
in America, ought to be imputed to Great Britain or
America. By John Roebuck... New ed. London, Printed
for J. Donaldson, 1776.
1 p.l., 73 p.   21 cm.

23547 Rogers, Howard S
History of Cass County, from 1825 to 1875. By Howard S.
Rogers. Cassopolis, Mich., W. H. Mansfield, Vigilant
Book and Job Print, 1875.
iv, [5]-406 p.   21 cm.

23548 Rogers, Robert 1731-1795.
Ponteach: or, The savages of America. A tragedy.
London, Printed for the author, and sold by J. Millan,
opposite the Admiralty, Whitehall, 1766.
110 p.   20 cm.

23549 Rogers, Woodes, d. 1732.
A cruising voyage round the world: first to the
South-seas, thence to the East-Indies, and homewards by
the cape of Good Hope. Begun in 1708, and finish'd in
1711. Containing a journal of all the remarkable transactions; particularly of the taking of Puna and Guiaquil,
of the Acapulco ship, and other prizes; an account of
Alexander Selkirk's living alone four years and four
months in an island; and a brief description of several
countries in our course noted for trade, especially in
the South-sea. With maps of all the coast, from the
best Spanish manuscript draughts. And an introduction
relating to the Sovth-sea trade. By Captain Woodes
Rogers, command in chief on this expedition, with the
ships Duke and Dutchess of Bristol. London, Printed for
A. Bell and B. Lintot, 1712.
xxi, [1], 428, 56, [14] p. incl. tables.   5 fold.
maps.   20 cm.

23550 [Rokeby, Matthew Robinson-Morris] 2d baron, 1713-1800.
Considerations on the measures carrying on with

respect to the British colonies in North America...
London, Sold by R. Baldwin [1774]
2 p.l., 160 p.   20 cm.

23551   [Rokeby, Matthew Robinson-Morris, 2d baron] 1713-1800.
A further examination of our present American measures
and of the reasons and the principles on which they are
founded. By the author of Considerations on the measures
carrying on with respect to the British colonies in
North America... Bath, Printed by R. Cruttwell, for R.
Baldwin etc. London, 1776.
3 p.l., 3-256 p.   21 cm.

23552   Rokeby, Matthew Robinson-Morris, 2d baron, 1713-1800.
Peace the best policy; or Reflections upon the appearance
of a foreign war, the present state of affairs at home and
the commission for granting pardons in America. In a
letter to a friend, by Matt. Robinson M. 2d ed. cor. by
the author. London, Printed for J. Almon, 1777.
1 p.l., 59 p.   21 cm.

23553   Roosevelt, Robert Barnwell, 1829-1906.
Florida and the game water-birds of the Atlantic coast
and the lakes of the United States, with a full account
of the sporting along our sea-shores and inland waters,
and remarks on breech-loaders and hammerless guns, by
Robert Barnwell Roosevelt... New York, Orange Judd
company, 1884.
443 p. incl. front. (port.) illus., plates.   19 cm.

23554   Ross, Harvey Lee, 1817-
The early pioneers and pioneer events of the state of
Illinois including personal recollections of the writer;
of Abraham Lincoln, Andrew Jackson and Peter Cartwright,
together with a brief autobiography of the writer. By
Harvey Lee Ross. Chicago, Eastman brothers, 1899.
xi, 199 p.   front. (port.)   21½ cm.

23555   Roux de Rochelle, Jean Baptiste Gaspard, 1762-1849.
États-Unis d'Amérique, par M. Roux de Rochelle...
Paris, Firmin Didot frères, 1837.
3 p.l., 400 p.   85 pl., 5 port., 3 maps (1 fold.)
4 plans, facsim.   21½ cm.   (Half-title: L'univers.
Histoire et description de tous les peuples. [t. 22])

23556   Rowlandson, Mrs. Mary (White)
Narrative of the captivity and removes of Mrs. Mary
Rowlandson, who was taken by the Indians at the des-

310

truction of Lancaster, in 1676. Written by herself.
Sixth edition. Lancaster [Mass.] Published by Carter,
Andrews, and co., 1828.
x, [11], 100 p.   14½ cm.

23557   Rundle, Thomas, 1688?-1743.
A sermon preached at St. George's church, Hanover Square,
on Sunday, February 17, 1733/4. To recommend the charity
for establishing the new colony of Georgia. Pub. at the
request of the Right Honourable the Lord Viscount Tyrconnel,
the Honourable Colonel Whitworth, churchwardens, and
several of the parishioners. London, Printed for T.
Woodward and J. Brindley, 1734.
24 p.   22½ cm.

23558   Rupp, Israel Daniel, 1803-1878.
The geographical catechism of Pennsylvania, and the
western states; designed as a guide and pocket companion,
for travellers and emigrants, to Pennsylvania, Ohio,
Indiana, Illinois, Michigan and Missouri; containing a
geographical and early historical account of these several
states, from their first settlement up to the present
time. By I. Daniel Rupp... Harrisburg, Pa., J. Wine-
brenner, 1836.
iv, 384 p.   16 cm.

23559   Russell, Sir William Howard, 1820-1907.
Pictures of southern life, social, political, and
military. Written for the London times, by William
Howard Russell... New York, J. G. Gregory, 1861.
143 p.   20½ cm.

23560   Rutherford, Samuel, 1600?-1661.
The due right of presbyteries or, A peaceable plea for
the government of the Church of Scotland, wherein is
examined 1. The way of the Church of Christ in New England,
in brotherly equality, and independency, or coordination,
without subjection of one church to another. 2. Their
apology for the said government, their answers to thirty
and two questions are considered. 3. A treatise for a
church covenant is discussed. 4. The arguments of Mr.
Robertson in his justification of separation are discovered. 5. His treatise, called, The peoples plea for
the exercise of prophecy, is tryed. 6. Diverse late
arguments against presbyteriall government, and the
power of synods are discussed, the power of the Prince
in matters ecclesiastical modestly considered, & divers
incident controversies resolved. By Samuel Rutherford...

311

Cant. 6. 10. [Three lines of Biblical quotations]
London, Printed by E. Griffin, for Richard Whittaker, and
Andrew Crook and are to be sold at their shops in Pauls
church yard, 1644.
12 p.l., 484 (i.e. 498), 185-468 p.   19 cm.

23561   Rutherford, Samuel, 1600?-1661.
A survey of the Survey of that summe of church-discipline
penned by Mr. Thomas Hooker, late pastor of the church at
Hartford upon Connecticut in New England. Wherein the
way of the churches of N. England is now re-examined;
arguments in favour thereof winnowed; the principles of
the way discussed; and the reasons of most seeming strength
and nerves, removed. By Samuel Rutherford... London,
Printed by J. G. for Andr. Crook, at the Green dragon in
St. Pauls churchyard, 1658.
1 p.l., [6], 521 (i.e. 519) p.   19 cm.

23562   Ryan, William Redmond.
Personal adventures in Upper and Lower California, in
1848-9; with the author's experience at the mines.
Illustrated by twenty-three drawings... By William
Redmond Ryan... London, W. Shoberl, 1850.
2 v.   fronts., plates.   19 cm.

S

23563   Sagard-Théodat, Gabriel, 17th cent.
Le grand voyage dv pays des Hvrons, situé en l'Amerique
vers la Mer douce, és derniers confins de la Nouuelle
France, dite Canada. Où il est amplement traité de tout
ce qui est du pays, des moeurs & du naturel des sauuages,
de leur gouuernement & facons de faire, tant dedans leurs
pays, qu'allans en voyages: de leur foy & croyance;
de leurs conseils & guerres, & de quel genre de tourmens
ils font mourir leurs prisonniers. Comme ils se marient,
& esleuent leurs enfans: de leurs medecins, & des remedes
dont ils vsent à leurs maladies: de leurs dances & chan-
sons: de la chasse, de la pesche, & des oyseaux &
animaux terrestres & aquatiques qu'ils ont. Des richesses
du pays: comme ils cultiuent les terres, & accommodent
leur menestre. De leur deüil, pleurs & lamentations, &
comme ils enseuelissent & enterrent leurs morts. Anee vn
Dictionaire de la langue huronne, pour la commodité de
ceux qui ont à voyager dans le pays, & n'ont l'intelligence
d'icelle langue. Par F. Gabriel Sagard Theodat, recollet

de S. François, de la prouince de S. Denys en France. A
Paris, Chez Denys Moreav, rue S. Lacques, à la salamandre
d'argent. M.DC.XXXII. Auec priuilege de roy.
12 p.l., 380, 12, [146] p.   17 cm.

23564 Sagra, Ramón de la, 1798-1871.
Cinq mois aux États-Unis de l'Amérique du Nord, depuis
le 29 avril jusqu'au 23 septembre 1835; journal de voyage
de M. Ramón de la Sagra. Tr. de l'espagnol par M. René
Baissas. Bruxelles, Société Typographique Belge, 1837.
484 p.   15 cm.

23565 St. Clair, Arthur, 1734-1818.
A narrative of the manner in which the campaign against
the Indians, in the year one thousand seven hundred and
ninety-one, was conducted, under the command of Major
General St. Clair, together with his observations on the
statements of the secretary of war and the quarter master
general, relative thereto, and the reports of the committees
appointed to inquire into the causes of the failure
thereof: taken from the files of the House of representatives in Congress. Philadelphia, Printed by Jane Aitken,
no. 71 North third street, 1812.
xix, [24], 273 p.   23½ cm.

23566 [Saint-Cricq, Laurent]
Travels in South America from the Pacific Ocean to the
Atlantic Ocean. By Paul Marcoy [pseud.] Illustrated by
five hundred and twenty-five engravings on wood, drawn by
E. Rion, and ten maps from drawings by the author...
London [etc.] Blackie & son, 1875.
2 v.   fronts., illus., plates, maps.   31½ cm.
Translated from the French by Elihu Rich.

23567 St. John, Peter, 1720-1811.
A dialogue between flesh and spirit: composed upon the
decease of Mr. Abijah Abbott, who was kill'd at the
raising of a building in New-York in the year 1768:
in the name of the bereaved widow. [n.p., 1768?]
broadside.   21 x 26½ cm.

23568 St. Louis.
Report of the celebration of the anniversary of the
founding of St. Louis, on the fifteenth day of February,
A.D. 1847. Prepared for the Missouri republican. [St.
Louis] Chambers & Knapp, 1847.
cover-title, 32 p.   24½ cm.

313

23569 St. Paul, Henry.
Our home and foreign policy. November, 1863.
[Mobile, Ala.] Printed at the Office of the Daily
Register and Advertiser, 1863.
23 p.   21 cm.

23570 [Sainte-Croix, Guillaume Emmanuel Joseph Guilhem de Clermont-
Lodève, baron de] 1746-1809.
De l'état et du sort des colonies, des anciens peuples.
Ouvrage dans lequel on traite du gouvernement des anciennes
républiques, de leur droit public, &c. avec des observations
sur les Colonies de Nations modernes, & la conduite des
Anglois en Amérique. Philadelphia, 1779.
xiv, 336 p.   21 cm.

23571 [Sanders, Daniel Clarke] 1768-1850.
A history of the Indian wars with the first settlers
of the United States, particularly in New-England. Written
in Vermont... Montpelier, Vt., Published by Wright and
Sibley. Wright & Sibley Printers, 1812.
319 p.   14 x 8 cm.
A severe criticism of this work, published in the Liberal
and philosophical repository immediately upon its
appearance, caused it to be suppressed and but few copies
were circulated. cf. Sabin, Bibl. amer. 76366.

23572 Sanderson, James M
My record in rebeldom, as written by Friend and foe.
Comprising the official changes and evidence before the
military commission in Washington, Brig. Gen'l J. C.
Caldwell, president, together with the report and finding
of the court. Printed for private circulation and future
reference. New York, W. E. Sibell, Stationer and Printer,
1865.
160, liv p.   23 cm.

23573 Sands, Robert Charles, 1799-1832.
The writings of Robert C. Sands, in prose and verse.
With a memoir of the author... 2d ed. New York, Harper
& brothers, 1835.
2 v.   front. (port.)   23½ cm.
Memoir by Verplanck. cf. Duyckinck, Cyclopaedia of
American literature.

23574 Sanford, Ezekiel, 1796-1822.
A history of the United States before the revolution:
some account of the aborigines. By Ezekiel Sanford.
Philadelphia, A. Finley, 1819.
cxiii, 341 p.   21½ cm.

23575   Sanson, Nicolas, 1600-1667.
        L'Amérique en plusieurs cartes nouvelles, et exactes,
        &c. en divers traitez de geographie, et d'histoire. Là où
        sont descrits succinctement, & avec une belle methode, &
        facile, ses empires, ses monarchies, ses estats, &c., les
        moeurs, les langues, les religions, le negoce et la
        richesse de ses peuples, &c. Et ce qu'il y a de plus beau
        de de plus rare dans toutes ses parties, & dans ses isles.
        Paris, Chez l'autheur [1657]
        15 double maps.   25 x 18 cm.

23576   Sargent, Winthrop, 1825-1870.
        The life and career of Major John André, adjutant-general
        of the British army in America. By Winthrop Sargent...
        Boston, Ticknor and Fields, 1861.
        xiv, 471 p.   front. (port.)   map.   19 cm.

23577   Sargent, Winthrop, 1753-1820.
        Papers, in relation to the official conduct of Governour
        Sargent. Published by particular desire of his friends.
        [Ornament] Printed at Boston, by Thomas & Andrews, Aug. 1,
        1801.
        iv, [5]-64 p.   20 cm.

23578   Say, Jean Baptiste, 1767-1832.
        A treatise on political economy; or, The production,
        distribution, and consumption of wealth. By Jean Baptiste
        Say. Tr. from the 4th ed. of the French, by C. R. Prinsep,
        M.A., with notes by the translator. New American ed.
        Containing a translation of the introduction, and additional
        notes. By Clement C. Biddle... Philadelphia, J. B.
        Lippincott & co., 1867.
        ix, [61]-488 p.   22½ cm.

23579   Schoolcraft, Henry Rowe, 1793-1864.
        Personal memoires of a residence of thirty years with
        the Indian tribes on the American frontiers: with brief
        notices of passing events, facts, and opinions, A.D.
        1812 to A.D. 1812. By Henry R. Schoolcraft. Philadelphia,
        Lippincott, Grambo and co., 1851.
        xlviii, [17]-703 p.   front. (port.)   23 cm.

23580   Scot, George d. 1685.
        The model of the government of the province of East-
        New Jersey in America; and encouragements for such as
        designs to be concerned there. Published for information
        of such as are desirous to be interested in that place.
        Edinburgh, Printed by John Reid, 1685.
        4 p.l., 272 p.   14½ cm.

23581   Scott, James Leander.
         A journal of a missionary tour through Pennsylvania,
         Ohio, Indiana, Illinois, Iowa, Wiskonson and Michigan;
         comprising a concise description of different sections of
         country; health of climate; inducements for emigration
         with the embarrassments; the religious condition of the
         people; meetings connected with the mission; and of the
         great western prairies. By Rev. James L. Scott. Provi-
         dence, The author, 1843.
         viii, [9]-203 p.   19 cm.

23582   Scott, John, of Centreville, Ind.
         The Indiana gazetteer, or Topographical dictionary,
         containing a description of the several counties, towns,
         &c. in the state of Indiana. Alphabetically arranged
         by John Scott. Centreville, J. Scott & W. M. Doughty,
         1826.
         143 p.   16 cm.

23583   [Scott, Thomas] 1580?-1626.
         A choice narrative of Count Gondamor's transactions
         during his embassy in England. By... Sir Robert Cotton...
         exposed to public light for the benefit of the whole
         nation. By a person of honour. London, Printed for J.
         Garfield, 1659; Re-printed and sold by G. Smeeton, 1820.
         iv, [5]-30 p.   front. (port.)   20½ x 16½ cm.

23584   Scott, Winfield, 1786-1866.
         Memoirs of Lieut.-Gen. Scott, LL.D. Written by himself.
         New York, Sheldon & company, 1864.
         1 p.l., xxii, 653 p.   2 port. (incl. front.)   25 cm.

23585   [Seabury, Samuel] bp., 1729-1796.
         An alarm to the legislature of the province of New-York,
         occasioned by the present political disturbances, in North
         America: addressed to the honourable representatives
         in General assembly convened... New York, Printed for
         James Rivington, 1775.
         13, 2 p.   20½ cm.

23586   [Seabury, Samuel] bp., 1729-1796.
         The Congress canvassed: or, An examination into the
         conduct of the delegates, at their grand convention,
         held in Philadelphia, Sept. 1, 1774. Addressed to the
         merchants of New York. By A. W. Farmer. Author of Free
         thoughts, &c. ... [New York] Printed in the year 1774.
         27, [1] p.   21 cm.

23587 [Seabury, Samuel] bp., 1729-1796.
Free thoughts, on the proceedings of the Continental
Congress, held at Philadelphia Sept. 5, 1774: wherein
their errors are exhibited, the reasonings confuted, and
the fatal tendency of their non-importation, non-export-
ation, and non-consumption measures, are laid open to the
plaintest understandings; and the only means pointed out
for preserving and securing our present happy constitution:
in a letter to the farmers, and other inhabitants of North
America in general, and to those of the province of New-
York in particular. By a farmer... New York Printed
in the year 1774.
24 p. 19½ cm.

23588 [Seabury, Samuel] bp., 1729-1796.
A view of the controversy between Great-Britain and
her colonies: including a mode of determining their
present disputes, finally and effectually; and of preventing
all future contentions. In a letter, to the author of
A full vindication of the measures of the Congress, from
the calumnies of their enemies... By A. W. Farmer.
Author of Free thoughts, &c. New York, Printed by James
Rivington, 1774.
37, 2 p. 20 cm.

23589 Seaver, James Everett, 1787-1827.
A narrative of the life of Mrs. Mary Jemison, who was
taken by the Indians, in the year 1775, when only about
twelve years of age, and has continued to reside amongst
them to the present time. Containing an account of the
murder of her father and his family; her sufferings; her
marriage to two Indians; her troubles with her children;
barbarities of the Indians in the French and revolutionary
wars; the life of her last husband, &c.; and many
historical facts never before published. Carefully taken
from her own words, Nov. 29th, 1823. To which is added,
an appendix, containing an account of the tragedy at the
Devil's Hole, in 1763, and of Sullivan's expedition; the
traditions, manners, customers, &c., of the Indians, as
believed and practised at the present day, and since
Mrs. Jemison's captivity; together with some anecdotes,
and other entertaining matter. By James E. Seaver.
Canadaigua, N. Y., Printed by J. D. Bemis and co., 1824.
xv, [17]-189 p. 15 cm.

23590 A selection of the patriotic addresses, to the President of
the United States. Together with the President's answers.
Presented in the year one thousand seven hundred and

317

ninety-eight, and the twenty-second of the independence of
America. Boston, Printed by John W. Folsom, no. 88,
Union-street, 1798.
v, [7]-360 p.   17½ cm.
Addresses to, and replies of, President John Adams.

23591 Semallé, René de.
Considerations on the establishment in the Indian
territory of a new state of the American union by R. de S.
Versailles, Printed by E. Aubert, 1876.
8 p.   21½ cm.

23592 Semmes, John Edward, 1851-
John H. B. Latrobe and his times, 1803-1891, by John E.
Semmes; with thirty-eight illustrations in color and
black and white. Baltimore, Md., The Norman, Remington
co. [c1917]
viii, 601 p.   plates (part co.) ports. (2 col., incl.
front.) coat of arms, facsim.   24½ cm.

23593 Semmes, Raphael, 1809-1877.
Croisières de l'Alabama et du Sumter. Livre de bord et
journal particulier du Commandant R. Semmes. Deuxième éd.
Paris, E. Dentu, 1864.
ii, 471 p.   front.   19 cm.

23594 A series of wisdom and policy: being a full justification
of all our measures ever since the year 1721, inclusive;
and especially of our late most honourable Convention
with Spain. [One line Latin quotation: Hor.] London,
Printed for T. Cooper, 1739.
63 p.   20½ cm.

23595 [Serle, Ambrose] 1742-1812.
Americans against liberty: or an essay on the nature
and principles of true freedom, shewing that the designs
and conduct of the Americans tend only to tyranny and
slavery... London, Sold by J. Mathews, 1775.
64 p.   23 cm.

23596 Sewall, Jonathan, 1729-1796.
A cure for the spleen. Or, Amusement for a winter's
evening; being the substance of a conversation on the
times, over a friendly tankard and pipe. Between Sharp,
---a country parson. Bumper, ---a country justice.
Fillpot, ---an inn-keeper. Graveairs, ---a deacon.
Trim, ---a barber. Brim, ---a Quaker. Puff, ---a late
representative. Taken in short hand, by Sir Roger de

Coverly [Two line Latin quotation: Hor.] [Boston]
America: Printed and sold in the year 1775.
1 p.l., [7]-43 p.   25½ cm.

23597 Sewall, Jonathan Mitchel, 1748-1808.
Eulogy on the late General Washington; pronounced at
St. John's church, in Portsmouth, New Hampshire, on
Tuesday, 31st December, 1799. At the request of the
inhabitants. By Jonathan Mitchell Sewall, esquire...
Portsmouth, N. H., Printed by William Treadwell [1800]
28 p.   21 x 17 cm.

23598 Sewall, Rufus King, 1814-1903.
Sketches of St. Augustine. With a view of its history
and advantages as a resort for invalids. New York, Pub.
for the author by G. P. Putnam, 1848.
69 p.   plates.   19 cm.

23599 Seward, Anna, 1742-1809.
Monody on Major André. By Miss Seward... To which
are added letters addressed to her by Major André, in the
year 1769. The 2d ed. Lichfield, Printed and sold by
J. Jackson, for the author [etc., etc.] 1781.
vi, 47, [1] p.   26½ x 21½ cm.

23600 [Seymour, Silas]
Incidents of a trip through the great Platte valley, to
the Rocky mountains and Laramie plains, in the fall of
1866, with a synoptical statement of the various Pacific
railroads, and an account of the great Union Pacific railroad excursion to the one hundredth meridian of longitude.
New York, D. Van Nostrand, 1867.
129 p.   18½ cm.

23601 Shaffner, Taliaferro Preston, 1818-1881.
The war in America: being an historical and political
account of the southern and northern states: showing
the origin and cause of the present secession war. With
a large map of the United States, engraved on steel. By
Colonel Tal. P. Shaffner... London, Hamilton, Adams,
and co. [1862]
vi, 418 p.   front. (fold. map)   18½ cm.

23602 Sharland, George.
Knapsack notes of Gen. Sherman's grand campaign through
the empire state of the South, by George Sharland...
Springfield, Ill., Jackson & Bradford, printers, 1865.
68 p.   21½ cm.

23603 Sharp, Granville, 1735-1813.
A declaration of the people's natural right to a share
in the legislature; which is the fundamental principle
of the British constitution of state. By Granville Sharp.
The 2d ed. London, Printed for B. White, 1775.
2 p.l., xl, 279, 4 p.   19½ cm.

23604 [Shebbeare, John] 1709-1788.
An answer to the printed speech of Edmund Burke, esq;
spoken in the House of commons, April 19, 1774. In which
his knowledge in polity, legislature, human kind, history,
commerce and finance, is candidly examined; his arguments
are fairly refuted; the conduct of administration is
fully defended; and his oratoric talents are clearly expose
to view. Addressed to the people... London, Printed for
T. Evans [etc.] 1775.
iv, 222 p.   21½ cm.

23605 [Shebbeare, John] 1709-1788.
A third letter to the people of England, on liberty,
taxes, and the application of public money. [Two line
Latin quotation] The second edition. London, printed
for J. Scott, at the Black-Swan, in Pater-noster-row,
1756.
1 p.l., 60 p.   22 cm.

23606 [Shebbeare, John] 1709-1788.
A fourth letter to the people of England. On the
conduct of the m---rs in alliances, fleets, and armies,
since the first differences on the Ohio, to the taking
of Minorca by the French... London, Printed for M.
Collier, 1756.
1 p.l., 69 p.   19½ cm.

23607 [Shebbeare, John] 1709-1788.
A fifth letter to the people of England, on the sub-
version of the constitution: and, the necessity of its
being restored.   Five lines of Greek and Latin quotations
The second edition. London, printed for J. Morgan in
Pater-noster-row, 1757.
2 p.l., 99 p.   22½ cm.

23608 [Shebbeare, John] 1709-1788.
A sixth letter to the people of England, on the progress
of national ruin; in which it is shown, that the present
grandeur of France, and calamities of this nation, are
owing to the influence of Hanover on the councils of
England.   [Three line Biblical quotation] London, printed

for J. Morgan in Pater-noster-row, 1757.
2 p.l., 121 p.   20 cm.
Treating especially of the reign of George I.

23609 Sheldon, Mrs. Electa M   (Bronson) d. 1902.
The early history of Michigan, from the first settlement
to 1815. By E. M. Sheldon. New York, A. S. Barnes &
company; Detroit, Kerr, Morley & co., 1856.
409 p.   4 ports. (incl. front.) 1 illus. (map)
21½ cm.

23610 Shepard, Thomas, 1605-1649.
The clear sun-shine of the gospel breaking forth upon
the Indians in New England. Or, An historicall narration
of Gods wonderfull workings upon sundry of the Indians,
both chief governors and common-people, in bringing them
to a willing and desired submission to the ordinances
of the gospel; and framing their hearts to an earnest
inquirie after the knowledge of God by Father, and of
Jesus Christ the Saviour of the world. By Mr. Thomas
Shepard... London, Printed by R. Cotes for J. Bellamy,
1648.
7 p.l., 38 p.   17½ x 14½ cm.

23611 Sherburne, Andrew, 1765-1831.
Memoirs of Andres Sherburne: a pensioner of the Navy
of the Revolution. Written by himself... Utica, W.
Williams, 1828.
5 p.l., [13]-262 p., 1 l.   18 cm.

23612 Sherburne, John Henry, 1794-1850?
Life and character of the Chevallier John Paul Jones,
a captain in the Navy of the United States during their
Revolutionary War, dedicated to the officers of the
American Navy, by John Henry Sherburne, Register of the
Navy of the United States... City of Washington, 1825.
Vanderpool & Cole, printers, N. Y.
viii, [9]-364 p.   24 cm.

23613 Sherburne, John Hern, 1794-1850?
The life of Paul Jones, from original documents in the
possession of John Henry Sherburne... London, J. Murray,
1825.
xii, 320 p.   19½ cm.

23614 [Sherman, John H   ]
A general account of Miranda's expedition. Including
the trial and execution of ten of his officers, and an

account of the imprisonment and sufferings of the
remainder of his officers and men who were taken prisoners.
Upon the authority of a person who was an officer under
Miranda... New York, Printed by M'Farlane and Long,
no. 308 Broadway, 1808.
120 p.   21 x 12½ cm.

23615 Shillibeer, John.
A narrative of the Briton's voyage, to Pitcairn's
island. By Lieut. J. Shillibeer, R.M. Illustrated with
eighteen etchings by the author from drawings on the
spot. London, Law and Whittaker, 1817.
3 p.l., 179, 2 p.   front., plates (part fold.)
21½ cm.

23616 [Shipley, Jonathan, bp. of St. Asaph] 1714-1788.
A speech, intended to have been spoken on the bill for
altering the charters of the colony of Massachusett's
bay. London, Printed for T. Cadell, 1774.
vii, 36 p.   20½ cm.

23617 Shute, Daniel, 1722-1802.
A sermon preached before His Excellency Francis Bernard,
esq: governor, His Honor Thomas Hutchinson, esq;
lieutenant-governor, the honourable His Majesty's Council,
and the honourable House of representatives, of the
province of the Massachusetts-Bay in New-England, May 25th,
1768. Being the anniversary for the election of His
Majesty's Council for said province. By Daniel Shute,
a.m., pastor of the Third church in Hingham. Boston,
New-England, Printed by Richard Draper, printed to His
Excellency the governor, and the honorable His Majesty's
Council, 1798.

23618 [Simcoe, John Graves] 1752-1806.
Remarks on the travels of the Marquis de Chastellux,
in North America. London, Printed for G. and T. Wilkie,
1787.
1 p.l., [2], 80 p.   20 cm.
The authorship has been attributed to Benedict Arnold
and Nonathan Boucher.

23619 Simms, William Gilmore, 1806-1870.
The social principle: The true source of national
permanence. An oration, delivered before the Erosophic
Society of the University of Alabama, December 13, 1842.
By William Gilmore Simms, of South Carolina. Tuscaloosa,
Published by the Society, 1843.
56 p.   23 cm.

23620 Simpson, Sir George, 1792-1860.
An overland journey round the world, during the years
1841 and 1842. By Sir George Simpson... Philadelphia,
Lea and Blanchard, 1847.
xiv, 1 l., [17]-273 p., 1 l., [17]-230 p.   21 cm.

23621 Sketches of "Sonewall Jackson," giving the leading events of
his life and military career, his dying moments, and the
obsequies at Richmond and Lexington. English ed.
Halifax, N. S., Printed by James Bowes & sons, 1863.
56 p.   22 cm.

23622 Sketches of the war, between the United States and the
British isles: intended as a faithful history of all the
material events from the time of the declaration in 1812,
to and including the treaty of peace in 1815, interspersed
with geographical [!] descriptions of places, and biographical notices of distinguished military and naval
commanders. Volumes I and II. Rutland, Vt., Published
by Fay and Davison, 1815.
iv, 496 p.   illus. (plans)   22 cm.

23623 A small testimony of that great honour due to the honourable
servant of God and his generation John Alden Esq; who
changed this life for a better, Sept. 12th. Anno Domini
1687. [Cambridge? Samuel Green?] 1687.
broadside.   20 x 36 cm.

23624 Smith, Daniel 1748-1818.
A short description of the Tennessee government or the
Territory of the United States south of the river Ohio,
to accompany and explain a map of that country. Philadelphia, Printed by Mathew Carey, bookseller, no. 118,
High-street, 1793.
20 p.   23½ cm.

23625 Smith, James F
The Cherokee land lottery, containing a numerical list
of the names of the fortunate drawers is said lottery,
with an engraved map of each district. By James F. Smith...
New York, Printed by Harper & brothers, 1838.
1 p.l., [v]-vi p., 1 l., [9]-413, [1] p.   59 maps.
23 cm.

23626 Smith, John, 1580-1631.
New England's trials. Declaring the successe of
80 ships employed thither within these eight yeares; and
the benefit of that countrey by sea and land. With the

present estate of that happie plantation, begun but by
60 weake men in the yeare 1620. And how to build a fleete
of good shippes to make a little nauie royall. Written
by Captaine Iohn Smith, sometimes gouernour of Virginia,
and admirall of New England. 2d ed. London, Printed by
W. Iones, 1622. [Cambridge, Mass., Printed by H. O.
Houghton and company, 1867?]
    [32] p.   28 x 19 cm.

23627   Smith, John, 1580-1631.
    The trve travels, adventvres and observations of
Captaine Iohn Smith, in Europe, Asia, Africke, and America:
beginning about the yeere 1593, and continued to this
present 1629... From the London ed. of 1629. Richmond,
Republished at the Franklin Press, William W. Gray,
Printer, 1819.
    2 v.   fronts. (v. 1, port.)   fold. plates, fold. map.
22 cm.

23628   Smith, Joshua Hett, 1736-1818.
    An authentic narrative of the causes which led to the
death of Major André, adjutant-general of His Majesty's
forces in North America. By Joshua Hett Smith... To
which is added a Monody on the death of Major André. By
Miss Seward. London, Printed for Mathews and Leigh, 1808.
    vii, 357, [1] p.   front. (port.)   plate, fold. map.
$20\frac{1}{2}$ cm.

23629   [Smith, Melancthon] 1744-1798.
    An address to the people of the state of New-York:
showing the necessity of making amendments to the
Constitution, proposed for the United States, previous
to its adoption. By a plebeian. Printed by Robert
Hodge, in New York in the state of New-York, 1788.
[Brooklyn, N. Y., 1788?]
    26 p.   20 cm.
    "Postscript remarks on a pamphlet entitled 'An address
to the people of the state of New-York, on the subject
of the new Constitution' [by John Jay]": p. [23]-26.

23630   Smith, Samuel, 1720-1776.
    The history of the colony of Nova-Caesaria, or New
Jersey: containing, an account of its first settlement,
progressive improvements, the original and present
constitution, and other events, to the year 1721. With
some particulars since; and a short view of its present
state. By Samuel Smith. Burlington, in New Jersey,
Printed and sold by James Parker: sold also by David
Hall, in Philadelphia, 1765.
    x, 573, [1] p.   22 cm.

23631   Smith, Samuel, 1720-1776.
        History of the province of Pennsylvania, by Samuel
        Smith; ed. by William M. Mervine. Pub. by the Colonial
        society of Pennsylvania. Philadelphia, Pa., Printed by
        J. B. Lippincott company, 1913.
        xiii, [3]-231, 4 p.   26 cm.

23632   Smith, Samuel, 1752-1839.
        Remarks of Mr. Smith, of Maryland, in the Senate of
        the United States, on the subject of discriminating
        duties. April 18, 1826. [Washington, 1826]
        15 p.   18 cm.

23633   Smith, Samuel, 1752-1839.
        Speech of the Hon. Samuel Smith, in the Senate of the
        United States, on the renewal of the charter of the Bank
        of the United States. Washington, Press of Gales and
        Seaton, 1832.
        6 p.   21½ cm.

23634   Smith, Samuel, 1759-1854.
        Memoirs of Samuel Smith, a soldier of the revolution,
        1776-1786. Written by himself. With a preface and notes,
        by Charles I. Bushnell. New York, Priv. print., 1860.
        41 p.   front. (port.)   pl.   25½ cm.   [Crumbs for
        antiquarians, by C. I. Bushnell, v. 1, no. 2]
        Originally published in Middleborough, Mass., 1853.

23635   Smith, Samuel, lecturer of St. Alban's.
        A sermon preach'd before the Trustees for establishing
        the colony of Georgia in America, and before the Asso-
        ciates of the late Rev. Dr. Thomas Bray, for converting
        the negroes in the British plantations, and for other
        good purposes. At their first yearly meeting, in the
        parish church of St. Augustin, on Tuesday February 23,
        1730/31. By Samuel Smith... Pub. at the desire of the
        trustees and associates. To which is annexed Some
        account of the designs both of the trustees and asso-
        ciates. London, Printed by J. March, 1733.
        42 p.   fold. map.   22 x 17½ cm.

23636   [Smith, Samuel] vicar of Lois Weedon.
        A word in season; or, How to grow wheat with profit.
        By the author of "Lois Weedon husbandry." 18th ed.,
        with a practical farmer's view of the plan.   London,
        J. Ridgway, 1861.
        63 p. incl. pl.   19 cm.

23637   Smith, Sydney, 1771-1845.
        Letters on American debts. By the Rev. Sydney Smith.

325

First printed in the "Morning chronicle". London, Longman, Brown, Green, & Longmans, 1843.
21 p.   23 cm.

23638 [Smith, William] 1727-1803.
A brief view of the conduct of Pennsylvania, for the year 1755; so far as it affected the general service of the British colonies, particularly the expedition under the late General Braddock. With an account of the shocking inhumanities, committed by incursions of the Indians upon the province in October and November; which occasioned a body of the inhabitants to come down, while the Assembly were sitting, and to insist upon an immediate suspension of all disputes, and the passing of a law for the defence of the country. Interspers'd with several interesting anecdotes and original papers, relating to the politics and principles of the people called Quakers: being a sequel to a late well-known pamphlet, intitled, A brief state of Pennsylvania. In a second letter to a friend in London... London, Printed for R. Griffiths in Pater-noster row; and sold by Mr. Bradford in Philadelphia 1756. Price one-shilling and six-pence.
88 p.   21 cm.

23639 [Smith, William] 1727-1803.
An historical account of the expedition against the Ohio Indians, in the year 1764, under the command of Henry Bouquet... Including his transactions with the Indians, relative to the delivery of their prisoners, and the preliminaries of peace. With an introductory account of the preceding campaign, and battle at Bushy-run. To which are annexed military papers, containing reflections on the war with the savages; a method of forming frontier settlements; some account of the Indian country; with a list of nations, fighting men, towns, distances, and different routes. The whole illustrated with a map and copper-plates. Published, from authentic documents, by a lover of his country. Philadelphia, Printed: London, Reprinted for T. Jefferies 1766.
1 p.l., xiii, 71 p.   front. (fold. map) 1 illus., 2 pl., 2 plans.   27 x 21 cm.

23640 Smith, William, 1728-1793.
History of New-York, from the first discovery to the year 1732. To which is annexed, a description of the country, with a short account of the inhabitants, their religious and political state and the constitution of the courts of justice... By William Smith, A.M. With a

continuation, from the year 1732, to the commencement of
the year 1814. Albany, Printed by Ryer Schermerhorn.
Sold by himself and G. Forbes, Albany; H. Stockwell,
Troy; A. Seward, Utica; and Andrus & Starr, Hartford...
1814.
xv, [17]-511, [1] p.   21½ cm.

23641   Somers, Robert, 1822-1891.
The southern states since the war. 1870-1. By Robert
Somers... London & New York, Macmillan and co., 1871.
xii, 286 p.   fold. map.   22½ cm.

23642   Soto, Hernando de, 1500(ca.)-1542.
Letter of Hernando de Soto, and Memoir of Hernando de
Escalante Fontaneda. Tr. from the Spanish, by Buckingham
Smith. Washington [Priv. print.] 1854.
67 p.   map.   38½ cm.

23643   South Carolina. Agricultural survey.
Report of the commencement and progress of the Agri-
cultural survey of South Carolina for 1843. By Edmund
Ruffin, agricultural surveyor of the state. Columbia,
A. H. Pemberton, state printer, 1843.
120, 55, [1] p.   illus., fold. tab.   21½ cm.

23644   South Carolina (Colony) Assembly. Committee, to enquire
into the causes of the disappointment of success, in the
expedition against St. Augustine.
The report of the committee of both houses of Assembly
of the province of South Carolina, appointed to enquire
into the causes of the disappointment of success, in the
late expedition against St. Augustine, under the command
of General Oglethorpe. Published by the order of both
houses. South Carolina, printed; London, reprinted for
J. Roberts, 1743.
2 p.l., 112 p.   20 cm.

23645   South Carolina. Commission to negotiate with the government
of the United States, 1860-1861.
The correspondence between the commissioners of the
state of So. Ca. to the government at Washington and the
President of the United States; together with the
statement of Messrs. Miles and Keitt. Printed by order
of the Convention. Charleston, Evans & Cogswell, printers
to the Convention, 1861.
26 p.   23 cm.

23646   South Carolina. General assembly. Senate.
Report of a special committee of the Senate, of South-

Carolina, on the resolutions submitted by Mr. Ramsay, on the subject of state rights. Columbia, S. C., Printed by Sweeny & Sims, state printers, 1827.
24 p.   22 cm.

23647   South Carolina (Colony) Provincial congress, February 1-April 11, 1776.
Journal of the Provincial congress of South Carolina, 1776. Pub. by order of the Congress. Charles-Town: printed; London, reprinted for J. Almon, 1776.
134 p.   21½ cm.

23648   Southern convention, Nashville, 1850.
Resolutions and address, adopted by the Southern convention. Held at Nashville, Tennessee, June 3d to 12th inclusive, in the year 1850. Pub. by order of the Convention. Nashville, Tenn., H. M. Watterson, printer, 1850.
21 p.   25 cm.

23649   Spain. Laws, statutes, etc., 1759-1788 (Charles III)
Reglamento y aranceles reales para el comercio libre de España a Indias de 12. de octubre de 1778. Madrid, Impr. de P. Marin [1778]
2 p.l., 19, 262 p.   front. (royal arms)   29½ cm.

23650   Sparks, Jared, 1789-1866.
The life of Gouverneur Morris, with selections from his correspondence and miscellaneous papers; detailing events in the American revolution, the French revolution, and in the political history of the United States. By Jared Sparks... Boston, Gray & Bowen, 1832.
3 v.   front. (port.)   23 cm.

23651   Squibb, Robert.
The gardener's calendar for the states of North-Carolina South-Carolina, and Georgia. By Robert Squibb. With appendix, containing a variety of particular and general information on husbandry and horticulture. Charleston, S.C., P. Hoff, 1827.
4 p.l., 176 p.   front.   19 cm.

23652   Staden, Hans, 16th cent.
Véritable histoire et description d'un pays habité par des hommes sauvages, nus, féroces et anthropophages, situé dans le novueau monde nommé Amérique, inconnu dans le pays de Hesse, avant de depuis la naissance de Jésus-Christ, jusqu'à l'année dernière. Hans Staden de Homberg, en Hesse, l'a connu par sa

propre expérience et le fait connaitre actuellement par
le moyen de l'impression. Marbourg, Chez André Kolben.-
1557... [Paris, A. Bertrand, 1837]
3 p.l., [3]-335 p.   21 cm.   (Added t.-p.: Voyages,
relations et memoires originaux pour servir à l'histoire
de la découverte de l'Amérique, pub... par Henri Ternaux.
[t. 3])

23653 Staples, William Read, 1798-1868.
Annals of the town of Providence, from its first settlement, to the organization of the city government, in
June, 1832. By William R. Staples. Providence, Printed
by Knowles and Vose, 1843.
vi p., 1 l., [9]-670 p.   23 cm.

23654 The state of the trade and manufactory of iron in Great-
Britain considered. [n.p.] 1750.
15 p.   19 cm.

23655 [Steele, Joshua] 1700-1791, supposed author.
An account of a late conference on the occurrences in
America. In a letter to a friend. London, Printed by
J. Almon, opposite Burlington House, in Piccadilly, 1766.
40 p.   21 cm.

23656 [Stephen, James] 1758-1832.
Observations on the speech of the Hon. John Randolph,
representative for the state of Virginia, in the general
Congress of America: on a motion for the non-importation
of British merchandize, pending the present dispute
between Great-Britain and America. By the author of War
in disguise. (London, printed) New York, Reprinted for
E. Sargeant, Wall-Street, opposite the Bank of the United
States, S. Gould, printer, 1806.
43 p.   20½ cm.

23657 [Stephens, Thomas]
The hard case of the distressed people of Georgia.
[London, 1742]
4 p.   37½ cm.

23658 Stephens, William, 1671-1753.
A journal of the proceedings in Georgia, beginning
October 20, 1737. By William Stephens, esq; to which
is added, A state of that province, as attested upon
oath in the court of Savannah, November 10, 1740...
v. 1-2. London, Printed for W. Meadows, 1742.
2 v.   21 cm.

23659 Stephens, William, 1671-1753.
Journal received February 4, 1741, by the Trustees
for establishing the colony of Georgia, in America, from
William Stephens, esq; secretary for the affairs of the
trust within the said colony: commencing September 22,
1741, and ending October 28 following. London, Printed
for W. Meadows, 1742.
[44] p.   19½ cm.

23660 Sterling, James, 1701?-1763.
Zeal against the enemies of our country pathetically
recommended: in a remarkable sermon, preached before His
Excellency the governor of Maryland, and both houses of
Assembly, at Annapolis. December 13, 1754. By James
Sterling, A.M., rector of St. Paul's parish, in Kent
County. Published at the request of the lower house of
Assembly. Annapolis, printed: London reprinted, for
J. Whiston [etc.] 1755.
1 p.l., 30 p.   19½ cm.

23661 Stevens, Benjamin, 1720-1791.
A sermon preached at Boston, before the great and
General court or assembly of the province of the
Massachusetts Bay in New England, May 27, 1761. Being
the day appointed by royal charter for the election of
His Majesty's Council for said province. By Benjamin
Stevens, A.M., pastor of the First church in Kittery.
N.B. Several passages omitted in preaching are inserted.
Boston, Printed by John Draper, printer to His Excellency
the governor and the honorable His Majesty's Council,
1761.
72 p., 1 l.   23 cm.

23662 Stevens, Charles.
Constitutional arguments indicating the rights and
policy of the southern states. By Charles Stevens.
Charleston, Printed by J. S. Burges, 1832.
24 p.   21 cm.

23663 Stiles, Ezra, 1727-1795.
A history of three of the judges of King Charles I.
Major-General Whalley, Major-General Goffe, and Colonel
Dixwell: who, at the restoration, 1660, fled to America;
and were secreted and concealed in Massachusetts and
Connecticut, for near thirty years. With an account of
Mr. Theophilus Whale, of Narragansett, supposed to have
been also one of the judges. By President Stiles...
Hartford, Printed by Elisha Babcock, 1794.
357 p., 1 l.   front. (port.) plates, (part fold.)
maps (part fold.)   17 cm.

330

23664 Stiles, Henry Reed, 1832-1909.
       The history of ancient Windsor, Connecticut, including
East Windsor, South Windsor, and Ellington, prior to
1768, the date of their separation from the old town;
and Windsor, Bloomfield and Windsor Locks, to the present
time. Also the genealogies and genealogical notes of
those families which settled within the limits of ancient
Windsor, Connecticut, prior to 1800. By Henry R. Stiles...
New York, C. B. Norton, 1859.
       xii, [2], 922 p.   front., illus., port., maps.   23 cm.

23665 Stillman, Samuel, 1738-1807.
       Death, the last enemy, destroyed by Christ. A sermon,
preached, March 27, 1776, before the Honorable Continental
congress: on the death of the Honorable Samuel Ward,
esq., one of the delegates from the colony of Rhode
Island, who died of the small-pox, in this city, (Philadelphia) March 26, aet. 52. By Samuel Stillman, M.A.
Philadelphia, Printed by Joseph Crukshank, in Market-
street, 1776.
       iv, [5]-28 p.   19 cm.

23666 Stillman, Samuel, 1738-1807.
       Good news from a far country. A sermon preached at
Boston, May 17, 1766. Upon the arrival of the important
news of the repeal of the Stamp-act. By Samuel Stillman...
Boston, Printed by Kneeland and Adams in Milk-Street,
for Philip Freeman, in Union-Street, 1766.
       34 p.   20½ cm.

23667 Stillman, Samuel, 1738-1807.
       A sermon preached before the honorable Council, and
the honorable House of representatives of the state of
Massachusetts-Bay, in New-England, at Boston, May 26,
1779, being the anniversary for the election of the
honorable Council. By Samuel Stillman, A.M. pastor of
the First Baptist church in Boston. Boston, New England,
printed by T. and J. Fleet, in Cornhill, and J. Gill,
in Court-street, 1779.
       38 p.   24 cm.

23668 Stobo, Robert, b. 1727.
       Memoirs of Major Robert Stobo, of the Virginia
regiment... Pittsburgh, J. S. Davidson, 1854.
       1 p.l., [v]-vi, [ix]-xii, [13]-92 p.   front. (fold.
plan)   14½ cm.

23669 Stockton, Richard, 1764-1828.
       Speech of the Hon. Richard Stockton, delivered in

the House of representatives of the United States, on
the 10th December, 1814, on a bill "To authorise the
President of the United States to call upon the several
states and territories thereof for their respective
quotas of eighty thousand four hundred and thirty militia
for the defence of the frontiers of the United States
against invasion". Georgetown, Published by Richards &
Mallory, 1814.
27 p.   21½ cm.

23670   [Stokes, Anthony] 1736-1799.
A narrative of the official conduct of Anthony Stokes,
of the Inner temple London... His Majesty's chief
justice, and one of his Council of Georgia; and of the
dangers and distresses he underwent in the cause of
government: some copies of which are printed for the
information of his friends. [London, 1784]
112 p.   19 cm.

23671   Stone, William Leete, 1792-1844.
Life of Joseph Brant (Thayendanegea) including the
border wars of the American revolution, and sketches of
the Indian campaigns of Generals Harmar, St. Clair, and
Wayne, and other matters connected with the Indian
relations of the United States and Great Britain, from
the peace of 1783 to the Indian peace of 1795. By
William L. Stone. Albany, N. Y., J. Munsell, 1865.
2 v.   illus., 2 plates (1 fold.) 4 port., fold. map.
23 cm.

23672   Stone, William Leete, 1792-1844.
The poetry and history of Wyoming: containing
Campbelle's Gertrude, and the history of Wyoming, from
its discovery to the beginning of the present century.
By William L. Stone... 2d ed., with an index. Albany,
J. Munsell, 1864.
1 p.l., xxiii, 406 p.   19½ cm.

23673   Sullivan, James, 1744-1808.
The history of the district of Maine. By James
Sullivan... Boston, Printed by I. Thomas and E. T.
Andrews, 1795.
vii, iv, [5]-421 p.   front. (fold. map)   21 cm.

23674   Sylvester, Nathaniel Bartlett, 1825-1894.
Historical sketches of northern New York and the
Adirondack wilderness: including traditions of the
Indians, early explorers, pioneer settlers, hermit
hunters, &c. by Nathaniel Bartlett Sylvester... Troy,

N. Y., William H. Young, 1877.
viii, [9]-316 p.   front. (port.)   22½ cm.

23675 Symmes, William, 1731-1807.
A sermon, preached before His Honor Thomas Cushing,
esq; lieutenant-governor, the honorable the Council,
and the two branches of the General court, of the
commonwealth of Massachusetts, May 25, 1785: being the
anniversary of general election. By William Symmes,
A.M., pastor of the First church in Andover. Boston,
Printed by Adams and Nourse, printers to the Honourable
the General court [1785]
28 p.   21 cm.

23676 Symonds, William, 1556-1616?
Virginia. A sermon preached at White-chapel, in the
presence of many, honourable and worshipfull, the
aduenturers and planters for Virginia. 25. April. 1609.
Pvblished for the benefit and vse of the colony, planted,
and to be planted there, and for the aduancement of
their Christian purpose. By William Symonds... London,
Printed by I. Windet for Eleazar Edgar and William
Welby, and are to be sold in Paules church-yard at the
signe of the windmill, 1609.
4 p.l., 54 p.   20½ cm.

T

23677 Tacitus, Cornelius.
The works of Cornelius Tacitus: with an essay on his
life and genius, notes, supplements, &c., by Arthur
Murphy... 2d American, from the London ed., with the
author's last corrections... New York, Printed for
P. A. Mesier [etc.] 1822.
6 v.   22 cm.

23678 Tanner, Henry Schenck, 1786-1856.
A new American atlas containing maps of the several
states of the North American Union. Projected and
drawn on a uniform scale from documents found in the
public offices of the United States and state governments and other original and authentic information.
By Henry S. Tanner. Philadelphia, 1823.
18 p.   maps (part fold. & part col.)   60 cm.

23679 Tappan, David, 1752-1803.
A sermon preached before His Excellency John Hancock,

esq., governour; the honourable the Council, Senate, and House of representatives, of the commonwealth of Massachusetts, May 30, 1792. Being the day of general election. By David Tappan, A.M., pastor of a church in Newbury. Printed in Boston, Massachusetts, at the State press, by Thomas Adams, printer to the honourable, the General court, 1792.
39 p.   21 cm.

23680 Tatham, William, 1752-1819, ed.
Communications concerning the agriculture and commerce of America: containing observations on the commerce of Spain with her American colonies in time of war. Written by a Spanish gentleman in Philadelphia, this present year, 1800. With sundry other papers concerning the Spanish interests. Ed. in London, by William Tatham. London, Printed for J. Ridgway, 1800.
viii, 120 p.   21 cm.

23681 [Taylor, George] 1820-1894.
Martyrs to the revolution in the British prison-ships in the Wallabout Bay. New-York, W. H. Arthur & co., 1855.
iv, [5]-64 p.   front. (fold. map)   21½ cm.

23682 [Taylor, John] 1753-1824.
Arator; being a series of agricultural essays, practical and political: in sixty one numbers. By a citizen of Virginia. Georgetown, Columbia, Printed and published by J. M. & J. B. Carter, 1813.
296 p.   18½ cm.

23683 Tea destroyed by Indians. [Boston, 1773?]
broadside.   32 x 20½ cm.
Poetry.

23684 The tears of the foot guards, upon their departure for America: written by an ensign of the army. London, Printed for G. Kearsly, 1776.
iv, [5]-12 p.   23 cm.

23685 Telltruth, Timothy, pseud.
The collected wisdom of ages, the most stupendous fabric of human invention, the English constitution. A true copy from the original, in the possession of William Pitt & co. By Timothy Telltruth... Philadelphia, Printed by James Carey, 1799.
xi, [13]-47 p.   21½ cm.

23686 Tennet, William, 1740-1777.
An address, occasioned by the late invasion of the

liberties of the American colonies by the British Parliament, delivered in Charlestown, South Carolina. By William Tennent, A.M. Philadelphia, Printed and sold by William and Thomas Bradford, at the London Coffee-House, 1774.
iii, [5]-30 p.   20½ cm.

23687   Ternaux-Compans, Henri, 1807-1864.
Bibliothèque américaine; ou, Catalogue des ouvrages relatifs à l'Amérique qui ont paru depuis sa découverte jusqu'à l'an 1700. Paris, Arthus-Bertrand, 1837.
viii, 191 p.   21 cm.

23688   The testimony of a number of New-England ministers met at Boston, September 25, 1745. Professing the ancient faith of these churches; inviting others who hold it, to unite in professing and maintaining the same; reciting and recommending an excellent act concerning preaching lately made by the General assembly of the Church of Scotland. [Six lines of Biblical quotations] Boston, Printed and sold by S. Kneeland and T. Green in Queen-street over against the Prison, and J. Winter in Union-street near the Town dock, 1745.
20 p.   18½ cm.

23689   [Thacher, Oxenbridge] 1720-1765.
The sentiments of a British American... Boston, Printed and sold by Edes and Gill, next to the prison in Queen-street, 1764.
16 p.   19½ cm.

23690   Thacher, Peter, 1752-1802.
An oration delivered at Watertown, March 5, 1776. To commemorate the bloody massacre at Boston: perpetuated March 5, 1770. By Peter Thacher, A.M. Watertown [Mass.] Printed and sold by Benjamin Edes, on the Bridge, 1776.
15 p.   23 cm.

23691   Thacher, Benjamin Bussey, 1809-1840.
Indian biography: or, An historical account of those individuals who have been distinguished among the North American natives as orators, warriors, statesmen, and other remarkable characters. New York, Harper & brothers, 1837.
2 v.   front. (port.)   15½ cm.

23692   Thévenot, Melchisédech, 1620-1692.
Recueil de voyages de M. Thevenot... Paris, Chez Estienne Michallet, 1681.

335

1 p.l., 169 p.   illus., 7 pl. (2 fold.)   2 fold.
maps.   17 cm.

23693   Thomas, Abel.
A brief memoir concerning Abel Thomas, a minister of
the Gospel of Christ in the Society of Friends, compiled
from authentic documents.   Philadelphia, Benjamin &
Thomas Kite, No. 20, North Third Street, 1824.
51 p.   20 cm.

23694   Thomas, Gabriel, 17th cent.
An historical and geographical account of the province
and country of Pensilvania; and of West New Jersey in
America.   The richness of the soil, the sweetness of the
situation, the wholesomness of the air, the navigable
rivers, and others, the prodigious encrease of corn, the
flourishing condition of the city of Philadelphia, with
the stately buildings, and other improvements there.
The strange creatures as birds, beasts, fishes, and
fowls, with the several sorts of minerals, purging waters,
and stones, lately discovered.   The natives, aborogmes [!]
their language, religion, laws, and customs; the first
planters, the Dutch, Sweeds, and English, with the
number of its inhabitants; as also a touch upon George
Keith's new religion, in his second change since he
left the Quakers.   With a map of both countries.   By
Gabriel Thomas, who resided there about fifteen years.
London, Printed for, and sold by A. Baldwin, 1698.
4 p.l., 55 p., 1 l., [9], 34 p.   fold. map.   17 cm.

23695   Thompson, David.
History of the late war between Great Britain and the
United States of America: with a retrospective view of
the causes...   to which is added an appendix, containing
public documents &c., relating to the subject.   By
David Thompson...   Niagara, U. C., Printed by T. Sewell,
1832.
vii, [9]-300 p.   17 cm.

23696   Thompson, Zadock, 1796-1856.
History of the state of Vermont, from its earliest
settlement to the close of the year 1832.   By Zadock
Thompson...   Bulington [!], E. Smith, 1833.
252 p.   17½ cm.

23697   [Thomson, Charles] 1729-1824.
An enquiry into the causes of the alienation of the
Delaware and Shawanese Indians from the British interest,
and into the measures taken for recovering their friend-

336

ship. Extracted from the public treaties, and other
authentic papers relating to the transactions of the
government of Pensilvania and the said Indians, for near
forty years; and explained by a map of the country.
Together with the remarkable Journal of Christian Frederic
Post, by whose negotiations, among the Indians on the
Ohio, they were withdrawn from the interest of the French,
who thereupon abandoned the fort and country. With notes
by the editor explaining sundry Indian customs, &c.
Written in Pensylvania. London, Printed for J. Wilkie,
1759.
184 p.   fold. map at end.   21 cm.

23698 Thomson, John, of New York.
An enquiry, concerning the liberty, and licentiousness
of the press, and the uncontroulable nature of the human
mind: containing an investigation of the right which
government have to controul the free expression of public
opinion, addressed to the people of the United States.
By John Thomson... New York, Printed by Johnson & Stryker,
for the author, 1801.
iv, [5]-84 p.   23 cm.

23699 Thornton, John Wingate, 1818-1878, ed.
The pulpit of the American revolution: or, The political
sermons of the period of 1776. With a historical introduction, notes, and illustrations. By John Wingate
Thornton... Boston, Gould and Lincoln; New York, Sheldon
and company; etc., etc. 1860.
xxxviii, [39]-537 p.   front. (port.) pl.   19½ cm.

23700 Three letters to a member of Parliament, on the subject of
the present dispute with our American colonies. London,
Printed for T. Lowndes, 1775.
1 p.l., 74 p.   20½ cm.

23701 [Tickell, Richard] 1751-1793.
La cassette verte de monsieur de Sartine, trouvée chez
mademoiselle du Thé... (5. éd. rev. & cor. sur celles de
Leipsic & d'Amsterdam) La Haye, Chez la veuve Whiskerfeld,
1779.
2 p.l., 71 p.   23 cm.

23702 Tomb, Samuel, 1766-1832.
An oration on the auspicious birth, sublime virtues,
and triumphant death of General George Washington;
pronounced Feb. 22, 1800; in Newbury Second parish. By
Rev. Samuel Tomb. To which are annexed, two odes and an

acrostic, commemorative of the birth and death of that
illustrious personage; composed by the same hand...
Newburyport, Printed by Edmund M. Blunt, 1800.
17, [3] p.   23 cm.

23703   The Tom-cod catcher.   [Boston, 1769]
broadside.   37½ x 25 cm.

23704   Tompson, Benjamin, 1642-1714.
The grammarians funeral, an elegy composed upon the
death of Mr. John Woodmancy, formerly a schoolmaster in
Boston: but now published upon the death of the venerable
Mr. Ezekiel Chevers [!] the late and famous schoolmaster of Boston in New England; who departed this life
the twenty-first of August 1708.   [Boston? n.d.]
broadside.   30 x 23 cm.

23705   T[ompson], B[enjamin] 1642-1714.
A neighbour's tears sprinkled on the dust of the amiable
virgin, Mrs. Rebekah Sewall, who was born December 30,
1704 and died suddenly, August 3, 1710.   Aetatis 3.
[Boston? n.d.]
broadside.   33 x 23 cm.

23706   [Toplady, Augustus Montague] 1740-1778.
An old fox tarred and feathered.   Occasioned by what is
called Mr. John Wesley's Calm address to our American
colonies...   Printed for William Baynes and son,
Edinburgh, H. S. Baynes, 1825.
19 p.   17 cm.
In Toplady's Works, v. 5, p. 441-59.

23707   [Torrens, Robert] 1780-1864.
The budget.   A series of letters on financial, commercial
and colonial policy.   By a member of the political economy
club...   London, Smith, Elder, and co., 1841.
226 p.   20½ cm.

23708   [Tracy, Uriah] 1755-1807.
Reflections on Monroe's View of the conduct of the
executive, as pub. in the Gazette of the United States,
under the signature of Scipio.   In which the commercial
warfare of France is traced to the French faction in
this country, as its source, and the motives of opposition,
&c.   [Philadelphia, 1797]
88 p.   20½ cm.

23709   Trescot, William Henry, 1822-1898.
The position and course of the South.   By Wm. H. Trescot.

Charleston [S. C.] Steam Power-Press of Walker & James, 1850.
20 p.   26 cm.

23710   Trevor, Richard, bp. of Durham, 1707-1771.
A sermon preached before the incorporated Society for the propagation of the gospel in foreign parts; at their anniversary meeting in the parish church of St. Mary-le-Bow, on Friday February 16, 1749 [i.e. 1750] By the Right Reverend Father in God, Richard, lord bishop of St. Davids. London, Printed by E. Owen and sold by J. Roberts [etc.] 1750.
71 p.   21½ x 17 cm.

23711   Trollope, Frances (Milton) 1780-1863.
The life and adventures of Jonathan Jefferson Whitlaw; or, Scenes on the Mississippi. With fifteen engravings. London, R. Bentley, 1836.
3 v.   15 plates.   19 cm.
Dedicated "to those states of the American Union in which slavery has been abolished, or never permitted."

23712   A true account of the most considerable occurrences that have happened in the warre between the English and the Indians in New-England, from the fifth of May, 1676, to the fourth of August last; as also of the successes it hath pleased God to give the English against them: as it hath been communicated by letters to a friend in London. The most exact account yet printed... London, B. Billingsley, 1676.
(In Drake, S. G., ed. The old Indian chronicle... Boston, 1836. 16 cm. p. 113 -143. front.)

23713   A trve declaration of the estate of the colonie in Virginia, with a confutation of such scandalous reports as haue tended to the disgrace of so worthy an enterprise. Published by aduise and direction of the Councell of Virginia. London, Printed for W. Barret, 1610.
1 p.l., 68 p.   18 cm.

23714   Trumbull, Benjamin, 1735-1820.
A complete history of Connecticut, civil and ecclesiastical, from the emigration of its first planters, from England, in the year 1630, to the year 1764; and to the close of the Indian wars... By Benjamin Trumbull... With an appendix, containing the original patent of New-England, never before published in America. New-Haven, Maltby, Goldsmith and co. and Samuel Wadsworth,

1818.
2 v. front. (port.) 22½ cm.

23715 [Trumbull, Henry]
    Life and adventures of Robert, the hermit of Massa-
chusetts, who has lived 14 years in a cave, secluded
from human society. Comprising, an account of his birth,
parentage, sufferings, and providential escape from
unjust and cruel bondage in early life - and his reasons
for becoming a recluse. Taken from his own mouth, and
published for his benefit. Providence, Printed for H.
Trumbull, 1829.
    36 p. port. 19½ cm.

23716 Trumbull, John, 1750-1831.
    The poetical works of John Trumbull, LL.D. Containing
M'Fingal, a modern epic poem, revised and corrected,
with copious explanatory notes; The progress of dulness;
and a collection of poems on various subjects, written
before and during the revolutionary war... Hartford,
Printed for Samuel G. Goodrich, by Lincoln & Stone, 1820.
    2 v. front. (port.) plates. 22 cm.

23717 Tucker, John, 1719-1792.
    A sermon preached at Cambridge, before His Excellency
Thomas Hutchinson, esq; governor: His Honor Andrew
Oliver, esq; lieutenant-governor, the honorable His
Majesty's Council, and the honorable House of representatives, of the province of the Massachusetts-Bay in
New-England, May 29th, 1771. Being the anniversary
for the election of His Majesty's Council for said
province. By John Tucker, A.M., pastor of the First
church in Newbury. Boston, New England, Printed by
Richard Draper, printer to His Excellency the governor,
and the honorable His Majesty's Council, 1821.
    63 p. 19½ cm.

23718 Tucker, Josiah, 1712-1799.
    Cui bono? or, An inquiry, what benefits can arise
either to the English or the Americans, the French,
Spaniards, or Dutch, from the greatest victories, or
successes, in the present war? Being a series of
letters, addressed to Monsieur Necker, late controller
general of the finances of France, 2d ed., cor. With a
plan for a general pacification. By Josiah Tucker, D.D.,
dean of Glocester. Glocester, Printed by R. Raikes, for
T. Cadell, in the Strand; sold also by Evans and Hazel,
in Glocester, 1782.
    141 p. 21 cm.

23719 Tucker, Josiah, 1712-1799.
Four letters on important national subjects, addressed
to the... Earl of Shelburne... By Josiah Tucker...
Dublin, Printed by R. Marchbank, for W. & H. Whitestone
[etc.] 1783.
vii, 72 p.   24 cm.

23720 Tucker, Josiah, 1712-1799.
Four tracts, together with two sermons, on political
and commercial subjects. By Josiah Tucker... Glocester,
Eng., Printed by R. Raikes, and sold by J. Rivington,
1774.
3 p.l., [v]-xv, 9-216, 35 p.   21 cm.

23721 Tucker, Josiah, 1712-1799.
An humble address and earnest appeal to those respectable personages in Great-Britain and Ireland, who,
by their great and permanent interest in landed property,
their liberal education, elevated rank, and enlarged
views, are the ablest to judge, and the fittest to decide,
whether a connection with, or a separation from the
continental colonies of America, be most for the national
advantage, and the lasting benefit of those kingdoms.
[One line Latin quotation: Hor.] Second edition, corrected. By Josiah Tucker... Glocester [Eng.] Printed
by R. Raikes; and sold by T. Cadell, in the Strand,
London, 1775.
93, [2] p.   fold. tab.   22 cm.

23722 Tucker, Josiah, 1712-1799.
A letter of Edmund Burke, esq; member of Parliament
for the city of Bristol, and agent for the colony of
New York, &c. in answer to his printed Speech, said to
be spoken in the House of commons on the twenty-second
of March, 1775. By Josiah Tucker... Glocester, Printed
by R. Raikes, and sold by T. Cadell, London, 1775.
58 p.   21½ cm.

23723 Tucker, Josiah, 1712-1799.
... The respective pleas and arguments of the mother
country, and of the colonies, distinctly set forth; and
the impossibility of a compromise of differences, or a
mutual concession of rights, plainly demonstrated.
With a prefatory epistle to the plenipotentiaries of the
late congress at Philadelphia. By Josiah Tucker...
Glocester, Printed by R. Raikes; and sold by T. Cadell
[etc.] London, 1775.
xvi, [9]-51 p.   21 cm.

23724   Tucker, Josiah   1712-1799.
         A series of answers to certain popular objections
         against separating from the rebellious colonies, and
         discarding them entirely; being the concluding tract
         of the Dean of Glocester, on the subject of American
         affairs. Glocester, Printed by R. Raikes, and sold by
         T. Cadell, London, 1776.
            xv, [ix]-xiv, [15]-108, 5 p.   21½ cm.

23725   Tucker, Josiah, 1712-1799.
        The true interest of Great Britain, set forth in
        regard to the colonies; and the only means of living in
        peace and harmony with them. By Josiah Tucker...
        Norfolk [Va.], Printed in the year, 1774.
           66 p.   18½ cm.

23726   Tudor, William, 1779-1830.
            Letters on the eastern states. By William Tudor.   2d
        ed. Boston, Wells and Lilly, 1821.
            viii, [9]-423 p.   22 cm.

                                  U

23727   U. S.   Army.   Continental Army.
            General orders of George Washington, commander-in-chief
        of the Army of Revolution, issued at Newburgh on the
        Hudson, 1782-1783. By Major Edward G. Boynton.
        Newburgh, N. Y., News company, 1909.
            128 p.   illus.   21 cm.

23728   U. S.   21st Cong., 1st sess., 1829-1830.
            Speeches on the passage of the bill for the removal
        of the Indians, delivered in the Congress of the United
        States, April and May, 1830. Boston, Perkins and Marvin,
        New York, Jonathan, 1830.
            viii, 304 p.   20½ cm.
            Edited by Jeremiah Evarts.

23729   U. S.   War dept.   Inspector general's office.
            Regulations for the order and discipline of the
        troops of the United States. Philadelphia, Published
        by M. Carey, no. 122, High-street, Alexander & Phillips,
        printers, Carlisle, 1809.
            5 p.l., 72 p.   viii fold. pl.   17½ cm.
            Compiled by Baron de Steuben, inspector general of the
        Army.

                                 342

23730 Upon the death of the virtuous and religious Mrs. Lydia
       Minot, (the wife of Mr. John Minot of Dorchester)...
       who died... January 27, 1667. [Cambridge, Mass.,
       Samuel Green? 1667]
          broadside.   22 x 35 cm.

                                  V

23731 Vail, Eugène A
          Notice sur les Indiens de l'Amérique du Nord, ornée de
       quatre portraits coloriés [!], dessinés d'après nature, et
       d'une parte, par Eugène A. Vail... Paris, A. Bertrand,
       1840.
          246 p.   col. ports., fold. map.   22½ cm.

23732 [Van Ness, William Peter] 1778-1826.
          A concise narrative of Gen. Jackson's first invasion of
       Florida, and of his immortal defence of New-Orleans:
       with remarks... 6th ed. [New York, 1828?]
          24 p.   23½ cm.

23733 Veech, James, 1808-1879.
          Mason and Dixon's line: a history. Including an out-
       line of the boundary controversy between Pennsylvania
       and Virginia. By James Veech... Pittsburgh, W. S.
       Haven, 1857.
          iv, [5]-58 p.   map.   23 cm.

23734 Velasco, Juan de, 1727-1819.
          Histoire du royaume de Quito, par don Juan de Velasco...
       Inédite. Paris, A. Bertrand, 1840.
          2 v.   21 cm.   (Added t.-p.: Voyages, relations
       et mémoires originaux pour servir à l'histoire de la
       découverte de l'Amérique... pub. ... par H. Ternaux-
       Compans. [t. 18-19])

23735 [Vernon, Edward] 1684-1757.
          Original papers relating to the expedition to Panama...
       London, Printed for M. Cooper, 1744.
          1 p.l., 224 p.   20½ cm.

23736 [Vernon, Francis V   ]
          Voyages and travels of a sea officer... Dublin,
       Printed by Wm. M'Kenzie, 1792.
          xxiv, [3]-306 p.   21½ cm.

23737 Vethake, Henry, 1792-1866.
          An address, delivered at his inauguration, as president

of Washington college, Lexington, Virginia, February 21st, 1835, by Henry Vethake. Lexington, Va., Printed by C. C. Baldwin, 1835.
   19 p.   21½ cm.

W

23738   Waldo, Samuel Putnam, 1780-1826.
   The tour of James Monroe, president of the United States, through the northern and eastern states, in 1817; his tour in the year 1818; together with a sketch of his life; with descriptive and historical notices of the principal places through which he passed... 2d ed. By S. Putnam Waldo... Hartford, Silas Andrus, 1820.
   xii, [13]-348 p.   front. (port.)   18½ cm.

23739   Walker, Francis Amasa, 1840-1897.
   The Indian question. By Francis A. Walker... Boston, James R. Osgood and company, 1874.
   268 p.   fold. map.   18 cm.
   Consists of three previously published articles: The Indian question, in the North American review, April, 1873; Indian citizenship, in the International review, May, 1874; An account of tribes, his report as Commissioner of Indian Affairs, 1872.

23740   [Walpole, Horatio Walpole, baron] 1678-1757.
   The grand question, whether war, or no war, with Spain, impartially consider'd: in defence of the present measures against those that delight in war. London, Printed for J. Roberts, 1739.
   32 p.   21 cm.

23741   Wansey, Henry, 1751-1827.
   The journal of an excursion to the United States of North America, in the summer of 1794. Embellished with the profile of General Washington, and an aquatinta view of the State house at Philadelphia... Salisbury, Printed and sold by J. Easton; [etc., etc.] 1796.
   1 p.l., [v]-xiii p., 1 l., 290, [12] p., 1 l.   front. (port.) pl.   21½ cm.

23742   [Ward, Nahum] 1785-1860.
   A brief sketch of the state of Ohio, one of the United States in North America: with a map delineating the same into counties. Giving the opinion of Thomas Hutchison

esq., geographer of the United States, and British
travellers in 1787, when that state was uninhabited by
civilized man. Likewise, exhibiting a view of the un-
paralleled progress of that state since 1789, to the
present day... By a resident of twelve years at Marietta,
in that state. Glasgow, Printed by J. Niven, and sold by
A. Penman & co., 1822.
   16 p.   front. (fold. map)   21½ cm.

23743 [Ward, Nathaniel] 1578?-1652.
   A religious retreat sounded to a religious army, by one
that desires to be faithful to his country, though
unworthy [!] to be named... London, S. Bowtell, 1647.
   13 (i.e. 15) p.   19½ x 15 cm.

23744 [Ward, Nathaniel] 1578?-1652.
   The simple cobler of Aggavvam in America. Willing to
help 'mend his native country, lamentably tattered, both
in the upper-leather and sole, with all the honest stitches
he can take. And as willing never to be paid for his
work, by old English wonted pay. It is his trade to
patch all the year long, gratis. Therefore I pray gentlemen keep your purses. By Theodore de la Guard [pseud.]
The fifth edition of some amendments. London, Printed
by J. D. & R. I. Reprinted at Boston in N. England for
Daniel Henchman at his shop in King street, 1713.
   2 p.l., 100 p.   19½ x 15½ cm.

23745 [Warden, David Bailie] 1772-1845.
   A chorographical and statistical description of the
District of Columbia, the seat of the general government
of the United States... Paris, Printed by Smith, 1816.
   vii, 212, [2] p. incl. fold. tables.   fold. pl.,
fold. map.   21 cm.

23746 Warden, David Bailie, 1772-1845.
   On the origin, nature, progress and influence of
consular establishments. Paris, Printed and sold by
Smith, 1813.
   3 p.l., [5]-331 p.   23 cm.

23747 Warren, Gouverneur Kemble, 1830-1882.
   An account of the operations of the Fifth army corps,
commanded by Maj. Gen. G. K. Warren, at the battle of
Five Forks, April 1, 1865, and the battles and movements
preliminary to it. By G. K. Warren... New York, W. M.
Franklin, printer, 1866.
   53 p. incl. diagr.   front. (fold. map)   23½ cm.

23748 Warren, Joseph, 1741-1775.
An oration delivered March 6, 1775, at the request of
the inhabitants of the town of Boston; to commemorate the
bloody tragedy of the fifth of March, 1770. By Dr. Joseph
Warren... Newport, Rhode Island; Reprinted and sold by
S. Southwick, in Queen street, 1775.
22 p.   21½ cm.

23749 Warren, Mercy (Otis) 1728-1814.
History of the rise, progress and termination of the
American revolution. Interspersed with biographical,
political and moral observations... By Mrs. Mercy Warren...
Boston, Printed by Manning and Loring, For E. Larkin,
No. 47, Cornhill, 1805.
3 v.   21 cm.

23750 Warren, Owen Grenliffe.
Dream of the highlands. A poem, by Owen Grenliffe
Warren... New York, Printed for private distribution
[J. Mackellar, printer] 1840.
xx, 76 p.   18 cm.

23751 Warren, Owen Grenliffe.
Xyclo of Argos: an epi-dramatic poem, in five parts.
By Owen G. Warren. New York, 1864.
v.   23 cm.
"Printed, not published, ten copies only, for purposes
of correction." With manuscript notes and corrections.
The publisher's name, "D. Appleton & co.", has been
supplied in pencil.

23752 Warren, Robert.
Industry and diligence in our callings earnestly
recommended. In a sermon preached before the Honourable
Trustees for establishing the colony of Georgia, in
America, and the Associates of the late Rev. Dr. Bray;
at their anniversary meeting, March 17, 1736-7, at the
parish-church of St. Bride, alias St. Bridget, in Fleet-
street, London. By Robert Warren... Pub. at the
unanimous request of the Trustees. London, Printed for
W. Meadows, 1737.
16 p.   23½ x 19 cm.

23753 Washington, George, pres. U.S., 1732-1799.
Facsimiles of letters from His Excellency George
Washington, president of the United States of America,
to Sir John Sinclair, Bart., M. P., on agricultural and
other interesting topics... Washington, published by

346

Franklin Knight, E. G. Dorsey, printer, Philadelphia, 1844.
   72 p.   illus.   27½ cm.

23754   Washington, George, pres. U.S., 1732-1799.
   Letters from His Excellency General Washington, to Arthur Young... containing an account of his husbandry, with a map of his farm; his opinions on various questions in agriculture; and many particulars of the rural economy of the United States. London, Sold by W. J. and J. Richardson [etc.] 1801.
   vi, 172 p.   fold. map.   22 cm.

23755   Washington, George, pres. U.S., 1732-1799.
   Official letters to the Honorable American Congress, written, during the war between the United Colonies and Great Britain, by His Excellency George Washington, commander in chief of the continental forces, now president of the United States. Copied, by special permission, from the original papers preserved in the office of the secretary of state, Philadelphia... London, Printed for G. G. and J. Robinson [etc.] 1795.
   2 v.   22 cm.

23756   [Washington, George] pres. U.S., 1732-1799.
   The President's address to the people of the United States, September 17, 1796, intimating his resolution of retiring from public service, when the present term of presidency expired. Philadelphia, Printed for W. Young, Mills & son, no. 52, Second-street, corner of Chestnut-street, 1796.
   16 p.   21½ cm.

23757   [Watterston, George] 1783-1854.
   Letters from Washington, on the Constitution and laws; with sketches of some of the prominent public characters of the United States. Written during the winter of 1817-18. By a foreigner. City of Washington, J. Gideon, junr., 1818.
   139 p.   19½ cm.

23758   Webster, Daniel, 1782-1852.
   An address delivered at the laying of the corner stone of the Bunker Hill monument. By Daniel Webster. Boston, Published by Cummings, Hilliard, and company, 1825.
   40 p.   23 cm.

23759   Webster, Daniel, 1782-1852.
   Speech of Daniel Webster, in reply to Mr. Hayne, of

South Carolina: the resolution of Mr. Foot, of Connecticut, relative to the public lands, being under consideration. Delivered in the Senate, January 26, 1830. Washington, Printed by Gales and Seaton, 1830.
  96 p.   23½ cm.

23760 Webster, Daniel, 1782-1852.
    Speech of Mr. Webster, upon the tariff; delivered in the House of representatives of the United States, April, 1824. Washington, Printed by Gales & Seaton, 1824.
  47 p.   22½ cm.

23761 Webster, Noah, 1758-1843.
    An American selection of lessons in reading & speaking; calculated to improve the minds and refine the taste of youth. To which is prefixed, rules in elocution, and directions for expressing the principal passions of the mind. By Noah Webster, esq. Hogan's seventh improved edition, carefully corrected. Philadelphia, Published and sold by David Hogan, no. 249, Market-street, Thomas T. Stiles, printer, 1814.
  1 p.l., [vii]-xii, [13]-230, [2] p.   18½ cm.

23762 Webster, Noah, 1758-1843.
    A compendious dictionary of the English language. In which five thousand words are added to the number found in the best English compends; the orthography is, in some instances, corrected; the pronunciation marked by an accent or other suitable direction; and the definitions of many words amended and improved. To which are added for the benefit of the merchant, the student and the traveller. I. Tables of the moneys of most of the commercial nations in the world... II. Tables of weights and measures, ancient and modern... III. The divisions of time among the Jews, Greeks and Romans... IV. An official list of the post-offices in the United States... V. The number of inhabitants in the United States, with the amount of exports. VI. New and interesting chronological tables of remarkable events and discoveries. By Noah Webster, esq. From Sidney's press. For Hudson & Goodwin, book-sellers, Hartford, and Increase Cooke & co., book-sellers, New Haven, 1806.
  xxiii, [1], 408 p.   18½ cm.
  First edition.

23763 [Webster, Pelatiah] 1725-1795.
    A dissertation on the political union and constitution

of the thirteen United States, of North-America: which is
necessary to their preservation and happiness, humbly
offered to the public, by a citizen of Philadelphia.
Philadelphia, Printed and sold by T. Bradford, 1783.
47 p.   20 cm.

23764 [Webster, Pelatiah] 1725-1795.
A seventh essay on free trade and finance; in which the
expediency of funding the public securities, striking
further sums of paper money, and other important matters,
are considered. By a citizen of Philadelphia. Philadelphia, Printed by E. Oswald, 1785.
38 p.   21½ cm.

23765 Webster, Samuel, 1719-1796.
A sermon preached before the honorable Council, and the
honorable House of representatives, of the state of the
Massachusetts-Bay, in New England. At Boston, May 28,
1777. Being the anniversary for the election of the
honorable Council. By Samuel Webster... [Eight line
Biblical quotation] Boston, Printed by Edes & Gill, in
Queen-street, 1777.
44 p.   19½ cm.

23766 Weems, Mason Locke, 1759-1825.
The bad wife's looking glass: or, God's revenge against
cruelty to husbands. Exemplified in the awful history
of the beautiful, but depraved Mrs. Rebecca Cotton,
who most inhumanly murdered her husband, John Cotton,
esq. for which horrid act God permitted her... to be cut
off by her brother, Stephen Kannady, May 5th, 1807...
2d ed., improved. Charleston, Printed for the author,
1823.
44 p.   23 cm.

23767 Weems, Mason Locke, 1759-1825.
God's revenge against adultery, awfully exemplified
in the following cases of American crim. con. I. The
accomplished Dr. Theodore Wilson (Delaware), who for
seducing Mrs. Nancy Wiley, had his brains blown out by
her husband. II. The elegant James O'Neale, esq. (North
Carolina) who for seducing the beautiful Miss Matilda
L'Estrange, was killed by her brother. 2d ed. Philadelphia, Printed for the author, 1816.
48 p.   front.   22 cm.

23768 Weems, Mason Locke, 1759-1825.
God's revenge against gambling. Exemplified in the

miserable lives and untimely deaths of a number of
persons of both sexes, who had sacrified their health,
wealth, and honour, at gaming tables. With curious
anecdotes of the following unfortunate gamblers: I.
Miss Fanny Braddock. II. Drisden Harwood. III. Jack
Gilmore. IV. T. Alston. V. Maria Antoinette. VI.
Other awful cases of young gamblers, and their untimely
ends. 4th ed. Philadelphia, Printed for the author,
1822,
    iv, [5]-47 p. front. 24 cm.

23769 Weems, Mason Locke, 1759-1825.
    The life of Benjamin Franklin; with many choice anecdotes
and admirable sayings of this great man, never before
published by any of his biographers. By M. L. Weems...
6th ed.... Philadelphia, H. C. Carey & I. Lea, 1822.
    264 p. front. (port.) 18 cm.

23770 [Weems, Mason Locke] 1759-1825.
    The life of Gen. Francis Marion, a celebrated partizan
officer, in the revolutionary war, against the British
and Tories in South Carolina and Georgia. By Brigadier
General P. Horry... Baltimore, Printed for the Rev.
M. L. Weems, by W. D. Bell & J. F. Cook, 1814.
    270 p. 18 cm.

23771 Weems, Mason Locke, 1759-1825.
    The life of George Washington; with curious anecdotes,
equally honourable to himself and exemplary to his young
countrymen... ninth edition, greatly improved. Embellishe
with seven engravings. By M. L. Weems, formerly rector
of Mount-Vernon parish. Philadelphia, Printed for Mathew
Carey, 1809.
    228 p. 6 pl. (incl. front.) port. 17½ cm.

23772 Weems, Mason Locke, 1759-1825.
    The philanthropist; or, A good twenty-five cents worth
of political love powder, for honest Adamites and
Jeffersonians; with the following recommendation by George
Washington... By the Rev. M. L. Weems (of Lodge No. 50)
Dumfries. [Dumfries? Va., 1799]
    2 p.l., [3]-30 p. front. (fold. facsim.) 24 cm.

23773 Weems, Mason Locke, 1759-1825.
    The true patriot: or, An oration, on the beauties and
beatitudes of a republic; and the abominations and
desolations of despotism. With an affectionate persuasive
to the American people, to fear God, and to honor their

rulers; to love one another, and to beware of discord. Delivered in the State-house, Trenton, before the Honorable the governor and Legislature, and printed at their request. Philadelphia, Printed by W. W. Woodward [1802]

 56 p.   20½ cm.

23774   Welby, Adlard.
  A visit to North America and the English settlements in Illinois, with a winter residence at Philadelphia; solely to ascertain the actual prospects of the emigrating agriculturist, mechanic, and commercial speculator. By Adlard Welby, esq.... London, Printed for J. Drury, Baldwin, Cradock, and Joy; and G. and W. B. Whitaker; Drury, Stamford, and Drury and son, Lincoln, 1821.
  xii, 224 p., front., 14 plates.   23 cm.

23775   Welles, Noah, 1718-1776.
  A vindication of the validity and divine right of Presbyterian ordination, as set forth in Dr. Chauncy's sermon at the Dudleian lecture, and Mr. Well's ! discourse upon the same subject, in answer to the exceptions of Mr. Jeremiah Leaming, containing in his late defence of the episcopal government of the church. By Noah Welles... Six line Biblical quotation New Haven, Printed by Samuel Green, for Roger Sherman, 1767.
  viii, 9-159 p.   19½ cm.

23776   Wesley, John, 1703-1791.
  Some observations on liberty: occasioned by a late tract. By John Wesley, M.A. [Ornament] London, Printed by R. Hawes, and sold at the Foundry, in Moorfields, and at the Rev. Mr. Wesley's preaching-houses in town and country, 1776.
  36 p.   17 cm.
  Written in answer to Richard Price's Observations on the nature of civil liberty.

23777   West, Samuel, 1731-1807.
  Greatness the result of goodness. A sermon, occasioned by the death of George Washington, late commander in chief of the armies, and first president, of the United States of America... By Samuel West, D.D., pastor of the church in Hollis street, Boston. Boston, From the printing-office of Manning & Loring [1800]
  40 p.   23 cm.

23778   West, Samuel, 1731-1807.
  A sermon preached before the honourable Council and the

351

honourable House of representatives, of the colony of
the Massachusetts-Bay in New England, May 29th, 1776.
Being the anniversary for the election of the honourable
Council for the colony. By Samuel West... [Fifteen lines
of Bibliical quotations] Boston, Printed by John Gill,
in Queenstreet, 1776.
    70 p.   22 cm.

23779 The Western traveler's pocket directory and stranger's guide;
exhibiting distances on the principal canal and stage
routes in the states of New-York and Ohio, in the territory
of Michigan, and in the province of Lower Canada, &c.
Containing also descriptions of the rail roads now building
and in contemplation in this state: with a list of broken
banks - rates of toll on the canals for 1834 - and a
variety of other matter, highly valuable to the traveling
community. Schnectady, Printed by S. S. Riggs for the
publisher, 1834.
    95, [1] p.   11½ cm.

23780 Wheelock, Eleazar, 1711-1779.
    A plain and faithful narrative of the original design,
rise, progress and present state of the Indian charity-
school at Lebanon, in Connecticut. By Eleazar Wheelock...
[Four lines of Biblical quotations] Boston, Printed by
Richard and Samuel Draper, in Newbury-street, 1763.
    viii, 9-55 p.   20 cm.

23781 Whitaker, Daniel Kimball 1801-1881.
    Sidney's letters to William E. Channing, occasioned by
his letters to Hon. Henry Clay, on the annexation of
Texas to the United States. Charleston, S. C., Printed
by Edward C. Councell, 1837.
    84 p.   19 cm.

23782 Whitaker, Nathaniel, 1732-1795.
    An antidote against Toryism. Or The curse of Meroz,
in a discourse on Judges 5th 23, by Nathaniel Whitaker...
Published at the desire of many who heard it. Dedicated
to His Excellency General Washington [Five line Biblical
quotation] Newbury-port, Printed by John Mycall, 1777.
    2 p.l., [3]-34 p.   19½ cm.

23783 [White, John] 1575-1648, supposed author.
    The planters plea. Or The grovnds of plantations
examined, and vsuall objections answered. Together with
a manifestation of the causes mooving such as have lately
vndertaken a plantation in Nevv-England: for the

satisfaction of those that question the lawfulnesse of
the action.   London, Printed by William Iones, 1630.
   2 p.l., 84 p.   18 cm.

23784 Whitefield, George, 1714-1770.
       An account of money received and disbursed for the
       orphan-house in Georgia. By George Whitefield... To
       Which is prefixed a plan for the building. London,
       Printed by W. Strahan for T. Cooper at the Globe in
       Pater-noster-row, and sold by R. Hett at the Bible and
       Crown in the Poultry, 1741.
          1 p.l., 45 p.   front. (port.)   fold. plan, tables.
       20 cm.

23785 Whitefield, George, 1714-1770.
       The Christian's companion: or, Sermons on several
       subjects... To which are added, several prayers. By
       George Whitefield... London, Printed and sold by the
       booksellers in town and country, 1739.
          264 p.   17½ cm.

23786 Whitefield, George, 1714-1770.
       Eighteen sermons preached by the late Rev. George White-
       field... Taken verbatim in short-hand, and faithfully
       transcribed by Joseph Gurney. Revised by Andrew Gifford,
       D.D. Printed at Newburyport, by Edmund M. Blunt, 1797.
          4 p.l., 368, [3] p.   18 cm.

23787 Whitefield, George, 1714-1770.
       A hymn composed by the Reverend Mr. Whitefield to be
       sung over his own corps. Taken from the original,
       May 1, 1764. [n.p., 1764?]
          broadside.   illus.   22½ x 36 cm.

23788 Whitefield, George, 1714-1770.
       A journal of a voyage from London to Savannah in
       Georgia. In two parts. Part I. From London to
       Gibraltar. Part II. From Gibraltar to Savannah. With a
       short preface, shewing the reason of its publication.
       London, Whittaker, Treacher and Arnot, 1829.
          13-274 p.   20 cm.

23789 Whitefield, George, 1714-1770.
       A letter from the Reverend Mr. George Whitefield,
       to the Reverend Mr. John Wesley, in answer to his sermon,
       entitled Free grace... Boston, Printed by G. Rogers,
       for S. Kneeland and T. Green in Queen-street, J. Edwards
       and S. Eliot in Cornhill, 1740.
          [3], [1] p.   15½ cm.

23790 Whitfield, Henry, 1597-1660? ed.
       The light appearing more and more towards the perfect
       day. Or, A farther discovery of the present state of the
       Indians in New-England, concerning the progresse of the
       gospel amongst them. Manifested by letters from such as
       preacht to them there. Published by Henry Whitfield...
       London, Printed by T. R. & E. M. for John Bartlet, 1651.
       4 p.l., 46 p.   19 cm.

23791 Whittier, John Greenleaf, 1807-1892.
       Poems written during the progress of the abolition
       question in the United States, between the years 1830 and
       1838. By John G. Whittier. Boston, I. Knapp, 1837.
       x p., 3 l., [17]-103 p. incl. illus., pl.   17 cm.

23792 Wigglesworth, Edward, 1732-1794.
       Calculations on Americal population, with a table for
       estimating the annual increase of inhabitants in the
       British colonies: the manner of its construction ex-
       plained: and its use illustrated. By Edward Wigglesworth...
       [Seven lines of quotations] Boston, Printed and sold by
       John Boyle in Marlboro'-street, 1775.
       24 p.   21 cm.

23793 Wilkes, George, 1280-1885.
       McClellan: who he is and what he has done. By George
       Wilkes. New York, S. Tousey, 1862.
       12 p.   19½ cm.

23794 Wilkie, Franc Bangs, 1832-1892.
       Davenport past and present; including the early industry,
       and personal and anecdotal reminiscences of Davenport;
       together with biographies, likenesses of its prominent
       men; compendious articles upon the physical, industrial,
       social and political characteristics of the city, full
       statistics of every department of note or interest, &c.
       By Franc B. Wilkie. Davenport, Publishing house of Luse,
       Lane & co., 1858.
       333, [1] p.   fold. front., plates, ports.   22 cm.

23795 Willard, Joseph, 1738-1804.
       An address in Latin, by Joseph Willard... and a
       discourse in English, by David Tappan... delivered before
       the anniversary in Cambridge, Feb. 21, 1800, in solemn
       commemoration of Gen. George Washington. Charlestown,
       Mass., E. typis Samuel Etheridge, 1800.
       31 p.   26 x 20½ cm.

23796 Williams, Abraham, 1726-1784.
       A sermon preach'd at Boston, before the great and General

court of assembly of the province of the Massachusetts-Bay
in New-England, May 26, 1762. Being the day appointed by
royal charter, for the election of His Majesty's Council
for said province. By Abraham Williams, A.M., pastor of
the church in Sandwich. Boston, Printed by S. Kneeland,
by order of the honourable House of representatives, 1762.
  2 p.l., 28 p.   23 cm.

23797 [Williams, Edward] fl. 1650.
  Virginia's discovery of silke-vvormes, with their
benefit. And the implanting of mulberry trees. Also
the dressing and keeping of vines, for the rich trade
of making wines there. Together with the making of the
saw-mill, very usefull in Virginia, for cutting of timber
and clapboard, to build withall, and its conversion to
other as profitable uses. [Vignette] London, Printed by
T. H. for John Stephenson, 1650.
  3 p.l., 75, [3] p.   illus.   17½ x 13 cm.

23798 Williams, John Lee.
  A view of West Florida, embracing its geography,
topography, &c. With an appendix, treating of its antiquities, land titles, and canals, and containing a map,
exhibiting a chart of the coast, a plan of Pensacola,
and the entrance of the harbour. By John Lee Williams.
Philadelphia, Printed for H. S. Tanner and the author,
1827.
  iv, [5]-178 p.   fold. map.   23 cm.

23799 [Williams, Roger] 1604?-1683.
  The blovdy tenent, a persecution, for cause of
conscience, discussed, in a conference betweene trvth
and peace. VVho, in all tender affection, present to
the High court of Parliament, (as the result of their
discourse) these, (amongst other passages) of highest
consideration. [London?] Printed in the year 1644.
  12 p.l., 247 p.   19 x 14½ cm.

23800 Williams, Roger, 1604?-1683.
  A key to the language of America: or, An help to the
language of the natives in that part of America, called
New-England. Together, with briefe observations on the
customes, manners and workships, &c. of the aforesaid
natives, in peace and warre, in life and death. On all
which are added spirituall observations, generall and
particular by the authour, of chiefe and speciall use
(upon all occasions,) to all the English inhabiting those
parts; yet pleasant and profitable to the view of all men:
By Roger Williams of Providence in New-England. London,

Printed by Gregory Dexter, 1643.
1 p.l., 17-163, [2] p.   23 cm.

23801 Williams, Samuel, 1743-1817.
The natural and civil history of Vermont. By Samuel
Williams... Published according to act of Congress.
Printed at Walpole, New Hampshire, by Isaiah Thomas and
David Carlisle, jun. Sold at their bookstore, in Walpole,
and by said Thomas, at his bookstore, in Worcester, 1794.
xvi, [17]-416 p.   front. (fold. map) tables.   20 cm.

23802 Williams, Stephen West, 1790-1855.
A biographical memoir of the Rev. John Williams, first
minister of Deerfield, Massachusetts. With a slight sketch
of ancient Deerfield, and an account of the Indian wars in
that place and vicinity. With an appendix, containing
the journal of the Rev. Doctor Stephen Williams, of Long-
meadow, during his captivity, and other papers relating to
the early Indian wars in Deerfield. By Stephen W. Williams.
Greenfield, Mass., Published and printed by C. J. J.
Ingersoll... 1837.
vi, [7]-127 p.

23803 Williamson, Hugh, 1735-1819.
The history of North Carolina. By Hugh Williamson...
Philadelphia, Published by Thomas Dobson, at the Stone
House, no. 41, South Second street. Fry and Kammerer,
printers, 1812.
2 v.   front. (fold. map)   22 cm.

23804 Williamson, Hugh, 1735-1819.
Observations on the climate in different parts of
America, compared with the climate in corresponding parts
of the other continent. To which are added, remarks on
the different complexions of the human race; with some
account of the aborigines of America. Being an introductory discourse to the History of North Carolina. By
Hugh Williamson... New York, Printed and sold by T. & J.
Swords, no. 160 Pearl-street, 1811.
viii, 199 p. incl. 2 plans.   22 cm.

23805 Williamson, William Durkee, 1779-1846.
The history of the state of Maine; from its first discovery, A.D. 1602, to the separation, A.D. 1820,
inclusive. By William D. Williamson... Hallowell,
Glazier, Masters & co., 1832.
2 v.   23½ cm.

23806 Wilson, James, 1742-1798.
  Commentaries on the Constitution of the United States
of America, with that Constitution prefixed, in which are
unfolded, the principles of free government, and the
superior advantages of republicanism demonstrated. By
James Wilson... and Thomas M'Kean... The whole extracted
from debates, published in Philadelphia by T. Lloyd.
London, Printed for J. Debrett [etc.] 1792.
  1 p.l., [5]-147, [2] p.   20½ cm.

23807 Wilson, John, d. 1667.
  A copy of verses made... on the sudden death of Mr.
Joseph Brisco, who was translated from earth to heaven
Jan. 1, 1657. [Cambridge, Mass., Samuel Green? 1657?]
  broadside.   20½ x 30 cm.

23808 Winchester, Elhanan, 1751-1797.
  A plain political catechism, intended for the use of
schools, in the United States of America; wherein the
great principles of liberty, and of the federal government,
are laid down and explained, in the way of question and
answer. Made level to the lowest capacities. By Elhanan
Winchester. Copyright secured. Norfolk, Printed for the
proprietor, by A. C. Jordan, & co., no. 3, Market-square,
1806.
  59 p.   16 cm.

23809 Winslow, Edward, 1595-1655.
  Hypocrisie unmasked; a true relation of the proceedings
of the governor and company of the Massachusetts against
Samuel Gorton of Rhode Island, by Edward Winslow, governor
of Plymouth colony. Reprinted from the original edition
issued at London in 1646; with an introduction by Howard
Miller Chapin. Providence, The Club of colonial reprints,
1916.
  xiv, [12], 103 p.   22½ cm.

23810 Winthrop, John, 1588-1649.
  A journal of the transactions and occurrences in the
settlement of Massachusetts and the other New England
colonies, from the year 1630 to 1644: written by John
Winthrop, esq., first governor of Massachusetts: and now
first published from a correct copy of the original
manuscript... Hartford, Printed by Elisha Babcock, 1790.
  3 p.l., 364, 4 p.   21 cm.

23811 Wirt, William, 1772-1834.
  Opinion on the right of the state of Georgia to extend

her laws over the Cherokee nation. New Echota, Printed
for the Cherokee nation at the Office of the Cherokee
Phoenix and Indians' Advocate, 1830.
27 p.   21½ cm.

23812   Wisconsin. State Historical Society.
First annual report and collections of the State Historical Society, of Wisconsin, for the year 1854. Volume
I. Madison, Bereah Brown, printer, 1855.
160 p.   21 cm.

23813   Wise, John, 1652-1725.
A vindication of the government of New-England churches.
Drawn from antiquity; the light of nature; Holy Scripture;
its noble nature: and from the dignity divine Providence
has put upon it. By John Wise, A.M., pastor of a church
in Ipswich... Boston, Printed and sold by John Boyles,
in Marlboro'-street, 1772.
80, 96, [1] p.   16½ cm.

23814   Wiswell, Ichadob, ca. 1637-1700.
Upon the death of the reverend and aged man of God,
Mr. Samuel Arnold, pastor of the church at Marshfield,
who deceased this life in the 71st year of his age, of
his ministry the 36th, September 1693. [n.p., 1693?]
broadside.   30 x 44 cm.

23815   [Witherspoon, John] 1723-1794.
The history of a corporation of servants. Discovered a
few years ago in the interior parts of South America...
Glasgow, Printed for J. Gilmour, 1765.
76 p.   21 cm.
A satire on the abuses prevalent in the Scottish church.

23816   Wolcott, Oliver, 1760-1833.
An address, to the people of the United States, on the
subject of the report of a committee of the House of
representatives, appointed to "examine and report,
whether monies drawn from the Treasury, have been faithfully applied to the objects for which they were appro-
priated, and whether the same have been regularly accounted
for," which report was presented on the 29th of April,
1802. By Oliver Wolcott... Boston, Printed by Russell
and Cutler, 1802.
112 p.   23 cm.

23817   Wolfe, James, 1727-1759.
General Wolfe's instructions to young officers: also

his orders for a battalion and an army. Together with
the orders and signals used in embarking and debarking
an army by flat-bottom'd boats, &c. And a placart to the
Canadians. To which is prefixed, the resolutions of the
House of commons for his monument; and his character,
and the dates of all his commissions. Also the duty for
an adjutant and quarter master, &c. 2d ed. London,
Printed for J. Millan, 1780.
1 p.l., ix, [3], 106 p.   19 cm.

23818   Wolley, Charles.
A two years journal in New York, and part of its
territories in America. By Charles Wooley, A.M. A new
ed., with an introduction and copious historical notes
by E. B. O'Callaghan... New York, W. Gowans, 1860.
97 p. incl. facsim.   25 cm.   (Added t.-p.: Gowans'
bibliotheca americana, 2)

23819   Wood, John, 1775-1822.
A correct statement of the various sources from which
the History of the administration of John Adams was
compiled, and the motives for its suppression by Col. Burr:
with some observations on a Narrative, by a citizen of
New York. By John Wood, author of the said history.
New York, Printed and sold, for the author, by G. F.
Hopkins, 1802.
49 p.   22 cm.

23820   Wood, John, 1775-1822.
The history of the administration of John Adams, esq.
late president of the United States. By John Wood...
New York Barlas and Ward 1802.
1 p.l., 506 p.   21 cm.

23821   Woodward, Augustus Brevoort, d. 1827.
Considerations on the government of the Territory of
Columbia. By Augustus B. Woodward. No. VII... Alexandria,
Territory of Columbia: Printed by S. Snowden & co.,
sold by Rapine and by Stickney, Washington, and Bishop,
Alexandria, where the previous numbers may be procured.
January, 1802.
25 p.   21½ cm.

23822   Woolman, John, 1720-1772.
A word of remembrance and caution to the rich. By
John Woolman, of Mount-Holly, in New Jersey... Dublin,
Printed by T. M. Bates, for R. M. Jackson, 1793.
1 p.l., [5]-91 p.   12½ cm.

23823 Wright, Edward, 1558?-1615.
Certain errors in navigation. Detected and corrected
by Edw. Wright. With many additions that were not in the
former editions. London, Printed by Joseph Moxon, 1657.
13 p.l., 224 (i.e. 212), 110, 20 p.   illus.   2 fold.
maps, tables, diagrs. (part fold.)   20 cm.

23824 Wright, John, fl. 1761-1765.
The American negotiator; or, The various currencies of
the British colonies in America; as well as the islands,
as the continent. The currencies of Nova Scotia, Canada,
New England, New York... and of the islands of Barbadoes,
Jamaica, St. Christophers... reduced into English money,
by a series of tables, suited to the several exchanges
between the colonies and Britain... With tables reducing
the currency of Ireland into sterling, and the contrary...
Also, a chain of tables, of the interchangeable reduction
of the currencies of the colonies... To which are added,
tables reducing gold and silver bullion of any degree of
coareness [!] or fineness into standard, and valuing the
same by the assay according to the mint price of the
Tower of London. By J. Wright, accomptant. The 2d ed.
London, Printed for the proprietor, 1763.
1 p.l., ii, 24, xvi, 464 p.   20½ cm.

23825 Wyoming, pseud.
The letters of Wyoming, to the people of the United
States, on the presidential election, and in favour of
Andrew Jackson. Originally published in the Columbian
observer... Philadelphia, S. Simpson & J. Conrad, 1824.
2 p.l., [3]-104 p.   23 cm.
A series of 12 letters, and "Finale" signed: Wyoming.

Y

23826 Young, Alexander, 1800-1854.
Chronicles of the Pilgrim fathers of the colony of
Plymouth, from 1602 to 1625. Now first collected from
original records and contemporaneous printed documents,
and illustrated with notes, by Alexander Young... Boston,
C. C. Little and J. Brown, 1841.
xvi, 504 p.   front. (port.) illus., maps.   23 cm.

23827   Zenger, John Peter, 1680?-1746, defendant.
        The tryal of John Peter Zenger, of New York, printer,
    who was lately try'd and acquitted for printing and
    publishing a libel against the government. With the
    pleadings and arguments on both sides... 2d ed. London,
    Printed for J. Wilford, 1738.
        1 p.l., 32 p.   24 cm.

23828   Zurita, Alonso de, b. 1511 or 12.
        Rapport sur les différentes classes de chefs de la
    Nouvelle-Espagne, sur les lois, les moeurs des habitants,
    sur les impôts établis avant et depuis la conquête,
    etc., etc....   (Inédit)   [Paris, A. Bertrand, 1840]
        xvi, 418 p.   21 cm.   (Voyages, relations et mémoires
    originaux pour servir à l'histoire de la découverte de
    l'Amérique, pub. ... par H. Ternaux-Compans [t. 11])

Along with Volumes 1 and 5 of The New Sabin, the present one is intended to be a full record of works recorded in Sabin (or which would have been recorded had they been known) which have been issued thus far in a microfiche edition by the Lost Cause Press. However, certain other series issued by the Lost Cause Press have included material in the original Sabin, and the numbers, as they appear in The New Sabin, are recorded below:

2585	6401	8768	17269
2959	6408	9004	17270
2967	6537	9090	17309
3027	6540	9406	17324
3061	6547	9409	17358
3197	6615	9621	17367
3209	6859	9622	17392
3236	6933	10033	17395
3375	6935	10273	17485
3605	6987	10485	17491
3610	6994	10683	17581
3765	6997	12455	17852
3808	6998	14993	
3826	7059	15499	
3837	7068	15806	
3909	7135	15942	
3954	7164	15965	
3969	7278	16214	
3976	7360	16222	
4034	7363	16227	
4061	7367	16342	
4320	7368	16394	
4332	7386	16470	
4362	7394	16562	
4383	7395	16580	
4388	7402	16731	
4417	7414	16748	
4496	7423	17019	
4536	7430	17040	
4595	7438	17060	
4598	7590	17076	
4696	7842	17097	
5052	8097	17107	
5072	8161	17133	
5167	8256	17154	
5169	8379	17188	
5308	8390	17194	
5343		17268	